Democracy

BLACKWELL READINGS IN PHILOSOPHY

Series Editor: Steven M. Cahn

Blackwell Readings in Philosophy are concise, chronologically arranged collections of primary readings from classical and contemporary sources. They represent core positions and important developments with respect to key philosophical concepts. Edited and introduced by leading philosophers, these volumes provide valuable resources for teachers and students of philosophy, and for all those interested in gaining a solid understanding of central topics in philosophy.

1 *God and the Problem of Evil*
   Edited by William L. Rowe

2 *Epistemology: Internalism and Externalism*
   Edited by Hilary Kornblith

3 *Free Will*
   Edited by Robert Kane

4 *Democracy*
   Edited by David Estlund

Democracy

Edited by
David Estlund

Copyright © Blackwell Publishers Ltd 2002
Editorial matter and organization copyright © David Estlund 2002

First published 2002

2 4 6 8 10 9 7 5 3 1

Blackwell Publishers Inc.
350 Main Street
Malden, Massachusetts 02148
USA

Blackwell Publishers Ltd
108 Cowley Road
Oxford OX4 1JF
UK

Library of Congress Cataloging-in-Publication Data
Democracy / edited by David Estlund.
p. cm. — (Blackwell readings in philosophy; 4)
Includes bibliographical references and index.
ISBN 0-631-22103-4 (alk. paper) — ISBN 0-631-22104-2 (pb. : alk. paper)
1. Democracy. 2. Democracy—Philosophy.   I. Estlund, David M. II. Series.

JC423. D43976 2001
321.8—dc21

2001037589

British Library Cataloguing in Publication Data
A CIP catalogue record for this book is available from the British Library.

Typeset in 10/12.5 pt Palatino
by Kolam Information Services Pvt. Ltd, Pondicherry, India
Printed in Great Britain by MPG Books Ltd, Bodmin, Cornwall

This book is printed on acid-free paper.

Contents

Acknowledgments vii

Introduction: *David Estlund* 1

Part I   Procedural Fairness 29

1   Democracy as Equality 31
Thomas Christiano
2   The Constitutional Conception of Democracy 51
Jeremy Waldron

Part II   Ideal Deliberation 85

3   Deliberation and Democratic Legitimacy 87
Joshua Cohen
4   Deliberative Politics 107
Jürgen Habermas

Part III   Wise Decisions 127

5   Open Government and Just Legislation 129
William Nelson
6   A Theory of Political Fairness 152
Charles Beitz

Part IV   Deliberation and Institutions 173

7   Political Quality 175
David Estlund

8 Difference as a Resource for Democratic Communication   213
   Iris Young

Part V Why Vote?   **235**

9 Toward a Democratic Morality   237
   Geoffrey Brennan and Loren Lomasky
10 A Causal Responsibility Approach to Voting   267
   Alvin Goldman

Part VI Formal Models and Normative Theory   **287**

11 Deliberative Democracy and Social Choice   289
   David Miller
12 Rousseau's General Will: A Condorcetian Perspective   308
   Bernard Grofman and Scott Feld

Bibliography   320

Index   333

Acknowledgments

Thank you to Steven Cahn for inviting me to put together this volume. I am grateful to Josha Bliss and Aaron Boyden for terrific work on the comprehensive bibliography at the end of the book, and for Tony Grahame's expert help preparing the manuscript.

The authors and publishers gratefully acknowledge the following for permission to reproduce copyright material:

1 American Political Science Association, for Bernard Grofman, Scott Feld, "Rousseau's General Will: A Condorcetian Perspective" from *American Political Science Review* 82:2, June 1988;
2 Blackwell Publishers Ltd., for David Miller, "Deliberative Democracy and Social Choice" from *Political Studies* 40 (1992), pp. 54–67; and Jeremy Waldron "The Constitutional Conception of Democracy" from *Journal of Political Philosophy* V (1998). Published by Blackwell Publishers;
3 Cambridge University Press, for Geoffrey Brennan, Loren Lomasky, "Toward a Democratic Morality" from *Democracy and Decision*. Published by Cambridge University Press, 1993;
4 Cambridge University Press inc., for Alvin Goldman, "A Causal Responsibility Approach to Voting" from *Social Philosophy and Policy* 16 (2), Summer 1999; and David Estlund, "Political Quality" from *Social Philosophy and Policy* 17 (1), winter 2000;
5 Joshua Cohen, for extract from *The Good Polity*, edited by Hamlin/Petit. Published by Blackwell, 1989;
6 MIT Press, for Jürgen Habermas, "Deliberative Politics" from *Between Facts and Norms: Contributions to a Discourse Theory of Law and Democracy*. Published by MIT Press, 1996; and Iris Young, "Difference as a

Resource for Democratic Communication" from *Deliberative Democracy*, ed. Bohman and Rehg. Published by MIT Press, 1997;

7   Perseus Books Group, for Thomas Christiano, "Democracy as Equality" from the *Rule of the Many*. Copyright © 1996 by Westview Press, a member of the Perseus Books Group;

8   Princeton University Press, for Charles Beitz, *Political Equality*. Copyright ©1989 by Princeton University Press. Reprinted by permisssion of Princeton University Press;

9   Taylor and Francis Books Ltd., for William Nelson, "Open Government and Just Legislation" in *On Justifying Democracy*. Routledge, 1980.

The publishers apologize for any errors or omissions in the above list and would be grateful to be notified of any corrections that should be incorporated in the next edition or reprint of this book.

Introduction

David Estlund

Democratic theory takes place across a range of academic disciplines including at least philosophy, political science, law, economics, and sociology. Guided by the title of this series of volumes, *Readings in Philosophy*, I have chosen readings that are distinctively philosophical (rather than predominantly historical, empirical, legal, policy-oriented, etc.) but readings that are accessible to students in other disciplines as well at an advanced undergraduate level or above. I have tried to present some diversity and some unity. On the side of diversity, as chapter headings indicate, the pieces are intended to cover a number of important issues in democratic theory. On the side of unity, I have chosen exclusively recent writings, all within the last 20 years. Also for unity these pieces generally (with several exceptions) emphasize normative questions about justification, legitimacy and obligation, and many of the authors engage each other directly. There is also no pretense of covering work originating in languages other than English, the only exception being Habermas. Readers can pursue these issues further by consulting the suggestions for further reading and the bibliography of all works cited in this volume. I have discussed several of the points in this introduction at greater length in other works which are cited *en route*.

I begin by setting the historical background for the recent work compiled here, and then turn to introducing the essays as I have grouped them into pairs. This long introduction is divided into sections which should be comprehensible either separately or all together. The sections after the one providing historical background correspond to the sections of the book consisting of pairs of readings, and all pieces are discussed in the order in which they appear in this collection.

Background

In the last fifteen years or so philosophical work on democracy has changed. For about the fifteen years before that distributive justice was a far more prominent topic than democracy in political philosophy.[1] Coming out of the anti-war and civil rights movements of the 1960s many were interested in ideals of participatory democracy (e.g., Pateman 1970), but as time went on much philosophical democratic theory concentrated on the analysis and justification of democracy from a broadly economic point of view, encouraged and provoked especially by the fascinating work of Kenneth Arrow and others in the "social choice" and "public choice" schools of social science (Arrow 1950, 1963, Sen 1970, Elster and Hylland 1986). Recently, the topic of democracy has taken on new life under the rubric of "deliberative democracy." There are several good collections specifically in that mold (Elster 1998, Bohman and Rehg 1997, Benhabib 1996), and so I have not used that as a selection criterion here. Still, the trend clearly shows itself here, so it is worth saying a little about the multiform idea of deliberative democracy and the contrast with other approaches.

The rise of theories of deliberative democracy has two main philosophical roots. One root (which obviously has a longer history as well) is a reaction to the alignment of political science and political theory with the methods of economics and its prevailing philosophical assumptions. The other, not unrelated, is the enormous influence of the fundamental and systematic political philosophies of John Rawls and Jürgen Habermas.

Social and political philosophy contains among its central concerns normative questions – questions about what rights and obligations citizens have, what distributions of goods are just, how political power ought to be arranged. To this extent it overlaps with normative moral philosophy which asks generally what is right and wrong, good and bad. In English-speaking philosophy, the most influential general moral theory in the last two centuries has been utilitarianism, the view that our overarching duty is to promote happiness and well-being. As a consequentialist theory utilitarianism raises questions about how happiness is affected by events in the world, questions that it is natural to hope might be addressed scientifically, by studying the ways of the world rather than reflecting in a philosophical mode. On the other hand, many have thought that a scientific approach would have no proper business pronouncing on the matter of what human happiness really is, and so there is a difficulty about how to proceed. Even apart from that, if the results of scientific study are to be put into action, many have thought – in a politically liberal vein – that they must be defensible on grounds that are neutral among different views of happiness. Otherwise, some people would be illegitimately imposing a view of the good on many people who may not share it. For these and other reasons the scientific study of the causes and effects of well-being – this is a rough description of a central task of welfare economics – has come to proceed on the methodological assumption that well-being is simply the satisfaction of whatever preferences people actually have. A further reason for this assumption is that a scientific view will want to predict and explain behavior, and many have thought that the simple assumption that people pursue their own self-interest would predict and explain a great deal. The combination of these ideas – utilitarianism, scientific value-neutrality, value-neutral political liberalism, and predictive egoism – goes a long way toward accounting for the influential view of political agents as maximizers of their own expected preference–satisfaction.

This economistic framework has generated important advances, as well as spawning a recent reaction. The economic approach to democracy flourished in the 1950s and '60s among social scientists and theorists. Among the great achievements were those of Anthony Downs (1957) and Arrow. Downs's views were of more immediate relevance for empirical than for normative theory, suggesting that viewing voters and candidates as economic agents seeking utility might allow clear and plausible predictions and explanations of behavior. Arrow's famous theorem in social choice theory attracted more philosophical attention for its apparent challenge to traditional normative democratic theory. It showed that several normatively plausible conditions on ways to aggregate individual preference rankings into a group preference ranking could not be met jointly. One interpretation, encouraged especially by William Riker (Riker 1982) concluded that there is no normatively compelling interpretation of democratic social choice at all. In the reading by David Miller, the Arrow model and its implications are explained and brought into engagement with more recent normative theory.

Beginning around 1971, the time of the publication of Rawls's *A Theory of Justice*, the economic model of political agency, rationality, and morality, came under increasing challenge. Rawls's own theory still owed much to that individual maximizing model, and yet it vividly presented a "veil of ignorance" as a normative device whose value did not rest on its ability to satisfy anyone's preferences but lay in its usefulness as a representation – or so Rawls hypothesized – of widely and firmly held convictions about freedom, equality, and justification. The enormous influence of Rawls's book revived a traditional approach to politics in which it was assumed that ascertaining the most effective means to satisfying people's desires was not the only way to reason about political matters. It reasserted the traditional objection to utilitarianism: that it could not seem to account for justice. There are still many writers inclined to the narrower conception of reason and value characteristic of the economic approach, and there is no shortage of brilliant utilitarian moral philosophers. But the broader view of reason and value characteristic of Rawls now plays a much larger role than before.

Around this same time the economists' conception of agency and value was influentially challenged by Amartya Sen (e.g., 1977). Sen's main challenge did not lie mainly in the presentation of a moral alternative to utilitarianism (though he also has offered such an alternative (e.g., 1984)). Rather, Sen's greatest influence on current political philosophy has been to challenge the narrow economic emphasis on the satisfaction of an agent's preferences. One side of the challenge, pursued also by others, is to argue that certain common ways of emphasizing preference–satisfaction give rise to an odd and incoherent view of human agency. Another side is to note the obvious ways in which a person's preferences can be nosy, or trivial (Scanlon 1975), uninformed (many), or irrationally formed in other ways (Elster 1983).

It may seem as though social choice theory could simply stay out of debates about which preferences should properly be counted, and then bring its impossibility theorem to bear on whatever preferences pass those prior tests. Indeed, in social choice theory preferences are taken at face value and not further evaluated as to their content or the circumstances of their formation. In the usual serene phrase, they are "taken as given." But this is far from clear, since Arrow's impossibility theorem assumes that an adequate social choice rule must be able to aggregate absolutely any possible profile of individual preferences. Passing individual preferences through prior filters in order to disqualify nosy or irrationally formed preferences may present social choice procedures with a limited and more manageable domain of preference profiles. (Miller discusses this idea in the essay in this volume.) Once the motley nature of brute preference is appreciated, social choice theory can come to look complacent, and attention naturally shifts from the aggregation procedure to the process through which preferences are formed.

Attention to preference formation may seem to call for theoretical and empirical investigations into individual and social psychology and pathology, a route that Elster and others pioneered to important effect. But thinking about preference formation was led in a different direction by the work of Habermas. Habermas's normative vision begins in an "ideal discourse" in which all affected parties join to discuss the merits of practical proposals under conditions of severe deliberative equality. The preferences that ought to matter, this tempts many to say, are those that are formed under that kind of egalitarian practical deliberation. The idea that preferences might be improved by public reasoning tends, moreover, to shift the focus away from preferences and toward reasoning. The equal status of citizens is often represented in their equal (opportunity for) cooperation in a public process of reasoned decision making rather than in having their preferences or interests equally counted. On these views, the role that preferences will play is a substantial issue to be settled by rational deliberation among political equals. This way of putting it increases the distance from utilitarian themes, but also, more generally, suggests a shift of emphasis from substantive justice to legitimate political procedure, a shift that Habermas heartily endorses. There are difficulties about translating these central Habermasian ideas into a normative theory of democracy, as we'll see below, but that project animates much of the work under the banner of "deliberative democracy."

Habermas's work and its suggestiveness for democratic theory required intermediaries. For one thing Habermas worked in German and was only translated into English after significant delays. For another thing, while many of Habermas's concerns are shared by philosophers writing in English, his work also drew on many less familiar sources, and proceeded in a style that many found overly complex and obscure. Nevertheless, his influence has been profound. Perhaps the most important intermediary was Joshua Cohen,[2] whose early papers drew parallels and built bridges between several central themes of Habermas and the ideas of Rawls (Rawls 1971, Elster 1986). Cohen's emphasis on democratic ideals, which are not prominent in Rawls, drew illuminating links between Rawls's liberalism and Habermas's socialism, and also between Rawls's emphasis on substantive justice and Habermas's emphasis on legitimate procedure. Partly as a consequence liberalism, which had nearly been discredited as a political philosophy by that time for its failure to address severe economic, racial, and gender injustices, is now thought by many to be compatible with "progressive," egalitarian, and social-democratic political agendas. The result has been a remarkable recovery for liberal political philosophy. Democratic theory is now typically pursued in a liberal context, taking for granted the existence of some fundamental rights, enshrined in a constitution, that limit the scope of legitimate democratic outcomes. Still, even among liberal democratic theorists there is hardly consensus around any particular account of the best form of liberal democracy. The limits of democratic prerogatives are still controversial. Waldron (more on this below), for one, doubts the usual liberal view that democratic legislatures must answer to courts with the power of judicial review. And while

liberalism has historically been associated with strong natural and constitutional rights to private property and a celebration and expansion of
economic markets, since Rawls liberalism is often taken to leave open the
choice between capitalism and socialism.

I turn now to some introductory remarks about the paired readings.

Part I: Procedural Fairness

An important question in recent normative democratic theory has been
how best to explain the moral importance of political equality. Political
equality is generally assumed to require at least such "formal" conditions as
equal legal rights to vote in elections and hold office. In addition, though,
the moral value of democracy apparently depends on a background that is,
at least, not too unequal. Some have sought to explain this further requirement as the only way to make the political process fair to all citizens. But
the idea of fairness is by no means self-explanatory and it is interpreted in
very different ways by different theorists. A good initial distinction, though,
is between (a) fairness as a procedure that gives an equal chance for each
participant to affect the outcome, and (b) fairness as a tendency of a
procedure to produce results that are just. This distinction tracks one of
the continuing fundamental divides among normative theories of democracy, and it runs through many of the readings in this collection.

On one side there are theories that hold that there is some available
standard by which political outcomes can be evaluated in a way that is
logically independent of whatever procedures produced it. An example
would be a utilitarian standard that says the best outcome is the one that
maximizes well-being. Another example would be an egalitarian standard
that says well-being or certain resources ought to be distributed as equally
as possible. And there are many other possibilities. Some will put the
independent standard in terms of treating people fairly, and others will
not. This first category of democratic theories designs and defends democratic institutions with an eye to promoting justice or the common good.
Among the readings collected here Nelson, Beitz, Estlund, and Young are
all in this category. Cohen and Habermas are difficult to locate, but Christiano and Waldron explicitly oppose it. Many have held that there is no
coherent account of what substantive justice or the common good would
mean, and the social choice tradition has been used by some in this way.
Others, including Christiano and Waldron, have emphasized that even if
there were a coherent account of it, there is too much disagreement about it
for it to be invoked in the justification of political arrangements. For

example, even if utilitarianism or egalitarianism were the correct account of substantive (procedure-independent) justice, they would remain highly controversial. As a result, these authors argue, we must back up to less controversial territory and settle for a fair procedure in which each is given an equal chance to determine the outcome. Procedural fairness is invoked as a weaker and more widely acceptable basis for political justification, and then it is argued that this supports some form of democratic legal and social institutions to implement the requisite procedural equality of persons.

Christiano takes a complex view of the relation between democracy and substantive (or not merely procedural) justice. In the end, democratic institutions are not recommended on the basis of any tendency to promote substantive justice, but on the basis that they are themselves dictated by principles of substantive justice. Justice, he thinks, requires treating every individual's interests equally, and this requires subjecting political decisions to collective choice procedures in which each person has an equal chance to advance his or her concerns. In short, justice requires fair social choice procedures, not procedures that aim at substantively just outcomes (on other matters).

There is a tension here, since among citizens' interests are interests in substantive justice on matters other than the structure of social choice procedures, such as economic distribution, racial and sexual discrimination, and many other things. Theorists such as Nelson, Beitz, Estlund, and Young argue that political procedures ought to aim at promoting just outcomes rather than merely giving each person a fair or equal role in the decision. Christiano rejects this move for reasons that also appeal to Waldron. Christiano and Waldron assume that there is no wide consensus on which outcomes are just and which are not. It would not immediately follow that a tendency to promote justice cannot or need not be a part of the justification of social choice procedures. Christiano suggests, though, that such an epistemic element would have no point unless there were enough consensus about justice that most citizens could come to be governed by what they held to be just policies (pp. 57–8). The fact of wide disagreement about justice, then, vitiates any rationale for an epistemic dimension of the authority of democratic arrangements. Christiano writes, "in the face of deep disagreements, individuals can still be treated fairly if they are treated as equals. Though they cannot be self-governing, they can be treated fairly and this is what is essentially attractive about democracy" (p. 42).

Waldron also rejects epistemic approaches because there is wide disagreement about justice. And he also opts for procedures that are fair to participants rather than procedures that aim at just outcomes.

Nevertheless, Waldron's reasoning is not quite the same as Christiano's. The importance of disagreement for Waldron lies in his evident acceptance of the principle that political arrangements must be justifiable to each individual in terms that they would not reject unless they were unreasonable.[3] Given wide reasonable disagreement about justice, it is difficult to see how an epistemic defense of democratic arrangements – a defense holding that they tend to promote substantive justice – might proceed. So Waldron's defense of democratic procedures appeals mainly to their giving each person a fair share of influence.

In the piece included here, Waldron considers arguments for and against letting a judicial branch of government have the final power of review of democratically produced legislation. It might seem that his skepticism about judicial review is predictable in light of his emphasis on fairness to all citizens in social decision making. Judges with the power of review have a higher order of power than the participants even in an otherwise egalitarian legislative procedure. But things cannot be this simple, since Waldron's comfort with representative legislative bodies shows that he is happy to let some citizens (at least elected representatives) have far more power over political outcomes than others (such as citizens who hold no high office). A good question to bring to Waldron's chapter is to ask what reason there is against judicial review that is not also an argument for direct rather than representative democracy. If the difference lies somehow in electoral authorization, would he drop his objections to judicial review if judges were elected? If the difference lies not in election but in the larger numbers of decision makers in a legislature, then should we prefer direct democracy to representative democracy?

A good way to study democratic theories that emphasize procedural fairness, taking Christiano and Waldron as good examples, is to look for their answers to a few natural questions: Can political justifications appeal to any controversial premises, doctrines, or principles? If this is not always impermissible, then exactly how do all substantive accounts of justice or common good get pushed aside in favor of a procedural treatment of justice for purposes of democratic theory? Or, if controversial doctrines always are impermissible in political justification, then are these authors prepared to say that their appeals to procedural fairness are, fortunately, uncontroversial? Certainly not everyone will accept their procedural accounts, but should that make their accounts unavailable? If only some controversy – say, "reasonable" or "good faith" controversy – is what must be avoided, then what is their argument that all substantive accounts of justice are subject to reasonable controversy and not just the same kind of unavoidable controversy that would plague even their procedural accounts? Waldron and Christiano are both aware of these challenges, but I leave it to the reader to decide how they propose to answer them, and how one author may differ from the other on this matter.

Part II: Ideal Deliberation

Cohen's paper explicitly acknowledges a debt to Habermas, and points out that other philosophers were also beginning to apply his ideas to theorizing about democracy around the same time. However, Habermas had not yet had much to say about the connection between his "ideal speech situation," and the structural organization of politics, the questions that Cohen emphasizes in this piece. It is useful then to say something about both Cohen's debt to Habermas, and also what turns out to be a fundamental difference. The distinction discussed just above, between theories that appeal to procedure-independent standards of justice or common good and theories that rest entirely on procedural fairness or justice, helps frame important interpretive questions about Habermas and Cohen.

Habermas has long argued that the substantial ethical standards of traditional societies have become unavailable in the modern world.[4] Among the reasons for this, some are purely philosophical: Habermas believes that appeals to theistic sources of moral law have been decisively defeated on philosophical grounds, and that many appeals to non-theistic standards that purport not to depend in any way on human faculties or practices are also unacceptable philosophically. A second strand of his rejection of strongly independent ethical standards rests on the increasing pluralism of modern societies, in which many traditions and outlooks overlap and interact in societies that nevertheless seek unity in a legitimate legal order. No sectarian account singled out from among the many competing ones can hope to provide the unity and stability pluralistic societies seek. For these and other reasons Habermas attempts to develop an account of moral normativity in which it arises within the structure of human capacities and practices rather than standing prior to and outside of them (as, say, God's will would), and yet is not tethered to any particular sectarian view of substantial goals. These are complex matters that cannot be closely examined here, but a few points help to set up Habermas's approach to democratic theory and its influence on Cohen and the deliberative approach to democracy generally.

Habermas proposes that objective moral norms are those that would be accepted by all affected parties in an ideal discourse. What is ideal about the discourse is, roughly, that participation is equally available to all affected and the outcome is determined only by the rational weight of the considerations advanced, and by unanimous acceptance of all participants. There are important similarities to the contractualist moral and political philosophies of Rawls and Scanlon, but also important differences.[5] One important difference is that Habermas denies that philosophers are in a position to ("monologically") determine what the outcome of such an ideal discourse would be. The standard is ideal discourse among *actual* people, and no philosophical idealization or simplification of the participants would be legitimate.

This naturally gives rise to the idea of attempting to approximate an ideal discourse among actual people, and Cohen's idea of deliberative democracy pursues this strategy. On Cohen's view the ideal deliberative situation (he is not committed to exactly Habermas's version of it) cannot be pondered by philosophers for its normative implications, but ought to be "mirrored" by social and political institutions. If this can be done there is the basis for a presumption that social decisions conform to what would be agreed to in ideal deliberation. This is Cohen's normative basis for democratic legitimacy, and it supports a broadly egalitarian theory of social justice.

The idea of mirroring the ideal deliberative situation is problematic, and Habermas's own view does not require it. Consider a deliberative situation in which one interest group has disproportionate control of the course of debate because of their superior social power. Under these conditions the value of unfettered freedom of expression may serve to irrationally favor the views of the powerful. The idea of mirroring the ideal deliberation provides no plausible guidance in this kind of case, since it seems to suggest that while the unequal power in this case is certainly a deviation from the ideal, any differential infringement of the speech of the powerful would be simply a further deviation, and so ought to be avoided.

Habermas suggests a different approach. Social institutions ought, still, to be arranged in order to ground the presumption that what is actually decided would have been agreed to in ideal discourse. But Habermas rejects Cohen's suggestion that society as a whole should "mirror" the ideal deliberative situation, since this is not automatically the best way to ground the relevant presumption. One reason for this might be that deviations from the ideal are unavoidable in society at large, and there is no reason for supposing that the best response would be to minimize further deviations. What best grounds this presumption may be to meet one deviation with another. An instructive example might be Herbert Marcuse's recommendation of "selective intolerance" of the repetitive statements of the views of those with disproportionate power over the deliberation.[6]

Their power is a deviation from the ideal, but it should (Marcuse says) be met with a countervailing deviation of interference with their public expression, even though the result will not more closely mirror an ideal deliberative situation.

Habermas does not discuss countervailing deviations from ideal discourse, but emphasizes the richness and openness of less rigidly structured communication. He argues that a more restrictive model applies only to a specifically political component of the larger social system, and depends for its value on a "wilder" social background. On this view the rigid conditions of ideal deliberation would be unfortunate even if they were followed without any deviation. Countervailing deviations from ideal discourse would be incompatible with Cohen's idea of mirroring the ideal discourse, but would still be compatible with Habermas's stated approach to democratic legitimacy. On this view, the case for liberal and majoritarian political institutions is more complicated than it would otherwise be. Even if the ideal discourse proceeds under guarantees that resemble certain liberal democratic legal norms, real discourse might best proceed in terms of very different norms – whichever ones would best ground the presumption that the results would be unanimously acceptable if discourse had been ideal.

It is not clear that the kind of political discourse recommended by deliberative democrats fits the mirroring model even under the best of conditions. Cohen follows Rawls (following Rousseau) in supposing that democratic participation ought to be guided by a conception of justice or common good of the kind that ideal discourse seeks to explicate. The ideal discourse itself, then, could not be made up of the same kind of participation. In real political discourse citizens ought, partly, to consider what justice requires, but in ideal discourse (as in Rawls's original position) this question is not available. What justice requires is explicated or defined by the device of the ideal discourse, and so participants in that imaginary context must be addressing other issues altogether, such as their interests. Perhaps a real politics that mirrors the ideal discourse would similarly avoid questions of justice, but this is neither descriptive of real politics, nor is it what theorists of deliberative democracy generally recommend.

A useful set of questions to bring to the Habermas and Cohen readings, then, are these: Is any real "mirroring" possible and desirable? If not, then what does the ideal deliberative situation imply for the structure of actual social and political institutions? Are there clear implications, and if so are they plausible? Indeed, are they recognizably democratic?

Part III: Wise Decisions

The readings collected here do not appear chronologically. William Nelson's book appeared in 1980, and was perhaps the leading edge of the turn toward the topic of democracy. Nelson's view anticipated the deliberative democracy movement in political theory by insisting that democratic institutions depended for their justification on the tendency of free and open democratic government to improve the quality of political decisions by independent moral standards. This strong epistemic emphasis remains a controversial view (as we saw in the discussion of Christiano and Waldron), but the emphasis on the processes of communication leading up to voting is what has come to be so typical of contemporary democratic theory. Still, it is important to see that the role of interpersonal deliberation in Nelson's own theory is smaller than might appear.

Nelson writes, "the tests that a law has to pass to be adopted in a constitutional democracy are analogous to the tests that a moral principle must pass in order to be an acceptable moral principle" (101). Nelson lays out a contractualist moral theory very similar to that of Scanlon and Habermas, in which a set of moral rules is acceptable if it is the object of a possible consensus. There are differences: For example, unlike Scanlon, Nelson does not explicitly deal with the possibility that some people may object to certain proposed moralities on unreasonable grounds such as malice or exaggerated self-concern. Still, the account of morality is recognizably contractualist, locating moral justification in the idea of a hypothetical situation in which all parties could agree.

There is a similarity to Cohen too. Cohen and Nelson both suggest democracy has the desirable feature of being structurally similar to the hypothetical contractualist initial situation, giving us reason to expect democratic decisions to tend to be ones that could have been accepted in the ideal situation. But again there are differences. Nelson's initial contractual situation is like Scanlon's, and unlike Cohen's in that there is no real place for interpersonal deliberation. The central function of the initial situation is to allow each individual to veto any proposals he finds unacceptable. There is no mention here of other effects of discussion such as a broadening of one's perspective, or a reshaping of one's values and interests themselves, not to mention the simple gathering of information, and the subjection of one's arguments to rational criticism. For Nelson, majority rule in an "open" government resembles the initial contractual situation in two main respects: (1) in such a system each person gets to register his acceptance or rejection of proposals, (2) since proposals can be rejected by others, advocates will tend to present proposals that they expect to be acceptable to others.

In following Mill, Nelson celebrates the tendency of advocates in an open government to *defend* their proposals by showing that they should be thought acceptable to all or most citizens. This kind of moralizing of public discourse may well be a good thing, and may well improve the expected moral quality of outcomes, but it is not clear that it has any analogue in the contractual initial situation as conceived by Nelson. He conceives of justification as involving showing that a proposal would or could be accepted in a contractual initial situation (as well as showing that it could be accepted by real people – this is his own twist on the familiar versions in Rawls and Scanlon). So justification is not a mode of discourse that takes place *within* the initial situation on this kind of view. Insofar as real democratic discourse does involve justificational argumentation rather than simple endorsements or rejections of proposals the analogy between Nelson's contractual situation and democratic procedures may be strained.

Nelson claims to model his view on Mill's celebration of the epistemic value of "open government." But Mill explicitly supposes that voters, despite inevitable bias toward self-interest, ought properly to address the question of the general good. "[T]he voter is under an absolute moral obligation to consider the interest of the public, not his private advantage, and give his vote, to the best of his judgment, exactly as he would be bound to do if he were the sole voter, and the election depended upon him alone" (Mill 1861, Chapter 10). Voters are not supposed to confine their political advocacy to the pursuit of their own interests. This is no inconsistency in Mill, since as a utilitarian he asserts no isomorphism between democracy and contractualism. So it makes perfect sense for Mill to speak of citizens and officials in open government "defending" the morality and justice of proposals. But insofar as Nelson wants the epistemic value of democracy to derive from what he calls the analogy between democracy and contractualism, this Millian conception of democratic practice would not be open to him.

Nelson and Charles Beitz have a lot in common. Both rely on an underlying contractualist understanding of justice, and both argue that a central virtue of democratic arrangements is that they tend to produce social decisions that are just by contractualist standards. Beitz relies heavily on the language of fairness, however, in a way that Nelson does not. Indeed, the structure of Beitz's view can be easily missed as a result.

Beitz says he seeks to determine fair procedures of political decision-making. While he assumes that procedures ought to be democratic, he argues that they need not be obsessively egalitarian. Unlike Christiano,

Beitz does not give any foundational argumentative role to the idea of equal social and political power for all. His argument rests on a deeper level of justification – a contractualist framework of moral justification – from which questions about the appropriate distribution of social, political, and economic power can be addressed. The contractualist approach reflects a certain way of regarding all citizens as equals, but it does not assume that institutions must be egalitarian in themselves.

What Beitz means by a "fair procedure" is whichever procedures would be acceptable to all reasonable citizens. And "political equality" and "egalitarianism" are likewise located at this deep justificatory level (99). This raises a question of terminology. On Beitz's view, if the rule of a wise elite could be justified in the contractual framework (he doesn't think it could be) then he would be prepared to categorize it as a fair and egalitarian procedure. This use of words can easily obscure the real thrust of his argument, which could just as well be described as a contractualist argument *against* the view that decision procedures must be fair and/or egalitarian. Rather than being mainly about the fairness or equality of political procedures, Beitz (like Nelson, unlike Christiano and Waldron) emphasizes their tendency to produce just decisions. But this instrumental or epistemic consideration is not morally basic either, since it would not be the only consideration from within the authoritative contractualist moral perspective. Despite all the talk about fairness, then, Beitz is not arguing that appropriate democratic procedures must be internally fair. He asks instead what procedures could be justified to each citizen, and allows that the answer might not match what we would independently recognize as (internally) a fair procedure.[7]

Consider an entrenched minority, such as African-Americans. In one sense, a fair procedure is one that gives each person equal power. But if the majority's power is chronically used to treat members of the minority unjustly, then, at least if there are appropriate alternatives, it is unfair to African-Americans to employ a procedure of equal individual power. By saying that this is unfair, Beitz means that it would be reasonable for African-Americans to object to such a system in view of the unjust consequences it would have for them. Thus, Beitz allows the choice of appropriate procedures to be determined partly by their tendency to produce substantively just decisions and outcomes. He calls this, somewhat misleadingly, a part of a theory of the procedure's fairness, but in any case he is explicit that he is "relativizing the requirements of fairness to underlying views about acceptable results" (112). Beitz acknowledges that his account of political fairness is a "reforming definition" (219), and that it means only that political arrangements are justifiable to all citizens (228). Beitz, then, does not assume that political procedures must give all an equal chance for influence (contrast Christiano), nor does he argue that they could or should mirror the hypothetical contractual situation (contrast Cohen). And unlike Habermas he does not even suppose that social institutions should be designed to produce the results that an ideal deliberation would have recommended. Rather, he takes the structure of political procedures to be one topic among others to be addressed from a contractualist standpoint, and the tendency to produce justice is one consideration among several that emerge as important from that contractualist point of view. One interesting question for Beitz is why the hypothetical contractors would not simply choose to empower (or, as Mill suggests, at least give extra voting power to) whichever set of rulers would be most adept at ascertaining and implementing substantive justice, even if this turns out to be a small privileged elite. He seems to say that this would be incompatible with a reasonable demand for equal respect, but what kind of respect? If it were simply assumed that it would be disrespectful to politically treat some citizens as more capable than others, then both Millian plural voting and rule by a wise elite would be ruled out by assumption and not explained by argument. What considerations might arise from the appropriate contractualist point of view that would count against such an epistemic elitism even though the aim of promoting substantive justice is held by Beitz to play such an important role?

Part IV: Deliberation and Institutions

Democratic deliberation, under certain conditions, is often held to have an improving effect on the quality of democratic decisions, though there are differing philosophical accounts of what kind of improvement it is. Deliberation is not an on/off affair, but comes in different quantities. In repressive regimes it is natural to expect the amount of political deliberation to be reduced across the board, while in regimes protecting expression, and in cultures that support and encourage it, we expect political deliberation to be more voluminous. Democratic theorists are not indifferent between these two scenarios, but tend to hold that more deliberation has better effects. This puts the case too baldly, of course, but with appropriate qualifications it is widely thought that the salutary effects of deliberation tend to increase and decrease with its quantity. In the piece on "Political Quality," I argue that this raises a fundamental question about the idea of political equality. What if the ideal of equal availability of political input conflicts with the goal of increasing the amount of input in ways that would improve the result? By analogy, there is a standard difficulty for simple egalitarian theories of economic justice, in the fact that it is possible to face a choice between distributive equality at a very low level, or modest inequality at levels that are vastly improved for everyone. Discussions of political equality have often proceeded as if input is a zero-sum, preventing the same dilemma from arising for a specifically political egalitarianism. I argue that it can indeed arise, and I defend the idea that strict equality of available political input is an unattractive ideal for this reason.

This might easily be misunderstood as an argument against efforts, in present circumstances, to promote equal political influence. But inequality of influence also damages the quality of political deliberation. The argument is not that the degree of equality should be ignored in favor of greater quantity of input, but only that both matter to the quality of the deliberation, and that the importance of quantity is often ignored in normative theories of democracy. I sketch a voucher arrangement that illustrates how modest inequality might promote overall input enough to plausibly be worth it. Such arrangements are often in tension with the value of constitutional protections of free expression. Even if the main line of argument is accepted, any practical implementation of the idea will require ingenuity, and readers might consider whether weaknesses or over-simplifications in the voucher scheme I describe could be remedied by other arrangements.

Theories that attend to political discourse as an epistemically fruitful process are often challenged by the specter of Plato, who might ask, why not let the wisest rule rather than the largest number? Aristotle replied that two heads are better than one when they reason together.[8] Of course, the process of reasoning together could only improve the view of any of the participants if in the reasoning process they encountered ideas or facts that they had not previously encountered, or at least had not considered in the same way. Interpersonal reasoning is impotent without differences among the participants. This epistemic value of difference is central to Iris Young's argument against historically familiar devices and institutions that exclude or marginalize many groups of people from the forum of democratic deliberation. Aristotle's simple point about the value of multiple people reasoning together opens the door to this point, but has long been domesticated by the forces of marginalization. The operative thought seems to have been that two rational, calm, leisured, informed, propertied, and educated heads are better than one.

Young seeks to explain the democratic value of a social attention to the wide variety of social groups. Some argue that if we pay too much attention to these differences society will become "balkanized," split into factions with so little common ground that politics will be no more than a fierce competition. Young rejects "identity politics", in which a person's political perspective derives from only one or two salient group identities, such as race, gender, or religion. The problem with this approach, she argues, is that it still suppresses too much of the diversity that really exists. Everyone is a member of many overlapping interest and identity groups; no one's position in the web of social connections is the same as anyone else's, except in one or another limited respect. A black male Cuban art student in New York is not simply black, nor simply male, nor simply Cuban, but a socially unique combination of each of these things, and many others.

Young suggests that the threat of balkanization is actually reduced by a social attention to a wider range of difference. She also argues that this more variegated attention to difference promotes the tendency of political decisions to be good and just. By identifying social groups in this finer way, one result is that the resulting groups will often be smaller and less compelling to their members. Young suggests that this will lead people, for strategic reasons, away from a competitive approach to politics and more toward a political discourse of justice. It might do this because smaller and more partial group identities will have less clout. It may seem that it would be even better to completely avoid group identification for the same reason, forcing people to put their political cases in universalistic terms. But Young's approach incorporates the obvious fact that many injustices cannot be effectively placed on the political agenda unless the victims and their supporters can get together, so to speak. The injustices suffered by homosexuals would not be politically addressed unless gays and lesbians had developed certain aspects of a shared culture, literature, and public presence as a group. The reason, on Young's view, is not that this gives them the numerical strength to win in a majority politics; their numbers are too small for that. Rather, by joining into a partial identity group they have managed to advance a more compelling case that they are victims of injustice. At the same time, it should be possible to avoid forcing everyone to choose one or two main affiliations, and so to avoid the problems of a balkanized identity politics. Gays are not just gay, and so need not devote their whole political energy to that one set of issues, thus competing with other totalizing identifications. But by acknowledging that being gay subjects a person to distinctive forms of injustice, gays can work together to present this moral case publicly. If being gay were politically invisible, this would be impossible. Young's conclusion is that civil institutions should encourage this more fine-grained and overlapping form of a politics of difference in the interest of democracy and justice. Some injustices, of course, are suffered by people who have been unjustly grouped in the first place.[9] Many argue that the social category of race is a grouping created, in the first instance, by racism. It would seem to be different in this way from, say, blindness or deafness. The injustices suffered by people who are blind are not primarily the result of hatred or discrimination against the blind. Rather, the injustice is largely one of culpable negligence in designing physical and cultural spaces without due attention to the needs of those who cannot see and hear. In these cases, a more salient group identification among the blind or the deaf has all the potential that Young suggests. But in the case of race, the perpetuation of race as a socially salient category is thought by some to be a problem in its own right. In that case, conceptualizing injustice in racial terms in order more effectively to address it has a downside as well, by tending to further entrench the social significance of racial identity. The same is sometimes said of gender, that ideally it should be eradicated as a social category (see Okin 1989). Conceptualization of injustice in terms of gender or race (even within Young's important emphasis on overlapping identities) would be, on that model, questionable at least as a long-term program. Some groups are treated unjustly, but some people are unjustly grouped. Many groups, such as homosexuals, seem to have aspects of both. Still, the difference raises interesting questions within Young's framework.

Part V: Why Vote?

One of the most intractable puzzles in normative democratic theory stems from the tiny chance that any voter has of changing the outcome. In any large election, the chance of my vote making the difference is linked to the tiny chance that all other votes would produce an exact tie. The US presidential election in 2000 came down to only a few hundred votes in Florida, probably a number too small to exceed the margin of error in counting the several million votes cast in Florida. Countless commentators drew the conclusion that every vote counts. But, of course, any single voter (or any group of a hundred), even in Florida, could have stayed home or changed their vote without changing the result. If, as economistic theories often assume, it is only rational to do what will best satisfy your own preferences, then it would seem to be rational to save the effort of voting and spend the time doing something of more consequence. On this view, it is hard to explain why so many people vote, apparently contrary to rationality.

One line of response to this challenge is to argue that you have a reason to vote if you have a duty to vote. And you might have a duty to vote even despite the small chance of making a difference. One approach says that even if your chance of making a difference is small, you are morally required to attend to the consequences for everyone, whether or not this reflects your actual preferences. Acting on a small chance of enormous overall consequences might well be a morally better choice than refraining from voting, still strictly on consequentialist grounds. (See Barry and Parfit citations in the Brennan and Lomasky piece.) A different approach would argue that not all of our duties derive simply from the aim of producing the best consequences. For example, it is wrong to collaborate in cruel Nazi medical research even if someone else would willingly take your place with consequences at least as bad. So perhaps there is a duty to vote even apart from the effects of voting.

Geoffrey Brennan and Loren Lomasky offer a theory of both the rationality and the morality of voting that fully faces the fact that no individual's vote has more than a negligible chance of making a difference. Their idea is that a voter gets a psychological kick, or boost, or thrill from voting. Just as you cheer for your favorite team even though it makes no difference, you may vote for your favorite candidate. It is satisfying to express yourself, and voting is rational as a means to this satisfaction. Then, why is it morally good to vote? Brennan and Lomasky suggest that it is morally good to visit a sick friend, even apart from its benefits to the friend, in the sense that it is part of a good moral character to care enough to be drawn to visit. Likewise, they say, a good citizen will care about politics and be drawn to express herself on the important matters of the day. There are difficulties here that bear further thought: What is expressive about voting anonymously in a secluded booth? Even if the character trait of caring about politics is intrinsically good, why is it good to manifest it or indicate it?

Alvin Goldman tackles the question how it is that my vote could be thought to contribute to the outcome even though the outcome would have been the same even without my vote. This is not quite the question about rationality or the question about morality, but a question about causality. But Goldman argues that if we are not even partially causally responsible for the outcome of an election we couldn't be to blame for it either. So in order to support the idea that you can be partially blamed for the election of an evil candidate if you vote for her, it must be shown that you can be held partially causally responsible.

Goldman's approach is built around a compelling example from a non-electoral context. Suppose you are on a firing squad, and each member fires a bullet into the heart of the victim at the same time. It seems obvious that each shooter is morally responsible, at least partly, for the death. For example, if you knew the victim was innocent of any crime, you would be guilty of a terrible wrong. Goldman thinks this judgment depends on each shooter's contributing, causally, to the innocent person's death. Since it is obvious that each shooter is guilty of a great wrong, this commits us to holding that each is partially causally responsible for the death even though none of the shots made a difference in the victim's fate. Even if you had not fired, the victim would have been shot to death anyway. Still, you are partly to blame, and so you must be partly causally responsible.

The story roughly parallels the case of voters who elect an evil candidate by a margin of more than one vote. No single vote made a difference, but each voter is partially causally responsible in the same way as each member of the firing squad is. Then each can also be partly to blame.

Goldman considers two accounts of partial or contributory causation that might allow us to hold voters responsible for the outcomes they vote for even when their votes make no difference. Rather than discuss the details, it is worth drawing attention to the pivotal assumption that (at least in cases sufficiently similar to voting) an agent bears no moral responsibility for an outcome unless he bears some causal responsibility for it. It is important not to confuse this with certain different but obvious facts. One is that in some cases a person's moral responsibility derives partly from their causal responsibility. Murder by a single shooter is plainly such a case. Another obvious fact is that if there is a murder by a single shooter, then if I am not the shooter I am (normally[10]) not causally responsible, and, for that reason, not morally responsible for the death. We cannot conclude from these observations that in general (or in shooting and voting cases anyway) an agent is not morally responsible for an outcome unless also causally responsible. The reason is that this is disputable in the case where the outcome is "overdetermined" – where the acts of some set of people cause the outcome, even though no single participant's act makes any difference, because the acts of the others would have been enough anyway.

We have several choices in such cases. We might hold that since none makes a difference, none is causally responsible, and so none is morally responsible. This seems absurd, as the firing squad case makes clear. So we might hold, as Goldman does, that since each is morally responsible each must be partly causally responsible even though none makes any difference to the outcome. Then we need an account of causal responsibility that does not depend on making a difference, as Goldman tries to supply.

But we might hold instead that each is morally complicit, and so potentially blameworthy, even if none of them is even partially causally responsible considered alone. (Notice that all sides agree that the shooters considered together are causally responsible.) This possibility is easy to overlook if the question is described in terms of whether a person is partly morally *responsible* for the outcome. That language is suited to cases where moral responsibility rests on causal responsibility, since it encourages us to run those two ideas together. But if we wonder whether this is so in all cases, we can simply ask whether a participant acted wrongly, or is morally blameworthy for their participation. Then the more general theoretical question becomes whether a person can be morally blameworthy for an act even apart from that act's causal consequences. If so, as legions of moral philosophers believe (and legions deny), then morally blaming each shooter or each voter does not require us to find a way to hold them causally responsible for the bad effects of the collection of acts in which they participated.

Even if the ethics of voting could be accounted for in terms other than the value of the outcomes to which one's vote does or does not causally contribute, the question of causality would remain important. Apart from the questions of moral praise or blame for voting in certain ways, much traditional democratic theory has followed Rousseau in holding that democratic government is the only legitimate kind because in a democracy the people rule. It could plausibly be held that no agent rules if her acts are not even partly causally responsible for the laws. So far, rule by the people might be possible even if individual people did not contribute to ruling. Suppose that the people rule only in an essentially collective way; as a group they are causally responsible for the laws (in the way that the firing squad is causally responsible for the death, roughly), even though no individual is even partly causally responsible. This would require an account of essentially collective action, so that the group could rule even when no individual did.

Even then there are remaining problems. It has often been argued that rule of some by others violates a natural right to liberty, but that in democracy the people rule themselves. This very demanding doctrine requires that each subject of the laws also rules, and that seems to require that each is at least partly causally responsible for the laws. The cases of causal overdetermination that occupy Goldman directly challenge the tenability of this demanding standard of political legitimacy, and Goldman's account of partial or contributory causation, if successful, would go a long way toward vindicating it.

Part VI: Formal Models and Normative Theory

Social choice theory's conceptualization of democracy as the aggregation and satisfaction of individual preferences has been criticized by many in the deliberative democracy genre. Many of these theorists appeal to principles of morality or political justice that stand outside of actual preferences and provide a basis for deciding which preferences are most important to satisfy. Rawls, Habermas, Cohen, and Beitz are drawn particularly to the idea (in various forms) that the relative moral importance of someone's preferences must be determined in a (real or imaginary) rational confrontation with the preferences of others in which some unanimous solution is sought. On this view, call it the broadly contractualist approach, real democratic processes should not be taken simply to aggregate reported preferences, but to arrive at an aggregate estimation of what laws and politics could meet that test of idealized unanimity. On other views, call them non-contractualist approaches to deliberative democracy, while the appropriate standards of justice may involve a simpler aggregation of preferences or interests – as in utilitarianism, for example – democratic processes transform individual preferences in a rational process of discussion and debate. Insofar as the deliberative democracy approach (of either kind) is a rejection of the economistic vision of politics embodied in social choice theory, it is fair to ask whether they give any reason for rejecting or ignoring social choice theory's troubling conclusions.

In non-contractualist versions of deliberative democracy, while preferences are shaped by democratic deliberation, in the end the resulting preferences are apparently to be somehow aggregated to determine the most satisfactory public policy. Social choice theory, then, enters the scene after the deliberation is over, gathers individual preferences (for example, through a voting procedure) and asks what rule should take us from the set of preferences to an aggregate preference ranking that will determine policy.

By contrast, contractualist versions of deliberative democracy simply talk less about preferences and their aggregation, and so might seem less vulnerable to social choice theory's grip. This is far from obvious. Even if voters do not (even ideally) simply report their own preference or interests but rather offer judgments on justice or the common good in the manner of contractualism, they must still arrive at rankings of the social alternatives according to that criterion. Perhaps one voter thinks A is more conducive to justice than B, and B more conducive than C, and so on, while other voters might order these alternatives differently. If so then social choice theory's question for advocates of democracy remains: by what rule should we convert these individual rankings into an aggregate ranking in order to determine public policy?

Either way, so far, social choice theory applies intact, and so we might expect all the skeptical results to survive as well. David Miller argues, however, that processes of deliberation tend to transform individual preferences in certain systematic ways that avoid the brunt of Arrow's argument that no aggregation rule is acceptable. Roughly (leaving details to Miller), if we seek to respect only preferences that have been shaped by public deliberative processes, then we can drop Arrow's condition requiring that our aggregation rule must generate an outcome for every logically possible set of individual preferences. The reason is that deliberation tends to produce preferences that, as a group, structure the choice in a shared way (in the technical term, the profile of individual preferences tends to become "single-peaked") which avoids Arrow's impossibility result. In other words, if our aggregation rule only handles single-peaked sets of preferences, it will nonetheless handle post-deliberative preference sets. So we should not regret the fact that it violates Arrow's requirement that it handle all possible preference sets.

Miller's second main point is that many issues on which preferences are not single-peaked can, in principle, be separated into several issues on which they are. He further argues that democratic deliberation can allow these issues to be taken up singly by a rule that handles only single-peaked preferences.

Social choice theory can be highly technical, proceeding in symbolized formulas and complicated proofs. Even Miller's argument, while relatively accessible, relies on some highly technical research by others. Still, it usefully illustrates at least two important points. First, it shows that even non-economistic theories that don't put much stock in unreflective preference might, nevertheless, involve individual rankings of social alternatives in a way that leaves the door open to social choice theory. Second, it shows that the admirable logical rigor characteristic of technical social choice theory should not deter philosophical reflection on the merits of the axioms and assumptions on which the results depend.

As we have seen there are philosophical reasons behind the (now receding) economistic phase in democratic theory, including an array of utilitarian argument, and various interpretations of liberal and scientific value-neutrality. In addition, however, it seems likely that the fascinating, if skeptical, result proven by Arrow in his Impossibility Theorem attracted so much attention and raised so many fruitful questions that the economistic conception of democracy came to crowd out more traditional alternatives. The more traditional approach, in which citizens act to promote the common good rather than merely to secure their own interests, had its most influential theorist in Rousseau. But under prevailing academic proclivities, the Rousseauean view came to seem hopelessly vague, or even utopian, or perhaps also dangerously seductive – the kind of thing ripe for scientific debunking. It didn't help matters that nothing in the Rousseauean approach seemed to have received the precise formal characterization that Arrow and others gave to the economic approach.

It turns out that this was not quite true. There was a relatively unknown mathematical result from the eighteenth century that (inadvertently, as far as we can tell) gave a rigorous statistical interpretation to many of the issues and claims in Rousseau's account of democracy and the general will. Condorcet's Jury Theorem, as we now call it, was rediscovered by Black (1958), and introduced into recent political theory first by Barry (1965). The theorem has attracted increasing interest as the trend in "deliberative democracy" has grown. In our final chapter, Bernard Grofman and Scott Feld draw a fascinating parallel between Condorcet's Jury Theorem and Rousseau's theory of democracy and the general will. It will be helpful here to explain the basis of the Jury Theorem itself, and to raise some questions about its value for normative democratic theory.

Begin with the fact that while a fair coin flipped a few times is not likely to produce a very equal head/tail ratio, with more tosses the ratio becomes more even. With just a few tosses, an outcome of, say 70% heads, 30% tails, would not be shocking. But with many tosses of a fair coin, a 70/30 split is almost out of the question. With enough tosses it becomes certain that the division will be almost exactly 50/50. This "Law of Large Numbers," is the core of the proof of the Jury Theorem.

Let us proceed in several small steps: first, change the coin from a fair one, to one weighted slightly in favor of heads, so in each toss it has a 51% chance of being heads. Now with enough tosses the percentage of heads is certain to be almost exactly 51%. The more tosses, the closer to exactly 51% it is likely to be. Now obviously the same would be true if instead of one coin flipped repeatedly, we considered many coins, all weighted the same way, each having a 51% chance of coming up heads. The more coins we flipped, the closer the frequency of heads would come to exactly 51%. Now, the same obviously would be true if we had individual voters instead of coins, where each will say either "heads" or "tails" but each has a 51% chance of saying "heads." The more such voters, the closer the frequency of "heads" answers would come to exactly 51%. Here is the payoff: if the frequency of "heads" is bound to be almost exactly 51%, then, of course, it is even more certain to be over 50%. So the chance that at least a majority will say "heads" is astronomical if the group is large, and it gets higher with the size of the group. It is also plainly higher if instead of 51%, each voter (or coin) has an even higher chance of saying "heads," say 55% or 75%.

So if voters each have an individual likelihood above 50% (call it (50 + n)%) of giving the correct answer (whatever it is) to a dichotomous choice (heads/tails, yes/no, true/false, better/worse, etc.), then in a large group the percentage giving the correct answer is bound to be exceedingly close to (50 + n%). Therefore, the chance that it will be *at least 50%*, is even higher, approximating certainty as the group gets larger or the voters are better. In summary, if voters are all 51% likely to be correct, then in a large number of voters it is almost certain that almost exactly 51% will be correct, and so even more certain that more than 50% will be correct. The results are very much the same if we weaken the assumption that all voters have the same competence, but assume only an average competence above 50%, so long as the individual competences that produce this average are distributed normally around the average. Abnormal distributions change the results significantly, sometimes for better, sometimes for worse.

Several problems arise once this result is used to support democratic political arrangements on epistemic grounds. One obvious difficulty is that the result assumes that voters are, on average, better than random with respect to the issue in question. This is far from obvious.[11] Second, the Jury Theorem assumes that each voter's input is statistically independent of the votes of others, a condition that might be widely violated in real democracies.[12] Third, the Jury Theorem applies only to dichotomous choices, those that take the form of yes/no, or better/worse, etc., while political choices do not obviously take this form.[13] Fourth, the Rousseauean use of the Jury Theorem still assumes that there is such a thing as the general will or the common good. It is natural to suppose that this must be some mathematical function of the interests – or the informed, post-deliberation interests – of individuals. But in that case the argument, in social choice theory, that there is no such function that meets all necessary normative criteria, must be confronted at this deeper constitutive level.[14]

A final problem for the Condorcetian epistemic approach is this: just as moral experts will be too controversial, even if they exist, to figure in any justification of authoritarian political arrangements, any particular set of criteria for determining whether the average voter is better than random (as, for example, the Jury Theorem requries) will be just as controversial. If the qualifications of an alleged moral expert will always be subject to reasonable disagreement, then so will any list of qualifications itself. So, even if you or I might sometimes have good reason to think the requirements of the Jury Theorem are met, and so have good reason to surrender our moral judgment to the majority outcome when we disagree with it, there will always be reasonable grounds for others to deny this by rejecting the criteria of moral competence that we have used (Estlund 1993).

Two final points. First, the Grofman and Feld piece might initially look to be a scholastic effort to discern influences between Condorcet and Rousseau. In fact it uses Condorcet's Jury Theorem to sharpen many of the issues that arise in assessing broadly Rousseauean approaches to democratic theory from a normative philosophical standpoint. Second, research on the mathematical properties of the Jury Theorem and related results is, like social choice theory, highly technical, and often deters students of political philosophy for this reason. But in both cases (as in much science) there are substantial philosophical positions at stake in the background of the technical apparatus, issues on which mathematicians and economists have no advantage over philosophers, to say the least. They should neither be dismissed as philosophically irrelevant, nor studied with a tunnel-vision in which they appear as self-sufficient philosophical systems conclusively pronouncing on the prospects of democracy.

Notes

1   A search of *Philosopher's Index* shows that articles with "democracy" in the subject were 40% as common as articles with "justice" in the subject from 1970 to 1984. From 1985 to 1999 they came to be 75% as common.

2   There are different ways of being an intermediary. Cohen is by no means a Habermas expositor, and his body of work suggests ambivalence about some of Habermas's ideas.

3   Waldron's commitment to this principle may not be clear from the reading included here (though see the paragraph about "good faith disagreement" at p. 72. I defend this interpretation and other interpretive claims I make here, and venture several criticisms in Estlund 2000.

4   For an influential overview of Habermas's work up to about 1982 see McCarthy 1982. For a more recent study of Habermas's moral and political thought, see Rehg 1997.

5   An exceptionally clear critical comparative treatment of Rawls's, Scanlon's, and Habermas's approach to moral philosophy is Kelly 2000.

6   I discuss this Marcusean idea in the context of deliberative democracy in Estlund 2001.

7   For more discussion of these different senses of the fairness of a procedure see the Estlund piece in this volume, in the section, "Is there an absolute right to equal influence?"

8   Aristotle's point is very different from the epistemic value of large numbers of voters as represented in Condorcet's Jury Theorem, discussed below in Part VI. For discussion of the Aristotle texts on this point see Waldron 1995.

9   I owe this important point to a discussion with my seminar on democracy authority at Brown University in Fall 2000.

10 Leave aside the possibility that I could have intervened but didn't.

11 For more discussion of this issue see Estlund 1993.

12 For more discussion of this issue see Estlund 1994.

13 List and Goodin (2001) extend the Jury Theorem to prove that even when there are more than two alternatives, the chance of the plurality

winner being correct increases with voter competence and the number of voters, and approaches certainty. It also increases with the number of alternatives.

14   At this constitutive level, Arrow's restriction of utility information to ordinal preference ranking without any measure of intensity is more easily challenged. See the essays in Elster and Hylland 1986.

Suggestions for Further Reading:

Books

Beitz, Charles (1989) *Political Equality*, Princeton, NJ: Princeton University Press.

Bohman, James (1996) *Public Deliberation: Pluralism, Complexity, and Democracy*, Cambridge, MA: The MIT Press.

Brennan, Geoffrey and Loren Lomasky (1993) *Democracy and Decision*, Cambridge: Cambridge University Press.

Chambers, Simone (1996) *Reasonable Democracy: Jürgen Habermas and the Politics of Discourse*, Ithaca, NY: Cornell University Press.

Christiano, Thomas (1996) *The Rule of the Many*, Boulder: Westview Press.

Dryzek, John (1990) *Discursive Democracy: Politics, Policy, and Political Science*, Cambridge: Cambridge University Press.

Fishkin, James (1991) *Deliberative Democracy*, New Haven, NJ: Yale University Press.

Gutmann, Amy and Dennis Thompson (1998) *Democracy and Disagreement*, Cambridge, MA: Harvard University Press.

Habermas, Jürgen (1996) *Between Facts and Norms: Contributions to a Discourse Theory of Law and Democracy*, Cambridge: Polity Press.

Mansbridge, Jane (1983) *Beyond Adversary Democracy*, Chicago: University of Chicago Press.

Nelson, William (1980) *On Justifying Democracy*, Boston: Routledge and Kegan Paul.

Nino, Carlos Santiago (1996) *The Constitution of Deliberative Democracy*, New Haven, NJ: Yale University Press.

Phillips, Anne (1993) *Democracy and Difference*, University Park: University of Pennsylvania Press.

Waldron, Jeremy (1999) *Law and Disagreement*, Oxford: Clarendon Press.

Young, Iris Marion (2000) *Inclusion and Democracy*, Oxford University Press.

Collections

Barry, Brian, and Russell Hardin, eds. (1982) *Rational Man and Irrational Society?* Sage Publications, Beverly Hills.

Benhabib, Seyla, ed. (1996) *Democracy and Difference. Contesting the Boundaries of the Political*, Princeton: Princeton University Press.

Bohman, James and William Rehg (1997) *Deliberative Democracy: Essays on Reason and Politics*, Cambridge, MA: MIT Press.

Copp, David, Jean Hampton, and John E. Roemer, eds. (1993) *The Idea of Democracy*, Cambridge: Cambridge University Press.

Elster, Jon, ed. (1998) *Deliberative Democracy*, Cambridge: Cambridge University Press.

Part I
Procedural Fairness

1

Democracy As Equality

Thomas Christiano

Society is organized by terms of association by which all are bound. The problem is to determine who has the right to define these terms of association. Democrats state that only the people have a right to rule over the society. And they argue that citizens ought to be equals in important respects in making these decisions. What is the basis of these views? We have seen that liberty accounts of democracy fail to provide a thorough understanding of the foundations of democratic decisionmaking. In large part this failure is due to the dependence of these conceptions on consensus within the society. They are unable to account for the basic democratic principle that when there are disagreements over what the terms of association are to be, that view that secures support from a majority of the citizens ought to be chosen. This is the problem of incompatibility. These theories also fail to account for the interests persons have in democratic decision-making that explain why a person ought to be allotted equal shares in political rule. This is the problem of trade-offs.

Although liberty over the common social world is incompatible with democracy, equality on its own may provide the basis. After all, democracy implies commitments to equality, such as equality in voting power as well as equality of opportunity to participate in discussion. Egalitarian theories attempt to derive a conception of democracy from a principle of equality among persons. They acknowledge fundamental conflicts of interests and convictions in society and assert that because of this lack of consensus, each person may demand an equal share in political rule.

At the same time an egalitarian conception of the foundations of democracy must include an important component of liberty views that is often left out by egalitarians. It ought to accommodate and explain the importance of the convictions citizens hold and the role of public discussion in democracy. Democratic decisionmaking is not merely a matter of each person voting his or her preference. Individual citizens' preferences are formed in society as a result of social interaction they have with others and the institutions that structure social interaction. It is important for them to reflect critically on and improve their preferences so as to have a sophisticated appreciation of their interests and ideals. A democratic theory ought to have something to say about what constitutes a reasonable and just context for the formation of these preferences. . . .

In this section we will look at an egalitarian approach to democracy that requires that each person's *interests* ought to be given equal consideration in choosing the laws and policies of a society.[1] This approach begins with Thomas Rainsborough's observation that "the poorest he that is in England has a life to live as the greatest he."[2] It goes on to claim that democracy is founded on this principle of equal consideration of interests.

Let us explore the distinction between judgments and interests and show how it is related to the principle of equality as well as sketch the relation of judgments and interests to democracy. First, an *interest* is something that is a component of a person's overall well-being. I have interests in pleasure, friendship, knowledge, health, and so on. I am better off when my interests are satisfied and worse off when they are not. An interest is not the same as the satisfaction of desire. I may desire many things that do not contribute to my own good. I may desire that peace and justice reign forever over the world, but I am not better off if ten thousand years from now there is peace and justice, though this does satisfy my desire. I may knowingly desire things that harm me because I am addicted to them or simply because I have been raised in a way that encourages masochism. Interests also differ from judgments. An interest is something that can be attributed to me whether I believe it or not. Someone can coherently say of me that it would be better for me if I had more pleasure in my life even if I, because of certain religious convictions, abhor pleasure and believe it to be bad. In this case, I may judge falsely what is in my interest. A judgment is a belief about a fact of the matter or a principle of justice or one's interests. Interests are one kind of fact about which we make judgments. Judgments can be correct or incorrect, whereas interests are not correct or incorrect; they are simply attributes of a person.

Equal consideration of interests means that advancing the interests of one person is as important as advancing the interests of any other person. There is no reason why one person should have a fundamentally better life than others, because "each has a life to live." To the extent that social institutions have a great influence on how people's lives go, they are unjust when they unnecessarily make some people's lives go worse than others.

It is an elementary requirement of justice that individuals ought to be treated equally if they are equal in the relevant ways and may be treated unequally if they are unequal in a relevant way. Each person has an equally important life to live, so there is a strong presumption in favor of his or her interests being given equal consideration. Furthermore, there is no good reason at the outset for arranging things so that some persons' lives will go better than others. Let us consider why some have thought that the lives of some individuals ought to go better than the lives of others. Some have maintained that race or sex ought to determine how a person's life can go. They have thought that women's or blacks' interests are less important than those of men or whites because of the natural differences between them and that the lives of these could be worse without injustice. But this is false; the fact that someone is a woman or black is of no relevance to issues of justice. They each have a life to live and interests to satisfy, and it would be unjust to treat their interests as less important. Social institutions that systematically make it harder for women or blacks to live flourishing lives than for others to are unjust. Others have thought that there is no injustice in the fact that the children of poor parents are not likely to do nearly as well as the children of the wealthy. That growing up in poverty and without the benefits of education makes it much harder and much less likely for a child to live a satisfying life implies that the institutions that permit these great disparities are unjust. The wealth or poverty of the family into which one is born hardly seem relevant to whether one's life ought to go well or not. This kind of argument can be generalized. We find injustice in any society that systematically ensures that some persons' lives go worse than others'. Thus, if we take the standpoint of considering each person's life as a whole, we see no relevant reason for treating anyone's interests unequally.

How does all of this apply to democracy? Democracy gives individuals equal abilities to advance their concerns when decisions concerning the terms of association are made. For instance, each person is provided with an equally weighted vote in deciding the outcome of an election. We cry "foul play" when some are prohibited from voting or when the votes of some are not counted. Also, the democratic method is usually to decide by majority rule. Whichever alternative gets the most votes is implemented. Majority rule is a genuinely egalitarian rule because it gives each person the same chance as every other to affect the outcome. Thus each person's concerns are treated equally by this method. In addition, each person is thought to have an equal opportunity to run for office and to have a say in public debate. Those who are systematically unable to make themselves heard because of poverty or race or sex are treated unjustly. If nothing else, democracy is a deeply egalitarian method of organizing social decisionmaking.

It is important, however, to get clear on the relation between democracy and the principle of equal consideration of interests; a large part of this chapter will pursue this issue. We might understand the principle to imply that everyone's interests are to be equally advanced or that everyone is to be made equally well-off by decisions. This is the *equal well-being* interpretation. On this account, justice demands that each person lives a life of the same total level of well-being as everyone else. But if we interpret the principle of equal consideration of interests as recommending that everyone be equally well-off, then the relation between it and democracy is rather unclear. Democracy is a method for making collective decisions in which everyone has an equal right to play a role. Democracy is an arrangement in which individuals have some equality in political power. But the principle of equal well-being is not concerned with the *method* by which decisions are made. It does not say anything about who has a right to rule. And it does not say anything about the distribution of power. Policies can be designed with an eye to making everyone equally well-off without their being democratically chosen. Such equality of well-being may be a good thing, but it is not the same as democracy. Democratic processes may be good methods to ensure that everyone's interests are equally satisfied, but such an argument for democracy would be instrumentalist and not an intrinsic argument of the sort we are pursuing. Again, to use a worn illustration, equal well-being is compatible with the institution of benevolent dictatorship.

So if we are to understand democracy as based on a principle of equal consideration of interests, we must have a different interpretation of that principle to work with. After the next section, I will lay out a different interpretation of equal consideration that provides a more defensible version of equality as well as a proper basis for democracy. . . .

Some have supposed that democratic participation is really a matter of formulating judgments about the best way to organize society. They argue that a democratic society is one in which I live under institutions that correspond to my judgment of what is best. I am free on this account when the institutions that constrain my life accord with my freely arrived at judgments about what is best. But in order for this approach to be relevant, there must be substantial consensus of judgment on the proper terms of association we live under. This condition, however, flies in the face of the common and pervasive experience we have of disagreement and conflict in society and thus, must fail as a strategy for defending democracy.

From the failure of the last view, we know that our conception of democracy must not ignore the facts of deep disagreement on matters of principle in modern society. We have seen that some egalitarian theorists of democracy have tried to accommodate the idea that participation is based on judgment with the fact of disagreement. Disagreement on matters of principle, they argue, must be resolved by fair compromise. Such a fair compromise is that each has a say in making decisions. A number of difficulties afflict this view, but the most serious is that it is self-defeating. If all disagreements on matters of principle are to be met with fair compromise, what are we to do if there is disagreement on what the fair compromise ought to be?

An Egalitarian Defense of Democracy

There are four steps in the basic argument that democracy is defensible in terms of a principle of egalitarian justice. First, justice requires that individuals be treated equally with regard to their interests. Second, there is a special category of interests that are deeply interdependent, so that what affects one, affects all; these are interests in the collective properties or features of society. Third, these interests can generally only be served through a collectively binding procedure. Fourth, the principle of equal consideration of interests requires equality of means for participating in deciding on the collective properties of society. Democratic decisionmaking is the embodiment of this equality of resources. Votes, campaign finances, and access to sources of information are all the kinds of resources that must be equalized in the process. Therefore, the principle of equal consideration of interests requires democratic decisionmaking on the collective attributes of society.

Collective properties

Let us start with an explanation of the interest in collective features of society. Examples of collective properties are the arrangement of public symbols and spaces, the level of environmental protection, the geographical disposition of various elements of the community by means of zoning laws, the system of defense, the system of education, the laws regulating property and exchange as well as the enforcement of these institutions, and finally the method by which all the above activities are financed. We also have to include the distribution of wealth in society and the basic structure of civil rights of citizens. A society can have any one of a variety of collective features. With regard to property, one collective feature is a highly regulated system of private property, an alternative feature would be an unregulated system, and another yet would be a system of collectivized property. With regard to environmental protection, a society can have regulations that limit the amount of pollution or it might choose to permit a considerable amount of pollution. A society must make choices among the above institutions. And the set of collective features is what defines the common world that people share in a society.

I define "collective property of the society" in the following way: A property of individuals' lives in a society is a collective property or feature if and only if in order to change one person's welfare with regard to this property one must change all or almost all of the other members' welfare with regard to it. This definition implies that collective properties have the following four characteristics. First, they satisfy a condition of *nonexclusivity*. It is not possible to affect one person's life without affecting the lives of the others. Pollution control is the most obvious example of this. One cannot generally limit pollution in a society for the benefit of some but not for others. Everyone benefits from pollution control or no one does. Of course, not all collective properties affect citizens in the same way; some collective properties may benefit some citizens and harm others. What is important is that everyone be affected by the change in a collective property. Zoning, or the lack thereof, is a property of the whole community in which it is done. When one zones a community, one arranges the various parts in a certain way. A change in a zoning law is a change of collective property for the community being zoned; in principle, everyone is affected by the change. The same is true for public monuments and institutions as well as limitations on publicly displayed behavior. These sorts of concerns are cultural in nature. They are collective properties, but there is conflict over the goods themselves.

The second condition is *publicity*. The point of saying that everyone's well-being is affected rather than that their preferences are satisfied is that it rules out the possibility that the property satisfies purely nosy preferences. For example, it might be thought that homosexuality is a collective property when some members of the society desire that others participate in or abstain from this activity. But insofar as I can participate in, or abstain from, homosexual activities without affecting other people's interests, I do not affect others' welfare with regard to this property even if those others have preferences about what I do. Hence, collective properties must be public objects.[3]

Third, the fact that individuals share such a common world is *inevitable*. For example, every society has a public environment; we have no choice about whether our community will have air and water of some quality or another. That environment is characterized by its collective properties. It can have different properties, just as a surface can be different colors. It will have some such properties necessarily.

Finally, the properties of this common world are *alterable*. The issue for us is which among the alternative possible properties society will have. We have no choice about whether the community is arranged geographically in a particular way, but we can choose which among the many possible ways it is arranged. Thus, we cannot avoid the existence of a common world in which each person shares, but we may be able to decide what that common world is like.

These four conditions describe a high level of interdependence of interests. To affect one person's interests is to affect everyone's interests. Individuals have interests in these properties of society because they play such an important role in defining the basic environment in which individuals live. The common world frames each's relations with others and structures the possible courses of life each can lead. These features are also a source of a sense of belonging inasmuch as citizens understand, recognize, and adhere to the cultural and moral norms of the social arrangements that frame their lives. They can also be a source of alienation to those for whom these conditions do not hold. For each person, there is a lot at stake in how the common world is arranged.

However, in modern society there is substantial conflict over what collective properties to bring about. There are disagreements about the norms of justice, there are different cultural traditions that citizens identify with, and there are disagreements about the appropriate level of provision of public goods. Finally, there is substantial disagreement as well as conflict of interest over the total packages of collective properties. Some may think that certain issues are more important than others. Thus there is no consensus on these goods.[4] I will not go into what is the basis of this diversity in society except to observe that modern societies are the products of large movements of diverse peoples, they include highly differentiated divisions of labor, and they tend to be very large geographically. More generally, people are different from each other inasmuch as they flourish in different kinds of environments. To some degree these different needs can be handled in more private circumstances and voluntary associations without affecting the interests of others, so I do not wish to deny the private–public distinction or the importance of individual liberty. However, the whole environment of the society is at stake in many conflicts of interests in collective properties. So collective features are defined in terms of a deep interdependence of interests in certain features of society, though there is no consensus on which properties to choose for organizing the society.

One choice a community must make is whether to decide these issues in a centrally coordinated way or to leave the determination of these properties up to the free play of social forces. In the case of collective properties, the latter method will often lead to unpalatable results for all. To allow these to develop in an uncoordinated fashion will often lead to results of which no one will approve. For example, it is better to have some legal system of property than none at all. The absence of such a system would lead to confusion and uncertainty for everyone. The likely result will be worse for everyone than almost all the alternatives. In order to have a legal system, however, a society must have an authoritative process by which to decide on what the laws are as well as how to enforce them and judge when individuals have violated them. If a society is to advance the interests of all its citizens, it must have a collective decision-making procedure that binds citizens to its decisions.

So far, this collective decision-making procedure need not be democratic in order to play the role of choosing collective properties. Kings can choose collective properties; aristocracies can also do this. The question for us is, Is there anything special about democratic methods of making decisions on these matters? As we noted earlier, equality requires that citizens' interests be given equal consideration, but we have not shown yet why democracy is a unique embodiment of this equal consideration.

A defense of equal distribution of political resources

The problem we need to address is, Why does equal consideration of the interests citizens have in collective properties imply that they ought to have equal votes in the collective decision-making process that chooses those properties? How can citizens complain of injustice if they are not given the means with which to influence the process of decisionmaking? A crucial step in the argument for democratic decisionmaking is to move beyond mere equal consideration of interests to equality in the process of decisionmaking. The reason for this is that democracy involves not just any equality, it requires equality in certain kinds of instruments or resources for achieving one's ends. For example, democracy is commonly thought to require that each person have one vote. A vote is a kind of instrument or resource for achieving one's aims. A vote is not by itself intrinsically desirable; it is not a piece of happiness or well-being itself. But it might help us achieve what is intrinsically worthwhile to us. If we have a vote in a decision, this vote will help us get the decision that we think best. Having equality in votes does not imply that there is equality in well-being; and having equality in well-being does not entail that there is equality in the vote. Our previous two conceptions of equality have failed to make the necessary move from equality to equality in the instruments for achieving one's aims that is required for a defense of democracy. Can this move be made? I believe it can.

What is the difference between equality in well-being and equality in resources? Here are some examples of this distinction. Well-being is usually thought to involve happiness, health, knowledge, friendship, pleasure, self-respect, and the respect of others, as well as a sense of belonging and community with others and a variety of other things that people desire for their own sakes. These are what make up a good life. They are the most basic interests that people have. On the other hand, resources are money, power, liberty, and opportunity, as well as votes and information that people usually desire for the sake of achieving greater well-being. They may be described as tools, instruments, or means for pursuing our aims. They do not by themselves make for a good life, but they are useful in helping us satisfy our interests.

Equality of well-being is equality in those things that make for a good life. Each person, in such a view, would have equal totals of pleasure, happiness, self-respect, and so on. Clearly the idea of equal consideration of interests is closely related to equality of well-being. However, equality of resources involves the equal distribution of money, power, opportunities, and so on. The relation between equal consideration of interests and equality of resources is more obscure. At the same time it is clear why democracy might constitute at least a partial realization of equality of resources since democracy involves the equal distribution of those means (e.g., votes) for influencing the collective decision-making procedure. We should note here that though resources themselves are not intrinsically desirable, equality in the distribution of resources may well be intrinsically just and valuable. If we start with a principle of equal consideration of interests, it is essential that we show that equality of resources is really the most plausible interpretation of this ideal.

Not only does equality of well-being not provide an account of democracy, I argue that egalitarian justice under circumstances of substantial disagreement and pluralism about well-being is best understood as equality of resources.[5] The problem with equality of well-being is that it runs afoul of a basic constraint in political theory. It appears to be a reasonable interpretation of the principle of equal consideration of interests, but upon closer inspection it is not. In political philosophy we cannot assume an equal well-being approach because we cannot make clear sense of the comparisons of well-being that must be made in order to sustain it. There is too little information about the alternatives and their comparisons, and there is a great deal of disagreement as to how they should be compared. First I will show how these claims are true, and then I will demonstrate their importance.

Three considerations motivate the rejection of equal well-being as a political principle with which to evaluate social and political institutions. The incompleteness of knowledge, the changeability of preference, and the contestability of comparisons of well-being all show that the distribution of well-being is not a reasonable standard for assessing social institutions. The main point is that equality of well-being and indeed any notion of equality in the satisfaction of interests is unintelligible as a political ideal. Thus it cannot provide an interpretation of equal consideration of interests for a political society.

The *incompleteness of knowledge* is that individuals do not have clear or fully worked out ideas of what their overall interests are. And no one else can have such an understanding about what individuals' overall interests are. But only if we do have such an understanding can we make sense of equality of well-being among citizens. There are two basic reasons for the incompleteness. The first reason is that human cognitive capacities are simply too weak to formulate such complex conceptions about all the possible interests persons have in all the relevant circumstances. The alternatives are themselves quite complex, and the number of possible different alternatives is very great, too great for a single mind to grasp. Let each person attempt to rank the goods I adumbrated above in all the different combinations in which they might arise. Each will find that they only have extremely crude ways of comparing the goods of love and self-respect as well as knowledge and pleasure. These ways are completely inadequate for attempting to evaluate many of the circumstances in which we find ourselves. This is so even when limited to the sphere of interests over collective properties of society.[6] It is not that we haven't tried to do this, it is simply that it is beyond our capacity to conceive of such a complicated ranking of all the different combinations of the things we think are important.

The second reason why knowledge of interests is incomplete is that individuals do not have complete understandings of most of their particular interests. Individuals are constantly in a process of improving and completing their judgments about what is good and just, and they do not come to an end in this process. It is ongoing and incomplete because of the cognitive limitations on persons. Much of our lives consists of learning new things about our good. None of us would claim that we have a full understanding of even the elements of our good. And if this is true of our knowledge of ourselves, it is even more true of our understanding of other people's interests. But if our knowledge of our own interests is so incomplete, then even if we have a metric for comparing interests, we do not have even the beginnings of a clear idea of what we are comparing. And if we do not know what we are comparing, then we certainly cannot say when we have equal amounts of those things.

To be sure, if we think of equal well-being as equal satisfaction of preferences, at least the second part of the above argument can be answered. It simply says that we ought to advance each person's preferences equally. But the *changeability* of preferences undermines this possible response. The problem is that persons base their preferences on their understanding of their interests and they are constantly changing their conceptions of their interests. Their understandings change as a consequence of the process of learning from experience and discussion with others, as well as from other causes. Their lives cannot be evaluated in terms of how well they live up to a preference ordering over a whole life because they cannot be identified with any single set of preferences since they change over time. Thus, even if we were to have a metric for measuring relative levels of preference satisfaction, we would not be able to figure out what equality of preference satisfaction for lives amounts to, given the mutability of these preferences.

The *contestability of comparisons argument* proceeds from the claim that there is considerable disagreement in any democratic society about what interests are most important as well as how to compare the relative worth of satisfying those interests. What constitutes an equal distribution for one person may not be equal in another's eyes. How to compare interests among individuals will be a deeply contested subject. The ideal of equality of well-being must be essentially ambiguous in a complex society. The same is true for any conception of welfare. What constitutes welfare is a matter on which persons will have serious disputes, and the metric for determining when people's interests are met is itself a matter of deep contestation.[7]

Hence, egalitarian institutions cannot depend on the notion of equal well-being to serve as a principle for solving political disputes. The metric for defining how much a person has gotten out of the democratic process must be essentially undefined since individuals cannot have fully articulated or constant preferences over results in general. There also cannot be uncontestable accounts of the bases of comparison on which any notion of equality of results must depend.

These difficulties may be thought to show that an outcome view like equality of welfare is a first-best solution, which, though unattainable, must be approximated by some second-best solution. On such an account equal well-being would be an unattainable but desirable political ideal and democratic equality would be merely a necessarily imperfect means to such an outcome. This would be much like a trial procedure which is thought to be an imperfect means to discovering the guilt or innocence of a person. Or some may think that economic markets are means for achieving efficient allocations of resources as well as technological progress. The market arrangement is not in itself just, these proponents would say, it is merely a good way to achieve good outcomes, given the ignorance of persons in figuring out how to do it in some other way. Similarly, these thinkers would argue that democratic institutions are not intrinsically fair or just, they merely are the best way to ensure a fair distribution of well-being. The fact that we do not know what such a fair distribution looks like in advance does not imply that it cannot produce it. Our ignorance is merely a contingent obstacle that ought not to come in at the level of defining the political ideal.

But in my view the rejection of equal well-being as a political ideal is not merely a matter of contingent fact. We are not merely ignorant of what the ideal would look like; we are ignorant of what increasing approximations to the ideal look like except in fairly crude cases. It is certainly as fundamental a fact as any that human beings are not able to come up with clear conceptions of their own interests and that they cannot compare those interests in any precise way amongst themselves. It would be absurd to evaluate political institutions on the basis of so unfathomable a standard.

One reason why this is absurd is that just institutions must not only be just by some standard, they must be capable of being manifestly just to each of the members. Partly this is because the justice of a social order ought not to be a complete mystery to the citizens of the society. No standard of justice can be in principle beyond the capacity of citizens to ascertain. It must be something they have a chance of knowing and celebrating; the justice of a society is a feature of that society that individuals can recognize and by which they can acknowledge each other as equals. Furthermore, each member of an egalitarian society has an interest in their equal public status being manifest to themselves and to everyone. Such *manifestness*[8] in equal status does not arise with the use of the inscrutable standard of equality in well-being or preference satisfaction for the various reasons identified above. But there is some reasonable chance that the manifestness of equality can arise as a consequence of the implementation of equality of resources. I can see if I have an equal vote with others. I can know if I am being discriminated against in an electoral scheme. I can have a sense of when the promotion of my interests and point of view have far less financial backing than those of others. Indeed, these are the stuff of the standard complaints of politics in a democratic society. These publicly observable inequalities are often raised against political systems as affronts to the principle that each person is to be treated and acknowledged as an equal citizen. But these complaints are related not to the distribution of well-being in the society but rather to the distribution of resources in the society. Hence, an egalitarian will be concerned to determine collective properties in accordance with an equality of resources scheme. That each person has a vote, has adequate means to acquire understanding of their interests, and has the means for making coalitions with others as well as getting equal representation in a legislature is a publicly manifest phenomenon. Without such manifest equality citizens cannot be assured of their membership in an egalitarian society.

Moreover, observe how we actually do evaluate institutions. Part of the function of political institutions is to distribute resources for collecting and processing information about interests. Ignorance is one of the reasons why human beings need political institutions. They serve as contexts in which individuals may learn about their interests. Institutions of education, delib-eration, and communication are designed in part to help individuals deter-mine where their interests and values lie. Because institutions are to provide the basis for discovering one's interests, and those institutions must treat individuals as equals, the idea of equality for such institutions must be defined in some other way than directly in terms of equality in interests. Indeed, the ideal of equality must be defined partly in terms of the re-sources that are necessary to undertake these learning tasks. Consider primary education. We do not evaluate it on the grounds of its ability to ensure that each has equal well-being in the end; that would be simply impossible. We judge the justice of primary educational institutions on whether they give each child an equal chance to learn. Generally we judge these institutions on whether they have devoted equal resources to each and every pupil. Sometimes we think more resources ought to go to the students who need more help as a result of previous deprivation in their backgrounds, but this involves compensating the students for the lack of resources in the past. Beyond that already difficult task we can-not go.

Furthermore, democratic institutions provide the means for fairly decid-ing on the relative importance of various interests once discussion and deliberation have failed to produce consensus. The question must be, when we must make a collective decision, How do we decide in the light of the fact that we disagree about considerations of justice as well as about the relative importance of various kinds of interests? If fairness in the method by which we decide these issues is important, it must be that the fairness is to be implemented by means of a distribution of resources and not on the grounds that one method is more likely to achieve the equal well-being outcome. The latter is something deeply contested, and the contest is part of the reason why we must make a decision.

We have shown the impossibility of establishing what people's interests are and the contestability of our ways of comparing people's interests, as well as the function of justice as publicly establishing the equal worth of the interests of each citizen in the society. The only publicly accessible way to implement equal consideration of interests is to give each citizen the means for discovering and pursuing his or her own interests. The only reasonable implementation of such a principle must be in the equal distribution of resources for making collective decisions. Such a distribution permits each of its members the chance to enhance their understanding of their interests as well as justice on a publicly available equal basis.

Justice, collective properties, and political equality

Now we are in a position to bring the strands of our argument together. A society must make certain collectively binding decisions about its collective properties in which each citizen has distinct and substantial interests. But consensus is not possible in a society; disagreement is inevitable. So how should that authority be shared among the citizens? Equal consideration of interests is a solution to the problem of the just division of benefits and burdens when there is a scarcity of goods. There is scarcity when the interests of individuals conflict and they cannot all be satisfied. For collective properties there is a serious problem of scarcity. For example, there is conflict over the level of provision of pollution control insofar as different levels of provision have different costs. In the case of the cultural goods, there is conflict over the very goods to be provided as well as the level of provision. And in the case of the laws of property and exchange, there is considerable disagreement as to what ought to be chosen. These concerns determine the whole nature of the community. Insofar as there is a diversity of opinion among the citizens on the issues of which collective properties to implement, few will get their way on any particular issue. Hence, there is a high demand (relative to what can be supplied) for having one's preferred possible collective property implemented.

These last claims provide reasons for thinking that collective properties ought to be subject to principles of just distribution. What does justice require in these circumstances, and why are properties that are not collective to be treated differently? Justice, we have seen, requires that each person's interests be given equal consideration. This equal consideration of interests implies that individuals be given equal resources with which to understand, elaborate, and pursue their interests. Insofar as individuals' interests are deeply interdependent concerning certain features of society and individuals cannot avoid conflicts of interests over those features, there ought to be collective decisionmaking about those features. Inasmuch as everyone has interests in making these decisions, the ideal of equality of resources ought to be applied to the collective decision-making procedure. Thus, each citizen ought to have equal resources to affect the outcomes of the collective decision-making procedure. This implies roughly that each ought to have an equal vote and other resources for participating in the collective decision-making procedure. This is the principle of *political equality*. Political equality implies that each and every citizen ought to have a say in the choice of collective features of society in a common decision procedure. Thus the principle implies a version of the idea of popular sovereignty. Who ought to make the decisions? The answer is, the people. How should they make these decisions? They ought to make the decisions in accordance with a principle of political equality so that each citizen has an equal say. To say that the people are sovereign is not to say that they all agree or that they all have a common will. It merely implies that all the citizens ought to come together in one group to make decisions together as a group.

Inevitably, many readers will have complaints with the argument that I have given. In what follows, I will show how my view avoids difficulties, such as the problem of regress and the trade-off problem, that I have observed in the other theories. I will show how justice in the distribution of resources for collective decisionmaking relates to issues of justice in the distribution of economic resources as well as civil justice. And I will show how my conception of democracy implies the best view of the function of social deliberation in democracy. After addressing these potential sources of difficulties, I will give a fuller elaboration of the nature of political equality, and, finally, I will show how my view avoids one of the main recent criticisms of democracy, the impossibility theorem of social choice theory.

Interests, Judgments, and Conflicting Conceptions of Justice

Democracy is a just way of making laws in the case of collective properties because citizens' interests are opposed on them. But here a difficulty arises. Society must make decisions on matters of civil and economic justice too. Citizens disagree on the justice of the laws of property, exchange, taxation, and the rights of citizens as well, and, clearly, these laws are about collective properties. But conceptions of civil and economic justice are not opposed in the same way that interests are. On the one hand, when there is a controversy on civil and economic justice, individuals try to get others to give up their conceptions by means of rational persuasion. Their first concern is to arrive at the right conception. So when two people disagree they are not primarily concerned that their own conception be advanced but that the right conception be advanced. Conceptions of justice are a matter of judgment. They can be correct or incorrect. The first interest of each person is to have the correct judgment. By analogy, if you and I disagree on the solution to a mathematical problem, we advance opposed conceptions of the solution. What we try to do is figure out who is right, if either of us is right. Our first interest in discussion and debate is not to advance our own view but to discover what is right. Each is willing to give up his or her view if he or she can be shown to be wrong. So it appears that there is no ultimate conflict of interest involved in controversies on civil and economic justice.

On the other hand, when our interests are genuinely opposed, there is no further possibility of rationally persuading one person to give up his or her interests as there is in the case of judgments. My interests are not correct or incorrect as judgments are. And it is precisely this irresolvability that leads to attempts to resolve the conflict by fair means of accommodation. For example, if two people go out while it is raining and they have only one umbrella, they have a conflict of interest in not getting wet. It would not make sense for one person to attempt to resolve the matter by persuading the other that her interest is incorrect or that she should give up her interest. What the two must do here is accommodate the opposing interests in some way.

So although the principle of equality applies to conflicts of interest and democratic decisionmaking is appropriate in these contexts, it is unclear how the principle applies to controversies over civil and economic justice. Since everyone has the same interest – to find the right conception of justice – there is apparently no conflict. If this is right, then the scope of democratic decisionmaking is severely limited since the issues of property, exchange, and taxation play a role in virtually every decision and these issues are almost always connected with matters of justice. If democracy is intrinsically just only in matters unrelated to civil and economic justice, then the thesis of the intrinsic justice of democracy is not a very important one. The effort to improve on Singer's idea of democracy as a fair compromise has eviscerated the view.

The way to show that the principle of equal consideration of interests does apply to such conflicts is to show that important interests do conflict when citizens advance opposed conceptions of justice. There are really four such interests. First, there is the interest in recognition. Each person has an interest in being taken seriously by others. When an individual's views are ignored or not given any weight, this undermines his or her sense of self-respect, in which each has a deep interest. Each has an interest in having his or her conception of justice heard and taken into account when there is irresolvable disagreement. These interests in recognition obviously conflict to the extent that individuals advance opposing conceptions of justice. Second, conceptions of justice often reflect disproportionately the interests of those who hold them. There is a tendency to cognitive bias in articulating and elaborating conceptions of justice, particularly in contexts of actual political conflicts. Cynicism is not necessary to observe this. Cognitive bias is natural given that individuals are likely to be more sensitive and understanding towards their own interests than those of others. And in a complex society where individuals' positions in society are quite different, this tendency to bias is increased. If many advance conceptions of justice that reflect their interests, those who lack opportunities to advance their own will lose out. To be sure, the process of rational persuasion should eliminate some of this cognitive bias, but it is unlikely to eliminate it all. Thus, serious conflict of interest is likely to accompany controversies on justice. A third interest associated with advancing a conception of justice is that a person will most likely experience a sense of alienation and distance from a social world that does not accord with any of her sense of justice. She will have a sense of nonmembership. That individuals have these kinds of difficulties can be seen from the experience of indigenous peoples in societies that are radically different from theirs. But this sense of alienation can be experienced to lesser degrees when there are lesser disagreements. The interest in a sense of membership is a source of conflict as well. A fourth interest is related to the interest in coming to have the right conception of justice. If persons are to be rationally persuaded, the arguments that lead them to the new belief must start by appealing to their initial beliefs. Persons are not persuaded by arguments based on premises they do not believe. As a consequence, the views of each person in a process of social discussion must be taken seriously if each is to have the opportunity to learn from that discussion. But a person's views will not be taken seriously in such a process if that person does not possess the power to affect political decisionmaking. Why should others try to convince someone who has no impact on the decision when there is so little time to persuade those who do have power? So each person has an interest in having his or her own view taken into account in discussion, and citizens' interests conflict to the extent that there is a limited space in which to discuss all views. The only way to treat these interests equally is to give them equal shares in political authority. I explore equality in discussion in more detail later in this chapter [and in Chapter 8].

These four interests suggest that there is some similarity between advancing conceptions of justice and advancing one's interests. They suggest that there is some basis for applying a principle of equal consideration of interests when there is substantial disagreement over conceptions of justice. So democratic decisionmaking is the proper way of resolving conflicts over conceptions of justice.

To avoid misunderstanding here, when I say that individuals have interests in advancing their own conceptions of justice, I do not mean to say that their conceptions of justice are mere masks for their own interests. I also do not mean to say that individuals' conceptions of justice are mere tools for pursuing their own interests. I take it as a fundamental fact that human beings are deeply concerned with matters of civil and economic justice and are concerned with having the most accurate understandings of these matters. Conflict in political society is often generated by pervasive but sincerely based disagreement on these matters. The four kinds of interests that I described above are interests that individuals pursue when advancing conceptions of justice; they are interests that are assured by giving each an opportunity to advance his or her own conception of justice in a world where there is uncertainty about the truth of any particular conception.

The contrast between interests and principles of justice drawn above was too great in another way. Citizens do not advance their interests directly; they advance what they believe to be their interests. So when there are conflicts of interests, they are conflicts between what citizens judge to be their interests. Of course, unlike issues of justice, they are not in conflict primarily because of disagreement as to how best to understand their interests; they are in conflict on the assumption that their conceptions of their interests are right. But the question still arises as to why it follows from a principle of equal consideration of interests that citizens ought to be given the right to advance what they *understand* to be their interests. Versions of the four reasons provided above give answers to this question. To treat a person as incompetent in discerning her interests is to undermine a fundamental support for her self-respect. It amounts to treating her as an inferior. Her interest in recognition gives us a reason to treat her as competent in judging her interests. Furthermore, individuals are more likely than others to understand their own interests. Obviously, each has a greater incentive to understand his or her own interests than those of anyone else. And each is better acquainted with the needs and vicissitudes of his or her life than anyone else. This is particularly true in a complex and highly diversified society wherein the contexts of people's lives are quite diverse.[9] Furthermore, analogs of the feelings of belonging and alienation accompany the lives of those who live in contexts that respond to their conceptions of their interests and those who live in circumstances that do not. Finally, people can learn best about their interests in discussions with others where their ideas are taken seriously.

We might ask what a person is more likely to understand about his interests than others. Some have a lot more technical and scientific knowledge than others. Many doctors probably understand many aspects of my health better than I do. But there are aspects even of my health that I understand best, such as how much time I wish to contribute to my health compared to other goods of mine or how well I feel. As Aristotle says: "There are some arts whose products are not judged of solely, or best, by the artists themselves, namely those arts whose products are recognized even by those who do not possess the art; for example, the knowledge of the house is not limited to the builder only; . . . the master of the house will even be a better judge than the builder . . . and the guest will judge better of a feast than the cook."[10] Thus, though citizens may not be the best judges of their interests in an unqualified way because they have little knowledge of how to satisfy them or the conditions under which they can best be preserved, they are the best judges with regard to certain essential features of their interests. Not all the aspects of my interests are a matter of technical knowledge that can be had by anyone. Some knowledge of a person's interests is essentially more available to him or her than to anyone else. Though each can improve on his or her knowledge of interests by reflection and even discussion with others, others are not likely to be better informed in general. An important task of democratic theory is to separate out those aspects of a person's interests that a person is likely to be most knowledgeable about and those that he or she is not.

Notes

1   See Robert Dahl, *A Preface to Democratic Theory* (Chicago: University of Chicago Press, 1956), pp. 64–7; Dahl, "Procedural Democracy," in *Philosophy, Politics, and Society*, 5th Ser., ed. James Fishkin and Peter Laslett (New Haven: Yale University Press, 1979), pp. 97–133, especially pp. 99–101 and p. 125; and Peter Jones, "Political Equality and Majority Rule," in *The Nature of Political Theory*, ed. David Miller and Larry Siedentop (Oxford: Oxford University Press, 1983), pp. 155–82, especially p. 166.

2   In Thomas Rainsborough's "The Putney Debates: The Debate on the Franchise (1647)," in *Divine Right and Democracy*, ed. David Wootton (Harmondsworth: Penguin Books, 1986), pp. 285–317, especially p. 286.

3   This argument does not require that there be a private realm that is to be protected from paternalistic uses of public power. It merely denies that there is intrinsic justification for democratic decisionmaking in these contexts. The fact that someone does something in his home that I do not like or that I do not approve of is not a reason for me to complain of injustice. Only if his actions impinge on my well-being and that of others in a way that is hard to escape is there a genuine collective property. There may be grounds for criticism and intervention in private actions that are not related to collective properties, but those grounds are not that I or others have been unjustly treated.

4   Those recent thinkers, such as Michael Sandel and Charles Taylor, who agree with me in their emphasis on the importance and value of community in the lives of citizens, have failed to adequately deal with the diversity of people and the lack of consensus on what the community should be like.

5   See Gerald Cohen, "On the Currency of Egalitarian Justice," *Ethics* July (1989): pp. 906–44, for a critical discussion of many of the theories on this subject.

6   See Herbert Simon, *Reason in Human Affairs* (Stanford: Stanford University Press, 1983) for this kind of claim.

7   See Ronald Dworkin, "What Is Equality? Part I: Equality of Welfare," *Philosophy and Public Affairs* 10 (Spring 1981): pp. 185–246, for a similar kind of argument concerning the impossibility of defining an agreed-upon metric for equality of welfare. Of course, he is not concerned with democratic equality where I think this problem is the most severe.

8   See Joshua Cohen, "Deliberation and Democratic Legitimacy," in *The Good Polity: Normative Analysis of the State*, eds. Alan Hamlin and Philip Pettit (New York: Basil Blackwell, 1989), p. 19, for a discussion on this concept.

9   See John Stuart Mill, *On Liberty* (Buffalo, N.Y.: Prometheus Books, 1986), for this principle. See also his *Considerations on Representative Government* (Buffalo, N.Y.: Prometheus Books, 1991), for the application of this principle to democratic theory.

10   Aristotle, *Politics*, trans. Benjamin Jowett, Book 3 of *The Basic Works of Aristotle*, ed. Richard McKeon (New York: Random House, 1941), p. 1282a.

2

The Constitutional Conception of Democracy

Jeremy Waldron

1. Democratic Rights

The idea of democracy is not incompatible with the idea of individual rights. On the contrary, there cannot be a democracy unless individuals possess and regularly exercise what we called in [Chapter Eleven of *Law and Disagreement*, from which the present chapter in this volume is taken] 'the right of rights' – the right to participate in the making of the laws. Not only that but, [as I argued at the end of Chapter Ten], there is a natural congruence between rights and democracy. The identification of someone as a right-bearer expresses a measure of confidence in that person's moral capacities – in particular his capacity to think responsibly about the moral relation between his interests and the interests of others. The possession of this capacity – a sense of justice, if you like[1] – is the primary basis of democratic competence. Our conviction that ordinary men and women have what it takes to participate responsibly in the government of their society is, in fact, the same conviction as that on which the attribution of rights is based.

[In Chapters Ten and Eleven], I invoked this connection in order to embarrass theorists of rights who professed apprehensions about or indifference towards the ideal of democratic decision-making. But the congruence between rights and democracy is a two-way street. A theorist of rights should not be in the business of portraying the ordinary members of a democratic majority as selfish and irresponsible predators. But equally a theorist of democracy should not affect a pure proceduralist's nonchalance about the fate of individual rights under a system of majority-decision, for many of these rights (even those not directly implicated in the democratic ideal) are based on the respect for individual moral agency that democracy itself involves.

Constitutional theorists like Ronald Dworkin are therefore quite correct when they say we are not entitled to appeal to any fundamental opposition between the idea of democracy and the idea of individual rights as a basis for criticizing a practice like American-style judicial review of legislation. There is no such fundamental opposition. If there is a democratic objection to judicial review, it must also be a rights-based objection. And that objection cannot be sustained unless we are prepared to answer some hard questions about how rights are supposed to be protected in a system of democratic decision-making.

The rights I want to emphasize in this chapter fall into two main categories: (a) rights that are actually constitutive of the democratic process, and (b) rights which, even if they are not formally constitutive of democracy, nevertheless embody conditions necessary for its legitimacy.

Consider first the rights required for the constitution of a democracy – (a). Theorists disagree about whether democracy is anything more than a procedural ideal,[2] but certainly it is *at least* the idea of a political procedure constituted in part by certain rights. Democracy requires that when there is disagreement in a society about a matter on which a common decision is needed, every man and woman in the society has the right to participate on equal terms in the resolution of that disagreement. The processes that this involves may be complex and indirect; there may be convoluted structures of election and representation. But they are all oriented in the end towards the same ideal: participation by the people – somehow, through some mechanism – on basically equal terms. This means that there cannot be a democracy unless the right to participate is upheld, and unless the complex rules of the representative political process are governed, fundamentally, by that right. If some are excluded from the process, or if the process itself is unequal or inadequate, then both rights and democracy are compromised.

A second set of rights – (b) – we have to consider takes us beyond issues of formal procedure. Apart from those that constitute the democratic process, there are many rights that may plausibly be represented as conditions for the legitimacy or moral respectability of democratic decision-making. No one thinks that any old bunch of people is entitled to impose a decision on others, simply on the ground that there are more individuals in favour of the decision than against it. Democracy and majority-decision make moral sense only under certain conditions. The most obvious of these conditions are free speech and freedom of association – rights which establish a broader deliberative context in civil society for formal political decision-making. But I have in mind also claims about rights that have little or no procedural aspect. In *Freedom's Law*, Dworkin argues that a person is not bound by the decisions of a democracy unless he is in some satisfactorily substantive sense a member of the community whose democracy it is. Membership is not just a matter of formal participation: it is also a matter of a person's interests being treated with appropriate concern. Even if he has a vote, he can hardly be expected to accept majority decisions as legitimate if he knows that other members of the community do not take his interests seriously or if the established institutions of the community evince contempt or indifference towards him or his kind (25).[3] And Dworkin makes a similar case for the importance of the community respecting the moral independence of its members. He thinks I cannot be a member of a community, in the suitably robust sense that generates legitimacy and political obligation, unless I can reconcile my membership with self-respect; and I can do that only if the community does not purport to dictate my fundamental ethical convictions (25–6).

I am not sure whether we should accept this last argument of Dworkin's. But no doubt *some* arguments work along these lines. There are surely some rights such that, if they were not respected in a community, no political legitimacy could possibly be accorded to any majoritarian decision-procedure. Is it not appropriate, then, for majority decision-making to be constrained by rights which satisfy this formula? One could hardly complain about such constraints in the name of democracy, for a democracy unconstrained by such rights would be scarcely worthy of the name. Such an objection would be directed against the establishment or protection of the very conditions that made democracy an ideal worth appealing to.

The relation between democracy and the conditions of its legitimacy may be represented as a relation between rights: that is, the rights under class (a) *presuppose* the rights under class (b). Sometimes when we talk about one set of rights presupposing another, it is because we think the rights in the second set are preconditions for the meaningful or effective exercise of the first. Thus, Henry Shue argues that the meaningful exercise of any right presupposes that the right-bearers have rights to subsistence and security and that these latter rights have been satisfied.[4] No doubt this applies to political rights as well: one cannot meaningfully exercise the right to vote in conditions of terror or starvation. But the relation I discussed in the previous paragraph is slightly different. It represents one set of rights as the conditions of the *legitimate* exercise of another. (It is a bit like saying that the right to sell an object presupposes that the seller owns the object.) Legitimacy is an issue because the exercise of participatory rights is not just a matter of freedom. When one votes, one exercises a Hohfeldian power[5] which (together with the exercise of that power by enough others) may alter the legal position of certain other people, perhaps against their wishes, perhaps to their disadvantage. Having this impact on others is permissible only under certain conditions, and those conditions may be represented as rights held by anyone who is liable to be subject to such impact.

Rights in classes (a) and (b) I shall call 'rights associated with democracy'. In a broader sense all rights are associated with democracy because, as I said at the beginning of this section, all rights require the same sort of respect for individuals which democracy also requires. Many theorists have sought to confine their argument for constitutional rights to those rights that are related directly or indirectly to the democratic process.[6] They imagine – wrongly, as we shall see – that no democratic objection can be sustained against right-based constraints concerned with the procedural integrity of democracy. And they believe – again, I think, wrongly – that the concerns a democrat ought to have about rights do not apply to what they call 'substantive rights' unrelated to the democratic process. In fact, the right-based argument for democracy cannot be separated off from other rights in this way. Based as it is on respect for persons as moral agents and moral reasoners, the premises of that argument will certainly yield substantive conclusions about what people are entitled to so far as personal freedom is concerned and it may well yield conclusions about affirmative entitlements in the realm of social and economic well-being. Sure, some of these conclusions are also related to the democratic process as constitutive elements or as conditions of its legitimacy. But the premises of the right-based case for democracy may provide a direct argument for substantive rights that bypasses the case for democracy. These rights, then, are associated with democracy not in the sense of being constitutive of it or presupposed by it, but in the sense of being other conclusions of the very premises that ground the rights-based case for democracy.

For most of this chapter, however, I shall confine my attention to classes (a) and (b). Rights in class (a) have been the focus of a well-known argument by John Hart Ely to the effect that no democratic objection can be sustained against judicial review to vindicate rights that are procedurally constitutive of democracy.[7] Dworkin thinks Ely is wrong to confine his attention to class (a), however, and I agree with him on that.[8] The argument I want to examine in the body of the chapter deals with both categories. Then, towards the very end, in sections 11 and 12, I shall return to the broader issue of democratic protection for rights in general.

2. Does Judicial Review Improve Democracy?

In the United States and in the United Kingdom, Ronald Dworkin has been a firm defender of the compatibility of democracy with constitutional rights and judicial review.[9] His recent book, *Freedom's Law* articulates a new version of that defence. Dworkin believes it is no accident that new democracies – in South Africa, for example, or in Central and Eastern Europe – turn almost instinctively to some version of the constitutional arrangements we are considering. They do so, he thinks, not because they are nervous or ambivalent about democracy, but because a system combining popular legislation, constitutional guarantees, and judicial review seems like the form of democracy that, in their circumstances, will offer the best assurance that the rights associated with democracy will continue to be respected. America chose a particularly attractive form of democracy at its birth, Dworkin argues (70–1). Its Founding Fathers invented the idea that the very *constitution* of a country – the document that establishes, empowers, and shapes the structures of government – should also be the guarantor of human rights.[10] This idea that government should be bound to the rights associated with democracy by the very authority that structures and empowers its democratic procedures is in Dworkin's view 'the most important contribution our [i.e. United States] history has given to political theory' (6). It would be a 'historic shame', he says, if Americans were to lose faith in this practice just as it is beginning to inspire the world (71).

In *Freedom's Law*, Dworkin does not merely defend the familiar claim that judicial review on the basis of constitutional principle makes a society more *just* than it would be without it. Sure, he does accept that familiar claim (at least so far as the United States is concerned), and he has defended it elsewhere.[11] The challenging thing about the *Freedom's Law* position is that Dworkin actually insists, without any qualification, that '[a] constitution of principle, enforced by independent judges, is not undemocratic' (123). There is no trade-off between rights and democracy, he insists. Instead he thinks that the practice of allowing a handful of unelected and unaccountable judges to strike down laws passed by a representative legislature helps constitute a distinctive and excellent form of democracy in the United States (15). What's more, his reason for believing this remarkable claim is no longer the reason we criticized at the beginning of Chapter Twelve – namely, that the practice is something the American people have chosen.[12] He now maintains that whoever chose it chose *an option favourable to democracy*.

In one or two places Dworkin goes beyond this, and gives the impression that he thinks a political system which allows ordinary majorities to make decisions about rights should not be regarded as genuinely democratic. He says any version of democracy that requires 'deference to temporary majorities on matters of individual right is ... brutal and alien, and many other nations with firm democratic traditions now reject it as fake' (71). Mostly, however, his position is less strident than that. The argument I want to criticize in this chapter is the argument intended to show that American-style constitutional arrangements are no less democratic on account of judicial review, not the argument that judicial review is actually *required* by democracy. In his most careful formulation, Dworkin says:

> I do not mean that there is no democracy unless judges have the power to set aside what a majority thinks is right and just. Many institutional arrangements are compatible with the moral reading, including some that do not give judges the power they have in the American structure. But none of these varied arrangements is in principle more democratic than others. Democracy does not insist on judges having the last word, but it does not insist that they must not have it. (7)

So, although Ronald Dworkin is among those who urge the introduction of American-style arrangements into the United Kingdom, I do not think he really wants to say that the Westminster system as it stands is brutally undemocratic or less democratic because it lacks a system of judicial review. Mostly what he wants to say is that if judicial review were introduced, Britain would be *no less democratic* in consequence. That's what I want to consider in this chapter: I want to ask one more time, in the light of Dworkin's arguments, whether there is in fact a loss to democracy when the elected legislature of a society is subjected to judicial power. Dworkin thinks there is not. I shall try to show that this is not established by his arguments in *Freedom's Law*.

3. Judicial Review and Justice

I want to begin this discussion with a word about the more familiar claim I mentioned – namely, that judicial review may make a society more just (whether or not it is compatible with democracy). As I said, Dworkin believes this too, certainly as far as America is concerned. 'The United States', he says, 'is a more just society than it would have been had its constitutional rights been left to the conscience of majoritarian institutions.'[13]

Should we accept this as a starting point? I have my doubts. Like any claim involving a counterfactual ('more just than it would have been if . . .'), it is an extraordinarily difficult proposition to assess. As we consider it, we think naturally of landmark decisions like *Brown v. Board of Education*,[14] and the impact of such decisions on desegregation and the promotion of racial equality. But it is not enough to celebrate *Brown*. Verifying the counterfactual would involve not only an assessment of the impact of that and similar decisions but also a consideration of the way in which the struggle against segregation and similar injustices might have proceeded in the United States if there had been no Bill of Rights or no practice of judicial review.[15] About the only evidence we have in this regard is the struggle against injustice in other societies which lacked these institutions. Many such societies seem to be at least as free and as just as the United States,[16] though of course it is arguable such comparisons underestimate the peculiarities of American politics and society. In addition, a proper assessment of the claim would require us to consider the injustice that judicial review has caused as well as the injustice it has prevented. It would require us to consider, for example, the injustice occasioned by the striking down by state and federal courts of some 150 pieces of legislation concerning labour relations and labour conditions in the period (now referred to as the *Lochner* era) from 1885 to 1930.[17] Not only that, but it would also require us to consider the longer term effects of the discrediting of parliamentary socialism within the American labour movement that resulted from repeated judicial obstruction of otherwise successful legislative initiatives.[18] One would have to balance all that against the good that the courts have done. Dworkin is aware that the record on judicial review is far from perfect, and he has very little positive to say about the jurisprudence of the *Lochner* era. I cannot help feeling however that he understimates the damage done in this period when he says that '[i]n fact, the most serious mistakes the Supreme Court has made, over its history, have been not in striking down laws it ought to have upheld, but in upholding laws it ought to have struck down'(388).[19]

The claim about justice may in the end be impossible to verify. And even were it true, it would still involve a problematic trade-off between justice and democratic ideals, unless the more ambitious claim of *Freedom's Law* could be sustained. For Dworkin acknowledges that democracy *would* be eroded if we were to give a bunch of unelected philosopher-kings the power to overrule legislation simply on the ground that they thought it unjust: 'Even if the experts always improved the legislation they rejected – always stipulated fairer income taxes than the legislature had enacted, for example – there would be a loss in self-government which the merits of their decision could not extinguish' (32). To reach the distinctive conclusions of *Freedom's Law*, Dworkin must therefore show that in some circumstances judicial review of legislation does not detract at all from, and maybe even enhances, the democratic character of the political system of which it is a part.

4. Improving Public Debate

One way he tries to show this is by considering the effect of constitutional adjudication on the character of public debate. Modern civic republicans and participatory democrats emphasize the importance of citizens engaging actively in political deliberation, and some of them have misgivings about judicial review because they think it tends to undermine this engagement by removing important decisions of principle from the democratic forum. Dworkin believes, however, that the quality of public debate may actually be better on this account:

> When an issue is seen as constitutional, . . . and as one that will ultimately be resolved by courts applying general constitutional principles, the quality of public argument is often improved, because the argument concentrates from the start on questions of political morality. . . . When a constitutional issue has been decided by the Supreme Court, and is important enough so that it can be expected to be elaborated, expanded, contracted, or even reversed by future decisions, a sustained national debate begins, in newspapers and other media, in law schools and classrooms, in public meetings and around dinner tables. That debate better matches [the] conception of republican government, in its emphasis on matters of principle, than almost anything the legislative process on its own is likely to produce. (345)

He cites as an example the great debate about abortion surrounding the Supreme Court's decision in *Roe v. Wade*,[20] saying it has involved many more people and has led to a more subtle appreciation of the complexities involved than in other countries where the final decision about abortion was assigned to elected legislatures. As a result of entrusting it to the courts:

> Americans better understand, for instance, the distinction between the question whether abortion is morally and ethically permissible, on the one hand, and the question whether government has the right to prohibit it, on the other; they also better understand the more general and constitutionally crucial idea on which that distinction rests: that individuals have rights that may work against the general will or the collective interest or good. (345)

In this way, Dworkin thinks, a system of final decision by judges on certain great issues of principle may actually enhance the participatory character of our politics.[21]

I am afraid I do not agree with any of this. Consider first what is said about political discussion. Dworkin acknowledges that he is making tentative empirical claims about the quality of public debate. My experience is that national debates about abortion are as robust and well-informed in countries like the United Kingdom and New Zealand, where they are not constitutionalized, as they are in the United States – the more so perhaps because they are uncontaminated by quibbling about how to interpret the text of an eighteenth century document. It is sometimes liberating to be able to discuss issues like abortion directly, on the principles that ought to be engaged, rather than having to scramble around constructing those principles out of the scraps of some sacred text, in a tendentious exercise of constitutional calligraphy. Think of how much more wisely capital punishment has been discussed (and disposed of) in countries where the debate has not had to centre around the moral reading of the phrase 'cruel and unusual punishment', but could focus instead on broader aims of penal policy and on dangers more morally pressing than 'unusualness', such as the execution of the innocent.[22] It is simply a myth that the public requires a moral debate to be, first of all, an interpretive debate before it can be conducted with any dignity or sophistication.

Or consider the debate about homosexual law reform initiated by the 1957 Wolfenden Report in Great Britain,[23] and sustained in the famous exchange between Lord Devlin and H. L. A. Hart in the 1960s.[24] Despite their focus on the decisions of a legislature (the British Parliament), these authors seemed to evince a perfectly adequate grasp of the distinction between whether something is morally permissible and whether government has the right to prohibit it. They did not need to be taught that by a court. Indeed, if the US Supreme Court's intervention on a similar issue is anything to go by, the American debate is actually impoverished by its constitutionalization. As Mary Ann Glendon has remarked, the decision in *Bowers v. Hardwick*[25] is remarkable for the 'lack of depth and seriousness of the analysis contained in its majority and dissenting opinions', compared with the discussion that has taken place in other countries.[26] If the debate that actually takes place in American society and American legislatures is as good as that in other countries, it is so *despite* the Supreme Court's framing of the issues, not because of it.

Still, suppose Dworkin is right that the quality of public discussion may be improved by citizens' awareness that the final disposition of some issue of principle is to be taken out of the hands of their elected representatives and assigned instead to a court. The idea that civic republicans and participatory democrats should count this as a gain is a travesty. Civic republicans and participatory democrats are interested in *practical political deliberation*, which is not just any old debating exercise, but a form of discussion among those who are about to participate in a binding collective decision.

A star-struck people may speculate about what the Supreme Court will do next on abortion or some similar issue; they may even amuse each other, as we law professors do, with stories of how *we* would decide, in the unlikely event that we were elevated to that eminent tribunal. The exercise of power by a few black-robed celebrities can certainly be expected to *fascinate* an articulate population. But that is hardly the essence of active citizenship. Perhaps such impotent debating is nevertheless morally improving: Dworkin may be right that 'there is no necessary connection between a citizen's political impact or influence and the ethical benefit he secures through participating in public discussion' (30). But independent ethical benefits of this kind are at best desirable side effects, not the primary point of civic participation in republican political theory.

5. Democratic Ends and Democratic Means

As I said, Dworkin acknowledges the tentativeness of his response to the civic republicans. His main argument for the claim that judicial review involves no cost in terms of democracy is somewhat different. It goes as follows.

Suppose a piece of legislation is enacted by an elected assembly and then challenged by a citizen on the ground that it undermines one of the rights associated with democracy. (The example Dworkin gives (32) is a statute prohibiting flag-burning.) And suppose the issue is assigned to a court for decision, and the court strikes down the statute, accepting the citizen's challenge. Is there a loss to democracy? The answer, Dworkin says, depends entirely on whether the court makes the right decision. If it does – that is, if the statute really was incompatible with the rights required for a democracy – then democracy is surely improved by what the court has done. For the community is now more democratic than it would have been if the anti-democratic statute had been allowed to stand. Of course, Dworkin adds,

> if we assume the court's decision was wrong, then none of this is true. Certainly it impairs democracy when an authoritative court makes the wrong decision about what the democratic conditions require – but no more than it does when a majoritarian legislature makes a wrong constitutional decision that is allowed to stand. The possibility of error is symmetrical. (32–3)

It follows, says Dworkin, that democratic constitutional theory ought to be oriented primarily to results (34). In every society, there will be questions whether enacted legislation conflicts with the fundamental principles of democracy. These questions should be assigned to whatever institution is likely to answer them correctly. In some countries, for all we know, this may be the legislature. But often there is reason to think the legislature is not the safest vehicle for protecting the rights associated with democracy (34). In that case, we should assign the issue to the courts, if we think they are a safer bet. We should not be deterred, says Dworkin, by the fact that courts are not constituted in a way that makes them democratically accountable. Accountability does not matter, he says. The crucial thing is that courts are reliable at making good decisions about democracy. That is all a partisan of democracy should care about.

That is the argument. Notice how it turns on an elision between a decision *about democracy* and a decision *made by democratic means*. Dworkin seems to be suggesting that if a political decision is about democracy, or about the rights associated with democracy, then there is no interesting or interestingly distinct question to be raised about the way in which (i.e., the institutional process by which) the decision is made. All that matters is that the decision be right, from a democratic point of view. In the case of social justice, that is not so: the right decision about social justice may have been reached, but – as Dworkin concedes (32) – it still matters whether it was reached democratically. In the case of a decision about democracy, how- ever, he thinks the distinction collapses.

I wonder whether, on reflection, Dworkin really means to collapse con- tent and legitimacy in this way. Suppose the United Kingdom became embroiled in a debate about the democratic merits of proportional repre- sentation (PR), and that in a moment of national exasperation with the inability of elected politicians to resolve this issue, the Queen were to announce that henceforth the electoral system would be organized on the basis of 'Single Transferable Vote'. Suppose also, for the sake of argument, that the Queen's decision was the right one: that the version of PR she chose really does make an electoral system more democratic than the old- fashioned 'first-past-the-post' system. Could this possibly be regarded as an exercise of democratic power on the ground that it confined itself to a question about the nature of the democratic process and answered that question correctly? In New Zealand a few years ago, the issue which we are imagining being settled in Britain by the Queen was settled in fact by two popular referendums, separated by a year or so of public education and careful debate. Is it really Dworkin's position that the Queen's intervention (in our imagined example) would be no less democratic a way of settling this issue than the popular referendums in New Zealand? Should we not rather say – would it not be much clearer to say – that in the imaginary

British case a democratic issue was settled *undemocratically*? And that there *was* therefore a loss in self-government, *even though the Queen got the answer right*?

Of course there is an additional difference: we are imagining the Queen intervening in a sort of unconstitutional *putsch*. A system of judicial review would presumably not have that character.[27] Actually that's not quite true: at the birth of judicial review in the United States, some jurists did regard it as constitutionally irregular; and certainly, if it were introduced into the UK, various English pedants could be relied on to make the point that any abrogation of parliamentary sovereignty was both unconstitutional and illogical. Anyway, whether something is constitutionally irregular is a separate question from whether it is undemocratic (though sometimes the latter is a ground for the former). If someone were to ask (in our hypothetical case) why the Queen's intervention was an *important* as opposed to a trivial irregularity, we would surely say that it was important because it compromised democracy, because she had usurped a decision that should properly have been taken by the people or their representatives. And that's the point I want to make: concerns about the democratic or non-democratic character of a political procedure do not evaporate when the procedure in question is being used to address an issue about the nature of democracy.

The same argument may be put more concisely. If a question comes up for political decision in a community, a member of the community might reasonably ask to participate in it on equal terms with his fellow citizens. Now there may be all sorts of reasons for denying his request, but it would surely be absurd to deny it on the ground that the question was one about democracy. That would be absurd because it would fail to address his concern that a question about democracy, as much as any political question, should be settled by democratic means.

So I do not think we should accept Dworkin's claim to have created 'a level playing field on which the contest between different institutional structures for interpreting the democratic conditions must take place' (33). The playing field is not level. There *is* something lost, from a democratic point of view, when an unelected and unaccountable individual or institution makes a binding decision about what democracy requires. If it makes the right decision, then – sure – there is something democratic to set against that loss; but that is not the same as there being no loss in the first place. On the other hand, if an institution which *is* elected and accountable makes the wrong decision about what democracy requires, then although there is a loss to democracy in the substance of the decision, it is not silly for citizens to comfort themselves with the thought that at least they made their *own* mistake about democracy rather than having someone else's mistake foisted upon them. Process may not be all that there is to democratic decision-making; but we should not say that, since the decision is *about* democracy, process is therefore irrelevant.

6. Disagreement, Again

Dworkin acknowledges that reasonable citizens may disagree about what democracy requires and about the rights that it involves or presupposes.[28] They disagree about details like the voting age, electoral laws, and campaign finance. And they disagree also about some of the fundamentals: the basis of representation and the connection between political and social equality. They certainly disagree about what democracy presupposes as conditions of legitimacy. For example: What are the issues on which we require a common decision? How much concern must different sections of the community have for one another, before minorities may reasonably be expected to trust the majority? How much moral independence for its members does an attractive conception of community presuppose? Even if they agree that democracy implicates certain rights, citizens will surely disagree what these rights are and what in detail they commit us to.

The persistence of these disagreements makes a difference to the way we are able to proceed in constitutional design. The suggestion in *Freedom's Law* is that we should use a results-driven criterion for choosing the institutions to which decisions about democratic rights should be entrusted:

> I see no alternative but to use a result-driven rather than a procedure-driven standard.... The best institutional structure is the one best calculated to produce the best answers to the essentially moral question of what the democratic conditions actually are, and to secure stable compliance with those conditions. [34]

But a citizenry who disagree about what would count as the right results are not in a position to construct their constitution on this basis. (That is why John Rawls's approach to constitutional design, in *A Theory of Justice*, is so misconceived.) Using a result-driven approach, different citizens will attempt to design the constitution on a different basis. A libertarian will seek participatory procedures that maximize the prospect of legislation that is just by his own free market standards, while a social democrat will seek participatory procedures that maximize the prospects for legislation embodying collective and egalitarian concern. How can they together design a political framework to structure and accommodate the political and ideological differences between them? The only way they can do that is if they have managed already to adopt a view that can stand in the name of them all about the results they should be aiming at. But if they have managed that, from a baseline of disagreement, they must have been in possession of decision-procedures that enable them to get to that result. And presumably their possession of *those* decision-procedures can be explained only on the basis of their use of something other than a results-driven test (for choosing procedures) in the past.

We seem, then, to be in a bind. It looks as though it is disagreement all the way down, so far as constitutional choice is concerned. On the one hand, we cannot use a results-driven test, because we disagree about which results should count in favour of and which against a given decision-procedure. On the other hand, it seems we cannot appeal to any procedural criterion either, since procedural questions are at the very nub of the disagreements we are talking about.

7. The Capacity to Think Procedurally

Someone may say, 'Well, what did you expect? Even if we buy the view that right-based respect for persons is also respect for their sense of justice and thus respect for their political capacity, it does not follow that the people are to be entrusted with procedural questions of constitutional design. Ordinary political competence cannot be expected to extend to the building and care of the framework within which ordinary political competence is to be exercised.' Something along these lines is at back of what I perceive as the very considerable popularity of the John Hart Ely view mentioned earlier: namely, that even if there is an affront to democracy when substantive issues are taken away from the people, there is no affront when *procedural* issues are taken away.[29]

But that will not do. I said earlier that there is a theoretical connection between respect for people's rights and respect for their capacities as political participators. Now there is no reason to suppose that the moral capacities respected in the idea of rights are only capacities to think substantively, as opposed to capacities to think reflectively about procedures. On the contrary, the emergence of rights-theories in the modern era was associated not just with the substantive self-confidence of individual reason, but also with a certain *epistemological* self-confidence, that is, a confidence on the part of individuals in their ability to reflect systematically on the procedures that knowledge and rational deliberation involved.[30]

Whether in the form of Descartes's self-imposed strictures of method in the *Discourse on the Method*, or in John Locke's patient enquiry in the *Essay* into 'what objects our understandings were, or were not, fitted to deal with',[31] enlightenment optimism on behalf of the individual mind was optimism at least as much in regard to its reflections upon methodology as in regard to its achievements of substance. This optimism was mirrored, in early modern political philosophy, in the assumption that the one decision that did have to be made by the people – deliberating and voting together, unaided by authority or tradition – was the choice of a political procedure for the civil society they were inventing.[32] Government might not end up being democratic; some theorists, like Hobbes, advised strongly against democracy.[33] But they had no doubt that the choice of a constitution – and thus the pondering of the very issues about what different political processes involved or presupposed – was one that could only be made by the people.[34]

So, working in this tradition of political thought, we will not get very far with any argument that limits the competence of popular self-government to issues of substance and stops it short at the threshold of political procedure, assigning questions about forms of government to a body of a different sort altogether. Democracy is in part *about* democracy: one of the first things on which the people demand a voice about, and concerning which they claim a competence, is the procedural character of their own political arrangements.

8. Judges in our Own Case?

Still, the problem we face may not be one of capacity. We have to consider the suggestion – implicit in Dworkin's argument – that allowing the majority to decide upon the conditions under which majority-decisions are to be accepted may be objectionable because it makes them judge in their own case. Those who invoke the principle of *nemo iudex in sua causa* in this context say that it requires that a final decision about rights should *not* be left in the hands of the people: it should be passed on to an independent and impartial institution such as the US Supreme Court.[35]

It is hard to see the force of this argument. Almost any conceivable decision-rule will eventually involve *someone* deciding in his own case, in one or maybe two different ways. First, unless it is seriously imagined that issues of right should be decided by an outsider – by a Rousseauian 'law-giver' perhaps,[36] or by some neo-colonial institution that stands in relation to a given community as (say) the British Privy Council stands in relation to

New Zealand – such decisions will inevitably be made by persons whose own rights are affected by the decision. Even a Supreme Court justice gets to have the rights that he determines American citizens to have. We too often forget this: often our scholarly talk about when 'the people' or 'the majority' may be entrusted (by us?) with decisions about rights has something of the haughty air of a John Stuart Mill talking *de haut en bas* about native self-government in India.

It is sometimes said that what *nemo iudex* implies is that a democratic majority should not have the final say as to whether its decision about rights is acceptable. If there is a question about whether the majority's decision is acceptable, then the majority should not adjudicate that question. This will not do either. Unless we envisage a literally endless chain of appeals, there will always be some person or institution whose decision is final. And of that person or institution, we can always say that since it has the last word, its members are *ipso facto* ruling on the acceptability of their own view. Facile invocations of *nemo iudex in sua causa* are no excuse for forgetting the elementary logic of authority: people disagree and there is need for a final decision and a final decision-procedure.

Invoking *nemo iudex* may be appropriate when one individual or faction purports to adjudicate an issue concerning its own interests, as opposed to those of another individual or faction or as opposed to the rest of the community. (Historically, those who have invoked it against democratic government have often tried to portray democracy as class rule, i.e., self-interested rule by the lower classes.) The objection in such cases to A being judge in his (or its) own case is that B (the other party in the dispute) is excluded from the process. But it seems quite inappropriate to invoke this principle in a situation where the community as a whole is attempting to resolve some issue concerning the rights of *all* the members of the community and attempting to resolve it on a basis of equal participation. There, it seems not just unobjectionable but *right* that all those who are affected by an issue of rights should participate in the decision (and if we want a Latin tag to answer *nemo iudex*, we can say, '*Quod omnes tangit ab omnibus decidentur*').

9. Begging the Question

Still, the impression of some sort of logical difficulty remains. Surely there is something question-begging in the idea of a democratic decision about democracy? Is there not something circular in assigning to the majority decisions about the nature and limits of majority decision-making? And if it is circular or question-begging, is that not a reason for assigning decisions of this sort to some other individual or institution?

I am not so sure. Let us think it through. Suppose the citizens of a country do not have the legal right to X and that some among them believe that a system of majority decision-making can have no legitimacy in a community whose members do not have that right. Others in the society, who are opposed to the right to X, deny this. If the issue between the pro-X and anti-X factions is dealt with by a majority vote in the legislature, confirming that people are not to have the right to X, the pro-X faction may reasonably refuse to accept the legitimacy of this result. I do not mean they are necessarily right about the relation between X and democracy. I mean that, given the disagreement about this between them and their opponents, any claim that the issue about the right to X was settled legitimately by the vote would indeed be question-begging.

Notice two things about this conclusion, however. First: if, in the absence of a right to X, a majority decision confirming that citizens do not have the right to X is problematic so far as its legitimacy is concerned, the same would have to be said of the opposite decision in these circumstances. So even if the majority had voted the other way – that is, even if they had voted to institute the right to X – that decision too would be tainted by the fact that it was taken among a citizenry who, as things stood, lacked this right thought by one faction to be so essential for legitimate majority decision-making. Pragmatically, of course, the pro-X faction might be expected to take its victories where it found them, and not worry too much about their legitimacy. But that does not make the process any the less tainted, on their own account of democracy.

Secondly, and much more importantly: the fact that a majoritarian process is arguably tainted by the absence of a right to X does not mean that other processes (such as judicial decision-making) are therefore preferable or legitimate. In most cases, the claim that the right to X is one of the conditions of legitimate democracy is unlikely to be true unless X is also one of the conditions of the legitimacy of *any* political system. Dworkin argues that 'a society in which the majority shows contempt for the needs and prospects of some minority is illegitimate as well as unjust' (25). But surely it follows from this, not only that majority decisions lack political legitimacy in that society, but that legitimacy cannot be accorded to *any* political decisions, made by *any* procedure, under the circumstances he mentions. The majority contempt Dworkin describes is liable to destroy the entire basis of political community for the society, depriving any group in it of the right to speak for the society as a whole. The legitimate basis for rule by a monarch would be undermined by the divisions and hatred he imagines, as would rule by an aristocratic elite or, for that matter, rule by the courts. If the circumstances are such as to warrant minority distrust of a dominant majority, they will certainly arouse misgivings about the basis on which judges are selected and the social and political culture that is likely to inform their decisions.

There is an important general point here. Sometimes we talk carelessly as though there were a *special* problem for the legitimacy of popular majority decision-making, a problem that does not exist for other forms of political organization such as aristocracy or judicial rule. Because the phrase 'tyranny of the majority' trips so easily off the tongue, we tend to forget about other forms of tyranny; we tend to forget that legitimacy is an issue that pertains to *all* political authority. Indeed it would be very odd if there were a *graver* problem of legitimacy for popular majoritarian decision-making. Other political systems have all the legitimacy-related dangers of popular majoritarianism: they may get things wrong; they may have an unjust impact on particular individuals or groups; in short, they may act tyrannically. But they have in addition one legitimacy-related defect that popular majoritarianism does not have: they do not allow a voice and a vote in a final decision-procedure to every citizen of the society; instead they proceed to make final decisions about the rights of millions on the basis of the voices and votes of a few.

Of the categories of rights I set out in section 1 of this chapter – (a) rights constitutive of democracy and (b) rights presupposed by democracy – I have concentrated in this section on rights in group (b). I did so because this group seemed most promising for Dworkin's claim that there is something question-begging about using majority procedures to determine what rights we have. But a similar conclusion can be reached concerning rights in group (a).

Suppose citizens disagree about the basis of suffrage, about campaign finance, or about proportional representation. In extreme cases, one side to the disagreement may claim that a majority-decision made in the absence of the constitutive right that they are arguing about has no legitimacy whatsoever. They may say, for example – quite plausibly – that a majority of men has no moral right to decide in the name of the whole community whether women shall have the right to vote. As before, it does not follow that some other body – the monarch or the courts – has the right to decide this issue simply because the male citizenry does not. What follows is that we are left in a legitimacy-free zone in which the best that we can hope for is that a legitimate democratic system emerges somehow or other. This is not the same as saying we are now using a results-driven test of legitimacy. It is rather a pragmatic expression of hope in circumstances where it is not open to us to use any communal criterion of legitimacy at all.

To repeat, then: the situation may be such that the legitimacy of *any* political decision about a right associated with democracy, by any procedure or institution, is thrown in doubt. That, I think, is undeniable. Does it not follow, then, that in these circumstances we *have* to appeal to a results-driven approach? It does not, for two reasons.

First, as we have already seen, the existence of controversy about the rights associated with democracy means that a results-driven approach is unavailable too, or unavailable to us as a political community. Individuals and factions may have their own result-based opinions of course, but then they will also have their own opinions about procedures (for example, their own opinions about the relation between democracy and the right in question). There is thus no advantage either way for a results-driven as opposed to a proceduralist approach.

Secondly, it is possible, as a matter of practical politics, to use an ordinary and familiar procedure like majority-decision to settle one of these questions, while leaving open the issue of legitimacy. Suppose, for example, that we use majoritarian procedure A to decide whether to continue with a procedure of that kind in our politics or to replace it with a somewhat different political procedure B. And suppose we vote to retain procedure A. We may accept that vote as a pragmatic matter, without investing it with democratic legitimacy in any particularly question-begging way. In other words, the fact that, pragmatically, we have to find some way of resolving disagreements about the rights associated with democracy does not mean that we have no choice but to adopt a results-driven test. The pragmatics may drive us instead to an informal and unfreighted use of some familiar decision-procedure, a use that does not beg the questions of legitimacy that are at issue. (Notice, of course, that all this can also be said about a results-driven test. If we can get away with using a partisan results-driven test such as the Rawlsian one, that too can be a purely pragmatic basis for constitutional design. In other words, the pragmatic possibility I am outlining in this paragraph is open to both sides. All I am insisting on in this section is that we are not *required* to adopt a results-driven approach: pragmatism, in this regard, is not necessarily the same as orientation to results.)

Sure, to a careless eye, it may look as though we are privileging one of the possible outcomes – namely, procedure A – by using *it* as the procedure for deciding among the possible outcomes. And – I have heard people say – if it makes sense to privilege one of the outcomes in this case, why does it not also make sense to privilege one of the outcomes in an ordinary case where substantive rather than procedural questions are at stake? But to decide among procedures A and B by using procedure A as our method is not to *privilege* procedure A; it is simply to use it. If we choose one of the procedures which are up for decision as the procedure for making that very decision, we do so simply because *we need a procedure* on this occasion and this is the one we are stuck with for the time being.

Remember, finally, that the fact that an issue concerns a right associated with democracy does not mean that we are necessarily brought to the impasse I have been discussing. For one thing, the right in question may be incidental rather than central to democratic legitimacy. Democracy is a complex and variegated ideal, and some of the rights associated with it in one type of system may be called in question without anyone thinking that therefore democracy as such is called in question. For another thing, even if the right in question is thought by one side to be essential to democracy, it does not follow that a majority-decision is question-begging. Suppose that the right to X is in question among the members of a community all of whom currently *do* have the right to X, and that some think, as before, that X is one of the conditions of legitimate democracy while others deny this. And suppose the people (or their representatives) vote by a majority for a bill that narrows or abrogates the right to X. Can *this* majority-decision be criticized by the pro-X faction as illegitimate? Is any claim about the legitimacy of *this* decision question-begging as between the proponents and the opponents of the right to X? Surely not. Unless there is some other problem with democracy in the society (a problem undisclosed in the terms of our hypothetical), the decision about X has been made under what the pro-X faction regard as the optimal conditions of legitimacy. People had their right to X and they made a collective decision (about that right). Certainly the pro-X faction will have their doubts about political decisions *subsequent* to this one, for they will think the abrogation of X has undermined the prospective legitimacy of majoritarianism in that community. But these doubts will affect *all* subsequent political decisions – on substantive as well as procedural matters – and (as before) decisions made by courts as much as decisions made by popular majorities. They will even affect the legitimacy of a future decision to restore the right to X. So we see once again there is nothing necessarily circular about majority decision-making on an issue concerning the rights associated with democracy.

10. Summa Contra Dworkin

The conclusions of this chapter so far may be summarized as follows. We examined Ronald Dworkin's arguments in *Freedom's Law* in favour of judicial review on the American model, and we accepted the following positions he defended: (1) there is an important connection between rights and democracy; (2) some individual rights must be regarded as conditions on the legitimacy of majority-decision, and (3) if people disagree about the conditions of democracy, an appeal to the legitimacy of majority-decision to settle that disagreement may be question-begging.

However, we also argued for the following claims, which contradict the inferences that Dworkin wanted to draw from (3). We argued (4) that if an appeal to the legitimacy of majority-decision to settle a disagreement about the conditions of democracy is question-begging, then an appeal to the legitimacy of judicial review (or any political procedure) to settle that disagreement is *also* likely to be question-begging; (5) the fact that an appeal to the legitimacy of majority-decision to settle a disagreement about the conditions of democracy is question-begging does not mean that we have no choice but to use a decision-procedure selected according to a results-driven test; and (6) in cases where an appeal to the legitimacy of majority-decision to settle a disagreement about the conditions of democracy is not question-begging, there is no reason to disparage majority-decision on the basis of *nemo iudex in sua causa*.

Against Dworkin's central argument in *Freedom's Law*, we argued (7) that there is always a loss to democracy when a view about the conditions of democracy is imposed by a non-democratic institution, even when the view is correct and its imposition improves the democracy. We also argued, near the beginning of the chapter, against a couple of incidental positions that Dworkin maintains. We argued (8) that there is no reason to think that judicial review improves the quality of participatory political debate in a society, and (9) that it is an open question whether judicial review has made the United States (or would make any society) more just than it would have been without that practice.

11. Is Everything Up for Grabs?

I have argued that there is nothing particularly question-begging about assigning issues about democracy to popular participatory procedures. There is nothing logically inappropriate about invoking the right to participate to determine issues about rights, including issues about participation itself. There is no reason, therefore, why each individual's claim to participate in the making of the laws by which he is governed should be arrested at the threshold of procedure. Logic does not require us to assign questions about political and constitutional arrangements for final decision to a non-participatory institution. On the contrary, there is something demo-cratically incomplete – certainly something unpleasantly condescending – about a constitution that empowers a small group of judges or other offi-cials to veto what the people or their representatives have settled on as their answers to disputed questions about what democracy involves.

Still, none of this assuages the worries with which we began. Granted there is nothing illogical in assigning disputes about the rights associated with democracy to a majoritarian procedure, what guarantee do we have that such rights would be respected? How can rights be secure if they are at the mercy of majority-decision? How is respect for rights consistent with a process that appears to place no a priori limits on political outcomes? Do the conclu-sions to which we have been driven not leave everything up for grabs?

The most straightforward answer is 'Yes – everything *is* up for grabs in a democracy, including the rights associated with democracy itself.' Or, certainly, everything is up for grabs which is the subject of good-faith disagreement. That's the key to the matter, for to say that something which was the subject of good-faith disagreement was nevertheless *not* up for grabs would be to imagine ourselves, as a community, in a position to take sides in such a disagreement without ever appearing to have done so. Suppose again that the members of a community disagree about whether people ought to have the right to X. To say that, nevertheless, the right to X should not be up for grabs in this community, is to say that the community has already taken a side in this disagreement. And one is entitled to wonder how exactly *that* came about (given the disagreement) without at some earlier stage the right to X having indeed been up for grabs in a decision procedure addressing the question of whether this right was something to which the community ought to commit itself.

The panic about everything being 'up for grabs' is of course in part a panic about self-government in the political realm. We are not sure of each other in the way we purport to be sure of ourselves. We want to govern ourselves – I mean govern ourselves politically, acting together, acting in the company of others – but we know we disagree about the principles on which such government should be conducted. Each of us therefore must face the prospect that the values *he* takes seriously, the priorities *he* has, the principles to which *he* has a strong attachment, may not be the values, priorities, and principles held by the voter in the next booth. We can try if we like to suppress these disagreements, to denigrate the other's views as selfish or irrational and exclude them as far as possible from our politics. But, as I have argued, we can hardly do this in the name of *rights*, if it is part of the idea of rights that a right-bearer is to be respected as a separate moral agent with his own sense of justice. If, on the other hand, we resolve to treat each other's views with respect, if we do not seek to hide the fact of our differences or to suppress dissent, then we have no choice but to adopt procedures for settling political disagreements which do not themselves specify what the outcome is to be.[37] In that sense, politics does leave things up for grabs in a way that is bound to be disconcerting from each individual's point of view. Respect for the opinions and consciences of others means that a single individual does not have the sort of control over political outcomes that his conscience or his own principles appear to dictate. That bullet, I think, simply has to be bitten.

'Up for grabs', however, may indicate a couple of other things, neither of which is entailed by the position that I have been arguing for.

'Grabs' can connote selfish pork-barrelling – a feeding frenzy of interest rather than a good faith disagreement of principle. Reasonable men and women will quite properly be alarmed by the prospects for rights in a society where each citizen and interest group is attempting to grab as much as it can. Rights generally would be in peril in such a situation, including of course the rights that are constitutive of democracy. My argument has proceeded on the premise that democratic politics need not be like that, and that it is in fact much less like that than the denigrators of popular majoritarianism tend to claim. I have insisted too that we should resist the temptation to say that it *is* like that simply because we find ourselves contradicted or outvoted on some matter of principle. We do not need to invoke self-interest to explain disagreement about rights, for it is sufficiently explained by the difficulty of the subject-matter and by what John Rawls called 'the burdens of judgment'.[38] If we ascribe someone's political difference with us to the influence of self-interest, that must be justified as a *special* explanation, over and above the normal explanation of human disagreement about complex questions.

I may be wrong about all this, of course: perhaps politics just is a clash of interests. (There is a danger, too, that this is what it is becoming around the world, as a sort of self-fulfilling prophecy evoked by the contempt for legislative politics exported triumphantly as the American contribution to democratic theory.) But if so, we should recognize that it is not just the reputation of popular majoritarianism that is in danger. If democratic politics is just an unholy scramble for personal advantage, then individual men and women are not the creatures that theorists of rights have taken them to be. If we think nevertheless that certain interests of theirs require special protection (against majorities and other kinds of tyrant), we shall have to develop a theory of justice and a theory of politics that does not associate the call for such protection with the active respect for moral capacity that the idea of rights has traditionally involved.

Mostly, however, what I want to insist on is this. The alternative to a self-interest model of politics is not a scenario in which individuals, as responsible moral agents, converge on a single set of principles which add up to *the truth* about justice, rights and the common good. That would not be a credible alternative from a social science point of view. The proper alternative to the self-interest model is a model of opinionated disagreement – a noisy scenario in which men and women of high spirit argue passionately and vociferously about what rights we have, what justice requires, and what the common good amounts to, motivated in their disagreement not by what's in it for them but by a desire to get it right. If we take *that* as our alternative model, we may be more inclined to recognize that real world politics are not necessarily governed by self-interest than if we think the only alternative to the self-interest model is one which has high-minded citizens converging on the truth. I have tried to show that we can construct a theory of politics for the model of opinionated disagreement – a theory of legitimate decision-procedures which works on the assumption that people who really care about justice and rights may nevertheless disagree about what they entail. Of course any political theory is bound to be something of an ideal-type in relation to the messiness of the real world.[39] A full and faithful account may require us to blend in elements from a variety of theories. What I am suggesting, however, is that if we want to do justice to that part of our political experience which involves people sometimes being prepared to consult their ideals as well as their utilities, then it is the model of disagreement, not the model of moral convergence, that we should reach for to blend with or qualify the more cynical model of interest.

The second sense of 'up for grabs' that I want to disown has to do with hasty, volatile, and impetuous 'grabbing'. That a certain right is 'up for grabs' in majoritarian politics may mean that it is respected today, abrogated tomorrow, and reinstated in an amended form on Monday morning. We alluded briefly [in Chapter Five] to Thomas Hobbes's suggestion that one of the most distinctive features of democratic politics is its inconstancy.[40] There are a variety of ways in which a democratic constitution may mitigate this inconstancy. The legislative process may be made more complex and laborious, and in various ways it may be made difficult to revisit questions of principle for a certain time after they have been settled. (Such 'slowing-down' devices may also be supported in the political community by values associated with 'the rule of law'.) None of this need be regarded as an affront to democracy; certainly a 'slowing-down' device of this sort is not like the affront to democracy involved in removing issues from a vote altogether and assigning them to a separate non-representative forum like a court. However, [as I argued in Chapter Twelve] democracy *would* be affronted by any attempt to associated such 'slowing down' with the idea that there is something pathological about one side or the other in a disagreement of principle. In that chapter, I argued against the 'Ulysses and the Sirens' model of precommitment, which presents constitutional constraints as a form of immunization against madness. We are not entitled to secure stability at the cost of silencing dissent or disenfranchising those who express it. And we should not use the ideas of constitutional caution or constitutional commitment as a way of precluding effective deliberation on a matter on which the citizens are still developing and debating their various views.

12. Disagreement About Limits

We know that if rights are entrusted to the people for protection they will be entrusted to men and women who disagree about what they amount to. It is tempting to infer, from the fact of such disagreement and from the processes (like voting) which will be necessary to resolve it, that this sort of protection in politics is as good as no protection at all. It is tempting to think that people who are prepared to countenance voting on matters of fundamental right, and to accept the view of the majority, simply do not take rights seriously.

Actually that is a temptation which is awfully *easy* to resist in certain contexts. For nobody thinks this about a tribunal like the United States Supreme Court. Surely the Justices on the Supreme Court take rights seriously if anybody does. Yet the Justices disagree about rights as much as anyone, and they resolve those disagreements by simple majority-voting. The established practice in America is that the people are to accept as authoritative a determination by the Court as to what rights they have, even when that determination is based on a knife-edge 5-to-4 vote among the Justices. We count heads on the court, we call for the appointment of a conservative or a liberal Justice, we talk about a particular Justice being the 'swing vote' on the court – and none of this seems to shake our confidence that rights are being addressed in the only way they could be addressed among articulate and opinionated individuals. We cannot therefore argue that rights are not being taken seriously in a political system simply on the ground that the system allows majority voting to settle disagreements as to what rights there are. On the contrary, a political culture – such as that which pervades and surrounds the US Supreme Court – may be a culture of rights, a culture in which rights are taken with the utmost seriousness, even though it is at the same time a culture of disagreement and a culture oriented to the idea that at the end of the day there may be nothing to do about a disagreement except count up the ayes and the noes.

Equally, I think we should not underestimate the extent to which the idea of rights may pervade legislative or electoral politics. The idea of rights is the idea that there are limits on what we may do to each other, or demand from each other, for the sake of the common good. A political culture in which citizens and legislators share this idea but disagree about what the limits are is quite different from a political culture uncontaminated by the idea of limits, and I think we sell ourselves terribly short in our constitutional thinking if we say that the fact of disagreement means we might as well not have the idea of rights or limits at all.

I want to end with two examples from the classics of liberal political philosophy, which will help to explain what I mean.

The first is the example of John Locke, well known as the founder of modern liberalism, and well known too for his insistence that the authority of the legislature is limited by respect for the natural rights – the lives, liberties, and property – of the people.[41] Legislators, said Locke, are not entitled to do just as they like. If they 'endeavour to invade the Property of the Subject, and to make themselves . . . Masters, or Arbitrary Disposers of the Lives, Liberties, or Fortunes of the People', they forfeit their authority. 'These are the bounds which the trust that is put in them by the Society, and the Law of God and Nature, have set to the Legislative Power of every Commonwealth.'[42] Yet Locke conjoined this classic liberal doctrine of the limited legislature with an insistence that '[i]n all Cases, whilst the Government subsists, the Legislative is the Supream Power . . . and all other Powers in any Members or parts of the Society [are] derived from and subordinate to it'.[43] The conjunction sounds curious to our jaded ears: how can he possibly mean what he says about a limited legislature, if he is not prepared to countenance any superior institution (like a court) to do the limiting? Is a theory of limits without institutional enforcement not the same as no theory of limits at all?

The question ignores the importance of political culture and public political understanding. 'To *understand* Political Power right' is the aim of the *Second Treatise*;[44] and the assumption on which Locke proceeds is that a polity pervaded by a right understanding will differ remarkably in its character and operations from a polity whose members are under wilful or negligent misapprehensions about the rights and basis of government.[45]

The idea of right-based limits is thus, in the first instance, a matter of political self-understanding. It seemed important to Locke that legislators should go about their task imbued with a moral and philosophical sense that there are limits to what they may do, and that they should commit themselves (as a matter of virtue or duty associated with their office) to ascertain what those limits are and whether or not they are contravened by the legislative proposals that come before them. It seemed to him also important for citizens to imbue their deference to the authority of the legislature with an exactly similar sense. They should act and respond to its dictates with an awareness that they are not required (by social contract etc.) to do *whatever* the legislature says, but that they are entitled to disobey or *in extremis* rebel when it goes beyond its limits. Accordingly citizens should understand that they, too, must try as hard as *they* can to understand what those limits are and whether or not the laws that are presented to them contravene those limits. Moreover, Locke wants to encourage a political culture in which people accompany these convictions with a sense that the matters in question are objective, and that they may get it wrong, and that if they do, they are answerable to God for their mistakes and for whatever havoc results.

Still – someone may respond – political culture and self-understanding are all very well; but why was Locke unwilling to countenance some arrangement like a supreme court to make a final determination about whether the legislature has betrayed its trust? Why would he not consider the option of the judicial review of legislation?

Scholars have noted that Locke says very little about the judiciary as a distinct branch of government. Peter Laslett argues that on Locke's account the judiciary was not a separate power at all: '[I]t was the general attribute of the state.'[46] To govern, on Locke's account, is to make a public judgement as to what natural law requires – both in general and in detail – and to set that judgement up as a basis for social coordination and enforcement. And that is what the Lockean legislature does. Unless one is proposing a bicameral legislature (something with which Locke had no difficulty),[47] there is no need for an *additional* institution to test whether the legislature's enactments are in accordance with natural law. That is what legislating *is*; that is the function that legislators are supposed to perform as they deliberate and vote. To the extent that members of the society disagree about this – to the extent that the natural law limits are controversial – legislation just *is* the adjudication of those controversies.

In theory, that function might be performed by a nine man junta clad in black robes and surrounded by law clerks. They might be the ones who deliberate and judge and vote on these issues. Locke's point here is more or less the same as Hobbes's:[48] whatever is the supreme power is in effect the legislature. But Locke puts it more carefully and democratically than Hobbes does. His position seems to be that, if there are controversies among us about natural law, it is important that a *representative* assembly resolve them.[49] He thinks it important that the institution which, by its representative character, embodies our 'mutual Influence, Sympathy, and Connexion'[50] should also be the one which determines our disagreements about justice, rights, the common good, and natural law. The institution which comprises our representatives and the institution which resolves our ultimate differences in moral principle should be one and the same. It is by combining these functions that the legislature embodies our deliberative virtue and our sense of mutual responsibility. 'This', as Locke says, 'is the Soul that gives Form, Life, and Unity to the Commonwealth', and this is why an assault on the integrity or position of the legislature (whether from inside or outside its ranks) is the most heinous attack on 'the Essence and Union of the Society'.[51]

I find this a powerful and appealing position. It embodies a conviction that these issues of principle are *ours* to deal with, so that even if they must be dealt with by some institution which comprises fewer than all of us, it should nevertheless be an institution that is diverse and plural and which, through something like electoral accountability, embodies the spirit of self-government, a body in which we can discern the manifest footprints of our own original consent.[52] It connects the themes we have been pursuing [in this part of the book] with the themes we pursued [in Chapters Two through Five] – the importance of matters on which there are different views and variegated opinions being settled by institutions which in their size and diversity pay tribute to the essential plurality of politics.

The second of the two examples I said I would invoke from the canon of political theory is the example of John Stuart Mill, in the argument about individual freedom that he presented in the essay *On Liberty*. When my students read *On Liberty*, they assume almost without thinking that it is a defence of the First Amendment, and a call for the institution of some similar constitutional constraint in Victorian England. It does not occur to them to take seriously Mill's insistence that he is not talking about laws and constitutions at all, that he is addressing himself to public opinion, that he is seeking to raise 'a strong barrier of *moral* conviction'[53] against 'an increasing inclination to stretch unduly the powers of society over the individual both by the force of opinion and even by that of legislation'.[54] In our modern preoccupation with mechanisms of enforcement, we tend to lose sight of the possibility that freedom of thought and discussion might be respected more on account of the prevalence of a spirit of liberty among the people and their representatives – a political culture of mutual respect – than as a result of formal declarations or other institutional arrangements.[55] That I think is serious short-sightedness. As the fate of scores of 'constitutions' around the world shows, paper declarations are worth little if not accompanied by the appropriate political culture of liberty. And political philosophy, if it has any effect in the world at all, is likely to have much more effect on political culture than it has on political institutions *per se*, even if that effect is more diffuse and less flattering to ourselves as would-be counsellors to the powerful.[56] In other words, I think that in political philosophy we should be as interested in the condition of political culture – the array of current understandings – as we are in having our own cherished principles institutionalized.

Certainly that was Mill's view. Individual liberty cannot be expected to hold its ground, said Mill, 'unless the intelligent part of the public can be made to feel its value'.[57] If we are concerned about individual liberty, then, the first thing we should do is not call for a Bill of Rights to be enforced by a court, but develop among ourselves a culture of liberty in which the idea is appreciated and taken seriously among those who will be participating in major social and political decisions. And – as I suggested [in Chapters Ten and Eleven] – this is what we should want to do anyway, if we really take liberty seriously. For we cannot seriously think that liberty in general is safe in a society in which it is an accepted political tactic to regard ordinary citizens as nothing but selfish and irresponsible members of predatory political majorities. Taking liberty seriously means taking each other seriously as holders of views about liberty.

But here's the twist. We cannot expect any idea – let alone the idea of liberty – to be taken seriously in society, we cannot expect the intelligent part of the public to feel its value, if it is not itself subject to vigorous debate and contestation. That is the argument put forward in defence of freedom of thought and discussion in Chapter Two of Mill's essay – the argument about the importance of disagreement in a vigorous and progressive culture. And obviously it applies reflexively to liberty itself. The principle of liberty and the principles underlying other rights are no exception to Mill's argument that, without genuine debate and disagreement, a creed adopted among the people tends

> to be received passively, not actively, . . . incrusting and petrifying [the mind] against all other influences addressed to the higher parts of our nature; manifesting its power by not suffering any fresh and living conviction to get in, but itself doing nothing for the mind or heart except standing sentinel over them to keep them vacant.[58]

Mill is notorious for the suggestion that it might even be necessary sometimes to actually manufacture disagreement, if dissent is not available to perform this invigorating function. If people did not disagree about an issue of right, we might have to provide 'some contrivance for making the difficulties of the question as present to [each person's] consciousness as if they were pressed upon him by a dissentient champion, eager for his conversion'.[59] Fortunately we are not in that situation. Since there *are* people who disagree about any given proposition of right, and who will voice that disagreement 'if law or opinion will let them, let us thank them for it, open our minds to listen to them, and rejoice that there is someone to do for us what we otherwise ought, if we have any regard for either the certainty or vitality of our convictions, to do with much greater labor for ourselves'.[60]

That, I think, is as good a place as any to finish. We *do* disagree about rights, and it is understandable that we do. We should neither fear nor be ashamed of such disagreement, nor hush and hustle it away from the forums in which important decisions of principle are made in our society. We should welcome it. Such disagreement is a sign – the best possible sign in modern circumstances – that people *take rights seriously*. Of course, as I have said a million times, a person who finds himself in disagreement with others is not for that reason disqualified from regarding his own view as correct. We must, each of us, keep faith with our own convictions. But taking rights seriously is also a matter of how we respond to contradiction by others, even on an issue of rights. Though each of us reasonably regards his own views as important, we must also (each of us) respect the elementary condition of *being with others*, which is both the essence of politics and the principle of recognition that lies at the heart of the idea of rights. When one confronts a right-bearer, one is not just dealing with a person entitled to liberty, sustenance, or protection. One is confronting above all a particular *intelligence* – a mind and consciousness which is not one's own, which is not under one's intellectual control, which has its own view of the world and its own account of the proper basis of relations with those whom it too sees as other. To take rights seriously, then, is to respond respectfully to this aspect of otherness and then to be willing to participate vigorously – but as an equal – in the determination of how we are to live together in the circumstances and the society that we share.

Notes

1   See Rawls, *Political Liberalism*, 19.
2   See, e.g., Beitz, *Political Equality*, Ch. 4. See also Ch. 5, s. 14, of *Law and Disagreement*.
3   In this chapter, numbers in parentheses are page references to Dworkin, *Freedom's Law*.

4   See Shue, *Basic Rights*, Ch. 1.

5   See Hohfeld, *Fundamental Legal Conceptions*, 50 ff.

6   The best known example is Ely, *Democracy and Distrust*.

7   *Idem.*

8   See Dworkin, *A Matter of Principle*, 59–69. See also Waldron, 'A Right-Based Critique of Constitutional Rights', 39–41.

9   See Dworkin, *A Matter of Principle*, 9–71, Dworkin, *A Bill of Rights for Britain*, and Dworkin, *Law's Empire*, Ch. 10.

10 See also Black, *A New Birth of Freedom*, 5 and 89.

11 Dworkin, *Law's Empire*, 356.

12 See Ch. 12, fn. 1 and accompanying text in *Law and Disagreement*. (Professor Dworkin has indicated in conversation that he does not now hold the view attributed to him in that passage.)

13 Dworkin, *Law's Empire*, 356.

14 *Brown v. Board of Education* 347 US 483 (1954).

15 Though see also Rosenberg, *The Hollow Hope*, 39–169.

16 See Dahl, *Democracy and its Critics*, 189.

17 For a list, see Forbath, *Law and the Shaping of the American Labor Movement*, Appendices A and C.

18 Ibid., 37–58.

19 For examples of the kinds of case Dworkin is referring to here, see those cited in Ch. 12, fn. 31, *Law and Disagreement*.

20 *Roe v. Wade*, 410 US 113 (1973).

21 This, Dworkin says, is particularly the case if the debate is oriented towards what he calls a 'moral reading' of the Constitution (7–15).

22 See also the discussion in Ch. 10, s. 4.

23 *Report of the Committee on Homosexual Offences and Prostitution*, Cmd. no. 247 (1957).

24 See Hart, *Law, Liberty and Morality* and Devlin, *The Enforcement of Morals*.

25 *Bowers v. Hardwick* 478 US 186 (1986).

26 Glendon, *Rights Talk*, 151.

27 I am grateful to Stephen Perry for this point.

28 See Dworkin, *Freedom's Law*, 34: 'People can be expected to disagree about which structure is overall best, and so in certain circumstances they need a decision procedure for deciding that question, which is exactly what a theory of democracy cannot provide. That is why the initial making of a political constitution is such a mysterious matter . . . '

29 Ely, *Democracy and Distrust*.

30 For the connection between liberal political theory and enlightenment optimism in epistemology, see Waldron, 'Theoretical Foundations of Liberalism'.

31 Locke, *An Essay Concerning Human Understanding*, Epistle to the Reader.

32 See Hobbes, *Leviathan*, Chapter 17, 120–1; Locke, *Two Treatises of Government*, II, paras. 95–8 and 132–3, 330–3 and 354–5.

33 Hobbes, *Leviathan*, Ch. 19.

34   See Hobbes, *The Elements of Law*, Part II, Ch. XXI: 'The first in order of time of these three sorts [of commonwealth] is democracy, and it must be so of necessity, because an aristocracy and a monarchy, require nomination of persons agreed upon; which agreement in a great multitude of men must consist in the consent of the major part; and where the votes of the major part involve the votes of the rest, there is actually a democracy.'

35   I am grateful to George Kateb for insisting that I confront this point.

36   See Rousseau, *The Social Contract*, Bk. II, Ch. 7, 76–9.

37   See Ch. 5, ss. 2 and 9, *Law and Disagreement*.

38   Rawls, *Political Liberalism*, 54–8. For a discussion of 'the burdens of judgment', see Ch. 5, s. 12 and Ch. 7, s. 2 of *Law and Disagreement*.

39   For this notion of ideal-type, see Weber, *Economy and Society*, Vol. I, 20–2.

40   Hobbes, *De Cive*, Ch. X, 137–8.

41   The paragraphs that follow are adapted from the first of my 1996 Seeley Lectures, 'Locke's Legislature'. (See Waldron, *The Dignity of Legislation*, Ch. 4.)

42   Locke, *Two Treatises of Government*, II, para. 142, 363.

43   Ibid., II, para. 150, 367–8. The conjunction is not inadvertent on Locke's part: it's not a matter of *our* juxtaposing two disparate parts of a patchwork manuscript. On the contrary, Locke makes it explicit in a single passage: 'Though the Legislative, whether placed in one or more, whether it be always in being, or only by intervals, tho' it be the Supream Power in every Commonwealth; yet, First, It is not, nor can possibly be absolutely Arbitrary over the Lives and fortunes of the People.' (Ibid., II, para. 135, 357.)

44   Locke, *Two Treatises of Government*, II, para. 4, 269 (my emphasis).

45   See ibid., II, para. 111, 343. See also Locke's insistence in the 'Preface' to the *Two Treatises of Government* that 'there cannot be done a greater Mischief to Prince and People, than the propagating wrong Notions concerning Government' (ibid., 138).

46   Laslett, 'Introduction' to Locke, *Two Treatises of Government*, 120.

47   See Locke, *Two Treatises of Government*, II, para. 213, 408.

48   Hobbes, *Leviathan*, Ch. XXVI, 184.

49   See especially Locke, *Two Treatises of Government*, II, para. 94, 329–30 and para. 143, 364.

50   Ibid., II, para. 212, 407.

51   *Idem.*

52   The phrase is from Pangle, *The Spirit of Modern Republicanism*, 254.

53   Mill, *On Liberty*, Ch. 1, 18 (my emphasis).

54   *Idem.*

55   Cf. Alexander Hamilton in *The Federalist Papers* LXXXIV, 476–7: The security of a right like freedom of the press, 'whatever fine declarations may be inserted in any constitution respecting it, must altogether depend on public opinion, and on the general spirit of the people and of the government. And here, after all, . . . must we seek for the only solid basis of all our rights.'

56 See Waldron, 'What Plato Would Allow' and also Waldron, 'Dirty Little Secret'.

57 Mill, *On Liberty*, Ch. 3, 90.

58 Ibid., Ch. 2, 49–50.

59 Ibid., Ch. 2, 53–4.

60 Ibid., Ch. 2, 55.

Part II

Ideal Deliberation

3

Deliberation and Democratic Legitimacy

Joshua Cohen

In this essay I explore the ideal of a 'deliberative democracy'.[1] By a deliberative democracy I shall mean, roughly, an association whose affairs are governed by the public deliberation of its members. I propose an account of the value of such an association that treats democracy itself as a fundamental political ideal and not simply as a derivative ideal that can be explained in terms of the values of fairness or equality of respect.

The essay is in three sections. In section I, I focus on Rawls's discussion of democracy and use that discussion both to introduce certain features of a deliberative democracy, and to raise some doubts about whether their importance is naturally explained in terms of the notion of a fair system of social cooperation. In section II, I develop an account of deliberative democracy in terms of the notion of an *ideal deliberative procedure*. The characterization of that procedure provides an abstract model of deliberation which links the intuitive ideal of democratic association to a more substantive view of deliberative democracy. Three features of the ideal deliberative procedure figure prominently in the essay. First, it helps to account for some familiar judgements about collective decision-making, in particular about the ways that collective decision-making ought to be different from bargaining, contracting and other market-type interactions, both in its explicit attention to considerations of the common advantage and in the ways that that attention helps to form the aims of the participants. Second, it accounts for the common view that the notion of democratic association is tied to notions of autonomy and the common good. Third, the ideal deliberative procedure provides a distinctive structure for addressing institutional questions. And in section III of the paper I rely on that distinctive structure in responding to four objections to the account of deliberative democracy.

I

The ideal of deliberative democracy is a familiar ideal. Aspects of it have been highlighted in recent discussion of the role of republican conceptions of self-government in shaping the American constitutional tradition and contemporary public law.[2] It is represented as well in radical democratic and socialist criticisms of the politics of advanced industrial societies.[3] And some of its central features are highlighted in Rawls's account of democratic politics in a just society, particularly in those parts of his account that seek to incorporate the 'liberty of the ancients' and to respond to radical democrats and socialists who argue that 'the basic liberties may prove to be merely formal'. In the discussion that follows I shall first say something about Rawls's remarks on three such features, and then consider his explanation of them.[4]

First, in a well-ordered democracy, political debate is organized around alternative conceptions of the public good. So an ideal pluralist scheme, in which democratic politics consists of fair bargaining among groups each of which pursues its particular or sectional interest, is unsuited to a just society (Rawls 1971, pp. 360–1).[5] Citizens and parties operating in the political arena ought not to 'take a narrow or group-interested standpoint' (p. 360). And parties should only be responsive to demands that are 'argued for openly by reference to a conception of the public good' (pp. 226, 472). Public explanations and justifications of laws and policies are to be cast in terms of conceptions of the common good (conceptions that, on Rawls's view, must be consistent with the two principles of justice), and public deliberation should aim to work out the details of such conceptions and to apply them to particular issues of public policy (p. 362).

Second, the ideal of democratic order has egalitarian implications that must be satisfied in ways that are manifest to citizens. The reason is that in a just society political opportunities and powers must be independent of economic or social position – the political liberties must have a fair value[6] – and the fact that they are independent must be more or less evident to citizens. Ensuring this manifestly fair value might, for example, require public funding of political parties and restrictions on private political spending, as well as progressive tax measures that serve to limit inequalities of wealth and to ensure that the political agenda is not controlled by the interests of economically and socially dominant groups (Rawls 1971, pp. 225–6, 277–8; 1982, pp. 42–3). In principle, these distributional requirements might be more stringently egalitarian than those fixed by the difference principle (1982, p. 43).[7] This is so in part because the main point of these measures is not simply to ensure that democratic politics proceeds under fair conditions, nor only to encourage just legislation, but also to ensure that the equality of citizens is manifest and to declare a commitment to that equality 'as the public intention' (1971, p. 233).

Third, democratic politics should be ordered in ways that provide a basis for self-respect, that encourage the development of a sense of political competence, and that contribute to the formation of a sense of justice;[8] it should fix 'the foundations for civic friendship and [shape] the ethos of political culture' (Rawls 1971, p. 234). Thus the importance of democratic order is not confined to its role in obstructing the class legislation that can be expected from systems in which groups are effectively excluded from the channels of political representation and bargaining. In addition, democratic politics should also shape the ways in which the members of the society understand themselves and their own legitimate interests.

When properly conducted, then, democratic politics involves *public deliberation focused on the common good*, requires some form of *manifest equality* among citizens, and *shapes the identity and interests* of citizens in ways that contribute to the formation of a public conception of common good. How does the ideal of a fair system of social co-operation provide a way to account for the attractiveness and importance of these three features of the deliberative democratic ideal? Rawls suggests a formal and an informal line of argument. The formal argument is that parties in the original position would choose the principle of participation[9] with the proviso that the political liberties have their fair value. The three conditions are important because they must be satisfied if constitutional arrangements are to ensure participation rights, guarantee a fair value to those rights, and plausibly produce legislation that encourages a fair distribution according to the difference principle.

Rawls also suggests an informal argument for the ordering of political institutions, and I shall focus on this informal argument here:

> Justice as fairness begins with the idea that where common principles are necessary and to everyone's advantage, they are to be worked out from the viewpoint of a suitably defined initial situation of equality in which each person is fairly represented. The principle of participation transfers this notion from the original position to the constitution ... [thus] preserv[ing] the equal representation of the original position to the degree that this is feasible. (Rawls 1971, pp. 221–2)[10]

Or, as he puts it elsewhere: 'The idea [of the fair value of political liberty] is to incorporate into the basic structure of society an effective political procedure which *mirrors* in that structure the fair representation of persons achieved by the original position' (1982, p. 45; emphasis added). The suggestion is that, since we accept the intuitive ideal of a fair system of co-operation, we should want our political institutions themselves to conform, in so far as it is feasible, to the requirement that terms of association be worked out under fair conditions. And so we arrive directly at the requirement of equal liberties with fair value, rather than arriving at it indirectly, through a hypothetical choice of that requirement under fair conditions. In this informal argument, the original position serves as an *abstract model* of what fair conditions are, and of what we should strive to mirror in our political institutions, rather than as an initial-choice situation in which regulative principles for those institutions are selected.

I think that Rawls is right in wanting to accommodate the three conditions. What I find less plausible is that the three conditions are natural consequences of the ideal of fairness. Taking the notion of fairness as fundamental, and aiming (as in the informal argument) to model political arrangements on the original position, it is not clear why, for example, political debate ought to be focused on the common good, or why the manifest equality of citizens is an important feature of a democratic association. The pluralist conception of democratic politics as a system of bargaining with fair representation for all groups seems an equally good mirror of the ideal of fairness.

The response to this objection is clear enough: the connection between the ideal of fairness and the three features of democratic politics depends on psychological and sociological assumptions. Those features do not follow directly from the ideal of a fair system of co-operation, or from that ideal as it is modeled in the original position. Rather, we arrive at them when we consider what is required to preserve fair arrangements and to achieve fair outcomes. For example, public political debate should be conducted in terms of considerations of the common good because we cannot expect outcomes that advance the common good unless people are looking for them. Even an ideal pluralist scheme, with equal bargaining power and no barriers to entry, cannot reasonably be expected to advance the common good as defined by the difference principle (1971, p. 360).

But this is, I think, too indirect and instrumental an argument for the three conditions. Like utilitarian defences of liberty, it rests on a series of highly speculative sociological and psychological judgements. I want to suggest that the reason why the three are attractive is not that an order with, for example, no explicit deliberation about the common good and no manifest equality would be unfair (though of course it might be). Instead it is that they comprise elements of an independent and expressly political ideal that is focused in the first instance[11] on the appropriate conduct of public affairs – on, that is, the appropriate ways of arriving at collective decisions. And to understand that ideal we ought not to proceed by seeking to 'mirror' ideal fairness in the fairness of political arrangements, but instead to proceed by seeking to mirror a system of ideal deliberation in social and political institutions. I want now to turn to this alternative.

II[12]

The notion of a deliberative democracy is rooted in the intuitive ideal of a democratic association in which the justification of the terms and conditions of association proceeds through public argument and reasoning among equal citizens. Citizens in such an order share a commitment to the resolution of problems of collective choice through public reasoning, and regard their basic institutions as legitimate in so far as they establish the framework for free public deliberation. To elaborate this ideal, I begin with a more explicit account of the ideal itself, presenting what I shall call the 'formal conception' of deliberative democracy. Proceeding from this formal conception, I pursue a more substantive account of deliberative democracy by presenting an account of an *ideal deliberative procedure* that captures the notion of justification through public argument and reasoning among equal citizens, and serves in turn as a model for deliberative institutions.

The formal conception of a deliberative democracy has five main features:

D1   A deliberative democracy is an ongoing and independent association, whose members expect it to continue into the indefinite future.
D2   The members of the association share (and it is common knowledge that they share) the view that the appropriate terms of association provide a framework for or are the results of their deliberation. They share, that is, a commitment to co-ordinating their activities within institutions that make deliberation possible and according to norms that they arrive at through their deliberation. For them, free deliberation among equals is the basis of legitimacy.
D3   A deliberative democracy is a pluralistic association. The members have diverse preferences, convictions and ideals concerning the conduct of their own lives. While sharing a commitment to the deliberative resolution of problems of collective choice (D2), they also have divergent aims, and do not think that some particular set of preferences, convictions or ideals is mandatory.

D4   Because the members of a democratic association regard deliberative procedures as the source of *legitimacy*, it is important to them that the terms of their association not merely *be* the results of their deliberation, but also be *manifest* to them as such.[13] They prefer institutions in which the connections between deliberation and outcomes are evident to ones in which the connections are less clear.

D5   The members recognize one another as having deliberative capacities, i.e. the capacities required for entering into a public exchange of reasons and for acting on the result of such public reasoning.

A theory of deliberative democracy aims to give substance to this formal ideal by characterizing the conditions that should obtain if the social order is to be manifestly regulated by deliberative forms of collective choice. I propose to sketch a view of this sort by considering an ideal scheme of deliberation, which I shall call the 'ideal deliberative procedure'. The aim in sketching this procedure is to give an explicit statement of the conditions for deliberative decision-making that are suited to the formal conception, and thereby to highlight the properties that democratic institutions should embody, so far as possible. I should emphasize that the ideal deliberative procedure is meant to provide a model for institutions to mirror – in the first instance for the institutions in which collective choices are made and social outcomes publicly justified – and not to characterize an initial situation in which the terms of association themselves are chosen.[14]

Turning then to the ideal procedure, there are three general aspects of deliberation. There is a need to decide on an agenda, to propose alternative solutions to the problems on the agenda, supporting those solutions with reasons, and to conclude by settling on an alternative. A democratic conception can be represented in terms of the requirements that it sets on such a procedure. In particular, outcomes are democratically legitimate if and only if they could be the object of a free and reasoned agreement among equals. The ideal deliberative procedure is a procedure that captures this principle.[15]

I1   Ideal deliberation is *free* in that it satisfies two conditions. First, the participants regard themselves as bound only by the results of their deliberation and by the preconditions for that deliberation. Their consideration of proposals is not constrained by the authority of prior norms or requirements. Second, the participants suppose that they can act from the results, taking the fact that a certain decision is arrived at through their deliberation as a sufficient reason for complying with it.

I2 Deliberation is *reasoned* in that the parties to it are required to state their reasons for advancing proposals, supporting them or criticizing them. They give reasons with the expectation that those reasons (and not, for example, their power) will settle the fate of their proposal. In ideal deliberation, as Habermas puts it, 'no force except that of the better argument is exercised' (1975, p. 108). Reasons are offered with the aim of bringing others to accept the proposal, given their disparate ends (D3) and their commitment (D2) to settling the conditions of their association through free deliberation among equals. Proposals may be rejected because they are not defended with acceptable reasons, even if they could be so defended. The deliberative conception emphasizes that collective choices should be *made in a deliberative way*, and not only that those choices should have a desirable fit with the preferences of citizens.

I3 In ideal deliberation parties are both formally and substantively *equal*. They are formally equal in that the rules regulating the procedure do not single out individuals. Everyone with the deliberative capacities has equal standing at each stage of the deliberative process. Each can put issues on the agenda, propose solutions, and offer reasons in support of or in criticism of proposals. And each has an equal voice in the decision. The participants are substantively equal in that the existing distribution of power and resources does not shape their chances to contribute to deliberation, nor does that distribution play an authoritative role in their deliberation. The participants in the deliberative procedure do not regard themselves as bound by the existing system of rights, except in so far as that system establishes the framework of free deliberation among equals. Instead they regard that system as a potential object of their deliberative judgement.

I4 Finally, ideal deliberation aims to arrive at a rationally motivated *consensus* – to find reasons that are persuasive to all who are committed to acting on the results of a free and reasoned assessment of alternatives by equals. Even under ideal conditions there is no promise that consensual reasons will be forthcoming. If they are not, then deliberation concludes with voting, subject to some form of majority rule.[16] The fact that it may so conclude does not, however, eliminate the distinction between deliberative forms of collective choice and forms that aggregate non-deliberative preferences. The institutional consequences are likely to be different in the two cases, and the results of voting among those who are committed to finding reasons that are persuasive to all are likely to differ from the results of an aggregation that proceeds in the absence of this commitment.

Drawing on this characterization of ideal deliberation, can we say anything more substantive about a deliberative democracy? What are the implications of a commitment to deliberative decisions for the terms of social association? In the remarks that follow I shall indicate the ways that this commitment carries with it a commitment to advance the common good and to respect individual autonomy.

Common good and autonomy

Consider first the notion of the common good. Since the aim of ideal deliberation is to secure agreement among all who are committed to free deliberation among equals, and the condition of pluralism obtains (D3), the focus of deliberation is on ways of advancing the aims of each party to it. While no one is indifferent to his/her own good, everyone also seeks to arrive at decisions that are acceptable to all who share the commitment to deliberation (D2). (As we shall see just below, taking that commitment seriously is likely to require a willingness to revise one's understanding of one's own preferences and convictions.) Thus the characterization of an ideal deliberative procedure links the formal notion of deliberative democracy with the more substantive ideal of a democratic association in which public debate is focused on the common good of the members.

Of course, talk about the common good is one thing; sincere efforts to advance it are another. While public deliberation may be organized around appeals to the common good, is there any reason to think that even ideal deliberation would not consist in efforts to disguise personal or class advantage as the common advantage? There are two responses to this question. The first is that in my account of the formal idea of a deliberative democracy, I stipulated (D2) that the members of the association are committed to resolving their differences through deliberation, and thus to providing reasons that they sincerely expect to be persuasive to others who share that commitment. In short, this stipulation rules out the problem. Presumably, however, the objection is best understood as directed against the plausibility of realizing a deliberative procedure that conforms to the ideal, and thus is not answerable through stipulation.

The second response, then, rests on a claim about the effects of deliberation on the motivations of deliberators.[17] A consequence of the reasonableness of the deliberative procedure (I2) together with the condition of pluralism (D3) is that the mere fact of having a preference, conviction or ideal does not by itself provide a reason in support of a proposal. While I may take my preferences as a sufficient reason for advancing a proposal, deliberation under conditions of pluralism requires that I find reasons that make the proposal acceptable to others who cannot be expected to regard my preferences as sufficient reasons for agreeing. The motivational thesis is that the need to advance reasons that persuade others will help to shape the motivations that people bring to the deliberative procedure in two ways. First, the practice of presenting reasons will contribute to the formation of a commitment to the deliberative resolution of political questions (D2). Given that commitment, the likelihood of a sincere representation of preferences and convictions should increase, while the likelihood of their strategic misrepresentation declines. Second, it will shape the content of preferences and convictions as well. Assuming a commitment to deliberative justification, the discovery that I can offer no persuasive reasons on behalf of a proposal of mine may transform the preferences that motivate the proposal. Aims that I recognize to be inconsistent with the requirements of deliberative agreement may tend to lose their force, at least when I expect others to be proceeding in reasonable ways and expect the outcome of deliberation to regulate subsequent action.

Consider, for example, the desire to be wealthier come what may. I cannot appeal to this desire itself in defending policies. The motivational claim is the need to find an independent justification that does not appeal to this desire and will tend to shape it into, for example, a desire to have a level of wealth that is consistent with a level that others (i.e. equal citizens) find acceptable. I am of course assuming that the deliberation is known to be regulative, and that the wealth cannot be protected through wholly non-deliberative means.

Deliberation, then, focuses debate on the common good. And the relevant conceptions of the common good are not comprised simply of interests and preferences that are antecedent to deliberation. Instead, the interests, aims and ideals that comprise the common good are those that survive deliberation, interests that, on public reflection, we think it legitimate to appeal to in making claims on social resources. Thus the first and third of the features of deliberative democracy that I mentioned in the discussion of Rawls (pp. 18–19 above) comprise central elements in the deliberative conception.

The ideal deliberative scheme also indicates the importance of autonomy in a deliberative democracy. In particular, it is responsive to two main threats to autonomy. As a general matter, actions fail to be autonomous if the preferences on which an agent acts are, roughly, given by the circumstances, and not determined by the agent. There are two paradigm cases of 'external' determination. The first is what Elster (1982) has called 'adaptive preferences'.[18] These are preferences that shift with changes in the circumstances of the agent without any deliberate contribution by the agent to that shift. This is true, for example, of the political preferences of instinctive centrists who move to the median position in the political distribution, wherever it happens to be. The second I shall call 'accommodationist preferences'. While they are deliberately formed, accommodationist preferences represent psychological adjustments to conditions of subordination in which individuals are not recognized as having the capacity for self-government. Consider Stoic slaves, who deliberately shape their desires to match their powers, with a view to minimizing frustration. Since the existing relations of power make slavery the only possibility, they cultivate desires to be slaves, and then act on those desires. While their motives are deliberately formed, and they act on their desires, the Stoic slaves do not act autonomously when they seek to be good slaves. The absence of alternatives and consequent denial of scope for the deliberative capacities that defines the condition of slaves supports the conclusion that their desires result from their circumstances, even though those circumstances shape the desires of the Stoic slaves through their deliberation.

There are then at least two dimensions of autonomy. The phenomenon of adaptive preferences underlines the importance of conditions that permit and encourage the deliberative formation of preferences; the phenomenon of accommodationist preferences indicates the need for favorable conditions for the exercise of the deliberative capacities. Both concerns are met when institutions for collective decision-making are modelled on the ideal deliberative procedure. Relations of power and subordination are neutralized (I1, I3, I4), and each is recognized as having the deliberative capacities (D5), thus addressing the problem of accommodationist preferences. Further, the requirement of reasonableness discourages adaptive preferences (I2). While preferences are 'formed' by the deliberative procedure, this type of preference formation is consistant with autonomy, since preferences that are shaped by public deliberation are not simply given by external circumstances. Instead they are the result of 'the power of reason as applied through public discussion'.[19]

Beginning, then, from the formal ideal of a deliberative democracy, we arrive at the more substantive ideal of an association that is regulated by deliberation aimed at the common good and that respects the autonomy of the members. And so, in seeking to embody the ideal deliberative procedure in institutions, we seek, *inter alia*, to design institutions that focus political debate on the common good, that shape the identity and interests of citizens in ways that contribute to an attachment to the common good, and that provide the favourable conditions for the exercise of deliberative powers that are required for autonomy.

III

I want now to shift the focus. While I shall continue to pursue the relationship between the ideal deliberative procedure and more substantive issues about deliberative democratic association, I want to do so by considering four natural objections to the conception I have been discussing, objections to that conception for being sectarian, incoherent, unjust and irrelevant. My aim is not to provide a detailed response to the objections, but to clarify the conception of deliberative democracy by sketching the lines along which a response should proceed. Before turning to the objections, I enter two remarks about what follows.

First, as I indicated earlier, a central aim in the deliberative conception is to specify the institutional preconditions for deliberative decision-making. The role of the ideal deliberative procedure is to provide an abstract characterization of the important properties of deliberative institutions. The role of the ideal deliberative procedure is thus different from the role of an ideal social contract. The ideal deliberative procedure provides a model for institutions, a model that they should mirror, so far as possible. It is not a choice situation in which institutional principles are selected. The key point about the institutional reflection is that it should *make deliberation possible*. Institutions in a deliberative democracy do not serve simply to implement the results of deliberation, as though free deliberation could proceed in the absence of appropriate institutions. Neither the commitment to nor the capacity for arriving at deliberative decisions is something that we can simply assume to obtain independent from the proper ordering of institutions. The institutions themselves must provide the framework for the formation of the will; they determine whether there is equality, whether deliberation is free and reasoned, whether there is autonomy, and so on.

Second, I shall be focusing here on some requirements on 'public' institutions that reflect the ideal of deliberative resolution. But there is of course no reason to expect as a general matter that the preconditions for deliberation will respect familiar institutional boundaries between 'private' and 'public' and will all pertain to the public arena. For example, inequalities of wealth, or the absence of institutional measures designed to redress the consequences of those inequalities, can serve to undermine the equality required in deliberative arenas themselves. And so a more complete treatment would need to address a wider range of institutional issues (see Cohen and Rogers 1983, chs 3, 6; Cohen 1989).

Sectarianism

The first objection is that the ideal of deliberative democracy is objectionably sectarian because it depends on a particular view of the good life – an ideal of active citizenship. What makes it sectarian is not the specific ideal on which it depends, but the (alleged) fact that it depends on some specific conception at all. I do not think that the conception of deliberative democracy suffers from the alleged difficulty. In explaining why not, I shall put to the side current controversy about the thesis that sectarianism is avoidable and objectionable, and assume that it is both.[20]

Views of the good figure in political conceptions in at least two ways. First, the *justification* of some conceptions appeals to a notion of the human good. Aristotelian views, for example, endorse the claim that the exercise of the deliberative capacities is a fundamental component of a good human life, and conclude that a political association ought to be organized to encourage the realization of those capacities by its members. A second way in which conceptions of the good enter is that the *stability* of a society may require widespread allegiance to a specific conception of the good, even though its institutions can be justified without appeal to that conception. For example, a social order that can be justified without reference to ideals of national allegiance may none the less require widespread endorsement of the ideal of patriotic devotion for its stability.

A political conception is objectionably sectarian only if its *justification* depends on a particular view of the human good, and not simply because its stability is contingent on widespread agreement on the value of certain activities and aspirations. For this reason the democratic conception is not sectarian. It is organized around a view of political justification – that justification proceeds through free deliberation among equal citizens – and not a conception of the proper conduct of life. So, while it is plausible that the stability of a deliberative democracy depends on encouraging the ideal of active citizenship, this dependence does not suffice to show that it is objectionably sectarian.

Incoherence

Consider next the putative incoherence of the ideal. We find this charge in an important tradition of argument, including Schumpeter's *Capitalism, Socialism, and Democracy* and, more recently, William Riker's work on social choice and democracy. I want here to say a word about the latter, focusing on just one reason that Riker gives for thinking that the ideal of popular self-government is incoherent.[21]

Institutionalizing a deliberative procedure requires a decision rule short of consensus – for example, majority rule. But majority rule is globally unstable: as a general matter, there exists a majority-rule path leading from any element in the set of alternatives to any other element in the set. The majority, standing in for the people, wills everything and therefore wills nothing. Of course, while anything can be the result of majority decision, it is not true that everything will be the result. But, because majority rule is so unstable, the actual decision of the majority will not be determined by preferences themselves, since they do not constrain the outcome. Instead decisions will reflect the particular institutional constraints under which they are made. But these constraints are 'exogenous to the world of tastes and values' (Riker 1982, p. 190). So the ideal of popular self-government is incoherent because we are, so to speak, governed by the institutions, and not by ourselves.

I want to suggest one difficulty with this argument that highlights the structure of the deliberative conception. According to the argument I just sketched, outcomes in majority-rule institutions reflect 'exogenous' institutional constraints, and not underlying preferences. This suggests that we can identify the preferences and convictions that are relevant to collective choices apart from the institutions through which they are formed and expressed. But that is just what the deliberative conception denies. On this conception, the relevant preferences and convictions are those that could be expressed in free deliberation, and not those that are prior to it. For this reason, popular self-government *premises* the existence of institutions that provide a framework for deliberation; these arrangements are not 'exogenous constraints' on the aggregation of preferences, but instead help to shape their content and the way that citizens choose to advance them. And, once the deliberative institutions are in place, and preferences, convictions and political actions are shaped by them, it is not clear that instability problems remain so severe as to support the conclusion that self-government is an empty and incoherent ideal.

Injustice

The third problem concerns injustice. I have been treating the ideal of democracy as the basic ideal for a political conception. But it might be argued that the ideal of democracy is not suited to the role of fundamental political ideal because its treatment of basic liberties is manifestly unacceptable. It makes those liberties dependent on judgements of majorities and thus endorses the democratic legitimacy of decisions that restrict the basic liberties of individuals. In responding to this objection I shall focus on the liberty of expression,[22] and shall begin by filling out a version of the objection which I put in the words of an imagined critic.[23]

'You embrace the ideal of a democratic order. The aim of a democratic order is to maximize the *power of the people* to secure its wants. To defend the liberty of expression you will argue that that power is diminished if the people lack the information required for exercising their will. Since expression provides information, you will conclude that abridgements of expression ought to be barred. The problem with your argument is that preventing restrictions on expression also restricts the power of the people, since the citizens may collectively prefer such restrictions. And so it is not at all clear as a general matter that the protection of expression will maximize popular power. So while you will, of course, not want to prevent everyone from speaking all the time, you cannot defend the claim that there is even a presumption in favour of the protection of expression. And this disregard for fundamental liberties is unacceptable.'

This objection has force against some conceptions on which democracy is a fundamental ideal, particularly those in which the value of expression turns exclusively on its role as a source of information about how best to advance popular ends. But it does not have any force against the deliberative conception, since the latter does not make the case for expression turn on its role in maximizing the power of the people to secure its wants. That case rests instead on a conception of collective choice, in particular on a view about how the 'wants' that are relevant to collective choice are formed and defined in the first place. The relevant preferences and convictions are those that arise from or are confirmed through deliberation. And a framework of free expression is required for the reasoned consideration of alternatives that comprises deliberation. The deliberative conception holds that free expression is required for *determining* what advances the common good, because what is good is fixed by public deliberation, and not prior to it. It is fixed by informed and autonomous judgements, involving the exercise of the deliberative capacities. So the ideal of deliberative democracy is not hostile to free expression; it rather presupposes such freedom.

But what about expression with no direct bearing on issues of public policy? Is the conception of deliberative democracy committed to treating all 'non-political expression' as second-class, and as meriting lesser protection? I do not think so. The deliberative conception construes politics as aiming in part at the formation of preferences and convictions, not just at their articulation and aggregation. Because of this emphasis on reasoning about preferences and convictions, and the bearing of expression with no political focus on such reasoning, the deliberative view draws no bright line between political speech and other sorts of expression. Forms of expression that do not address issues of policy may well bear on the formation of the interests, aims, and ideals that citizens bring to public deliberation. For this reason the deliberative conception supports protection for the full range of expression, regardless of the content of that expression.[24] It would violate the core of the ideal of free deliberation among equals to fix preferences and convictions in advance by restricting the content of expression, or by barring access to expression, or by preventing the expression that is essential to having convictions at all. Thus the injustice objection fails because the liberties are not simply among the topics for deliberation; they help to comprise the framework that makes it possible.[25]

Irrelevance

The irrelevance objection is that the notion of public deliberation is irrelevant to modern political conditions.[26] This is the most important objection, but also the one about which it is hardest to say anything at the level of generality required by the present context. Here again I shall confine myself to one version of the objection, though one that I take to be representative.

The version that I want to consider starts from the assumption that a direct democracy with citizens gathering in legislative assemblies is the only way to institutionalize a deliberative procedure. Premising that, and recognizing that direct democracy is impossible under modern conditions, the objection concludes that we ought to be led to reject the ideal because it is not relevant to our circumstances.

The claim about the impossibility of direct democracy is plainly correct. But I see no merit in the claim that direct democracy is the uniquely suitable way to institutionalize the ideal procedure.[27] In fact, in the absence of a theory about the operations of democratic assemblies – a theory which cannot simply stipulate that ideal conditions obtain – there is no reason to be confident that a direct democracy would subject political questions to deliberative resolution, even if a direct democracy were a genuine institutional possibility.[28] In the absence of a realistic account of the functioning of citizen assemblies, we cannot simply assume that large gatherings with open-ended agendas will yield any deliberation at all, or that they will encourage participants to regard one another as equals in a free deliberative procedure. The appropriate ordering of deliberative institutions depends on issues of political psychology and political behaviour; it is not an immediate consequence of the deliberative ideal. So, far from being the only deliberative scheme, direct democracy may not even be a particularly good arrangement for deliberation. But, once we reject the idea that a direct democracy is the natural or necessary form of expression of the deliberative ideal, the straightforward argument for irrelevance no longer works. In saying how the ideal might be relevant, however, we come up against the problem I mentioned earlier. Lacking a good understanding of the workings of institutions, we are inevitably thrown back on more or less speculative judgements. What follows is some sketchy remarks on one issue that should be taken in this spirit.

At the heart of the institutionalization of the deliberative procedure is the existence of arenas in which citizens can propose issues for the political agenda and participate in debate about those issues. The existence of such arenas is a public good, and ought to be supported with public money. This is not because public support is the only way, or even the most efficient way, of ensuring the provision of such arenas. Instead, public provision expresses the basic commitment of a democratic order to the resolution of political questions through free deliberation among equals. The problem is to figure out how arenas might be organized to encourage such deliberation.

In considering that organization, there are two key points that I want to underscore. The first is that material inequalities are an important source of political inequalities. The second point – which is more speculative – is that deliberative arenas which are organized exclusively on local, sectional or issue-specific lines are unlikely to produce the open-ended deliberation required to institutionalize a deliberative procedure. Since these arenas bring together only a narrow range of interests, deliberation in them can be expected at best to produce coherent sectional interests, but no more comprehensive conception of the common good.

These two considerations together provide support for the view that political parties supported by public funds play an important role in making a deliberative democracy possible.[29] There are two reasons for this, corresponding to the two considerations I have just mentioned. In the first place, an important feature of organizations generally, and parties in particular, is that they provide a means through which individuals and groups who lack the 'natural' advantage of wealth can overcome the political disadvantages that follow on that lack. Thus they can help to overcome the inequalities in deliberative arenas that result from material inequality. Of course, to play this role, political organizations must themselves be freed from the dominance of private resources, and that independence must be manifest. Thus the need for public funding. Here we arrive back at the second point that I mentioned in the discussion of Rawls's view – that measures are needed to ensure manifest equality – though now as a way of displaying a shared commitment to deliberative decisions, and not simply as an expression of the commitment to fairness. Second, because parties are required to address a comprehensive range of political issues, they provide arenas in which debate is not restricted in the ways that it is in local, sectional or issue-specific organizations. They can provide the more open-ended arenas needed to form and articulate the conceptions of the common good that provide the focus of political debate in a deliberative democracy.

There is certainly no guarantee that parties will operate as I have just described. But this is not especially troubling, since there are no guarantees of anything in politics. The question is how we can best approximate the deliberative conception. And it is difficult to see how that is possible in the absence of strong parties, supported with public resources (though, of course, a wide range of other conditions are required as well).

IV

I have suggested that we take the notion of democratic association as a fundamental political ideal, and have elaborated that ideal by reference to an ideal deliberative procedure and the requirements for institutionalizing such a procedure. I have sketched a few of those requirements here. To show that the democratic ideal can play the role of fundamental organizing ideal, I should need to pursue the account of fundamental liberties and political organization in much greater detail and to address a wide range of other issues as well. Of course, the richer the requirements are for institutionalizing free public deliberation, the larger the range of issues that may need to be removed from the political agenda; that is, the larger the range of issues that form the background framework of public deliberation rather than its subject matter. And, the larger that range, the less there is to deliberate about. Whether that is good news or bad news, it is in any case a suitable place to conclude.

Notes

I have had countless discussions of the subject matter of this paper with Joel Rogers, and wish to thank him for his unfailingly sound and generous advice. For our joint treatment of the issues that I discuss here, see Cohen and Rogers (1983), ch. 6. The main differences between the treatment of issues here and the treatment in the book lie in the explicit account of the ideal deliberative procedure, the fuller treatment of the notions of autonomy and the common good, and the account of the connection of those notions with the ideal procedure. An earlier draft of this paper was presented to the Pacific Division Meetings of the American Philosophical

Association. I would like to thank Loren Lomasky and the editors [of this collection; *The Good Polity*] for helpful comments on that draft.

1   I originally came across the term 'deliberative democracy' in Sunstein (1985). He cites (n. 26) an article by Bessette, which I have not consulted.
2   For some representative examples, see Sunstein (1984, 1985, 1986), Michelman (1986), Ackerman (1984, 1986).
3   I have in mind, in particular, criticisms which focus on the ways in which material inequalities and weak political parties restrict democracy by constraining public political debate or undermining the equality of the participants in that debate. For discussion of these criticisms, and of their connections with the ideal of democratic order, see Cohen and Rogers (1983), chs 3, 6; Unger (1987), ch. 5.
4   In the discussion that follows, I draw on Rawls (1971, esp. sections 36, 37, 43, 54; 1982).
5   This rejection is not particularly idiosyncratic. Sunstein, for example, argues (1984, 1985) that ideal pluralism has never been embraced as a political ideal in American public law.
6   Officially, the requirement of fair value is that 'everyone has a fair opportunity to hold public office and to influence the outcome of political decisions' (Rawls 1982, p. 42).
7   Whatever their stringency, these distributional requirements take priority over the difference principle, since the requirement of fair value is part of the principle of liberty; that is, the first principle of justice (Rawls 1982, pp. 41–2).
8   The importance of democratic politics in the account of the acquisition of the sense of justice is underscored in Rawls (1971), pp. 473–4.
9   The principle of participation states that 'all citizens are to have an equal right to take part in, and to determine the outcome of, the constitutional process that establishes the laws with which they are to comply' (Rawls 1971, p. 221).
10   I assume that the principle of participation should be understood here to include the requirement of the fair value of political liberty.
11   The reasons for the phrase 'in the first instance' are clarified below at pp. 22–3.
12   Since writing the first draft of this section of the paper, I have read Elster (1986a) and Manin (1987), which both present parallel conceptions. This is especially so with Elster's treatment of the psychology of public deliberation (pp. 112–13). I am indebted to Alan Hamlin for bringing the Elster article to my attention. The overlap is explained by the fact that Elster, Manin and I all draw on Habermas. See Habermas (1975, 1979, 1984). I have also found the discussion of the contractualist account of motivation in Scanlon (1982) very helpful.
13   For philosophical discussions of the importance of manifestness or publicity, see Kant (1983), pp. 135–9; Rawls (1971), p. 133 and section 29; Williams (1985), pp. 101–2, 200.
14   The distinction between the ideal procedure and an initial-choice situation will be important in the later discussion of motivation formation and institutions.

15 There are of course norms and requirements on individuals that do not have deliberative justification. The conception of deliberative democracy is, in Rawls's term, a 'political conception', and not a comprehensive moral theory. On the distinction between political and comprehensive theories, see Rawls (1987), pp. 1–25.

16 For criticism of the reliance on an assumption of unanimity in deliberative views, see Manin (1987), pp. 359–61.

17 Note the parallel with Elster (1986a) indicated in note 12. See also the discussion in Habermas (1975), p. 108, about 'needs that can be communicatively shared', and Habermas (1979), ch. 2.

18 For an interesting discussion of autonomous preferences and political processes, see Sunstein (1986 pp. 1145–58; 1984, pp. 1699–700).

19 Whitney *vs*. California, 274 US 357 (1927).

20 For contrasting views on sectarianism, see Rawls (1987); Dworkin (1985), pt 3; MacIntyre (1981); Sandel (1982).

21 See Riker (1982); for discussion of Riker's view see Coleman and Ferejohn (1986); Cohen (1986).

22 For discussion of the connection between ideals of democracy and freedom of expression, see Meiklejohn (1948), Tribe (1978; 1985, ch. 2) and Ely (1980, pp. 93–4, 105–16). Freedom of expression is a special case that can perhaps be more straightforwardly accommodated by the democratic conception than liberties of conscience, or the liberties associated with privacy and personhood. I do think, however, that these other liberties can be given satisfactory treatment by the democratic conception, and would reject it if I did not think so. The general idea would be to argue that other fundamental liberties must be protected if citizens are to be able to engage in and have equal standing in political deliberation without fear that such engagement puts them at risk for their convictions or personal choices. Whether this line of argument will work out on the details is a matter for treatment elsewhere.

23 This objection is suggested in Dworkin (1985), pp. 61–3. He cites the following passage from a letter of Madison's: 'And a people who mean to be their own Governors, must arm themselves with *the power which knowledge gives*' (emphasis added).

24 On the distinction between content-based and content-neutral abridgements, the complexities of drawing the distinction in particular cases, and the special reasons for hostility to content-based abridgements, see Tribe (1978), pp. 584–682; Stone (1987), pp. 46–118.

25 I am not suggesting that the deliberative view provides the only sound justification for the liberty of expression. My concern here is rather to show that the deliberative view is capable of accommodating it.

26 For an especially sharp statement of the irrelevance objection, see Schmitt (1985).

27 This view is sometimes associated with Rousseau, who is said to have conflated the notion of democratic legitimacy with the institutional expression of that

ideal in a direct democracy. For criticism of this interpretation, see Cohen (1986a).

28   Madison urges this point in the *Federalist Papers*. Objecting to a proposal advanced by Jefferson which would have regularly referred constitutional questions 'to the decision of the whole of society', Madison argues that this would increase 'the danger of disturbing the public tranquillity by interesting too strongly the public passions'. And 'it is the reason, alone, of the public that ought to control and regulate the government . . . [while] the passions ought to be controlled and regulated by the government'. I endorse the form of the objection, not its content. (*Federalist Papers* 1961, pp. 315–17.)

29   Here I draw on Cohen and Rogers (1983), pp. 154–7. The idea that parties are required to organize political choice and to provide a focus for public deliberation is one strand of arguments about 'responsible parties' in American political-science literature. My understanding of this view has been greatly aided by Perlman (1987), and, more generally, by the work of my colleague Walter Dean Burnham on the implications of party decline for democratic politics. See, for example, Burnham (1982).

4

Deliberative Politics

Jürgen Habermas

Normative versus Empiricist Models of Democracy

I begin by assuming that the conceptual relation between political power and law becomes empirically relevant through the conceptually unavoidable pragmatic presuppositions of legitimate law-making and through the institutionalization of a corresponding practice of self-governance by citizens. This assumption might be tendentious, because it excludes an empiricist approach from the start. Empiricism purges the concept of power of just that normative authority it gains through its internal connection with legitimate law. Empiricist theories of power, whether conceived at an action level or a systems level, do not ignore the normative character that permeates the legal forms for the exercise of political power, but they do reduce the latter to social power. According to one reading, "social power" expresses itself in the ability to prevail of superior interests that can be pursued more or less rationally; "political power" can then be conceived as a more-abstract and permanent form of social power that licenses access to "administrative power," that is, to various government offices. When one takes the empiricist's observer perspective, one uses *different* terms than one would from the participant perspective to describe both the claim to legitimacy expressed by the legal form of political power, as well as the need for legitimation that requires recourse to specific standards of validity: the conditions for the acceptability of law and political authority are transformed into conditions of actual acceptance, while conditions of legitimacy become conditions for the stability of a generally held belief in the government's legitimacy. As we will see, an analysis conducted with these or similar conceptual instruments allows one to subject the normative self-understanding of constitutional democracy to a rather illuminating critique.[1]

However, it is an entirely different undertaking when a theory of democracy with normative intentions merely *borrows* the objectivating view and empiricist strategy from the social sciences. This cryptonormative approach aims to demonstrate that democratic practices can be legitimated from the perspective of the participants themselves in terms of descriptive empiricist categories. Starting with the assumption that the normative validity claims of politics and law lack a cognitive meaning, such a theory attempts to explain how the individual interests of elites and citizens could nevertheless provide them with good reasons for making their contribution to the normatively demanded legitimation game of liberal mass democracies. If such a model of democracy could be justified, then our question concerning the external relation between facticity and validity would, quite elegantly, become pointless. One would no longer need to take the normative substance of the constitutional state at face value.

In section 1.1, I will first examine the consistency of Werner Becker's proposal for an empiricist justification of the democratic rules of the game. The unsatisfactory result will force us back to the three normative models of democracy that we have already encountered (sec. 1.2).

1.1

Becker avails himself of empiricist materials in building a normative theory of democracy, that is, one designed for purposes of justification. Just as power in general is displayed in the empirical superiority of the stronger interest or will, so also political power is displayed in the sheer stability of a political order. Legitimacy is considered a measure for stability, for the legitimacy of the state is objectively measured by de facto recognition on the part of the governed. Such legitimacy can range from mere toleration to free consent (*Zustimmung*). Here the consent that creates legitimacy is based on subjective reasons that claim to be valid inside the currently accepted "ideological frame"; but these reasons resist objective assessment. One legitimation is as good as another, so long as it sufficiently contributes to stabilizing a given political order. According to this view, even a dictatorship must be considered legitimate so long as a socially recognized framework of legitimation enables the government to remain stable. From this perspective of the theory of power, the quality of the reasons are without empirical significance: "It is an illusion of liberals and democrats to think that dictatorships can only survive under the 'protection of the bayonet.' "[2]

Becker then introduces the concept of democracy through the rules governing universal and equal suffrage, party competition, and majority rule. Of course, in the background lies an empiricist understanding of social norms, according to which the "validity" of norms only signifies their connection with sanctions effective for stability. As a result, Becker cannot define his task as that of *normatively* justifying this arrangement. Rather, his theory only aims to demonstrate that even if the participants describe themselves in empiricist categories, they can have good reasons for adhering to the rules of the game for mass democracy. This explains, in the first place, the observance of these norms by the parties that hold power: "The party in power never seeks to restrict the political activity of the citizens or parties as long as they do not attempt to overthrow the regime by violence." Correspondingly, the losers keep their peace: "The parties that lost the election never resort to violence or other illegal means to prevent the victorious party from assuming office."[3] Under these conditions, a peaceful transfer of power is secured.

Becker's justification can be reconstructed as a sequence of three steps, each of which has two parts. In each case, the first half step is an objective explanation, whereas the second consists in the attempt to translate this explanation from the observer perspective into a rational-choice explanation *for the participants themselves*. The argument aims to reach that "indifference point" where the objective explanation can also be accepted as a sufficient explanation from the participant perspective.

(a) In a pluralist democracy, legitimacy stems from a majority vote reached in elections that are free, equal, and secret. This idea is supposed to acquire its plausibility from a specifically modern worldview and self-understanding, which are grounded in what Becker calls "ethical subjectivism." On the one hand, ethical subjectivism secularizes the Judeo-Christian understanding of the equality of each individual before God and assumes the fundamental equality of all individuals. On the other hand, it replaces the transcendent origin of obligatory commands with an immanent validity; that is, it considers the validity of norms to be anchored solely in the subject's own will. In the empiricist reading, the modern understanding of freedom means, among other things, that "the validity of . . . the norms accepted by the individual human being is generated by the individual himself through his free consent."[4] The individuals themselves are the ones who deliberately produce normative validity through a free act of consent. This voluntaristic understanding of validity corresponds to a positivist view of law: law includes everything that a duly chosen political lawgiver posits as law, and only that. This view agrees with critical rationalism, in the sense that modern convictions are not rationally justified in any sense but rather express a decision or a cultural shaping that in fact has become dominant.[5]

If participating citizens want to make this explanation their own, then they are at first tempted to look for ways of grounding ethical subjectivism. They might seek this grounding in human rights, or they might look to a deontological elucidation of the moral point of view, according to which the only valid norms are those that *all* could will. But empiricism teaches them that such rationalistic escapes would lead them away from the specific insight into the irreducible contingency of what they consider normatively valid. However, precisely this awareness of contingency renders the proffered objective explanation unsatisfactory for the participants in the democratic process. They need at least a purposive-rational explanation for why the norms passed by the majority should be accepted as valid by the outvoted minority.

(b) On voluntaristic premises, the validity claim raised by majority decisions cannot be grounded by appealing to the common good, forecasts of collective utility, or practical reason, for each of these would require objective standards. Instead, Becker explains the acceptance of majority rule in terms of a domesticated struggle for power. If one presupposes, with ethical subjectivism, that each individual has equal power, then a majority of votes is an impressive numerical expression of superior strength: "If one views the matter this way, then this justification of democratic procedures is based on . . . the threat of the majority to revoke the agreement to renounce violence, when things do not go according to its will. . . . According to this view, democracy means nothing other than that one part of the people rules the other part for a set time."[6] If one considers how a threat on the part of the numerically and at least symbolically stronger party can, against the background of the latent danger of a civil war, have an intimidating effect, then temporally limited majority rule seems to recommend itself as an "acceptable solution of the power question" for the minority as well.

This Hobbesian interpretation of majority rule can also gain a certain plausibility from the participant perspective if the goal of domesticating violent disputes has priority for all. Nonetheless, the explanation remains unsatisfactory for the participants in the democratic process as long as it remains unclear how minorities can be protected from the tyranny of the majority, even a peaceful tyranny. In addition, it must be guaranteed that the disputing parties will in fact submit to majority rule.

(c) In order to protect minorities, Becker has recourse to the classical basic liberties. Majority approval for such guarantees of minority interests is explained by the current majority's fear of becoming a minority itself. This by itself should preclude the danger that tyrannical majorities could become permanent, because both the majority, with its anxiety over the loss of its power, and the minority, with its prospects for a change in power, should be motivated to observe the established rules of the game. The conditions for a transfer of power between incumbents and opposition can now be satisfied in that the competing elites split the electorate into several camps according to ideological standpoints. In doing this, the elites aim to win majorities by programmatic means – as a rule, with promises of social rewards interpreted in particular ways. Thus the process of gaining legitimation boils down to an interplay between "ideologicopolitical" and "socio-political" means. This interplay is partly explained by the fact that the satisfaction of societal interests by distributive measures is, in the final analysis, not something objective but rather requires a convincing interpretation.

However, this explanation of the protection of minorities and the transfer of power is tailored entirely to the interest positions of elites concerned with acquiring and maintaining power. But what these elites consider plausible will not necessarily convince the citizens. The public of citizens will hardly be moved to take part in the democratic process, or at least to tolerate it benevolently, as long as this public can be viewed only as the ideological plunder of competing parties. This public wants to be *convinced* that the one party offers the prospect of better policies than does the other party; there must be good reasons for preferring one party to the other. Here one finally reaches the point where something that looks plausible from the observer perspective can no longer be translated into an argument that looks plausible to participants in the same way. The attempt at such a translation leads, under empiricist premises, to contradictions.

(d) From the objectivating viewpoint of the empiricist model, the struggle of parties for political power lacks a validity dimension. Becker does not cease to reiterate the point that political arguments are exhausted by their *rhetorical* functions. Political arguments are intended not to be rationally acceptable but to be perlocutionarily effective: "In democracy it is not a question of ascertaining the 'objective truth' of political policies. It is rather a matter of establishing conditions for the democratic acceptability of the goals that the parties pursue. To this extent, the function of political arguments is . . . more that of advertising, or 'weapons' that circumvent the use of physical force, than that of assertions one could interpret as providing support for 'true' theories."[7] The normatively laden but vague terms of political debate have rather an emotional significance: they are intended to create mass commitments. Accordingly, political speech has "a social-psychological, not a cognitive, function."[8]

Becker must explain why citizens, and not just the elites, see through the emotional meaning of pseudoargumentative advertising – and nonetheless accept it. It is assumed that the empiricist self-description does not have deleterious effects on their motivation to participate, because enlightened citizens already have a no-nonsense view of the political process as compromise formation. But even compromises must be grounded, and what grounds the acceptance of compromises? On the one hand, there are no normative standards by which the fairness of compromises could be assessed. Social justice, for instance, is relegated to the sphere of public-relations rhetoric: "In the political reality of liberal democracies this [i.e., social justice] is a systematically superfluous idea." On the other hand, participants should still have good reasons for entering into compromises: "Under the conditions of a competitive political and social pluralism, 'social justice' simply means a fair [!] balance among the interests of social groups." This contradiction does not arise by accident. In the end, Becker must smuggle in something like "fairness" as a standard for evaluating compromises, though he cannot declare this as such: "The rules of the game for balancing interests must include 'parity of weapons'. However, contrary to what the concept of 'social justice' suggests, one does not need a unitary standard to evaluate the outcome of a balancing of interests."[9] True, bargaining partners need not accept the outcome of successful bargaining for the *same* reasons. But the prudential considerations that each side weighs from its point of view tacitly presuppose the common recognition of normative reasons. These reasons justify the procedure itself as impartial by explaining why outcomes reached in conformity with the procedure may count as fair.

In the final analysis, therefore, the chasm between what can be asserted from the perspective of an observer and what can be accepted from the perspective of participants cannot be bridged by purposive-rational considerations alone. This reflects the performative self-contradiction that ensnares an empiricist theory of democracy with normative intentions – in fact, a self-contradiction Becker already indicates in the subtitle of his book: the "decision for democracy" recommended by the book may not be understood, on the book's own premises, as a *rationally grounded* decision. If, however, it is a matter of sheer decision, then as a reader one must wonder what kind of text one is dealing with in this book. At first sight, it seems to propose a philosophical theory that explains and justifies the rules of liberal democracy. After becoming acquainted with the theory, however, one realizes that the author, if he is consistent, can understand his theory at most as an ideological *advertisement* for liberal constitutionalism.

1.2

To summarize the results of our analysis, we can say that if rational citizens were to describe their practices in empiricist categories, they would not have sufficient reason to observe the democratic rules of the game. Obviously, a theory with justificatory intentions must not suppress the genuinely normative sense of the intuitive understanding of democracy. Empiricist redefinitions thus do not give us a way to avoid the question of how norm and reality are related. If this is the case, then we must return to those normative models of democracy already introduced and ask whether their implicit conceptions of society offer any points of contact with available sociological analyses.

Our reflections from the standpoint of legal theory revealed that the central element of the democratic process resides in the procedure of deliberative politics. This reading of democracy has implications for the concept of society presupposed in the received models of democracy, that is, the view of society as centered in the state. The reading proposed here differs both from the liberal conception of the state as guardian of an economic society and from the republican concept of an ethical community institutionalized in the state.[10]

According to the liberal view, the democratic process is effected exclusively in the form of compromises among interests. Rules of compromise formation are supposed to secure the fairness of results through universal and equal suffrage, the representative composition of parliamentary bodies, the mode of decision making, rules of order, and so on. Such rules are ultimately justified in terms of liberal basic rights. According to the republican view, on the other hand, democratic will-formation takes the form of ethicopolitical self-understanding; here deliberation can rely on the substantive support of a culturally established background consensus shared by the citizenry. This socially integrative pre-understanding can renew itself in the ritualized recollection of the founding of the republic. Discourse theory takes elements from both sides and integrates these in the concept of an ideal procedure for deliberation and decision making. Democratic procedure, which establishes a network of pragmatic considerations, compromises, and discourses of self-understanding and of justice, grounds the presumption that reasonable or fair results are obtained insofar as the flow of relevant information and its proper handling have not been obstructed. According to this view, practical reason no longer resides in universal human rights, or in the ethical substance of a specific community, but in the rules of discourse and forms of argumentation that borrow their normative content from the validity basis of action oriented to reaching understanding. In the final analysis, this normative content arises from the structure of linguistic communication and the communicative mode of sociation.

In the present context, it is interesting that these descriptions of the democratic process also set the stage for a normative conceptualization of state and society. All we need presuppose is a type of public administration that emerged in the early-modern period with the European nation-state and developed functional ties with the capitalist economy.

According to the republican view, the citizens' opinion-and will-formation forms the medium through which society constitutes itself as a political whole. Society is, from the very start, political society – *societas civilis* – for in the citizens' practice of political self-determination the community becomes conscious of itself, as it were, and acts upon itself through the citizens' collective will. Hence democracy becomes equivalent to the political self-organization of society as a whole. This leads to an offensive *understanding of politics directed against the state apparatus*. In Hannah Arendt's political writings, one can see where republican argumentation directs its salvos: in opposition to the civil privatism of a depoliticized population and in opposition to the production of mass loyalty through parties that have become arms of the state, the political public sphere should be revitalized to the point where a regenerated citizenry can, in the forms of a decentralized self-governance, (once again) appropriate bureaucratically alienated state power. In this way society would finally develop into a political totality.

Whereas the separation of the state apparatus from society elicits a polemical response from the republican side, according to the liberal view the gap cannot be eliminated but only bridged by the democratic process. Naturally, the regulated balance of power and interests needs to be channeled by the rule of law. The democratic will-formation of self-interested citizens has comparatively weak normative connotations, and it forms only one element in a complex constitution. The constitution is supposed to curb the administration through normative provisions (such as basic rights, separation of powers, and statutory controls); in addition, the constitution is meant to motivate the state, through the competition among political parties and between incumbents and opposition, to take adequate account of societal interests and value orientations. This *state-centered understanding of politics* can forego the unrealistic assumption of a citizenry capable of collective action. It is oriented not toward the input of a rational political will-formation but toward the output of government activities that are successful on balance. Liberal argumentation aims its salvos against the potential for disruption posed by an administrative power that hinders the spontaneous social commerce of private persons. The liberal model hinges not on the democratic self-determination of deliberating citizens but on the constitutional framework for an economic society that is supposed to guarantee an essentially nonpolitical common good by satisfying personal life plans and private expectations of happiness.

Discourse theory invests the democratic process with normative connotations stronger than those found in the liberal model but weaker than those
found in the republican model. Once again, it takes elements from both
sides and puts them together in a new way. In agreement with republicanism, it gives center stage to the process of political opinion- and will-
formation, but without understanding the constitution as something sec-
ondary; rather, as we have already seen, it conceives constitutional principles as a consistent answer to the question of how the demanding
communicative forms of democratic opinion- and will-formation can be
institutionalized. According to discourse theory, the success of deliberative
politics depends not on a collectively acting citizenry but on the institutionalization of the corresponding procedures and conditions of communication, as well as on the interplay of institutionalized deliberative processes
with informally developed public opinions. Proceduralized popular sovereignty and a political system tied into the peripheral networks of the
political public sphere go together with the image of a decentered society.
At any rate, this concept of democracy no longer has to operate with the
notion of a social whole centered in the state and imagined as a goal-
oriented subject writ large. Nor does it represent the whole in a system of
constitutional norms mechanically regulating the balance of power and
interests in accordance with a market model. Discourse theory drops all
those motifs employed by the *philosophy of consciousness* that lead one either
to ascribe the citizens' practice of self-determination to a macrosocial
subject or to refer the anonymous rule of law to competing individual
subjects. The former approach views the citizenry as a collective actor
that reflects the whole and acts for it. In the latter approach, individual
actors function as dependent variables in power processes – processes that
operate blindly because beyond individual choice there can be at most
aggregated, but not consciously formed and executed, collective decisions.

Discourse theory reckons with the *higher-level intersubjectivity* of processes
of reaching understanding that take place through democratic procedures
or in the communicative network of public spheres. Both inside and outside
the parliamentary complex and its deliberative bodies, these subjectless
communications form arenas in which a more or less rational opinion-
and will-formation can take place for political matters, that is, matters
relevant to the entire society and in need of regulation. The flow of communication between public opinion-formation, institutionalized elections,
and legislative decisions is meant to guarantee that influence and communicative power are transformed through legislation into administrative power.
Like the liberal model, discourse theory respects the boundaries between
"state" and "society," but it distinguishes civil society, as the social basis of

autonomous public spheres, from both the economic system and public administration. From a normative standpoint, this understanding of democracy requires a realignment in the relative importance of the three resources from which modern societies satisfy their needs for integration and steering: money, administration, and solidarity. The normative implications are obvious: the socially integrating force of solidarity,[11] which can no longer be drawn solely from sources of communicative action, must develop through widely diversified and more or less autonomous public spheres, as well as through procedures of democratic opinion- and will-formation institutionalized within a constitutional framework. In addition, it should be able to hold its own against the two other mechanisms of social integration, money and administrative power.

This view has implications for how one understands legitimation and popular sovereignty. On the liberal view, democratic will-formation has the exclusive function of *legitimating* the exercise of political power. Election results are the license to assume the power of governing, whereas the governing incumbents must justify the use of this power to the public and parliament. On the republican view, democratic will-formation has the significantly stronger function of *constituting* society as a political community and keeping the memory of this founding act alive with each election. The incumbent Government is not only empowered by an election between competing elites to exercise a predominantly free mandate. It is also programmed by voters to carry out certain policies. More a committee than an arm of the state, it is part of a self-governing political community and not the head of a separate branch of government. Once again, discourse theory brings another idea into play: the procedures and communicative presuppositions of democratic opinion- and will-formation function as the most important sluices for the discursive rationalization of the decisions of an administration bound by law and statute. *Rationalization* means more than mere legitimation but less than the constitution of power. The power available to the administration alters its aggregate condition as long as it remains tied in with a democratic opinion- and will-formation that does not just monitor the exercise of political power ex post facto but more or less programs it as well. Nevertheless, only the political system can "act." It is a subsystem specialized for collectively binding decisions, whereas the communicative structures of the public sphere constitute a far-flung network of sensors that react to the pressure of society-wide problems and stimulate influential opinions. The public opinion that is worked up via democratic procedures into communicative power cannot "rule" of itself but can only point the use of administrative power in specific directions.

The concept of *popular sovereignty* stems from the republican appropriation and reevaluation of the early-modern notion of sovereignty initially coupled with the absolute ruler. The state, which monopolizes the means for the legitimate application of force, is presented as a concentration of power able to overcome all the other powers of this world. This motif, which goes back to Jean Bodin, was carried over by Jean-Jacques Rousseau to the will of the united people. He fused it with the classical idea of the self-rule of free and equal persons and incorporated it in the modern concept of autonomy. Despite this sublimation, the concept of sovereignty remained bound to the notion of embodiment in the (at first even physically present) people. According to the republican view, the people, who are at least potentially present, are the bearers of a sovereignty that in principle cannot be delegated: in their sovereign character, the people cannot have others represent them. Constitutive authority is grounded in the citizens' practice of self-determination and not in their representatives. Liberalism counters this with the more realistic view that in a constitutional democracy, political authority emanating from the people is exercised only "by means of elections and voting and by specific legislative, executive, and judicial organs" (as we read, for example, in art. 20, sec. 2, of the Basic Law of the Federal Republic of Germany).

Of course, these two views exhaust the alternatives only if one dubiously conceives state and society in terms of the whole and its parts, where the whole is constituted either by a sovereign citizenry or by a constitution. By contrast, the discourse theory of democracy corresponds to the image of a decentered society, albeit a society in which the political public sphere has been differentiated as an arena for the perception, identification, and treatment of problems affecting the whole of society. Once one gives up the philosophy of the subject, one needs neither to concentrate sovereignty concretely in the people nor to banish it in anonymous constitutional structures and powers. The "self" of the self-organizing legal community disappears in the subjectless forms of communication that regulate the flow of discursive opinion- and will-formation in such a way that their fallible results enjoy the presumption of being reasonable. This is not to denounce the intuition connected with the idea of popular sovereignty but to interpret it intersubjectively.[12] Popular sovereignty, even if it becomes anonymous, retreats into democratic procedures and the legal implementation of their demanding communicative presuppositions only in order to make itself felt as communicatively generated power. Strictly speaking, this power springs from the interactions among legally institutionalized will-formation and culturally mobilized publics. The latter, for their part, find a basis in the associations of a civil society quite distinct from both state and economy alike.

Read in procedural terms, the idea of popular sovereignty refers to social-boundary conditions that, although enabling the self-organization of a legal community, are not immediately at the disposition of the citizens' will. The normative self-understanding of deliberative politics certainly requires a discursive mode of sociation *for the legal community*, but this mode does not extend to the whole of society in which the constitutionally organized political system is *embedded*. Even on its own self-understanding, deliberative politics remains part of a complex society, which, as a whole, resists the normative approach practiced in legal theory. In this regard, the discourse-theoretic reading of democracy has a point of contact with a detached social-scientific approach that considers the political system neither apex nor center nor even the structural core of society, but just *one* action system among others. On the other hand, because it provides a safety mechanism for solving problems that threaten social integration, politics must be able to communicate through the medium of law with all the other legitimately ordered spheres of action, however these happen to be structured and steered. The political system depends on the performance of other systems, such as the fiscal performances of the economic system, in more than just a trivial manner. What is more, deliberative politics is internally connected with contexts of a rationalized lifeworld that meets it halfway. This is true both for the politics governed by the formal procedures of an institutionalized opinion- and will-formation and for the politics that occurs only informally in the networks of the public sphere. It is precisely the deliberatively filtered political communications that depend on lifeworld resources – on a liberal political culture and an enlightened political socialization, above all on the initiatives of opinion-building associations. To a large extent, these resources form and regenerate spontaneously, and in any case they are not readily accessible to direct interventions of the political apparatus.

2 Democratic Procedure and the Problem of Its Neutrality

The discourse concept of democracy, having jettisoned received notions of a politically constituted society, is not obviously incompatible with the form and mode of operation of functionally differentiated societies. All the same, one can still ask whether and, if so, how the discursive social relations assumed for an association of free and equal citizens, and hence the self-organization of the legal community, are at all possible under the conditions for the reproduction of a complex society. For a sociologically informed resolution to this question, it is important to operationalize the procedural core of democracy at the right level. In democratic procedure, the ideal content of practical reason takes a pragmatic shape; the realization of the system of rights is measured by the forms in which this content is institutionalized. The *sociological translation* of the procedural understanding of democracy must, in regard to this normative content of the constitutional state, start neither too low nor too high.

In the introduction to his theory of democracy, Norberto Bobbio pursues a deflationary strategy.[13] He first notes some global social changes that contradict the promise of classical conceptions. First and foremost, a polycentric society of large organizations has emerged, in which influence and political power pass into the hands of collective actors and can be acquired and exerted less and less by associated individuals. In addition, competing interest groups have multiplied, making impartial will-formation difficult. Furthermore, the growth of state bureaucracies and their functions fosters the domination of experts. Finally, apathetic masses have become alienated from the elites, who become independent oligarchies that paternalize voiceless citizens. These skeptical diagnoses lead Bobbio to a cautious formulation of the democratic rules of the game: "My premise is that the only way a meaningful discussion of democracy, as distinct from all forms of autocratic government, is possible is to consider it as characterized by a set of rules . . . which establish *who* is authorized to take collective decisions and which *procedures* are to be applied."[14] Democracies satisfy the necessary "procedural minimum" to the extent that they guarantee (a) the political participation of as many interested citizens as possible, (b) majority rule for political decisions, (c) the usual communication rights and therewith the selection from among different programs and political elites, and (d) the protection of the private sphere.[15] The advantage of this minimalist definition lies in its descriptive character. It grasps the normative content of political systems as they already exist in Western-type societies organized as nation-states. For this reason, Bobbio can reach this conclusion: "The minimal content of the democratic state has not been impaired: guarantees of the basic liberties, the existence of competing parties, periodic elections with universal suffrage, decisions which are collective or the result of compromise . . . or made on the basis of the majority principle, or in any event as the outcome of open debate between the different factions or allies of a government coalition."[16]

At the same time, this operationalization by no means exhausts the normative content evident in democratic procedure when one adopts the reconstructive vantage point of legal theory. Although public controversies among several parties are mentioned as a necessary condition for the democratic mode of decision making, the proposed definition does not touch the core of a genuinely proceduralist understanding of democracy.

The point of such an understanding is this: the democratic procedure is institutionalized in discourses and bargaining processes by employing forms of communication that promise that all outcomes reached in conformity with the procedure are reasonable. No one has worked out this view more energetically than John Dewey: "Majority rule, just as majority rule, is as foolish as its critics charge it with being. But it never is *merely* majority rule ... 'The means by which a majority comes to be a majority is the more important thing': antecedent debates, modification of views to meet the opinions of minorities. ... The essential need, in other words, is the improvement of the methods and conditions of debate, discussion and persuasion."[17] Deliberative politics acquires its legitimating force from the discursive structure of an opinion- and will-formation that can fulfill its socially integrative function only because citizens expect its results to have a reasonable *quality*. Hence the *discursive level* of public debates constitutes the most important variable. It must not be hidden away in the black box of an operationalization satisfied with crude indicators. Before taking up a proposal that considers this aspect, I would like first to develop the concept of a two-track deliberative politics (sec. 2.1) and then defend this concept against communitarian and liberal objections (sec. 2.2).

2.1

Joshua Cohen has elucidated the concept of deliberative politics in terms of an "ideal procedure" of deliberation and decision making that should be "mirrored" in social institutions as much as possible. It seems Cohen has still not completely shaken off the idea of a society that is deliberatively steered *as a whole* and is thus politically constituted:

> The notion of a deliberative democracy is rooted in the intuitive ideal of a democratic association in which the justification of the terms and conditions of association proceeds through public argument and reasoning among equal citizens. Citizens in such an order share a commitment to the resolution of problems of collective choice through public reasoning, and regard their basic institutions as legitimate in so far as they establish the framework for free public deliberation.[18]

In contrast to Cohen, I would like to understand the procedure from which procedurally correct decisions draw their legitimacy – a procedure I will specify more closely in what follows – as the core structure in a separate, constitutionally organized political system, but not as a model for all social institutions (and not even for all government institutions). If deliberative politics is supposed to be inflated into a structure shaping the totality of society, then the discursive mode of sociation expected in the *legal system* would have to expand into a self-organization of *society* and penetrate the latter's complexity as a whole. This is impossible, for the simple reason that democratic procedure must be embedded in contexts it cannot itself regulate.

However, Cohen plausibly characterizes the procedure itself in terms of the following postulates: (a) Processes of deliberation take place in argumentative form, that is, through the regulated exchange of information and reasons among parties who introduce and critically test proposals.[19] (b) Deliberations are inclusive and public. No one may be excluded in principle; all of those who are possibly affected by the decisions have equal chances to enter and take part. (c) Deliberations are free of any external coercion. The participants are sovereign insofar as they are bound only by the presuppositions of communication and rules of argumentation.[20] (d) Deliberations are free of any internal coercion that could detract from the equality of the participants. Each has an equal opportunity to be heard, to introduce topics, to make contributions, to suggest and criticize proposals. The taking of yes/no positions is motivated solely by the unforced force of the better argument.[21]

Additional conditions specify the procedure in view of the *political character* of deliberative processes: (e) Deliberations aim in general at rationally motivated agreement and can in principle be indefinitely continued or resumed at any time. Political deliberations, however, must be concluded by majority decision in view of pressures to decide. Because of its internal connection with a deliberative practice, majority rule justifies the presumption that the fallible majority opinion may be considered a reasonable basis for a common practice until further notice, namely, until the minority convinces the majority that their (the minority's) views are correct.[22] (f) Political deliberations extend to any matter that can be regulated in the equal interest of all. This does not imply, however, that topics and subject matters traditionally considered to be "private" in nature could be a fortiori withdrawn from discussion. In particular, those questions are publicly relevant that concern the unequal distribution of resources on which the actual exercise of rights of communication and participation depends.[23] (g) Political deliberations also include the interpretation of needs and wants and the change of prepolitical attitudes and preferences. Here the consensus-generating force of arguments is by no means based only on a value consensus previously developed in shared traditions and forms of life.[24]

Every association that institutionalizes such a procedure for the purposes of democratically regulating the conditions of its common life thereby constitutes itself as a body of citizens. It forms a particular legal community, delimited in space and time, with specific forms of life and traditions. But this distinctive cultural identity does not designate it *as* a political community of citizens. For the democratic process is governed by *universal* principles of justice that are equally constitutive for every body of citizens. In short, the ideal procedure of deliberation and decision making presupposes as its bearer an association that agrees to regulate the conditions of its common life *impartially*. What brings legal consociates together is, *in the final analysis*, the linguistic bond that holds together each communication community.[25]

This image of deliberative politics does not just omit some important internal differentiations. It is also silent about the relation between decision-oriented deliberations, which are regulated by *democratic procedures*, and the informal processes of opinion-formation in the public sphere. To the extent that these procedures, unlike general elections, do not simply organize the voting that *follows* informal opinion-formation, they at least regulate the composition and operation of assemblies that "convene" for a "sitting" in which an agenda is "negotiated" and resolutions are passed if necessary. In setting up parliamentary procedures, decision-making powers (and assigned political responsibilities) provide the reference point from which socially bounded and temporally limited publics are constituted. They also determine how deliberations are structured through argument and specified in regard to the matter at hand. Democratic procedures in such "arranged" publics structure opinion- and will-formation processes with a view to the cooperative solution of practical questions, including the negotiation of fair compromises. The operative meaning of these regulations consists less in discovering and identifying problems than in dealing with them; it has less to do with becoming sensitive to new ways of looking at problems than with justifying the selection of a problem and the choice among competing proposals for solving it. The publics of parliamentary bodies are structured predominantly as a *context of justification*. These bodies rely not only on the administration's preparatory work and further processing but also on the *context of discovery* provided by a procedurally unregulated public sphere that is borne by the general public of citizens.

This "weak" public is the vehicle of "public opinion."[26] The opinion-formation uncoupled from decisions is effected in an open and inclusive network of overlapping, subcultural publics having fluid temporal, social, and substantive boundaries. Within a framework guaranteed by constitutional rights, the structures of such a pluralistic public sphere develop more or less spontaneously. The currents of public communication are channeled by mass media and flow through different publics that develop informally inside associations. Taken together, they form a "wild" complex that resists organization as a whole. On account of its anarchic structure, the general public sphere is, on the one hand, more vulnerable to the repressive and exclusionary effects of unequally distributed social power, structural violence, and systematically distorted communication than are the institutionalized public spheres of parliamentary bodies. On the other hand, it has the advantage of a medium of *unrestricted* communication. Here new problem situations can be perceived more sensitively, discourses aimed at achieving self-understanding can be conducted more widely and expressively, collective identities and need interpretations can be articulated with fewer compulsions than is the case in procedurally regulated public spheres. Democratically constituted opinion- and will-formation depends on the supply of informal public opinions that, ideally, develop in structures of an unsubverted political public sphere. The informal public sphere must, for its part, enjoy the support of a societal basis in which equal rights of citizenship have become socially effective. Only in an egalitarian public of citizens that has emerged from the confines of class and thrown off the millennia-old shackles of social stratification and exploitation can the potential of an unleashed cultural pluralism fully develop – a potential that no doubt abounds just as much in conflicts as in meaning-generating forms of life. But in a secularized society that has learned to deal with its complexity consciously and deliberately, the communicative mastery of *these* conflicts constitutes the sole source of solidarity among strangers – strangers who renounce violence and, in the cooperative regulation of their common life, also concede one another the right to *remain* strangers.

Notes

1 See chap. 8, sec. 8.1, in *Between Facts and Norms: Contributions to a Discourse Theory of Law and Democracy*, from which the present chapter in this volume is taken.

2 W. Becker, *Die Freiheit, die wir meinen: Entscheidung für die liberale Demokratie* (Munich, 1982), p. 61 (in subsequent quotations from this book, Becker's original emphasis has been removed).

3 Becker, *Freiheit*, p. 68.

4 Becker, *Freiheit*, p. 38.

5 Becker, *Freiheit*, p. 58.

6 Becker, *Freiheit*, p. 77.

7   Becker, *Freiheit*, p. 101.

8   Becker, *Freiheit*, p. 104; cf. pp. 155f.: "An ideological pluralism is desirable because democratic legitimation is not a matter of theoretical discussion directed toward ascertaining the 'truth' of this or that philosophical or religious view. Rather, legitimation only has to do with how such views, by being disseminated, function as ideologicopolitical means for bringing about a majority's assent to the state's guarantee of individual liberties. It would not be desirable to stage public discussions of these different or even opposed worldviews and ethical approaches in an attempt to ferret out which one is 'right' and which one is 'wrong.'"

9   Becker, *Freiheit*, p. 186f.

10   D. Held, *Models of Democracy* (Oxford, 1987). As in the previous chapter, when I refer to "liberal" conceptions of the state, I use the term in the narrow sense of the tradition going back to Locke. "Liberals" like Dworkin or Rawls cannot be confined to this tradition.

11   As in the first two chapters of *Between Facts and Norms*, I am using "solidarity" here not as a normative but as a sociological concept.

12   On the concept of popular sovereignty, see I. Maus, *Zur Aufklärung der Demokratietheorie* (Frankfurt am Main, 1992), pp. 176ff.

13   N. Bobbio, *The Future of Democracy*, trans. R. Griffin (Cambridge, 1987).

14   Bobbio, *Future*, p. 24.

15   Bobbio, *Future*, p. 56: "Parallel to the need for self-rule there is the desire not to be ruled at all and to be left in peace."

16   Bobbio, *Future*, p. 40.

17   J. Dewey, *The Public and Its Problems* (Chicago, 1954), pp. 207f. [Dewey's quote is taken from Samuel J. Tilden. Trans.]

18   J. Cohen, "Deliberation and Democratic Legitimacy," in A. Hamlin and P. Pettit, eds., *The Good Polity* (Oxford, 1989), pp. 17–34; here p. 21.

19   "Deliberation is reasoned in that parties to it are required to state their reasons for advancing proposals, supporting them or criticizing them. . . . Reasons are offered with the aim of bringing others to accept the proposal, given their disparate ends and their commitment to settling the conditions of their association through free deliberation among equals." Cohen, "Deliberation," p. 22.

20   "Their consideration of proposals is not constrained by the authority of prior norms or requirements." Cohen, "Deliberation," p. 22.

21   "The participants are substantively equal in that the existing distribution of power and resources does not shape their chances to contribute to deliberation, nor does that distribution play an authoritative role in their deliberation." Cohen, "Deliberation," p. 23.

22   "Even under ideal conditions there is no promise that consensual reasons will be forthcoming. If they are not, then deliberation concludes with voting, subject to some form of majority rule. The fact that it may so conclude does not, however, eliminate the distinction between deliberative forms of collective choice and forms that aggregate by non-deliberative preferences." Cohen, "Deliberation," p. 23.

23 "Inequalities of wealth, or the absence of institutional measures to redress the consequences of those inequalities, can serve to undermine the equality required in deliberative arenas themselves." Cohen, "Deliberation," p. 27; cf. also J. Cohen and J. Rogers, *On Democracy* (New York, 1983), chap. 6, pp. 146ff.; W. E. Connolly, *The Terms of Political Discourse* (Lexington, Mass., 1974).

24 "The relevant conceptions of the common good are not comprised simply of interests and preferences that are antecedent to deliberation. Instead, the interests, aims and ideals that comprise the common good are those that survive deliberation, interests that, on public reflection, we think it legitimate to appeal to in making claims on public resources." Cohen, "Deliberation," p. 23.

25 Cf. Michael Walzer's treatment of integration problems created in modern societies by the growing mobility of marriage partners, residences, social status, and political loyalties. These "four mobilities" loosen ascriptive bonds to family, locality, social background, and political tradition. For affected individuals, this implies an ambiguous release from traditional living conditions that, though socially integrating and providing orientation and protection, are also shaped by dependencies, prejudices, and oppression. This release is ambivalent, because it makes an increasing range of options available to the individual, and hence sets her free. On the one hand, this is a negative freedom that isolates the individual and compels her to pursue her own interests in a more or less purposive-rational fashion. On the other hand, as positive freedom it also enables her to enter into new social commitments of her own free will, to appropriate traditions critically, and to construct her own identity in a deliberate way. According to Walzer, in the last instance only the linguistic structure of social relations prevents disintegration: "Whatever the extent of the Four Mobilities, they do not seem to move us so far apart that we can no longer *talk* with one another. . . . Even political conflict in liberal societies rarely takes forms so extreme as to set its protagonists beyond negotiation and compromise, procedural justice and the very possibility of *speech*." "The Communitarian Critique of Liberalism," *Political Theory* 18 (1990): 13f.

26 Cf. N. Fraser, "Rethinking the Public Sphere: A Contribution to the Critique of Actually Existing Democracy," in C. Calhoun, ed., *Habermas and the Public Sphere* (Cambridge, Mass., 1992), p. 134: "I shall call *weak* publics publics whose deliberative practice consists exclusively in opinion formation and does not also encompass decision making."

Part III

Wise Decisions

5

Open Government and Just Legislation

William Nelson

Morality and Just Government

The most important question about the system of laws and institutions making up the state is whether they satisfy the conditions morality lays down for such systems. Morality determines the limits of the permissible for systems of laws and institutions as well as for individual conduct. It has been said that 'justice is the first virtue of institutions'.[1] If this is so, it is so because a reasonable moral theory assigns a kind of priority to considerations of justice or because, in such a theory, considerations referred to as considerations of justice are just those relevant to the assessment of institutions. I have no objection to this way of speaking, but it leaves us with the following question: when it is true that legal, political or economic institutions are just, what does this involve? This is a substantive moral question. It can be answered only within a substantive theory. I shall argue for democracy, here, on the ground that it tends to produce specific laws and policies that are just. I am assuming that this kind of argument is sufficient to justify a political system, or at least to create a strong presumption in its favor. Suppose someone says that this kind of argument is irrelevant – that the crucial question concerns not the effects of the system, but its intrinsic features, whether it is fair, for example. I have no *general* argument against this position. I have attempted to reply to specific theories of this type [in earlier chapters]. I hope to establish [in this chapter], at least the possibility of a coherent, plausible justification in terms of effects. Skepticism about the possibility of such a theory, as voiced by Dahl for example, may well be one reason for the prevalence of 'procedural' theories.

If we are to argue that democracy satisfies principles of justice, and if this requires us to argue that democracy is well designed to produce just laws and policies, we clearly must say something about what justice, and morality in general, require. One way to carry out a defense of democracy along these lines would be this: offer an account of which laws are morally good laws, and then try to show that democracies tend to have good laws and that other governments do not. (Dahl used something analogous to this procedure to discredit Madison's contention that democracy is necessary for good government.) There are other possibilities, however. When Buchanan and Tullock argue that certain kinds of democratic procedure will lead to Pareto optimal outcomes, or to Pareto improvements on the status quo, they do not proceed by examining governments of various kinds and establishing correlations. Instead, they begin with a reasonably precise, abstract specification of the goals to be achieved and of the system they have in mind, and then, given more or less standard motivational assumptions, *deduce* the consequence they seek from their definitions, assumptions and certain well-known results in economic theory. Of course, their argument is not as formal as I make it sound here, and my argument will not be as formal as theirs; but my argument will be more like theirs than like the other alternative mentioned. The mechanics of democracy are such, I shall argue, that, given certain assumptions about human nature, democracy will automatically tend to produce morally acceptable results. Now this kind of argument, like the others I have mentioned, seems to presuppose a clear account of which laws are morally good laws. I shall have something to say along these lines, but most of my argument will proceed at a higher level of abstraction. Instead of offering anything like a complete account of what morality requires, I shall suggest an account of what a (reasonable) morality is. This account will embody conditions which must be satisfied by any acceptable moral principles. I shall then argue that, following the procedures of (a kind of) constitutional democracy, we will tend to come up with laws that are justifiable in terms of principles satisfying the conditions of acceptability for moral principles. *The general idea is this: the tests that a law has to pass to be adopted in a constitutional democracy are analogous to the tests that a moral principle must pass in order to be an acceptable moral principle.*

What conditions must a principle satisfy in order to be an acceptable moral principle? What conditions must a set of principles satisfy if they are to constitute an adequate morality? What principles are true moral principles? It is natural to think that the answer to these questions depends on an account of the function of morality: true moral principles are principles that perform the function of moral principles. Looking at the problem in this way generates difficult questions. If two distinct sets of principles would equally well perform the function of morality, for example, is each set a set of true principles? More fundamental, however, is the question whether there is any such thing as *the* function(s) of morality. And how do we know when we have found it (them)? I do not have definitive answers to these questions. Nevertheless, I shall propose an account of morality in terms of its functions. The account I offer is not the only possible account of its kind. Others have been, or might be, offered. But neither is my account idiosyncratic. My suggestions about the function of morality should seem familiar both to theorists (since it is borrowed from other theorists) and to ordinary people. I think they are plausible suggestions. More important, whether or not what I offer here correctly captures the 'essence' of morality seems to me *relatively* unimportant. What is more important is that we have reason to be interested in morality as I conceive it. The functions of morality, on my account, are important functions. We have reason to be interested in principles or rules performing these functions, and we have reason to be interested in the truth or falsity of judgments made with respect to these rules. In any case, I believe it is better to leave off these preliminary discussions and turn to the account itself. We will be in a better position to decide what to do with the account when we have it before us.

A Conception of Morality

Minimally, a morality can be described by a system of rules or principles proscribing some kinds of harmful or dangerous conduct and enjoining certain kinds of beneficial conduct. Such rules constitute a system of constraints or boundaries determining the limits of the permissible. To speak of these rules as constraints is to emphasize their overriding character; when moral considerations conflict with other considerations, moral considerations take precedence. Moral rules, as so far described, can be usefully distinguished into two groups: (1) Some rules proscribe or enjoin actions that are either harmful or useful in themselves, regardless of what other people are doing; (2) Some rules enjoin actions which will either prevent harm or promote benefits just in case they are generally performed.[2] Rules of type (2) may be either direct rules, enjoining specific types of conduct, or indirect rules requiring simply that people adhere to whatever specific rules or conventions are being generally adhered to.[3] When I speak here of rules governing actions, I include actions establishing or altering institutional structures. When I speak of rules requiring that we benefit or refrain from harming people, I do not mean to exclude rules requiring that we benefit some at the expense of others. Thus, moral rules can include rules for settling disputes when one gains only at the expense of another, and they can also include rules governing the distribution or redistribution of goods.

Even if any morality includes rules of the sort described here, it does not follow that such rules exhaust the content of morality, nor, more importantly, does it mean that any such set of rules constitutes an *adequate* morality. What more is necessary? Let me begin by considering John Rawls's notion of a 'well-ordered society'. A society is well-ordered, he says, when it is 'effectively regulated by a public conception of justice'. More specifically, '(1) everyone accepts and knows that the others accept, the same principles of justice, and (2) the basic social institutions generally satisfy and are generally known to satisfy these principles'. In a well-ordered society, 'while men may put forth excessive demands on one another, they nevertheless acknowledge a common point of view from which their claims may be adjudicated'. The shared, public system of principles constitutes 'the fundamental charter of a well-ordered human association'.[4]

Pretty clearly, the notion of a well-ordered society admits of degrees. Consensus on principles can be more or less perfect, and institutions can vary in the degree to which they satisfy the conditions laid down in the shared moral principles. In a perfectly well-ordered society, though, there will be complete agreement on principles for evaluating actions and common institutions. Moreover, I take it, there will be agreement that these principles are final (Rawls, 135–6). These principles are the *fundamental charter* of a well-ordered association. When these principles apply to a specific decision, they are taken to override any other considerations that might also apply. Thus, the shared, public system of rules in a well-ordered society plays the same role in the life of the community earlier assigned to moral rules in general. It is regarded as a system of *constraints* determining the limits of the permissible.

When a proposal is agreed to be contrary to the shared system of principles, it will be rejected by all. On the other hand, there may well be disagreement about the acceptability, *all things considered*, of proposals consistent with the shared morality. Nor is this the only source of disagreement and strife. While there is agreement, in a well-ordered society, on fundamental principles, there may not be agreement on the consequences of their application to particular cases. Typically, there will be agreement on what is relevant to a given decision, but there may well be disagreement on the truth or falsity of some statement that all regard as relevant. Nevertheless, the knowledge that there is agreement on ends strengthens 'the bonds of civic friendship' (Rawls, 5), and mitigates the otherwise divisive effects of disagreement on specific matters of policy.

I want to suggest that one important function of a morality is to serve as the public system of constraints on action agreed to by citizens in a well-ordered society. A test for an *adequate* morality is that its principles be able to perform this function. The more stable a system of principles – the greater its capacity to continue to perform this function as a society grows and changes – the more adequate it is.

In general, then, those parts of a morality relevant to the assessment of laws and institutions consist of a system of final rules compliance with which tends to prevent harm or produce benefits. An adequate morality is a system of such rules on which there could be an enduring consensus. It is a system of rules that could be accepted by all members of society as principles determining the absolute limits of the permissible. Now, the idea of focusing on what could be agreed to or on what could constitute a consensus is like the idea that seems to underlie much moral theory in the social contract tradition.[5] There are, of course, differences within that tradition. Some theorists, for example, see moral principles as principles that *would* be agreed to in more or less idealized situations. Others hold that moral principles are principles actually agreed to in actual situations. The position I have sketched here is like those theories emphasizing hypothetical agreement since it asserts that an adequate morality is a system of principles that could be accepted by everyone, even if none is accepted now. On the other hand, it is like theories emphasizing an actual agreement in that it says a morality constitutes a possible consensus among actual people. There is precedent for this kind of combination. Indeed, I believe there is a plausible interpretation of Rawls's contract theory in which the notion of a well-ordered society plays the central role it plays in mine. On this reading of Rawls, a morality (or, anyway, principles of justice) constitutes a possible, public conception of justice in a well-ordered society. The appeal to the original contract – to the 'original position' in Rawls's theory – is designed to establish the *possibility* of consensus on principles of justice. When we find out that people in the original position would agree to certain principles, we find out that consensus, at least for a time, among some people, is possible. When we find out what they would agree to, we find out something about what kind of principles might form the basis of an *enduring* consensus. Principles people would agree to, in an initial situation of equality, behind a veil of ignorance, will be the kind of principles they would continue to accept in spite of changes in their prospects or other circumstances. But *full* justification of moral principles, on this interpretation, requires more than a demonstration that these principles would be chosen in the original position. It requires a demonstration that people in real societies are, or could become, sufficiently like people in the original position that principles chosen by the latter people could constitute a consensus among the former.[6]

One way in which my theory resembles other contract theories is that it seems to be subject to some of the same criticisms. Consider this question: why should we believe that real people ought to comply with the principles that ideal people would agree to in some hypothetical situation? This objection corresponds to the question about my theory, why should we believe that people ought to comply with rules that could, or even do, constitute a consensus on fundamental constraints on conduct? This question could be interpreted in different ways. (1) It might be the question whether we have any reason to be interested in the requirements of such systems of rules. (2) It could be the question whether what people would agree to has anything to do with what *morality* requires of them, or (3) it could be the question how, logically speaking, we can *derive* an 'ought' judgment from the mere existence of some system of principles or rules. To this last question, I believe, the most plausible response is in terms of something like the theory of 'ought' judgments developed by Roger Wertheimer in *The Significance of Sense*.[7] According to Wertheimer, roughly, all 'ought' judgments refer implicity to some system of rules or principles. To say that *x* ought to do *y* is to say: (1) There is an adequate and relevant system of rules; (2) According to some rule of that system, were *x* in some situation *s*, *x* would (ideally or actually) *y*; and (3) *x* is in situation *s*. A system is a relevant system if it is a system of the type to which the speaker means to refer. It is an adequate system if it satisfies the conditions of adequacy for systems of its type.[8] Now, given an account of 'ought' judgments along these lines, there is no particular logical problem about how we could derive such judgments, given a system of rules of the sort discussed here. But do we have reason to be interested in rules that constitute a possible consensus, and would those rules be adequate moral rules? I shall comment first on the latter question and then turn to the former.

I have suggested that we think of a morality as a system of overriding constraints on action compliance with which tends to produce benefits or prevent harm and which could serve as the fundamental character of a well-ordered society. I have not said that any system of rules with these two properties is an adequate morality. The properties mentioned are necessary conditions. Are there other necessary conditions? The question whether the rules imagined here would be a morality no doubt stems partly from the feeling that the class of acceptable rules needs to be narrowed down further. At the very least, one might say, a set of principles is an adequate morality only when it represents a possible consensus *among free and independent persons*. We could imagine a kind of slave society in which the slaves themselves are so dehumanized that they would accept the slaveholders' rationale for their common institutions. But, given the modification suggested here, that would not show that these institutions were morally acceptable. To show this, we would have to show that principles permitting such institutions *would* be acceptable to all concerned even if they were free from its dehumanizing effects.

The requirement that a set of principles be a potential *stable* consensus – a consensus that would endure over time – will tend to rule out some seemingly unfair sets of principles in some societies. When there is social mobility, so that any person (or any person's child) might occupy most any position in society, people will be reluctant to accept principles giving special, permanent advantages even to their own social class. And, if they do, consensus on those principles will tend to break down as people who have known those advantages come to occupy less advantageous positions. However, in a rigid caste society, we would find neither of these kinds of check on the adoption of principles that look grossly unfair. A caste society with a caste morality may be a stable, well-ordered society. It does make some difference, then, whether we make it a necessary condition for a morality's being adequate that it constitute a possible, stable consensus among free and independent persons. But should we say this?

I shall argue here that people generally have reason to promote and comply with principles satisfying the conditions I have so far laid down; and I shall argue that people generally have a greater interest in such principles when those principles would be acceptable under conditions of freedom and independence. I do not believe this is a *proof* that principles satisfying the conditions in question constitute an adequate morality. If one holds that, by definition, moral principles are principles on which people have a reason to act, then my argument is relevant to such a proof. Be that as it may, the argument does serve as a partial justification of the kind of principles I have in mind, at least to those who share a certain ideal of social cooperation. Moreover, if I am correct, morality as I conceive it can perform what might be regarded as one of its characteristic functions: people can successfully appeal to its principles in order to criticize the conduct of others or to justify their own.[9]

With or without the added requirement that principles be acceptable to free and independent persons, what reason do we have to take an interest in moral principles as described here? Suppose, to begin with, that we are in a well-ordered society. If so, there will be a set of fundamental principles on which people agree, and it will be agreed that these principles determine the limits of the permissible. They entail a set of constraints on conduct within which, it is agreed, we must confine ourselves. They will require that we refrain from harming one another in various ways, and they will require that we benefit one another in various ways. Also, in a well-ordered society, legal, political and economic institutions will be justifiable from the perspective of these shared principles, and it will be agreed that this is so. Now, on these assumptions, we will want others to comply with our shared principles insofar as we stand to benefit (or to avoid harm) as a result of their compliance. More interesting, it will generally be in the interest of each individual to conform to those shared principles himself and to develop the general disposition to do so. It will also generally be in the interest of each that basic institutions continue to be justifiable in terms of the society's shared principles. The argument for these conclusions is pretty straightforward. Given a general belief in certain fundamental constraints, and given a normal interest in the opinions of others, each will want to *appear* to limit his behavior by those constraints. But the easiest way to appear to conform to principles, usually, is to conform to them! And, if one has an interest in such general conformity, one has an interest in developing the general disposition to conform. Moreover, given an interest in conforming to shared principles, each has an interest in minimizing conflict between the requirements of these principles and the constraints and requirements of institutions. When one benefits from institutional constraints on others, one wants to be able to justify those constraints. When one is able to make use of institutions to his advantage, one wants to be able to justify one's conduct to others. All this requires, however, that the institutions themselves be justifiable in terms of shared, public principles.

In a well-ordered society, under plausible assumptions about human motives, people generally have a reason to conform to shared principles of morality. Do they have *more* reason to conform to principles acceptable to free and independent persons than to principles that are not? Most people are concerned about the opinions of others, and this concern, at the very least, makes them want to appear to conform to shared principles. The reasons for this will vary from person to person. Some, perhaps, will simply want to avoid criticism. Even then, they will do well to cultivate a general disposition to conform, since actual conformity virtually guarantees the appearance of conformity, and alternative strategies can involve costly calculation and planning. But most of us, to a greater or lesser degree, do not want merely to appear to comply with generally accepted standards. We want, in Philippa Foot's nice phrase, 'to live openly and in good faith with [our] neighbors'.[10] Not only do we want to avoid the consequences of hypocrisy (always being on guard, trying to keep our lies consistent and so on), but we find lying and deceit intrinsically unpleasant. We do not want to have to conceal; we want our lives to be able to stand inspection. All this, of course, strictly requires only that we comply with whatever restrictions people actually believe in. But if it makes us feel uncomfortable to have to conceal our conduct from others, it will hardly satisfy us to know that we can justify our conduct to others only because they have come to accept certain principles under duress or some psychological constraint. At least the latter attitude seems a natural extension of the former. For many of us, then, some of the same considerations that lead us to take an interest in the requirements of shared principles will lead us also to take a greater interest in requirements that would be acceptable to people choosing freely and independently.

I have argued so far only that people in a well-ordered society have a reason to comply with generally accepted principles. But I have said that a morality consists of a set of principles that *would* perform the function of the public conception of justice in a well-ordered society. Do we have a reason to take an interest in a morality – in principles that would serve this function – when we are not in a well-ordered society? Does this property of a morality give us a reason to take an interest in it when it is not generally accepted? Most of us, I think, do have a reason to want principles to be generally accepted, and to comply with principles that could be generally accepted even when no such principles are now accepted. So long as we wish to be able to justify our conduct to others, we have reason to comply with rules that others *could* be led to accept; we also have reason to try to get those principles accepted. To this point, the argument is like the argument for complying with rules actually accepted in a well-ordered society. But suppose many people accept principles – racist principles might be an example – that are *inconsistent* with principles that could be generally accepted. In this case, conduct that *could* be justified to everyone, in the long run, could not be justified to many people in the short run. In this kind of situation, it is far from clear that individuals have a reason to care about what morality requires. At least, whether a given person has reason to act according to principles that could be generally accepted will depend to a far greater extent on particular motives and features of his situation that are likely to differ from those of others. It will depend on the extent to which he must deal with members of racial minorities, for example; and it will depend on whether his desire to be able to justify his conduct to others is based on a mere desire to avoid ostracism and reprisals, or on a respect for persons as persons.

Aside from the desire to be able to justify our conduct to others, it should be remembered, we have other reasons to want certain kinds of general principles adopted and complied with. According to the theory under consideration, a morality is not just any system of principles that can be generally accepted and publicly avowed. It is a system of principles requiring some beneficial conduct and proscribing some harmful conduct. But then, insofar as we stand to benefit (or avoid harm) from compliance on the part of others, we have reason to want them to comply. Thus, we have an additional, independent reason to push for the acceptance of principles that could gain general acceptance and that people could therefore have a reason to comply with. One reason people have for complying with rules depends on the acceptability of those rules to other people. So, our interest in compliance on the part of others also gives us an interest in the general acceptability of those rules. It leads us to try to find systems of constraints that are, intuitively speaking, fair as well as beneficial.

Let me summarize. An adequate morality, I have suggested, can be described by a set of principles or rules having, at least, the following properties: (1) Compliance with the principles tends to produce benefits or prevent harm; (2) The principles could serve as the shared, public principles constituting a stable, 'fundamental charter of a well-ordered human association' as Rawls understands this notion; and (3) The principles could perform this function in a society of free and independent persons. The idea is that it is a necessary condition for a system's being an adequate morality that it satisfy these conditions, but I did not argue for this conclusion directly. What I argued is that we have reason to want *some* such set of principles accepted and generally complied with. If some set is accepted and complied with, we have reason to comply ourselves and to urge continued compliance on the part of others. We have reason to treat them with the seriousness normally accorded a morality.

It should be emphasized that the arguments in this section depend on empirical assumptions, and that the conclusions hold only other things being equal. First, the arguments depend clearly on assumptions about human motives and interests, like the assumption that we are not generally indifferent to the opinions of others; and they depend on assumptions about our circumstances, like the assumption that it is costly and difficult to conceal one's conduct. These assumptions *could* be false, but I think they are not. Second, the extent to which one has a reason to comply with the directives of morality (as conceived here) will depend on the extent to which others accept and comply with those directives. If no one accepted principles with the properties of an adequate morality, people would have much less reason to try to develop and comply with such principles. Still, it is hard to imagine a complete lack of consensus on principles within subgroups in a society anyhow; and, in the absence of a rigid caste structure, people would tend to comply with principles most widely accepted and therefore most widely acceptable. The long run tendency is toward general compliance with, and general acceptance of, principles that have the properties of an adequate morality. But, even if this is right, it does not follow at all that each person will always have an overriding reason to comply with such principles in particular cases.[11]

At the beginning of the section before this one, I asked what conditions a political system had to satisfy in order to be morally acceptable, and I said that this question is itself a substantive moral question. In this section, I have offered a partial account of the nature of an adequate morality, but I have said virtually nothing about its substantive content. If I am right, of course, the substantive requirements of morality will depend on what kinds of principles people can agree to under certain conditions and for certain purposes. What I shall argue in the next two sections is that familiar institutions of representative democracy tend to foster consensus on adequate principles of morality, and consequently tend to produce law and policy decisions consistent with these principles. The argument will depend in part on the precise nature of representative institutions and it will also presuppose some of the motivational assumptions I have introduced in this section in arguing that people have reason to care about the requirements of an adequate morality. The idea that this argument constitutes a *justification* for democracy depends on an assumption about what the substantive requirements of an adequate morality would be. Specifically, I assume that an adequate morality will include requirements that laws and social policy must satisfy, and I assume that it will not require anything of political decision procedures other than that they tend to produce acceptable laws and policies.

Democracy and Just Government: Mill's Argument

In this section I shall offer an interpretation and defense of the theory of democracy John Stuart Mill presented in *Considerations on Representative Government*.[12] I think Mill's justification of representative government is, in its main lines, reasonable. Other philosophers have suggested similar arguments, and Mill's argument needs to be supplemented at certain points; but I shall begin with Mill here, partly because he has sometimes been misinterpreted, and partly because, properly interpreted, he makes the case about as well as anyone.

According to Mill, the 'ideally best form of government', the 'form of government most eligible in itself', is representative government (Mill, 35–6). What does Mill mean by 'most eligible in itself', and what, in his view, are the criteria for good government in general? Basic to Mill's theory of government is the idea that different systems of government are appropriate in different societies and in different stages in the development of a given society. The form of government ideally best in itself, then, is not the form of government best under all circumstances. Instead, the idea is this: We consider all possible states of society, and we suppose that each is governed by the form of government best for that state of society. Each form of government, then, is operating in its most propitious circumstances, and we say that the society that is best governed has the form of government that is best in itself. In Mill's words, that government is 'most eligible in itself... which, if the necessary conditions existed for giving effect to its beneficial tendencies, would, more than all others, favor and promote not some one improvement, but all forms and degrees of it' (Mill, 35).

That form of government is best in itself which, given propitious circumstances, has the best effects. Government, according to Mill, is a *means* to certain ends (Mill, 15). But to what ends? What is the function of government? In Mill's view, there are two *criteria* for a good government. On the one hand, government must 'promote the virtue and intelligence of the people' in the community. On the other hand, the 'machinery' of government must be 'adapted to take advantage of the amount of good qualities which may at any time exist and make them instrumental to the right purposes' (Mill, 25–6). As many commentators have noted, Mill tends to emphasize the first of these criteria. What has not generally been noticed is that possession of these criteria – of these *marks* of good government – is not what *makes* the government good. What *makes* the government good is its having good effects. Virtuous citizens and appropriate governmental 'machinery' are marks of good government because they are what makes it possible for government to produce the right effects. This is quite clear from the way in which Mill introduces the idea of concentrating on the personal qualities of the citizenry. He begins by considering the problem of the administration of justice. An effective and fair judicial system requires intelligent, honest and fair-minded citizens: witnesses must be reliable, judges must refrain from taking bribes, jurors must be willing and able to consider the merits of a case dispassionately, and so on (Mill, 24). Mill uses the same example in order to explain the importance of the 'machinery' of government.

> The judicial system being given, the goodness of the administration of justice is in the compound ratio of the worth of the men composing the tribunals, and the worth of the public opinion which influences or controls them. But all the difference between a good and a bad system of judicature lies in the contrivances adopted for bringing whatever moral and intellectual worth

exists in the community to bear upon the administration of justice and making it duly operative on the result. (Mill, 26)

The tendency of a government to promote the virtue of its citizens, together with the quality of its 'machinery', are *criteria* of good government because governments that promote virtue and have the right machinery tend to perform the function of governments well. But the *function* of a government is to produce good decisions and good legislation – in general, to promote 'the aggregate interests of society' (Mill, 16). An ideal form of government, then, will be a government that is in harmony with itself. It will consist of institutions that affect people's character in such a way that people with that kind of character, operating those institutions, will tend to produce the best laws and decisions. To show that a form of government is desirable, one would need, in principle, to begin with an account of the goals to be achieved – an account of good legislation, for example. One would then have to demonstrate that, given the machinery of government, and given the effects of that form of government on the citizenry, we could expect good laws and policies.

Mill is a utilitarian. He holds, as noted above, that government should be so designed that it promotes 'the aggregate interests of society'. Why does he think that representative government is the form of government most likely to achieve this goal? In part, of course, the answer is that representative government is not the best form of government under *all* conditions. If, for example, citizens have acquired neither the willingness to acquiesce in *necessary* authority, nor sufficient will to take an active role in government, representative government will fail (Mill, Chapter IV). Nevertheless, Mill holds, once the requisite conditions have been satisfied, representative government is superior to any other form of government, under *any* conditions. Why?

The 'ideally best form of government', Mill says,

is that in which the sovereignty, or supreme controlling power in the last resort, is vested in the entire aggregate of the community, every citizen not only having a voice in the exercise of that ultimate sovereignty, but being, at least occasionally, called on to take an actual part in the government by the personal discharge of some public function, local or general. (Mill, 42)

This kind of government, Mill says, will both make good use of people as they are, and will tend to improve them in such a way that they will govern even better as time passes. People will be secure from bad government because they will be 'self-*protecting*' and they will be able to improve their collective lot because they will become 'self-*dependent*' (Mill, 43). In a popular form of government, the chance of injustice will be reduced because each person will stand up for his own rights. And no one stands up for a person's rights better than that person himself. Moreover, a system in which people have some control over their political situation breeds an active, vigorous citizenry. According to Mill, not only will active persons do a better job of protecting their rights, but also, active as opposed to passive persons will promote the long term interests of society. Self government protects people against abuses, it breeds the type of citizen who will be vigilant in protecting himself, and it breeds in everyone the attitudes that a society must have in its rulers if it is to advance (Mill, 43–52).

Parts of Mill's position – the idea that democracy protects individuals against injustice by giving them a chance to stand up for their own rights, for example – are familiar to most of us.[13] But the question is whether it is really *true* that individual rights are protected in a democracy. In what kind of a democracy, operating under what kinds of voting rules, do rights get protected? Throughout most of Chapter 3, Mill seems to be thinking of a direct democracy. He concludes the chapter thus:

> it is evident that the only government that can fully satisfy all the exigencies of the social state is one in which the whole people participate; that any participation, even in the smallest public function is useful; that the participation should everywhere be as great as the general degree of improvement of the community will allow; and that nothing less can be ultimately desirable than the admission of all to a share in the sovereign power of the state. But since all cannot, in a community exceeding a single small town, participate personally in any but some very minor portions of the public business, it follows that the ideal type of a perfect government must be representative. (Mill, 55)

This is a non sequitur. If direct democracy is ideal, but unfeasible, it does not follow that the feasible alternative most similar, namely representative democracy, is therefore the best of the feasible alternatives. It may be the best, but we need further argument to show this. Specifically, we would need to show that it will perform functions like that of protecting the rights of individuals as well as any alternative. There are clearly difficult questions here. For example, will everyone be represented, or represented equally well, in a representative democracy? And will it make a difference whether Parliament operates on a simple majority rule or on some alternative kind of rule?

Even if we imagine that some kind of direct democracy is possible, and assume that people are vigorous in the protection of what they take to be their own rights and interests, it does not follow that each person's rights *will* be protected in a direct democracy. [In Chapter V,] we looked at some attempts to predict the outcome of democratic decision-making processes under various assumptions about voting rules, and on the assumption that each individual would be vigorous in trying to achieve his own ends. Mill does not offer anything like this kind of analysis of democratic decision-making, but our earlier discussions should remind us that there is no guarantee that everyone will get his way. Quite the contrary. The problem of majority tyranny is still a serious problem.

As it happens, Mill does devote some later chapters (Chapter 7, especially) to the problem of designing a method of representation in which all shades of opinion achieve representation in Parliament. However, everyone's being represented in Parliament does not guarantee that everyone's rights will be respected in parliamentary decisions. After all, even direct democracy does not guarantee protection for everyone, since people may have diametrically opposed opinions as to what their rights are, and there is no reason to believe, a priori, that the person who is correct will prevail.

Mill would reply, I believe, that this objection is based on a misunderstanding of the way in which democracy works to protect people's rights. It is not because everyone has a vote that each person's rights are protected. Having a vote does not guarantee being on the winning side. The important thing about democratic government – whether direct democracy or representative democracy – is that the processes of decision-making and administration are carried out in the *open*. It is not that everyone will always have his or her way, but that whatever is done will be done in *public*. Administrators and legislators will be forced to *defend* their actions in public.

The proper function of a representative parliament, according to Mill, is not to administer, nor even to legislate, if by this we mean to write bills and enact statutes. If only because it is too large and diverse, it is ill suited to these tasks (Mill, 71–7). Its proper function is:

> to watch and control the government: to throw the light of publicity on its acts; [and] to compel a full exposition and justification of all of them which anyone considers questionable; ... Parliament [is] at once the nation's Committee of Grievances and its Congress of Opinions – an arena in which not only the general opinion of the nation, but that of every section of it, and as far as possible of every eminent individual whom it contains, can produce itself in full light and challenge discussion; where every person in the country may count upon finding somebody who speaks his mind, as well or better than he could speak it himself, not to friends and partisans exclusively, but in the face of opponents, to be tested by adverse controversy; where those whose opinion

> is overruled feel satisfied that it is heard and set aside not by a mere act of will, but for what are thought superior reasons . . . (Mill, 81–2)

Why think that this kind of open government, open debate of public policy, willingness to consider grievances seriously and respond to them, will lead to good government? Why think, for that matter, that representatives will properly discharge their responsibility to publicize the activities of government, to publicize criticism of the government, and to debate the issues seriously? Won't there be a temptation, for example, simply to ignore demands for justification when they proceed from small minorities? There are two kinds of questions here. On the one hand, there are questions about the likelihood that elected representatives will perform the functions expected of them according to the theory. On the other hand, there is the question whether, even if they do, the result will be morally good government. Mill offers, at best, only partial answers to these questions.

In a way, each of the two questions I have raised here is a question concerning the character of citizens. How will they respond to demands for justification from others? What will they regard as an acceptable justification? When will they be willing to limit their demands on others? To what extent will they feel that they need to justify their conduct to others? The questions I have raised above are also questions about what morality requires. What is the relation between a policy's being acceptable to members of a community – its being justifiable in the sense that it is acceptable – and its being *morally* justifiable?

Now, in Mill's view, a major advantage of democracy is that it improves the character of its citizens. On the one hand, he thinks it will produce active, self assertive persons concerned with improving their environment. Perhaps more important, when citizens are required 'to exercise, for a time and in their turn, some social function', this mitigates the fact that there is little 'in most men's ordinary life to give any largeness either to their conceptions or to their sentiments'. When a person is required to serve on juries, or to serve in local office, '[he] is called upon, while so engaged, to weigh interests not his own; to be guided, in case of conflicting claims, by another rule than his private partialities; to apply, at every turn, principles and maxims which have for their reason of existence the common good' (Mill, 53–4).

As I read Mill, assumptions something like these are crucial to his theory. The open and public character of government in a representative democracy is a *desirable* feature of that kind of government only if we assume that open discussion of governmental policy tends to result in good policy choices, or at least tends to prevent bad choices. The plausibility of this assumption depends, in turn, on assumptions about the kind of policy that citizens will find acceptable. What Mill wants to claim is that the very process of open discussion leads people to adopt reasonable moral principles. It works both directly and indirectly. To the extent that citizens already have good character, public discussion of governmental policy alternatives results in good policy. To the extent that citizens lack good character, public discussion and debate tends to improve their character by leading them, for example, to appreciate the situation of others.

The question is whether any of this is true. If Mill wishes to claim that participating in government, listening to public debate of political issues, discussing these issues with acquaintances and so forth, will lead people to adopt any specific set of moral principles – utilitarian principles, for example – it is not clear how he could defend his claim. But it may be possible to provide a plausible defense of a less specific claim. Recall Rawls's conception of a 'well-ordered society' discussed in the preceding section: A well-ordered society is a society governed by commonly accepted principles of justice. Now, it does seem plausible that, when matters of public policy are subject to frequent public debate, and when most individuals are called upon, from time to time, 'to exercise some public function', that citizens will attempt to formulate principles in terms of which they will be able to defend their positions to others. Similarly, to the extent that political leaders must defend their positions publicly, they will have to formulate principles and conceptions of the common good in terms of which they can justify their positions. At least, given open institutions, and given the kind of motivational assumptions discussed in the preceding section, public functionaries will attempt to formulate coherent justifications for their policies; and these justifications will have to be capable of gaining widespread public acceptance. Such justifications will have to represent a kind of possible consensus – a possible 'fundamental charter of a well-ordered society'. But principles like this satisfy at least a necessary condition for adequate moral principles. And if we assume a populace sufficiently well educated to understand the consequences of legislative proposals, laws that can pass the test of public justifiability will tend to be morally justifiable laws.

Summary, Objections and Qualifications

Mill's theory of representative government, I have claimed, embodies a justification of the kind appropriate for a system of government. The argument is that representative government tends to produce morally acceptable laws and policies. At least, it tends to produce laws and policies within the bounds of the permissible as determined by reasonable moral principles. The argument needs to be filled out with a general account of moral principles; and I have attempted to provide a partial account which, when conjoined with Mill's argument, makes the argument plausible. The idea is this: Morality is a system of constraints on conduct which people could jointly acknowledge as the constraints determining the form of their association together. Thus, a good system of government is a system that leads people to formulate mutually agreeable conceptions of fundamental constraints, and it is a system that leads them to adopt laws and policies compatible with such constraints.[14] A system of representative government with an educated, responsible citizenry, and with representatives who understand their responsibility to promote serious, open discussion of governmental policy – a *public* government, we might call it – should have these consequences.

Is public government, as conceived here, feasible? This question could have different meanings. Many recent disputes about the feasibility of democratic institutions have focused on the difference between representative systems and direct democracy of one kind or another. Thus, those more or less sympathetic to current institutions have objected to advocates of greater participation – the town meeting model – that it is just impossible to operate a national government that way.[15] But clearly there is no such problem about a system of representative government. We already have one. On the other hand, existing institutions and practices are not above criticism from the perspective of the kind of theory suggested here. If there is a single idea that is central to Mill's theory, it is the idea of *open* government. In a society of any great size it is clear that the ideal of open government depends for its realization on a variety of institutions. A vigorous free press, free not only from legal limitation, but also from more subtle forms of intimidation, is clearly essential. Open meetings laws – 'Sunshine Laws' – are also a natural step toward this ideal, as are proposals to broadcast congressional hearings and even sessions of congress. Such changes, evidently desirable in terms of this theory, are also possible.

The real problems of feasibility are not problems about the possibility of necessary institutions. They have to do with whether people – both citizens and officials of government – will comply with the spirit of open government. There is a nest of problems here. People I have claimed, naturally want to be able to justify their conduct to others. They want their own actions and their institutions to be acceptable from the perspective of mutually acceptable principles. If Mill is right, the institutions of representative government, especially when they require some citizen participation at least at some level, tend to foster the development of this natural desire.

When this desire is prevalent, open government conducted in a spirit of candor and openness tends to be good government. But, the prevalence of this desire does not itself guarantee that government will be so conducted. Quite simply, well-meaning elected officials, wanting to enact justifiable policies, may lack faith in the public, and thus may decide to act undemocratically. In the short run, at least, they will not necessarily be acting wrongly. The argument for democracy, as conceived here, is an argument in terms of its long run tendencies. In the short run, it requires faith. Even in a society of well-meaning persons, democracy is not necessarily stable; it is liable to degenerate into nondemocratic alternatives.

Another kind of instability afflicts democracies. The advantage of democracy is that it *moralizes* the process of government.[16] It encourages both citizens and representatives to think of legislation and policy-making in terms of what can be justified; and it leads them to formulate principles and conceptions of the common good in terms of which they can carry out the process of justification. The result, at best, is a stable, well-ordered society, as Rawls understands this notion, with virtual unanimity on fundamental principles underwriting common laws and institutions. But another possibility is a politics built around entrenched, irreconcilable ideologies: a society divided into warring camps. What *morality* requires in a case like this cannot be specified in the abstract. Perhaps one of the ideologies is actually a reasonable morality. Perhaps neither is. In any case, there is no guarantee that the democratic process will result in reasonable laws and policies under these conditions, and it is possible that democracy itself will not long survive.[17]

A good question for empirical study is the question under what conditions the 'moralizing' tendencies of democratic politics will tend to produce desirable results and under what conditions they will not. One might think that a crucial variable would be the method of voting. Specifically, one might think, a simple majority rule, either in the election of representatives or in the legislative process itself, would encourage the development of ideologies with less than universal appeal. Something closer to a unanimity rule seems more appropriate, given the emphasis on unanimity in my theory. But, as we have seen in earlier chapters, the unanimity rule is equivalent to the rule of one when that one happens to favor the status quo. Unless we assume that the status quo has some privileged status in morality, the unanimity rule is not clearly preferable to the majority rule. The ideal of democratic politics sketched here is that, whatever policies we adopt, they will have to be *justifiable* in terms of widely acceptable principles. Under majority rule, a decision *not* to change is subject to the same requirement.

Variables other than voting rules may well be even more important. The size of the community and the quality of communications, the character and educational level of citizens, and the presence or absence of castes or patterns of segregation are all likely to influence the quality of political debate and, hence, the quality of legislation. Again, it will take empirical investigation to determine just what variables affect the *moral* quality of legislation as I understand this notion here. It seems to me likely, for example, that the pressures for just legislation will be greater in a society to which people feel committed than in a society from which emigration is easy or attractive. But this conjecture requires verification.[18]

It is worth recalling, briefly, Dahl's criticism of Madison. Madison claimed, according to Dahl, that American constitutional procedures are strictly *necessary* if we are to avoid tyranny, and Dahl ridiculed that idea. I think it is also clear that no system of political institutions, by itself, is *sufficient* to prevent tyranny. I suspect Dahl would agree fully. But if there is reason to believe that democratic institutions are morally preferable to nondemocratic alternatives, they must increase the likelihood that laws and policies will conform to the requirements of an adequate morality. Whether they will do so in a particular case probably depends on factors of the kinds I have mentioned.

Many theorists have argued for democracy on the ground that it tends to protect the rights of individuals, and, in general, to produce just laws and policies. But the arguments tend to be weak. True, people have a chance to express their grievances, argue for their rights, and exercise their franchise in defense of their positions. But what we need to know is whether legitimate claims will tend to prevail and illegitimate claims to lose. Why think that? I have offered a way to strengthen the argument by suggesting assumptions about human motivation, about the dynamics of representative government, and about the nature of morality. The argument depends especially on these assumptions about morality. I have assumed that an adequate morality constitutes a kind of possible point of agreement among people concerning the limits of the permissible in their common affairs. At the beginning of this chapter, I suggested that other attempted justifications of democracy tend to assume the value of what they are trying to justify. When they assume a moral theory, for example, the moral theory is just what critics of democracy are likely to regard as in need of justification. Now, I can imagine someone objecting to the conception of morality advanced here in much the same way: The idea that what is morally right has anything to do with what people believe, or are willing to accept, or whatever, might well seem to be presupposed by a belief in democracy; and that presupposition is what bothers critics of democracy. I have some sympathy with this objection. It is probably correct, and worth noting, that unless there is *some* systematic connection between people's needs, preferences, etc., and what morality requires, then it is doubtful that democracy can be morally justified. On the other hand, we need not assume, and I do not assume here, that morality simply requires doing what the majority prefers, or that all preferences and desires need to be given equal weight, or even that they be weighted in proportion to their subjective intensity. It is more complicated than that. Moreover, I have made at least some effort to show that the conception of morality assumed here is reasonable on independent grounds.

Notes

1   John Rawls, *A Theory of Justice* (Cambridge, Mass., Harvard University Press, 1971), 3.
2   Trivial examples include such rules as 'everyone stop on red and go on green'. Some examples are instances of coordination problems in which everyone gains *if and only if* everyone follows some rule. Other examples are analogous to the prisoners' dilemma in which universal cooperation is sufficient, but not necessary for the production of some shared benefit. The latter cases, of course, present serious problems of instability. For an interesting discussion of coordination problems, see David Lewis, *Convention* (Cambridge, Mass., Harvard University Press, 1969). For the prisoners' dilemma, see Luce and Raiffa, *Games and Decisions* (New York, Wiley, 1957), Ch. 5. On the relation between these problems and the requirements of morality, see David Gauthier, 'Morality and Advantage', *Philosophical Review*, LXXVI, No. 4 (October 1967), 460–75.
3   The so called 'Principle of Fairness' is an example of such a rule. See Rawls, *op. cit.*, Section 18.
4   Rawls, *op. cit.*, 5. (Subsequent references in the text to 'Rawls' are to this volume.)
5   Among modern writers, Rawls is the best known proponent of a kind of hypothetical contract theory, though there are others. Gilbert Harman conceives of morality as a kind of actual agreement among actual persons. See 'Moral Relativism Defended', *Philosophical Review*, LXXXIV, No. 1 (January 1975); *The Nature of Morality* (New York, Oxford University Press, 1977), Chs. 5–8; and 'Relativistic Ethics: Morality as Politics', *Midwest Studies in Philosophy*, III (University of Minnesota, Morris, 1978), 109–21.
6   Thomas Nagel has criticized Rawls on the ground that decisions reached in the original position are not neutral with respect to all conceptions of the good. The 'primary goods', a fair distribution of which is required by the principles chosen in the original position, 'are not equally valuable in pursuit of all conceptions of the good'. Thus, what may seem agreeable to those in the original position may not be mutually acceptable to actual people in an actual society. (See 'Rawls on

Justice', *Philosophical Review*, LXXXII, 2 (April 1973), 228.) Rawls agrees that his theory incorporates a certain ideal of the person and is not neutral among different persons with different conceptions of the good. He argues, however, that no theory is completely neutral in these respects. (Rawls, 'Fairness to Goodness' *Philosophical Review*, LXXXIV, No. 4 (October 1975), Sec. VI esp. p. 549.) If this is so, then it would seem that morality, conceived as a kind of public consensus, will be possible only to the extent that some people are willing either to alter their conceptions of the good or, at least, to treat some of their interests as not constituting a valid claim on others. (For some further remarks on this point, see the discussion of economic theories later in this chapter.)

7   Roger Wertheimer, *The Significance of Sense* (Ithaca, New York, 1972, Cornell University Press), Ch. III.

8   *Ibid.* The definition of 'ought' is on page 109. I suspect Wertheimer would not accept the account of adequacy I offer here. See his Chapter IV.

9   For the distinction between *proof* and *justification* I have in mind, see Rawls, *A Theory of Justice*, Sec. 87, esp. 580–1.

10   Philippa Foot, 'Morality as a System of Hypothetical Imperatives', *Philosophical Review*, LXXXI, No. 3 (July 1972), 314. The argument in the text relies heavily on Mrs Foot's work, especially on the concluding pages of her 'Moral Beliefs', *Proceedings of the Aristotelian Society*, 58 (1958–9). See also Rawls, *A Theory of Justice*, *op. cit.*, Sec. 86.

11   One person's belief that others comply with the rules does not, in itself, necessarily give that person a reason to comply himself. For some people, at least, complying with the rules, by itself, is not a convention in David Lewis's sense of the term. (See 'Languages, Language and Grammar' in G. Harman (ed.), *On Noam Chomsky: Critical Essays* (New York, 1974, Doubleday), 255.) Conformity to some moral rules is unstable, at least among some people: while each benefits if everyone complies, universal conformity is not necessary. (See the references in Note 2 above, together with the accompanying text.) But, it may well be true, in most groups, that, if each complies with *and* professes belief in the rules, each thereby has reason to profess belief in *and* comply with the rules. This conjunctive regularity may come to have the status of a convention.

12   I shall rely here on the Bobbs-Merrill edition (Indianapolis and New York, 1958). References in the text to Mill are to this volume.

13   See, for example, Benn and Peters, *The Principles of Political Thought* (New York, Free Press, 1965), 414ff; and Carl Cohen, *Democracy* (Athens, Ga., University of Georgia Press, 1971), Section 14.3.

14   Compare Rawls, *A Theory of Justice*, *op. cit.*, 'Justice as fairness begins with the idea that where common principles are necessary and to everyone's advantage, they are to be worked out from the viewpoint of a suitably defined initial situation of equality...the constitutional process should preserve the

equal representation of the original position to the degree that this is feasible' (221–2).

15 See Robert Dahl, *After the Revolution* (New Haven and London, Yale University Press, 1970) and 'Democracy and the Chinese Boxes' in H. Kariel, ed., *Frontiers of Democratic Theory* (New York, Random House, 1970).

16 Benn and Peters, *op. cit.*, 416.

17 Some writers, it seems to me, are excessively concerned about this prospect and hold that moralizing or ideological tendencies should be resisted in favor of the politics of compromise among (mere) interest groups. At least, this is the impression I get from S. M. Lipset, 'The Paradox of American Politics', *The Public Interest*, 41 (Fall 1975).

18 For discussion of this idea, see Albert Hirschman, *Exit, Voice and Loyalty* (Cambridge, Mass., Harvard University Press, 1970).

6

A Theory of Political Fairness

Charles Beitz

As Hobbes recognized, the members of political society occupy two distinct roles: they are both the "makers" and the "matter" of government, its agents and its objects, its producers and its consumers.[1] Each role constitutes a point of view from which political arrangements can be judged. Hobbes's innovation was to relegate persons conceived as "makers" to a hypothetical act of "authorization" establishing a form of government where there is no place for participation in the choice of leadership or policy, no occasion for political deliberation, no sharing of information, no compromise, no voting, indeed no organized *public* life at all. The measure of a government's success, according to Hobbes, is its ability to induce its people to accept the conception of their political identity implicit in this vision – to accept, that is, the legitimacy of institutions designed to replace the desire to participate in public life with a desire to enjoy a felicitous private one. A government that succeeds in protecting the lives and promoting the satisfaction of the private desires of its people does all that they can reasonably require of it.[2]

The democratic ideal stands in contrast to Hobbes's vision. Its aspiration is a form of government continuously justifiable from both points of view. That political decisions take fair account of each person's prospects is not enough; for, in theory at least, this could be the case in a perfectly impartial dictatorship. As a generic form, democracy is distinguished from the other traditional forms of government by provisions for the regular participation of its citizens in political decisions. The "making" of policy is a shared function of the many, not the exclusive province of one or a few. The uniqueness of democratic forms lies in the fact that the set of rulers and the set of the ruled – the "makers" and the "matter" of politics – for the most part coincide.

This fact defines the philosophical problem to which a theory of political equality is a response, and it explains why any adequate theory must be complex. Popular participation in political decisions is possible only within an institutional framework that organizes and regulates it. But many such frameworks can be imagined, and the basic idea of democracy – that the people should rule – is too protean to settle the choice among them. A theory of political equality must resolve this indeterminacy by identifying the features that institutions for political participation should possess if they can truly be said to treat citizens as equals.

An adequate solution to this problem must be complex because the status of democratic citizenship is complex. The terms of participation in democratic politics should be fair to persons conceived as citizens. However, as both the "makers" and the "matter" of politics, citizens occupy multiple roles and so can judge their institutions from more than one point of view. We must not suppose that the interests of citizens conceived from one of these points of view will always harmonize with their interests conceived from the other or that an effort to secure one kind of interest will not put the other in jeopardy. For example, we can hardly assume a priori that the conditions of participation that would be optimal for the making of responsible judgments about public affairs will be the same as those that would generate political outcomes that would be best for those to whom they apply. Indeed, we must not suppose that either of these points of view, taken separately, defines a single consistent set of aims; either could dissolve on examination into a series of disparate, and potentially conflicting, concerns. It would be a mistake to assume (though in the end, it may prove to be true) that fairness to persons conceived as citizens names a simple, univocal criterion. We may understand it better as a complex criterion that brings together a plurality of values corresponding to both the active and the passive dimensions of citizenship.

Outline of the Theory

These remarks summarize the lessons to be learned from the criticisms of conventional conceptions of political equality [presented in earlier chapters]. I turn here to the more constructive task of formulating an alternative theory that takes account of these lessons. In form, the theory I shall set forth is a hybrid version of the procedural theory; thus, it differs not only from best result and popular will theories but also from simple versions of proceduralism that identify fair participation with procedural equality. To distinguish it from these other views, I call this theory *complex proceduralism*.

The central idea is this. Institutions for participation should be justifiable to each citizen, taking into account the interests that arise from both aspects of citizenship. We should be able to regard the terms of participation as the object of an agreement that it would be reasonable to expect every citizen to accept. Institutions that satisfy this condition can be said to be egalitarian in the deepest sense: being equally justifiable to each of their members, they recognize each person's status as an equal citizen.

The notion of reasonable agreement is an application of the idea of a social contract to the subject of political equality. As we shall see, this idea has normative consequences: it will rule out any arrangement for participation in political decisions for which no justification of the appropriate form is plausibly available. However, this is not likely to be enough to settle many practical disputes about the structure of democratic institutions. Often, what is at issue is not the *form* of the justification but its *content*; various reasons might be advanced to show why some arrangement is acceptable to all, and the question is whether these reasons ought to be seen as compelling. Hence, the formal conception of contractualist justification needs to be supplemented by a generalized account of the kinds of reasons we are prepared to recognize as grounds for refusing to accede to any particular arrangements for participation.

In complex proceduralism, this account is provided by a doctrine of *regulative interests of citizenship*. These are higher-order interests that represent within the theory the plurality of regulative concerns that arise in connection with the complex status of democratic citizenship. Paramount among these are interests in *recognition, equitable treatment*, and *deliberative responsibility*. Each defines a category of interest it would be reasonable to take into account in assessing the arrangements for participation. Taking the formal and the substantive elements of the theory together, complex proceduralism holds that *the terms of participation are fair if no one who had these ("regulative") interests and who was motivated by a desire to reach agreement with others on this basis could reasonably refuse to accept them.*

Unlike best result and popular will theories, complex proceduralism does not seek criteria for identifying the uniquely best or most desirable institutions; its aim is to identify grounds on which some of the feasible arrangements might reasonably be ruled out. To put it somewhat differently, it seeks criteria that any procedural arrangement should satisfy in order to be regarded as acceptable. Moreover, unlike the simpler versions of proceduralism considered earlier, complex proceduralism does not embrace any single value (such as the conservation of power) as definitive of political fairness; it recognizes a plurality of reasons why a procedural regime might be judged to be unfair. Its main concern is to devise a method for characterizing these reasons more precisely and for guiding judgment when they conflict.

The Idea of a Social Contract

A more detailed account of complex proceduralism should provide an explanation of both its formal and its substantive elements and of the important relationship between them.

Beginning with the social contract framework, there are three questions. First, in view of the variety of interpretations of the contract idea, why adopt so informal a conception as that employed in complex proceduralism? For example, why not impose informational constraints (a "veil of ignorance") on the parties to the agreement? Second, why should we take any interest in the contract idea, so understood? In particular, how is it connected to the traditional aspirations of democratic reform? Third, what is the normative force of this idea? What difference does it make that our conception of political fairness is based on contractualist reasoning rather than on reasoning of some other kind?

There are many ways to understand the idea of a social contract, each importantly different from the others. Later we will note some of the differences; for the moment we concentrate on the common elements. The social contract doctrine is first of all a view about the form that the justification of political principles should take. Like other moral conceptions, contractualism holds that principles should be justifiable from the perspective of everyone affected by them. What is special in contractualism is the attempt to understand this perspective as that of several distinct individuals, combined so that the separateness of each person's point of view is retained. In the classical social contract theories, this idea was expressed metaphorically in the requirement that the original agreement be unanimous. To remove the metaphor, we might say, following Scanlon, that contractualism regards moral principles as principles that "no one could reasonably reject as a basis for informed, unforced general agreement," provided they were moved by a desire to reach such an agreement.[3]

The requirement of unanimity reflects what might be called a distributive conception of justification: contractualist principles should be reasonable from each individual point of view. By way of comparison, views in the tradition of classical utilitarianism embody an aggregative conception: the perspective of everyone affected is interpreted as that of society at large, and principles are held to be justified when they are shown to be better, for the community as a whole, than any others, even if from some individual perspectives they appear less reasonable than some alternatives. Thus, although aggregative conceptions hold that principles should be acceptable from the perspective of society, this does not imply that they should be acceptable from the perspective of everyone, taken seriatim. In contrast to contractualist conceptions, utilitarian views might therefore be seen as an application of the idea of rule by the majority.[4]

It may help to compare this understanding of the essentials of the contract idea with a different one, which sees the idea of reciprocity rather than that of reasonable agreement as the central feature. According to this view, the unity of the social contract tradition, and what distinguishes it from utilitarianism, is (roughly) the insistence that the net benefit that social institutions confer on each of their members should be greater by a similar amount than what each could expect in a nonsocial "state of nature."[5] When this condition is met, people can regard the sacrifices their institutions call upon them to make as justified by the advantages they may expect to derive, in turn, from the sacrifices of others. The basis of political justice is the reciprocal expectation of benefit. This conception of the contract idea is natural enough if the description of society as "a cooperative venture for mutual advantage" is taken literally.[6] However, I believe the conception is too narrow. As a historical matter, it is inapt: none of the writers in the tradition, arguably (although implausibly) with the exception of Hobbes, regarded the original agreement as justified by considerations of parity of benefit.[7] Their views converge, instead, on the notion of reasonable consent.[8] As a philosophical matter, the conception confuses species and genus. Under some circumstances, reciprocity may not be necessary to show that a social arrangement is reasonably acceptable from all points of view, and under other circumstances it may not be sufficient: an agreement could be reasonable from each person's perspective without conferring equivalent net benefits, and it could confer equivalent net benefits without being reasonable on all sides. A condition of reciprocal benefit imports a specific normative criterion into the notion of a social contract that the form of that notion does not require. The core idea is better conceived as that of reasonable agreement.

So understood, the contract doctrine describes a conception of justification that is particularly compatible with the aspirations of modern democratic culture.[9] The Leveller defense of an expanded suffrage was perhaps the first important attempt to invoke these aspirations on behalf of political reform.[10] Commenting on Colonel Rainsborough's famous words, Lindsay wrote: "The poorest has his own life to *live*, not to be managed or drilled or used by other people."[11] The poorest and the richest are equally responsible for the conduct of their own lives and the choice of an individual good and should have equal authority over the public decisions that affect them. Of course, this aspiration would be fully realized only if unanimous consent were required for political decisions and then only if there were grounds for supposing that the status quo ante were itself unanimously accepted; otherwise, someone might find himself coerced to accept, or at least to accommodate himself to, political decisions affecting the conduct of his life that were taken without his consent. Contractualism arises in democratic theory once it is acknowledged that this degree of agreement will not normally obtain on political matters; indeed, it will not normally obtain even at the level of constitutional choice. The most that can be hoped is that institutions will be compatible with principles that no one could reasonably reject, supposing that they were motivated by a desire to find principles that each could justify to everyone else. Then, when someone complains that a procedural arrangement may disappoint her interests, it can be replied that this is the unavoidable result of acting on principles that her fellow citizens could reasonably expect her to accept. Institutions that can be justified in this way come as close as possible to the ideal of respect for each person's final authority over the conduct of her own life.[12]

There are many ways of interpreting the contract idea for normative purposes consistently with this understanding of the source of its appeal. For example, there are more and less formal conceptions, which differ according to the degree to which the background and setting of the original agreement are constrained by counterfactual assumptions about the knowledge, interests, and motivation of the parties. Rawls's theory is an instance of a relatively formal view, which proceeds by offering an account of the circumstances of agreement with sufficient normative content to enable principles to be derived, ideally, by deduction. On the other hand, the theory described by Scanlon is considerably less formal; the parties are imagined to be motivated by a desire to come to agreement but are otherwise conceived as having the knowledge and interests of the actual persons whom they represent. The theory consists of a generalized description of the point of view from which the justification of principles is to be sought and invites substantive argument about the reasons that would be sufficient to justify someone who took up this point of view in rejecting any particular principle. Because the structure of the theory incorporates less normative content than more formal views, it is less determinate in its consequences.[13]

In this sense, complex proceduralism is a relatively informal conception. One reason for adopting such a formulation is that any theory that included sufficient constraints to resolve the main institutional problems concerning political fairness would seem excessively artificial. Another is that the more informal view facilitates a clearer presentation of the considerations relevant to various interpretations of fair participation, and it forces the resolution of conflicts among these considerations into the open, so to speak, rather than allowing them to be concealed within the structure of a more formal theory.

Complex proceduralism is not, however, without significant normative content. We stipulate that the parties have certain regulative interests, that these are higher-order interests in the sense of being controlling in matters of procedural choice, and that the parties are motivated by a desire to reach an agreement that no one who had *these* interests would have sufficient reason to reject in preference to any feasible alternative. These assumptions are clearly significant additions, for they limit the range of considerations that the parties can be imagined to bring to bear on the choice of political procedures. Later, we will consider the basis of these constraints. For the moment, the point to stress is that complex proceduralism is nonetheless an informal view in at least two respects. First, in the construction of the contract situation we do not attempt to correct for the influence of knowledge of people's natural endowments or social situation by imposing informational limitations like the "veil of ignorance."[14] It is true that the regulative interests have a similar effect but only to the extent of preventing the parties from seeking procedural advantages for themselves that conflict with these interests which all are assumed to share. Counterfactual assumptions are made about the motivation of the parties but not about their knowledge of individual circumstance and social context, which is allowed to influence judgments about procedural fairness from the start. Second, no attempt is made to frame the contract situation so that the technical devices of the theory of rational choice can be brought to bear. Thus, for example, there is no claim that the interests of the parties can be represented as individual utility functions or that their reasoning can be meaningfully described as maximizing the satisfaction of these interests. Whereas the first point shows that in complex proceduralism the interests that explain agreement function as substantive constraints on the deliberations of the parties rather than as structural elements of the model itself, the second indicates that the problem of combining these interests to yield a decision on any particular issue of procedural design must be treated as a freestanding moral issue to be worked out more or less intuitively in a way that takes account of the historical circumstances in which the procedures are to operate. By leaving so much to be worked out by moral reasoning of the ordinary kind, we forbear from representing the agreement, so to speak, as the output of an axiomatic decision procedure or from claiming that the model is capable of generating by its own rules determinate decisions in the choices facing the parties.

These remarks provide answers to the first two of our questions about the contract idea – why we should interpret it so informally and why, so interpreted, its consequences should matter to us. However, the effect is to make the third question – about the normative force of contractualism – more pressing. For in view of what I have said thus far, the following objection will arise. The substantive elements of the theory – that is, the regulative interests – appear to do all of the normative work. These interests furnish the main basis for resolving disputes about procedural design; the contractualist framework seems not to contribute anything of its own. One might therefore wonder why it should not be seen as empty: a mere formality serving only to rationalize conclusions that would be fully determined by the regulative interests alone.

The answer to this objection has two parts. First, there is no need to deny that the doctrine of regulative interests has normative content. However, to grant this is not also to agree that the contract idea is empty. As a contractualist view, complex proceduralism holds that institutions should be justifiable to *each* person who comes under their sway; it should be possible to say to each person that the terms of participation are acceptable from her own point of view, given her social and historical circumstances, when this point of view is conceived as that of an equal citizen of a democratic society. As I have argued, it may be relevant, but it cannot be enough, that institutions yield outcomes that are best for society at large or that they generate decisions that accord with a technical construction of the popular will. For neither condition ensures that each citizen would have reason to accept the institutions when they are regarded from her own point of view. This would be true even if what is "best for society at large" could somehow be interpreted as a function of the regulative interests: complex proceduralism does not seek to maximize the aggregate, societywide level of satisfaction of these interests. It is true that by postulating a set of higher-order interests that motivate the choices of the parties, we restrict the bounds of possible agreement. But what is being restricted are the bounds of possible *agreement*: it is the set of procedural arrangements one could reasonably expect each of his fellow citizens to accept. There is no reason to believe that arrangements that satisfy this requirement will normally, if ever, yield the highest level of interest-satisfaction in society at large.

Second, and more basically, the regulative interests themselves stand in need of justification. Otherwise, the claim that they should be assigned a privileged position in reasoning about political fairness would seem arbitrary: we would have provided no special reason to care about them. I have said that these interests represent within the theory various elements of an ideal of democratic citizenship. But this ideal is not, so to speak, imposed on the theory from the outside; as we shall see, the theory seeks to provide an account of its appeal by connecting it with values we are prepared to accept as reasonable grounds for objecting to a procedural arrangement. The regulative interests themselves have a contractualist justification. Their prominence within the theory is not, therefore, an indication that the contractualist framework is normatively empty; indeed, it is only by accepting the framework that their prominence can be accounted for.

Regulative Interests of Citizenship

An explanation of the interests in recognition, equitable treatment, and deliberative responsibility should specify their content and show why it is reasonable to regard them as furnishing grounds for refusing to accept a procedural regime.

Imagine that citizens could meet to establish the terms of participation that their institutions should embody. We assume that the institutions are generically democratic; the question is not whether people should be entitled to participate in political decisions but how the mechanism of participation is to be arranged. What kinds of considerations would it be reasonable to take into account in assessing the alternatives?

It would be convenient if a catalog of these considerations could be exhibited as a systematic deduction from some more abstract and widely accepted conception of democratic citizenship. As no such deduction presents itself, we must proceed inductively, attempting to construct such a conception from more particularistic judgments. Thus, we might reflect on various procedural arrangements that would be widely agreed to be objectionable. We may regard such cases as *paradigmatic*[15] of procedural unfairness; they are ones about which most people's judgments converge. They might include, for example, weighted voting by race, systems of representation that favor certain minority interests (say, those of the landed gentry), unrestricted majority rule and the idea of majority tyranny, ballot access regulations that exclude popular candidates or positions from consideration, or imbalances in election campaign resources that give a decisive advantage to incumbents.

In considering each case, we should try to explain at a general level the reasons that would justify someone in objecting to the procedural arrangement in question. Any such explanation must be *constructive*. That is, we do not aim for a description of the actual basis of people's objections to the kinds of unfairness found in the paradigmatic cases; instead, we seek an account that seems maximally plausible in view of the characteristics of the case at hand, keeping in mind the desire to produce a more general conception of political fairness that coheres with the accounts that can be provided for the other cases as well. Accordingly, judgments about the reasonableness of objections to paradigmatic cases of unfairness will normally have a two-level structure. First, a weight must be assigned to the interest motivating the objection (the "harm"), reflecting its objective importance or urgency. By "objective" I mean, roughly, that the weight of the harm should reflect the degree of importance or urgency one could expect others in society to accord to it. It is not sufficient to rely on an agent's own subjective valuations; someone who detests being awake while the sun shines should have less weight attached to his objection to daytime voting hours than someone whose fourteen-hour-a-day job keeps him at work from dawn to dusk, even if each attaches equal subjective importance to his objection.[16] Second, the harm must be compared with the harms to other interests that might be anticipated under the feasible alternative arrangements, again taking into account their objective importance. For, clearly, supposing that everyone is moved by a desire to reach *some* agreement, it would not be reasonable to refuse to accept an institutional arrangement, even if it would do harm, if the alternatives would be even worse.

The three categories of values I have identified as regulative interests arise from reflection about paradigmatic cases of procedural unfairness. Each interest represents a type of reason that would justify someone in refusing to accept a procedural arrangement.

The interest in *recognition* involves the public status or identity that procedural roles assign to those who occupy them.[17] Political procedures define the terms on which citizens recognize each other as participants in public deliberation and choice. In the extreme case, when some people are excluded entirely from any public role (as, for example, with the wholesale denial of the franchise to blacks in the antebellum South), it has been said that those excluded "are not publicly recognized as persons at all" and might be described as "socially dead."[18] Something similar occurs when procedural roles are assigned in a way that conveys social acceptance of a belief in the inferiority or lesser merit of one group as distinct from others – as, for example, with racially weighted voting or efforts to dilute the votes of racial minorities through the use of gerrymandering techniques. Those singled out as less worthy are demeaned and insulted; they are encouraged to feel that patterns of disrespect that exist in society at large enjoy official sanction. It would be reasonable for anyone to object to procedural arrangements that had this effect. This is not simply because, from a subjective point of view, it is unpleasant or painful to be assigned a demeaning role in public procedures, although this is certainly true. The objection has a more objective foundation – not because it rests on some transcendent or immutable standard of value, but rather because it is a fixed point in a democratic culture that public institutions should not establish or reinforce the perception that some people's interests deserve less respect or concern than those of others simply in virtue of their membership in one rather than another social or ascriptive group. The political roles defined by democratic institutions should convey a communal acknowledgment of equal individual worth.[19]

Because it bears so directly on the definition of the procedural roles in which people participate in public decisions, the interest in recognition corresponds to the point of view of citizens as "makers." The interest in *equitable treatment* corresponds instead to that of citizens as "matter." The basic idea is that citizens might reasonably refuse to accept institutions under which it was predictable that their actual interests – that is, the satisfaction of their needs and the success of their projects – would be unfairly placed in jeopardy, at least if there were alternatives that would avoid these effects without imposing even worse risks on others. Normally we rely on democratic mechanisms themselves to guard against the oppressive use of state power; however, recognizing that these may not always be sufficient, we are prepared to supplement them with further constraints such as a bill of rights, judicial review, and the like. Without these further protections, democratic forms might reasonably be seen as so dangerous as to be unacceptable.

The idea of equitable treatment is difficult to render more precisely, primarily because it is uncertain how the notion of an interest's being "unfairly placed in jeopardy" should be interpreted. It seems clear that procedural interpretations will not suffice; one ought not to say, for example, that a person's interests are unfairly jeopardized when institutions accord the person less than an equal share in power or influence over the relevant class of decisions. This follows from our earlier observations about power: many manipulable factors can affect a person's prospects in a procedural regime; the extent of his power is only one (and ordinarily not the most important) of these. As the example of entrenched minorities illustrates, one's interests might be placed in great jeopardy even when power is equal. The interest in equitable treatment needs a more substantive interpretation.

One possibility is to identify equitable treatment with the principle that political decisions should aim to generate equal increments of preference-

or interest-satisfaction. However, here we face a familiar difficulty: whereas any such principle must presuppose that the *ex ante* distribution was morally satisfactory, as a general matter we have no reason to believe this. People would not necessarily be justified in objecting to participatory mechanisms that lead to unequal increments in preference- or interest-satisfaction if the inequalities worked to the benefit of those whose most urgent needs would otherwise be placed in jeopardy. Suppose, for example, that a choice was to be made between two systems of legislative representation, each of which guaranteed everyone equal procedural opportunities to influence the choice of representatives. If those with the greater or more urgent needs would tend to do better in one system than in the alternative, those who would fare worse in that system could not reasonably complain simply because another system would be better for them.[20] Since what is at issue is the contribution of particular decisions to each person's global situation rather than the distributive characteristics of individual political decisions viewed in isolation, there seems to be no alternative to relying on substantive views concerning social justice to render a complete account.[21] Political decisions could then be said to satisfy the interest in equitable treatment when, over time, they promote (or do not systematically detract from) a distribution that accords with the requirements of justice, which are themselves to be worked out from a point of view in which each person's prospects are taken equally into account.

It may be surprising that a theory of political fairness should incorporate a concern for the substantive characteristics of political outcomes. For people's conceptions of equity differ; if the present view were widely accepted, then disagreement about the meaning of political fairness would be endemic. But this hardly seems consistent with the notion that a main function of the idea of fairness is to regulate the social processes through which substantive disagreements are adjudicated, or at least compromised.

In response, there are two points. First, it is no misrepresentation of our pre-theoretical views about political fairness to hold that result-oriented considerations sometimes play a role. Consider, for example, the traditional democratic concern about the dangers of majority tyranny and the protection of minority rights.[22] The idea that fair institutions should contain safeguards against the oppressive use of state power by popular majorities would be incomprehensible unless the concept of oppression had some substantive content. Moreover, as a matter of descriptive accuracy, it does not seem wrong to characterize some procedural disputes as reflections of underlying disagreements about the nature of the outcomes that procedures should produce.[23] The account I have offered recognizes this by relativizing the requirements of fairness to underlying views about acceptable results. (To say this is not *also* to say that the underlying disagreements are incapable of principled resolution.)

Second, the direction of political decisions is determined by a great variety of factors, among which the structure of the system of political participation plays at best a subordinate role. It is unrealistic to think that, by a series of fine manipulations of this structure, small improvements in the distributive characteristics of political outcomes could often be guaranteed. Hence, the interest in equitable treatment is likely to operate more selectively and at a greater remove. It will justify a refusal to accept an institutional scheme mainly when it seems likely that the scheme will give rise to (or perpetuate) serious and recurring injustices and when there is an alternative available that would be less likely to do so without introducing countervailing harms of other kinds. Thus, in the context of reasoning about political procedures, the interest in equitable treatment will normally appear as an interest in safeguarding one's urgent or vital interests in the face of the threat that they might be systematically subordinated to the competing but less urgent claims of others. While there may be considerable disagreement in society about conceptions of social justice and the common good, it seems likely that the prospects of convergence are greatest in connection with the most vital of human interests. So, although the chances that substantive disagreement will generate procedural controversy cannot be ruled out, they need not pose too great a difficulty.

Now the central virtue of democratic forms is that, in the presence of a suitable social background, they provide the most reliable means of reaching substantively just political outcomes consistently with the public recognition of the equal worth or status of each citizen.[24] Democratic forms succeed in achieving this aim, when they succeed at all, less because they aggregate existing preferences efficiently than because they foster a process of public reflection in which citizens can form political views in full awareness of the grounds as well as the content of the (possibly competing) concerns of others.[25] It is a mistake to conceive democracy as a crude hydraulic device, moving society in the direction of the greater power. Instead, we must understand it as a deliberative mechanism that frames the formation and revision of individual political judgments in a way likely to elicit outcomes that treat everyone's interests equitably. The characteristics of preference-aggregating devices are clearly significant for an assessment of the fairness of the system as a whole, but they should be seen as parts of a larger deliberative framework.

These observations illustrate the significance of the third regulative interest, in *deliberative responsibility*: democratic institutions should embody a common (and commonly acknowledged) commitment to the resolution of political issues on the basis of public deliberation that is adequately informed, open to the expression of a wide range of competing views, and carried out under conditions in which these views can be responsibly assessed. This is important for reasons connected with both of the points of view characteristic of citizenship. Citizens conceived as participants in public decisions (Hobbes's "makers") will wish to regard their judgments as the most reasonable ones possible under the circumstances; such judgments should be formed in light of the relevant facts and should be defensible in the face of the conflicting views held by others in the community. If individual judgment could not be seen as justifiable in this way, it would be indistinguishable from prejudice; and this should be intolerable for anyone who takes seriously her responsibility for her own beliefs. On the other hand, for citizens conceived as the objects of public policy (its "matter"), the awareness that institutions encourage responsible deliberation is a necessary basis of confidence in the integrity of political decisions and, indeed, of the system of participation itself. Without this, the supposed tendency of democratic mechanisms to elicit equitable outcomes would be no more than a pious hope, and an important ground of the stability of democratic regimes would be lacking.

The interest in deliberative responsibility has two elements, which may be in conflict. The first is openness: deliberation should not be constrained by the exclusion of positions that would gain substantial support if they were sufficiently exposed to public scrutiny.[26] Thus, someone might reasonably object if widely supported candidates or positions were excluded from the political arena by such mechanisms as restrictive ballot access regulations or a distribution of campaign resources that gave some parties or positions a decisive advantage in access to the principal fora of public debate. Such an objection would be reasonable partly because exclusionary provisions could prevent people from representing their own interests in public deliberation; but even if this were not the case, exclusion of positions widely held by others would be objectionable because it would suppress information and points of view that would be essential for all citizens in reaching responsible judgments about the public good. The other element involves the quality of the deliberative process itself: the conditions of public deliberation should be favorable to the thoughtful consideration and comparative assessment of all of the positions represented. Citizens should be enabled to reach political judgments on the basis of an adequately informed and reflective comparison of the merits of the contending positions. Only then will they have reason to conduct themselves as cooperating members of a public deliberative enterprise, to exercise the capacities for judgment and choice in the public realm, and to regard others as similarly equipped and motivated.

Both elements are part of the nature of responsible deliberation. The potential for conflict arises from the fact that the conditions of public deliberation may be maximally favorable to the thoughtful assessment of the alternatives only if the number of alternatives to be considered is not too large. There is no guarantee that the range of alternatives that elicit non-trivial numbers of adherents will always fall within this limit. The interest in seeing a wide range of positions represented argues for openness, but the interest in conditions of public deliberation in which political judgments can be adequately informed and reflective argues, at least under some circumstances, for constraint. It is not easy to generalize about how such conflicts are most appropriately to be reconciled. In practice, as we shall see, any reconciliation will be heavily influenced by local considerations concerning the context in which the conflict arises and the impact that one or another way of resolving it seems likely to have on satisfaction of the other regulative interests. However such conflicts are resolved (and they may of course not arise at all), the interest in deliberative responsibility clearly expresses an important requirement on the choice of institutions for political participation and one which is distinct from those embodied in the other regulative interests.

The interests I have identified function within the theory as the criteria by which political institutions and procedures are to be assessed when they are regarded from each person's point of view. Although it would be surprising if things were otherwise, there is no claim that all citizens, in fact, conceive themselves as having these interests or are motivated to accord them a controlling position in actual political deliberation. This fact gives rise to an objection we have already anticipated: why not regard the regulative interests as no more than an arbitrary selection from the much wider range of values reflected in people's actual aims and preferences? And why endow them with a higher-order status, so that they eclipse people's more particularistic concerns in informing judgments about procedural design?

The answer is that these interests give theoretical expression to certain aspects of a normative conception of democratic citizenship, which is implicit in our ordinary judgments about political fairness and which we are prepared to accept as determining in matters of procedural choice. The list of regulative interests, and their interpretations, is derived from a consideration of cases of procedural unfairness that we may regard as paradigmatic. The diversity of the interests reflects the complexity of the status of membership in a democratic society, and the desire to realize this status on terms compatible with a similar realization by everyone else is taken to be the fundamental motivation for concern about procedural fairness. If the distinctive egalitarianism of the view is found in its contractualist framework, its distinctive idealism lies in this motivational aspect.

Finally, as I have suggested, a choice among institutions must rest on a consideration of how the alternatives affect all three kinds of interests. However, there is no reason to believe that the regulative interests will always coincide; indeed, it would be surprising if they did not occasionally conflict. A possible response would be to deny that, under the circumstances, *any* institutions could be fair. Perhaps there are cases so extreme that this is what we must say. However, this need not always be true: a degree of sacrifice in one interest may be a reasonable expectation, particularly when it is made up by gains in another. Because the regulative interests are irreducibly plural, it is unlikely that any systematic mechanism can be set forth for reconciling conflicts; one is forced to rely on an intuitive balancing of competing values. This is not an insuperable difficulty, particularly when the range of interests that enter at the foundational level is restricted and the grounds of their importance are reasonably clear. In part 2, I shall illustrate this by considering how complex proceduralism applies to several controversial problems of institutional design. Here, I note a related point. One must recall that we are driven to adopt a theory like complex proceduralism by a recognition of the diversity of the considerations it seems natural to take into account in assessing political institutions. It is neglect of some of these, and excessive concentration on others, that gives rise to the critical defects of more conventional theories of political equality. The need to rely on intuitive comparisons of conflicting and irreducible interests may seem less than satisfactory from a theoretical point of view, but it is an unavoidable reflection in democratic theory of the variety of ways in which political institutions touch people's lives.

Contrasts with Other Views

Complex proceduralism differs [from the views discussed in earlier chapters] in several respects. First, unlike best result and popular will theories, the form of proceduralism I have sketched is not in any straightforward sense instrumentalist. Fair terms of participation are not conceived as those most likely to succeed at producing outcomes that strike some independently identified target, whether this is described in terms of the substantive characteristics of desirable political decisions or the relationship of the decisions actually taken to the political preferences held by the people. Of course, both types of concerns may play a role in complex proceduralism, but this role is neither definitive nor morally basic; there are always further questions about why a given kind of outcome-oriented concern should matter and how it should be balanced against the other regulative concerns with which it may conflict.

Moreover, as I have emphasized, there is no a priori reason to assume that these interests will always be complementary, and it may be necessary to balance them against one another. Now the weights it would be appropriate to assign to these interests when they conflict may depend in part on a society's historical circumstances. For example, the interest in protecting against the political effects of racial bigotry and prejudice will be more weighty where its legacy is more pronounced. Hence, the theory contains some residual indeterminacy. Of course, the application of any abstract conception of political fairness will require some reference to the circumstances of the society in question. What is different about complex proceduralism is where, within the theory, historical considerations play a role: here they may enter at the foundational level of the theory – in judgments about appropriate weights for the regulative interests – as well as at the level of application. In other words, the theory's conception of fairness may itself remain partially indeterminate until the context of its application is taken into account. This does not seem to me to be objectionable; in fact, it might be seen as a virtue of a theory of political equality that it takes account of historical considerations in a way that more faithfully represents their actual effects on intuitive judgments about fair participation.

Third, this theory is primarily negative. It does not attempt to describe ideal conditions that institutions should strive to satisfy; rather, it seeks an account of the forms of unfairness that they should strive to avoid. (Of course, it need not follow that considerations of fairness *operate* only negatively, for example, by ruling out institutions with this or that objectionable feature; sometimes the avoidance of unfairness requires institutional provisions that might be characterized as affirmative.) I believe this feature of the theory is consistent with the characteristic role of political equality in controversy about the structure of democratic institutions: it is invoked more often to support criticism of the established order than as a description of a constructive ideal. Moreover, I believe that it accords with our intuitions about a variety of questions of policy: when a particular procedure is uncontroversially unfair, it is frequently possible to give an account of the reasons for the unfairness without committing oneself to a view about the nature of a uniquely preferable alternative.

This points to a fourth contrast to other theories.[27] According to at least the more familiar versions of the best result and popular will theories, there is always a uniquely best solution (or, in the case of indifference, class of solutions) to the problem of social choice. Thus, the fact that under certain circumstances a decision procedure operating on the same utility or preference information might produce either of two (or more) inconsistent outcomes must be deeply embarrassing: it shows either that there is some deficiency in the theory or that under those circumstances the ideal of fair participation is unattainable.[28] As we noted earlier, some such reasoning explains the unease with which the Arrow result is viewed in the theory of social choice. A consequence of the negative character of complex proceduralism is that its requirements may be satisfied in more than one way; several institutional structures, each perhaps likely to have different or even inconsistent political results, may be equally fair. But this need not be cause for concern. Because institutions are not evaluated simply with respect to the outcomes they are likely to produce, it is no occasion for unease, for example, that institutions that are equally fair according to the theory might generate inconsistent outcomes given identical information about people's preferences. This is not to say that it will never be occasion for concern *within* the theory: if, for example, considerations of stability indicate that institutions should normally produce outcomes that bear a predictable relationship to the political preferences in society, then the possibility that a particular decision procedure may give rise to inconsistency will count against that procedure. It will be one among many factors to be taken into account in comparing that procedure with the feasible alternatives. Moreover, the fact that several institutional configurations may be equally fair does not mean that they will be equally desirable overall; for example, considerations relevant to the vitality of political culture might incline toward one or another alternative. What complex proceduralism requires is that these considerations operate within the range of equally fair alternatives. It is no reason for embarrassment that there may be more than one of these.

Notes

1   Thomas Hobbes, *Leviathan* [1651] (New York: Collier Books, 1962), pp. 19, 229 (the passages occur in the "Author's Introduction" and chap. 28). The centrality of the distinction in Hobbes's thought was first made clear to me by Michael Walzer in a lecture presented in Princeton in 1973.
2   This is reflected in Hobbes's conception of the social contract as an undertaking in which people surrender their power to a sovereign (an "alienation" contract), rather than as one in which their power is merely "loaned," subject to certain

conditions on its use (an "agency" contract). For this distinction, see Jean Hampton, *Hobbes and the Social Contract Tradition* (Cambridge: Cambridge University Press, 1986), pp. 3–4, 256–79.

3   T. M. Scanlon, "Contractualism and Utilitarianism," in *Utilitarianism and Beyond*, ed. Amartya Sen and Bernard Williams (Cambridge: Cambridge University Press, 1982), p. 110. My interpretation of the social contract idea is greatly indebted to this article throughout.

4   Thomas Nagel, "Equality," in *Mortal Questions* (Cambridge: Cambridge University Press, 1979), p. 112.

5   For such a view, see David Gauthier, *Morals by Agreement* (Oxford: Clarendon Press, 1986), pp. 8–13.

6   John Rawls, *A Theory of Justice* (Cambridge: Harvard University Press, 1971), p. 4.

7   Indeed, the characterization fits Hume, the great opponent of contractualism, better than it fits anyone within the contract tradition as it is normally understood. See David Gauthier, "David Hume, Contractarian," *Philosophical Review* 88 (1979), pp. 3–38.

8   Jeremy Waldron, "Theoretical Foundations of Liberalism," *Philosophical Quarterly* 37 (1987), pp. 135–40.

9   The contractualist formula has also been advanced as a general characterization of the subject matter of morality, or of the grounds of moral truth (most influentially by Scanlon in "Contractualism and Utilitarianism," esp. pp. 110–15). Whether this is correct is a question I cannot consider here. Our concern is the more traditional conception of the social contract as a basis of *political* justification.

10 Quoted on page 3 of *Political Equality*, from which the present chapter in this volume is taken. On the character of the Leveller position as it was represented at Putney, see Austin Woolrych, *Soldiers and Statesmen: The General Council of the Army and Its Debates, 1647–1648* (Oxford: Clarendon Press, 1987), esp. chap. 9. On the Levellers' conception of democracy, see J. C. Davis, "The Levellers and Democracy," *Past and Present*, no. 40 (1968), pp. 174–80; and Keith Thomas, "The Levellers and the Franchise," in *The Interregnum: The Quest for Settlement 1646–1660*, ed. G. E. Aylmer (London: Archon, 1972), pp. 57–78. There is an accessible survey in Brian Manning, *The English People and the English Revolution* (London: Heinemann, 1975), pp. 286–317.

11 A. D. Lindsay, *The Essentials of Democracy*, Lectures on the William J. Cooper Foundation of Swarthmore College (Philadelphia: University of Pennsylvania Press, 1929), p. 13 (emphasis in original). Although historians of the Leveller movement have been particularly concerned with the question of the franchise, it does not appear to have been central to the Leveller program; what was more important – and more radical – in their thought was the idea that the legitimacy of the political order derives from the agreement of the people (by which they meant adult males who had not forfeited their birthright). Woolrych, *Soldiers and Statesmen*, pp. 221, 236.

12 This interpretation of the appeal of contractualism derives from Kant. See "On the Common Saying: 'This May be True in Theory, but it does not Apply in Practice'" [1793], in *Kant's Political Writings*, ed. Hans Reiss and trans. H. B. Nisbet (Cambridge: Cambridge University Press, 1970), pp. 77–81.

13 Scanlon, "Contractualism and Utilitarianism," pp. 123ff. See also Scanlon, "Liberty, Contract, and Contribution," in *Morals and Markets*, ed. Gerald Dworkin, Gordon Bermant, and Peter G. Brown (Washington, D.C.: Hemisphere, 1977), pp. 63–4.

14 As in Rawls's theory. See *A Theory of Justice*, pp. 136–42; and "Kantian Constructivism in Moral Theory," *Journal of Philosophy* 77 (1980), pp. 515–72.

15 The term is used this way by Ronald Dworkin: *Law's Empire* (Cambridge: Harvard University Press, 1986), p. 75.

16 For a more general argument that social judgments should be based on objective rather than subjective valuations, see T. M. Scanlon, "Preference and Urgency," *Journal of Philosophy* 72 (1975), pp. 655–69. On the idea of objectivity, see also Thomas Nagel, *The View from Nowhere* (New York: Oxford University Press, 1986), pp. 138–63.

17 On procedural roles as a basis of status, see T. H. Marshall, "Citizenship and Social Class" [1949], in *Class, Citizenship, and Social Development* (Garden City, N.Y.: Doubleday, 1964), pp. 84ff.

18 John Rawls, "Justice as Fairness: Political not Metaphysical," *Philosophy and Public Affairs* 14 (1985), p. 243. For the idea of "social death," see Orlando Patterson, *Slavery and Social Death* (Cambridge: Harvard University Press, 1982).

19 For the idea of communal acknowledgment of individual worth, see Jack Lively, *Democracy* (Oxford: Basil Blackwell, 1975), pp. 134–5. The connection between institutional roles and self-respect is clearest in Rousseau, *The Social Contract* [1762], in *The Social Contract and Discourses*, trans. G. D. H. Cole (London: J. M. Dent, 1973), bk. 1, chaps. 8–9, bk. 2, chaps. 2–3.

20 I discuss issues about the structure of representation at greater length in chapter 7 of *Political Equality*.

21 As William Nelson argues. See *On Justifying Democracy* (London: Routledge & Kegan Paul, 1980), chap. 6.

22 See, e.g., Giovanni Sartori, *The Theory of Democracy Revisited* (Chatham, N.J.: Chatham House, 1987), vol. 1, pp. 131–7, esp. the references to Madison, Jefferson, and Tocqueville.

23 We will consider some examples [in part 2] in connection with legislative districting and political finance. See *Political Equality*.

24 This is a comparative judgment; it need not presuppose any very optimistic non-comparative view about the tendency of democratic institutions to produce just outcomes.

25 As Pericles famously (if, perhaps, self-servingly) put it, "... instead of looking on discussion as a stumbling-block in the way of action, we think it an

indispensable preliminary to any wise action at all..." Thucydides, *The Peloponnesian War*, trans. John H. Finley, Jr. (New York: Modern Library, 1951), II. 40, p. 105.

26   This is a preliminary formulation of a complicated idea. For a further discussion, see chapter 8 of *Political Equality*.

27   I am grateful to Thomas Scanlon for pointing this out.

28   The latter view is advanced in William Riker, *Liberalism Against Populism* (San Francisco: W. H. Freeman, 1982), chap. 4 and pp. 233–41.

Part IV

Deliberation and Institutions

7

Political Quality

David Estlund

I. Introduction

Political equality is in tension with political quality, and quality has recently been neglected. My thesis is that proper attention to the quality of democratic procedures and their outcomes requires that we accept substantive inequalities of political input in the interest of increasing input overall. Mainly, I hope to refute *political egalitarianism*, the view that justice or legitimacy requires substantive political equality, specifically equal availability of power or influence over collective choices that have legal force.[1] I hope to show that political egalitarianism exaggerates individual rights in the conduct of political procedures, and neglects the substantive justice of the decisions made through those procedures. Some unequal distributions of influence may better promote just decisions, and without reliance on any invidious comparisons such as the relative wisdom of the wealthy or the educated.

Put in general terms, the goal is to find an acceptable stopping point between merely formal political equality on the one hand, which places no limits on substantive political inequality, and equal availability of political influence on the other, whose distributive constraints are too severe. The principled basis I offer for such a point is a theory of democratic legitimacy that gives a significant role to the epistemic value of democratic procedures – their tendency to produce decisions that are correct by the appropriate independent moral standards.[2] This approach requires more than merely formal equality, since great substantive inequality in political input will be damaging to the procedure's ability to arrive at just decisions. In this it not only accommodates a traditional criticism of classical liberalism, but makes a closely related point against the political-egalitarian ideal of equal *availability* of political influence, since that too is insensitive to the distribution of *actual* influence, and to the epistemic consequences of that distribution. The epistemic approach, then, seeks to structure politics so as to promote the quality of political decisions, but without relying on invidious comparisons between citizens or groups.[3] I defend the epistemic approach to democracy more fully elsewhere. Here my claim is that epistemic considerations should lead us to reject the goal of substantive equality of (available) influence. I thus draw out an implication of the epistemic view of democratic legitimacy for the issue of political equality.

Briefly, it is worth noting that this argument can be extended beyond the concern with epistemic value, though I will not develop these points in much detail. First, even for theories that accept that there is such a thing as epistemic value for some democratic decisions, it is plausible to hold that for other decisions there is no independent standard but only procedural justice. It may seem that the quantity of deliberation is worthless in those cases and all that matters is fairness. Second, some theorists will make no room for such a thing as independent standards for democratic decisions at all. In both these cases it may seem as if all that matters in democratic procedure is procedural fairness, and that my epistemic arguments for inequality would not apply. Notice, however, that in that case we should be satisfied with some random choice procedure. That we would not be satisfied even in the absence of epistemic considerations stems, I think, from the fact that quantity of deliberation, within certain distributional bounds, has other value even in addition to any tendency it might have to promote the discovery of truth. Some will put it in terms of the rationality of the decision, others in terms of letting participants be better informed about their genuine interests, and so on. My point here is only that tension between equality and quantity of input is not limited to contexts or theories where epistemic value is at stake. However, I will mainly press the point in the epistemic context.

Political egalitarianism requires equalizing opportunity for, or availability of, political influence, not actual political influence. This is because a citizen is in no way mistreated by the inequality resulting from her own free choice not to exercise all her available influence. My criticism is based on the value that more political deliberation has, other things being equal, on the quality of political decisions. But these epistemic consequences, as I call them, stem from facts about the amounts of actual input and participation rather than from facts about the amounts of input that are available. Thus, for some purposes below, the actual/available distinction will be important; but for other purposes it is not important. In much of what follows, I will speak of influence or input without specifying whether it is actual or available, and in those contexts I mean what I say to apply equally to both. When I mean one or the other I will be specific. I explicitly consider the difference at several points below.

Political egalitarianism may seem to be an extreme and implausible view, not requiring great efforts to refute it; but there is a plausible case to be made for it, even though, on reflection, it should be rejected. Here is one way of finding political egalitarianism tempting. Disputes over such things as distributive justice are deep and pervasive. Whatever the correct resolution of those disputes may be, we hope that a political decision about distributive justice can be legitimate, even if not just, on the basis of certain features of the political procedure, and not simply on the basis of whether the decision is morally correct, since the latter issue will be too deeply contested.[4] But now imagine a process in which those who have more money than others have more influence over the process. Such a process can easily seem unfair, depleting it of the moral capacity to render the outcomes of the process legitimate. At least if the process were fair, the outputs could be said to be fair in that procedural sense. A fair procedure, some argue, requires equal availability of input, or at least insulation of influence from things like differential wealth. It is natural to conclude that whether or not justice requires economic equality, legitimacy requires substantive political equality – equal availability of political influence – so as to keep the political process fair. Egalitarianism, then, is held to be the proper stance at least with respect to political input. For reasons that vary among its advocates, political egalitarianism is a popular and formidable normative theory of political legitimacy, one not to be easily dismissed.[5]

Put in simplest terms, I will argue that equality of input may come at the cost of quantity, and that both are important to the quality of the process and its outcomes. That is why substantive equality of influence is not a proper goal or constraint for the design of democratic political institutions.

A brief taxonomy of competing approaches may help avoid certain misunderstandings.

In what I shall call *authoritarian* theories of political legitimacy, invidious comparisons between people have often been used to justify unequal political rights and liberties even at the formal legal level, such as unequal legal rights to vote or hold office, ostensibly in the interest of high-quality political rule.[6] Another traditional view makes no invidious comparisons and thus accepts equal formal political rights and liberties, but rejects the goal of equalizing substantive political influence – equal availability of political input, including whatever resource distribution this requires. Call this mixed view the *formalist* view of political equality. Some hold, for example, that substantive political equality (in addition to formal political equality) is not compatible with due respect for an individual's right to property, or to freedom of speech, or, more generally, one's liberty to do as one chooses. This version of the formalist view, which I will call *libertarian*,[7] is not based on any claims about the resulting quality of decisions.

Call the principle requiring both formal and substantive equality of political influence, *political egalitarianism* – a view that I will argue wrongly neglects the quality of political decisions. My purpose is not to oppose formal political equality, much less democracy itself, nor to rely on either invidious comparisons among citizens or on strong rights to property or speech. I defend a formalist view, but not on a libertarian basis. On the other hand, the inequality of influence that I will defend does, like the property-based or liberty-based arguments, tend to allow specifically the wealthy to have more political influence than others (though not as much more as they now have). It shares this feature with libertarian theories, but its basis is entirely different.

Political egalitarianism and formalist views (including libertarian views) are anti-authoritarian, or liberal theories. The view I defend is also liberal, and formalist rather than egalitarian, but on an epistemic rather than a libertarian basis (sharing the epistemic concern with some authoritarian views). Call this view a *liberal epistemic view* of political equality (see figure 7.1). The liberal epistemic view is formalist because it accepts formal (but rejects substantive) equality of political influence. But formalist views need not say that distribution of substantive political influence does not matter at all (we might call that *strict formalism*; some libertarian views take this form). The liberal epistemic view does have the resources to criticize extreme inequality of influence, but rejects *equal* substantive influence as an appropriate goal. It is a *moderate formalism* in rejecting substantive equality, while not assuming that mere formal equality is enough.

My alternative to political egalitarianism diverges from it in approximately the way that John Rawls's difference principle diverges from a strictly egalitarian principle of distributive justice.[8] Rawls's view is often regarded as egalitarian, even though not strictly so. Likewise, the position taken here condemns great substantive (not only formal) political inequalities, but also finds decisive reasons to permit or require unequal influence

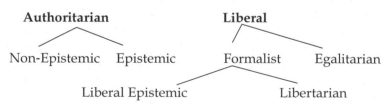

Figure 7.1

under certain conditions. It is certainly more egalitarian with respect to substantive political influence than authoritarian or libertarian theories.

While this parallel with Rawls's theory of justice is instructive, the view defended here is also a criticism of a certain Rawlsian argument, and it may be less egalitarian than Rawls's view in one respect. In Rawlsian theory, the liberties to participate in politics must be equal for all. First, they must be formally equal, giving each citizen equal status under the law.[9] But second, they must also be substantively equal (or approximately so) in the sense that people should not have substantially greater opportunity to influence political outcomes as a result of their having a greater share of other primary social goods. While unequal influence would be compatible with formal political equality (formalist views), it is disallowed by a separate provision in Rawls's inviolable principle of equal liberty: each person's political liberties ought to be guaranteed a fair (approximately equal) value in addition to being formally equal under the law. Rawls's political egalitarianism is much stronger than his economic egalitarianism, since the former recognizes no justification for divergence from the roughly equal value of the political liberties.[10] Specifically, the Pareto-style argument used by Rawls to justify (in principle) economic inequality seems to be denied application to the case of political influence. I begin, shortly, by asking why this is so.

Political egalitarianism neglects the fact that a small and limited discussion is not as valuable a guide to important practical decisions as is fuller, more extensive discussion.[11] There is something to be said for procedural fairness, but also something to be said for applying human intelligence more extensively to political problems. Some writers acknowledge this point,[12] but still avoid the hard question by assuming that equality need not reduce the total quantity of public deliberation. The point I want to urge is that if equal influence can only be achieved at lower levels of input, then the epistemic advantages of a wider discussion might, from any reasonable point of view, outweigh the disadvantages of some degree of unequal influence. This is not just a logical possibility but a real possibility in democratic politics. For this reason, equal political influence, and, more specifically, the complete insulation of political influence from differential wealth, are not appropriate goals in the design of deliberative democratic institutions.

II. Paretianism and Political Input

It is far from clear what equal political influence would mean. It is relatively clear what insulation of influence from differential wealth would mean. But the latter would typically still involve great inequality of influence, since money is not the only route to influence. Social connections, good looks, debating skill, and an eye for good points can all give a person more influence in political discussion than other people. On the other hand, a simple majority vote, without any discussion of the issue at hand, would, if such a thing were even remotely possible, embody pure equal influence. So would a coin flip to decide among the available alternatives, whether or not discussion had occurred.

Several of the sources of unequal influence mentioned above may well be regrettable. The one that apparently is not regrettable, and not regretted by any democratic theorist I know of, is the extra influence a person has by virtue of offering good reasons in a context where good reasons are appreciated and have influence. That some people are better at this than others is clear from the utter political ignorance or perversity of some people. If they are worse, some are better. How can this unequal influence be allowed or even celebrated by theorists who espouse the theory that equal influence is called for by the principle of equal respect for persons? I do not doubt that extra influence of better reasons is called for, in some way, by equal respect for persons. But I do doubt that the principle that each person is owed equal political influence can cohere with these other ideas. Unequal influence through rational persuasion is one kind of unequal influence. If there are good reasons, deriving from or at least consistent with equal respect, to allow unequal rational influence, then unequal influence does not, in general, violate equal respect. If it does, then unequal rational influence does too.

In what follows, then, I shall interpret the ideal of equal political influence to mean specifically *the insulation of political influence from differential wealth or social rank*. This more familiar and attractive thesis is what I hereafter mean by "political egalitarianism." Still, I think it is mistaken.

I begin with a story some philosophers tell, and which I will criticize, about why opportunities for political influence ought to be equalized among adult citizens. It is true, they grant, that if distributing some good unequally will allow more of that good to be given to everyone, then, at least in many contexts, it would be irrational to insist on an equal distribution. For example, Rawls argues that justice allows distributing primary social goods unequally if and only if doing so benefits all (or at least, for simplicity, the worst off). There might well be a way to do just that if extra social productivity can be induced by giving people incentives for producing more. If more social goods are produced by giving a larger share to the most productive citizens, then perhaps the incentive will still work if some portion of it is channeled to benefit the less well off. If so, who could complain about the productive citizens getting more than the others get, since this benefits everyone?[13] Thus, it is granted that if opportunity for political influence could be improved for everyone by giving some more than others, this would perhaps be justified. But, the argument goes, political influence does not work like that: it is a competitive good. There is no way to increase the quantity available to all by giving some people more than others. So there is no justification for deviating from an equal distribution.[14] I believe this story goes wrong in several ways.

A quick terminological point: One distribution is normally said to be *Pareto-superior* to another just when it is better for some and worse for none. Call a distribution that is better for everyone *strongly Pareto-superior*. Since only the stronger concept concerns us here, I shall use "Pareto-superior" to mean strongly Pareto-superior throughout. I simply do not consider whether weak Pareto-superiority has anything to recommend it in the contexts discussed here.

The first problem with the argument just sketched is that it does not even consider whether any unequal distribution of influence would be *better* for everyone. It asks only whether it could produce more influence for everyone. Even if it could not, though, it might yet be better for everyone, and so perhaps might be justified on that basis. We should distinguish between two ways in which political inequality might be claimed to be Pareto-superior: (a) it might be Pareto-superior with respect to all goods taken together (call this *true Pareto-superiority*); or (b) it might be Pareto-superior specifically with respect to (availability of) political influence or input (call this *political Pareto-superiority*).[15] The argument sketched above inexplicably assumes that political inequality could only be justified by political Pareto-superiority. But why couldn't it be justified by true Pareto-superiority even if this did not satisfy political Pareto-superiority? All might be made better off, even if not all are given more political input or influence. This objection will not be pursued here. I mention it only to introduce the distinction between true and political Pareto-superiority.

Second, the argument supposes that political influence is a competitive good:[16] no one can get more of it without someone getting less. If a person's share of the total quantity of influence exerted is expressed as a fraction of that total, then influence would be a competitive good. But, of course, if one's share of wealth were expressed as a fraction, then wealth too would be a competitive good. We know wealth can be increased for some without decreasing the wealth of others, and thus a person's share can be understood in absolute as well as comparative terms. The same is apparently true of political influence, or if the word "influence" suggests otherwise, it is true of political *input*. Let *input* stand for an individual's absolute quantity of political participation (measured, for simplicity, in money),[17] and let *influence* stand for a person's fraction of the total political input. If everyone wrote more letters to their congressional representative annually than they now do, the total quantity of input would increase and no person's absolute quantity of input would decrease. Even if influence is a constant sum, the quantity of input is not. The comparative idea of one's share of influence, and the absolute quantity of input, are both important, and the argument below proceeds by taking the latter idea more seriously than usual.

If the total quantity of input can be increased, then we can ask whether there might be any way, beginning from an equal distribution of input, to increase everyone's amount of it by distributing it less equally. Here are two ways it might happen. One way would rely on reasoning familiar from the incentive argument justifying economic inequality on the grounds that it improves everyone's condition. Suppose that the promise of unequally large amounts of political influence for the wealthy increased the desire for wealth and the influence it brings. This, combined with economic incentives for greater social productivity, could be expected to induce more productivity than would exist in the absence of this promise of extra influence. Then perhaps the extra could be taxed or otherwise allocated to subsidize input for those with less influence. Political inequality would be accompanied by political Pareto-superiority. A second way unequal influence might increase everyone's input would be if citizens had to pay a surcharge on each purchased marginal unit of political input, which payment could be used to subsidize increased input for others. I leave aside the details of such a scheme for now, but I will return to the subject later.[18] In principle, this is another way unequal influence could produce more input for all, or political Pareto-superiority. In both of these cases, while everyone's input increases, some will have lost influence (fraction of input) while others will have gained it, and that will have to be figured into our evaluation of the situation. My point here is only that with respect to input, political Pareto-improvement (that is, movement to a Pareto-superior state) is theoretically possible. Later I will argue that it is also really possible, and that it is sometimes justified.

Political inequality and substantive justice

Suppose that unequal input was not mutually beneficial as compared with an equal distribution – that it did not produce more input for all or more social goods for all – but that the unequal scheme did lead more reliably to just decisions. Just decisions will not necessarily benefit everyone, or even anyone, least of all anyone who has so far been benefiting unjustly. But whether or not it is mutually beneficial, the greater substantive justice of the outcomes of the unequal distribution looks like a powerful reason in its favor. It is a separate standard from either true or political Pareto-superiority.

Can inequality of political influence promote the substantive justice of political decisions? Here is one way it might do so: Suppose that the only way to achieve equal (available) influence is by leveling down – preventing those who would otherwise have the most influence from having any more influence than those who would otherwise have the least influence. If this low level is very low, the reduction in the total volume of deliberation might damage its epistemic value. Think of a choice between two debates and their epistemic value for an onlooker: in one debate the pro side speaks for a total of sixty minutes, and the con side for only fifty. In the alternative debate they are given equal time: two minutes each. The epistemic value of the second debate is probably much lower than the first.[19] Something analogous is theoretically possible in political participation. If equality can only be achieved at a very low level, the epistemic value of the process might be greater under some unequal distribution of political influence. Notice that this reasoning employs no invidious comparisons between participants. And here the Pareto-improvement in input is only indirectly relevant in that it plausibly improves the epistemic value of the procedure.

If we ask what is wrong with equalizing political input at the very lowest level, say at the level of a coin-flip, it is natural to object that political decisions are not likely to be well made by any random choice from among the alternatives. Political decisions are too important to be left to chance. Some procedure that gives citizens the opportunity to influence political decisions will be more likely to lead to wise decisions than would a random choice. This is the epistemic value of a particular arrangement of political influence.[20] By raising the question of an arrangement's epistemic value, we can account for our alarm about the coin-flip method, and thus we can explain why the absolute amount of input is important. Under the right conditions, more input tends to produce more epistemic value.

Epistemic value accounts for a concern about quantity, but can it place any constraints on distribution? If one person has the wisdom it takes to make better decisions than would be made under any more equal distribution of influence, the simple criterion of increasing epistemic value would require empowering this person as the sole political decision-maker. This epistocracy, as I call it, is highly inegalitarian, to say the least. This epistemic approach, then, might seem to be no better at explaining plausible distributive constraints than would a maximizing principle or a Pareto criterion.

The epistemic goal need not be the only relevant consideration, of course. Even granting that some people might be far better at making the morally and technically best political decisions, such invidious comparisons among citizens are bound to be open to reasonable disagreement. I propose to place the following constraint on political justification: that it may not make use of doctrines or principles or assertions that can be rejected even by conscientious, cooperative, reasonable citizens. (In this I follow Rawls's liberal principle of legitimacy.)[21] No test or criterion for distinguishing the better from the worse judges of justice and the common good would be acceptable from all reasonable and conscientious points of view. Since reasonable people can reject invidious comparisons, such comparisons should play no part in political justification.[22] No basic formal or substantive inequality of political influence may be justified on the grounds of the superior skill or wisdom of any individual or group.[23]

Might it not turn out, even without invidious comparisons, that the greatest total quantity of deliberation could only be produced if some citizens had vastly more opportunity for input than others had? If greater total deliberation increases the procedure's epistemic value, then the epistemic approach, even limited by the proscription of invidious comparisons, would not place any limits on permissible inequality of influence. In reality, however, it is doubtful that the epistemic value of a political decision procedure simply increases with the total quantity of input regardless of its distribution. Those with the ability to slant the system in their own favor will often do so, sometimes willfully, sometimes out of ignorance of the legitimate interests of others. As inequality of influence increases, the opportunity for this kind of abuse increases. The epistemic criterion places limits on acceptable inequality all by itself, without any help from the idea that equal influence is intrinsically valuable or required by fairness or equal respect for persons. In the context of political participation, inequality tends to diminish epistemic value even as the total quantity of participation, suitably distributed, promotes it.[24] In light of these countervailing tendencies, the epistemic approach seems bound to steer between a strict political egalitarianism on the one hand, and an utter insensitivity to inequality of influence on the other.

Is there an absolute right to equal influence?

The outlines of my objection to political egalitarianism are now clear. Before going into more detail, it is worth considering whether epistemic considerations are simply irrelevant because they are trumped. Is there a moral right to equal political influence that goes beyond the right not to be the victim of invidious comparisons in political justification? Two arguments for such a right are commonly seen, but both appear to be fallacious.

First, it is often argued that inequality of political influence expresses disrespect for citizens as equals, or expresses the view that some are inferior or less worthy than others in some way.[25] Certainly, unequal political institutions often do express disdain, or condescension. But this is a contingent matter. Inequality does not express disrespect unless it is owed to disrespect. When it is, that is a moral failing of the particular societies involved, not a defect of unequal political influence itself. Unequal influence can, in principle, exist entirely for other reasons.

More to the point, how does the charge of disrespect fare against an argument that advocates inequality of influence only when it will give everyone more input and thereby increase the substantive justice of political decisions? Toward whom does this theory express disdain, condescension, or disrespect? The requirement of equal respect does not directly support a requirement of equal political influence (or its availability) any more than it directly supports the right to an equal income, an equally fulfilling job, or an equally quiet neighborhood.

Second, it is often argued that equality of influence is a requirement of justice because it is fundamentally unjust for some citizens to be deprived of the resources and education required to understand their own authentic values, or to articulate them clearly in public, or to understand the important issues that are at stake in politics.[26] We may grant that such deprivation is unjust; nevertheless, none of these three considerations is a comparative matter, and so none supports equality of influence. No one's self-understanding suffers just because some people understand themselves even better. No one becomes less articulate just because some are more articulate than he or she is. Each of these important considerations supports *improving* cognitive, economic, and other resources. This is precisely the kind of consideration that I think presses *against* a requirement of equal influence, since equality may often mean preventing some from more fully understanding their own values, or from becoming more articulate, if there is no way of getting everyone to a higher equal level. A more frankly egalitarian argument for the egalitarian conclusion would have to say that what is most important is not that people understand their own values, but that each person understand or misunderstand them equally. But that implausible argument has not, to my knowledge, been offered.

Even if unequal opportunity for input does not disrespect those with less, there is still the question of whether it is *unfair*. Political egalitarianism is often presented as required by *fair proceduralism*, the view that democratic outcomes get their legitimacy from the fairness of the political procedure. I have argued against the latter view elsewhere,[27] and have argued here that political egalitarianism is, in any case, unacceptable. And yet, the idea of some citizens having more influence than others can still seem to be unfair to those with less influence. Now if influence were equally available, and those with less had less voluntarily, then the charge could be easily dismissed. But on the liberal epistemic approach defended here, influence would be more readily available to those with more money. How could this be fair?

We need to make several distinctions. First, departures from fairness are not always unfair. Second, there is a difference between a procedure that is internally governed by standards of fairness, and a procedure that (whether fair in the internal sense or not) it is fair to have. Each point requires some elaboration.

Departures from fairness are not always unfair. Consider a decision about which of two people should receive a certain indivisible good. This meager description often inclines us to think that fairness must guide the decision. But if the two people are drowning, and one is my son, fairness is not the operative moral idea. I ought to save my son, and this conclusion cannot be gotten from the idea that my decision process treats the two fairly. I ought to treat my son specially. Doing so is not based on fairness, nor is it unfair. Treating the two fairly would be wrong, though hardly unfair. We can call the right decision fair if all we mean is that it is not unfair, but fairness is still no guide in that case.

Similarly, the liberal epistemic view allows and requires departures from substantive procedural fairness, but this does not make the procedures it recommends unfair. A procedure is unfair only if it *wrongly* departs from fair procedure. Below, in Section III, I defend an "Epistemic Difference Principle" which, I believe, rightly departs from procedural fairness.

Second, a procedure can be thought of as fair to participants[28] in different senses. *Internal procedural fairness* of a decision procedure consists in roughly equal influence. Such a procedure may or may not be the morally right one to use in a given circumstance. A second kind of fairness of a decision procedure is present when the procedure is a fair one to have, whether or not it is internally procedurally fair. A popular way of elaborating this idea says that a procedure is a fair one to have if it is a procedure that would be agreed to in a hypothetical decision procedure in which all affected are represented and treated fairly in the internal procedural sense. This idea is best known from Rawls and Thomas Scanlon, and Charles Beitz analyzes political fairness in just these terms.[29] Beitz argues persuasively that this *external procedural fairness* (my term) may or may not end up endorsing actual internally fair decision procedures. Thus, if external procedural fairness is the proper standard of what procedure we ought to have, internal procedural fairness is of no independent moral significance.

How should authority be distributed in the classroom, or in the economic market? Fairly? We can now see that the issue of fairness applies at two levels. As for internal procedural fairness, it is not an appropriate standard for distributing decision-making authority in a classroom or in the market. This does not mean that departures from a fair distribution are *unfair*, since they do not depart from fairness wrongly. Furthermore, the inegalitarian distributions might be fair in the external procedural sense that they are procedures that it is fair to have if they are beyond reasonable objection suitably understood.

It is not obvious that external fairness is always the appropriate standard for what decision process there ought to be, and I will not consider that question. I will simply assume that this *is* so in the case of decision proced-ures for electing legislators and making laws for the basic legal structure of a society.

Political egalitarianism, then, calls for an internally fair political decision procedure, but I argue that it is morally mistaken to do so. A fair procedure neglects epistemic considerations and thus could be reasonably rejected in a hypothetical internally fair procedure for choosing actual political pro-cedures. The scheme of Progressive Vouchers discussed below (in Section V) instantiates the liberal epistemic view, and it is not internally fair since extra influence can be bought by those who can afford it. But it is not unfair, and it is a fair procedure to have if the improvement it brings in the epistemic value of the procedure would be acceptable to all in a fair hypothetical choice procedure.

Last, some may hold that social relations must rest on interactions in which wealth or rank bring no extra influence. One might take this simply as basic, or one might be led to this by the thought that only if there is a basic institutional level characterized by equal influence over politics could other inequalities, such as those in the economic realm, ever be justified by their source in those more equal political procedures. It would be a good reply to show that from a suitably formulated hypothetical decision procedure in which influence is pristinely equal, people would accept the inequalities of input required to improve the epistemic value of the political process. I will not attempt any such demonstration here, but I take this point to weaken the objection at hand. Some might have taken it as similarly basic that economic goods ought to be distributed equally, before considering the possibility of inequalities that benefit all. Then it becomes necessary to give some more specific argument about who could legitimately complain. I intend the points about the epistemic value of unequal but more voluminous public political input to raise a similar challenge.

Input as money

For purposes of quantifying input, I will assume it can be measured by money spent on politics. This is most appropriate for the case of a campaign contribution, and more complicated for other kinds of participation whose market value may not be entirely determinate, such as volunteering, writing books, or joining demonstrations or political parties. Money, of course, has only relative value. If the absolute amount of money goes up in a closed economy, its value merely decreases. Money's value depends on the demand for it, just as with any other exchangeable good. So how can the absolute amount of political input go up if it is measured in money? The answer is that we are only looking at one segment of the economy: money spent on politics. When I speak of, say, twice as much being spent on politics, I am assuming that the overall amount of money in the economy has stayed roughly the same. So a dollar has retained its value, and twice as much value is being devoted to politics.

Concentrating on money is a very useful simplifying move, but it has several difficulties. First, *which money* counts as an expenditure on politics? My purposes are at a high enough level of abstraction that my points do not depend on specifying this in much detail. The only problem would be if there were reasons to doubt that any such distinction could usefully be drawn. Certainly there is no sharp line here. The clearest cases would be candidates for office and political parties. Next would be advocacy groups that intentionally and expressly influence officials and voters, such as the American Civil Liberties Union, environmental groups, and so on. What about groups that seek mainly to educate the public about an issue? These are often on the borderline. Public education about the dangers of nuclear deterrence leans, perhaps, in the direction of the political. Perhaps education about how to have safe sex leans away. There will be borderline cases, but I do not see this issue as especially troubling. Numerous doctrines and policies depend on roughly identifying those activities and groups that should count as political for certain purposes, and I readily grant that the present approach would eventually need to rise to that challenge with more specificity.

The second difficulty is the problem of non-money input. It must be asked whether there are so many routes of political influence that cannot be subsumed under the concept of money contributions that the value of the overall model is very limited. Sidney Verba, Kay Lehman Schlozman, and

Henry E. Brady, for example, compare contributions of *time* and *money* as different modes of participating in politics.[30] Even this is too simple to capture everything. Those who contribute "time," for example, will have varying degrees of strength, energy, intelligence, experience, and knowledge to contribute in any given period of contributed time. Again, however, this general point does little damage to my argument. It can be put this way: certain important resources employed in politics are such that equalizing their availability might well reduce the epistemic value of the overall process so much as to not be worth it. Money is the paradigmatic example, and is also perhaps the single most significant measure of political resources. Insofar as there are other political resources that do not obey the logic I apply to money, then my conclusions do not apply to them.

Political egalitarianism faces similar challenges, however. Even if it does not concentrate on money, but chooses some probabilistic notion of influence (for example, equal probability of being decisive), its egalitarian principle is impossible to interpret in practice unless more is said about how to measure these probabilities. What gives one person a greater probability of changing the outcome than another? Obviously, we know there are certain things that make such a difference, such as, notably, the amount of money donated to parties and candidates. But if that is a distorting oversimplification, then what are the other important factors, and why can't they be accommodated by the arguments I offer about the epistemic value of quantity, etc.? Answers to these questions may well place qualifications on the conclusions I defend here.

III. The Epistemic Value of Equality and Quantity of Input

Epistemic considerations may cast doubt on fair proceduralism, upon which political egalitarianism often rests, but it might be thought that epistemic considerations themselves end up favoring political egalitarianism on other grounds. Fair proceduralism says that outcomes of democratic choice derive their legitimacy from the fairness of the democratic process. But political egalitarianism could instead rest itself on claims about the value of equal political input from an epistemic point of view.[31] It is natural to think that inequality in political input increases opportunities for oppression and discriminatory ignorance, and in these ways decreases the expected quality of democratic outcomes. In this section I want to grant quite a strong epistemic value to equality of input, and to attempt to formulate it in fairly precise terms. The reason is that in the next section I will argue that there are still important cases in which inequality of political input would be justified if there were offsetting increases in the quantity. So, in fact, I will be granting perhaps implausibly much to the epistemic importance of equality of input, but doing so will only strengthen my argument that, nevertheless, political egalitarianism fails.

The assumptions discussed in this section are just that: assumptions. They are not obviously correct, certainly not in all circumstances, nor can their merits be fully discussed here. I attempt to forestall objections but then proceed to show what can be derived from the assumptions. If the results are interesting, this raises the stakes about whether and in what circumstances these assumptions, or something close to them, can ultimately be defended.

I will assume that there is epistemic value to having an equal distribution of input, and that the epistemic value increases with the degree of equality, other things being equal. Thus, the epistemic approach has a place for the value of equality of political input:

> *Epistemic Value of Equality*: Given a quantity of input, a more equal distribution of that input has more epistemic value.[32]

Of course, giving more input to people who are more likely to promote the best decision would be a counterexample. Nevertheless, we are assuming that there is no politically legitimate basis for such invidious comparisons – for holding that some citizens are wiser in this way – since this will always be open to reasonable disagreement. Thus, no distribution of input can be epistemically evaluated by considering *which* citizens are at which levels of input. We proceed for these purposes as if everyone were equally wise, even though none of us need believe that. Under this assumption it is natural and common to hold that inequality of input is harmful to the expected quality of the decision.

Next, it is also natural to assume that under the right conditions more discussion and participation is epistemically better. This is more controversial, and I consider objections shortly.[33] Assume:

> *Epistemic Value of Quantity*: For any given level of equality of input, a greater quantity of input at the same level of equality has more epistemic value.[34]

Note that despite the simplifying name, this does not state that more quantity is always epistemically better. That would be a stronger and less plausible assumption. I assume only that where increases do not increase (or decrease) inequality they promote the expected quality of the decision.

Now each of these two factors, quantity and equality, has some power to compensate for a lack in the other. If increased equality improves quality for any given quantity, then (unless the slightest decrease in the quantity is epistemically catastrophic) there is the possibility of a reduction in the quantity small enough that it could be made up by increased equality of distribution. Likewise, a slightly less equal distribution can be, I will assume, epistemically compensated by a sufficiently great increase in the quantity.

I propose to assume, then:

Compensation of Quantity for Inequality: For an equal distribution E of a given quantity of input, and any degree of inequality i, there is some (logically possible) arrangement of a greater quantity that has degree of inequality i, and is also epistemically superior to E (unless E was already epistemically infallible, producing the best possible outcome all the time).

We already know that if the inequality were kept the same or decreased (starting from equality, of course, inequality cannot be reduced), then the epistemic value would be increased by raising the quantity. This much follows from the first two principles alone. This third principle says that even if inequality is increased, and no matter how much, the epistemic damage can be offset by a sufficiently increased quantity. This does not follow from the other two principles, since they leave it unsettled how much epistemic value an increased quantity has at very high levels. If this stayed constant at all levels, then the compensation principle would follow. If the marginal epistemic value of quantity of input decreases too fast, then some degrees of inequality might do more epistemic damage than can be offset by increasing the quantity.

Notice that we are forced to accept that the marginal epistemic value of input decreases at least at very high *ex ante* levels of epistemic value, since there is not much road to travel to get to infallibility. For any given degree of epistemic improvement, then, there is some high *ex ante* level of epistemic value that is so close to infallibility that such an improvement is logically impossible. Now perhaps very low levels of *ex ante* epistemic value (or, alternatively, low levels of input) have special features, but let us put that aside and assume that there is, at all levels, decreasing marginal epistemic value of input. Quantity will still always be capable of compensating for inequality so long as the marginal rate does not cause increased quantities to converge on some epistemic value short of infallibility. So long as there is always a quantity great enough to bring epistemic value arbitrarily close to infallibility, then inequality can always be epistemically offset by some increase in quantity. Think of it this way: Begin with an equal distribution of some quantity of input. Now introduce some degree of inequality, thus causing epistemic damage. Now keep the level of inequality constant but increase the total input. There is no logical upper bound on input; thus, if increasing input converges on infallibility (despite a decreasing marginal rate of epistemic value), then it eventually epistemically surpasses the original equal distribution.[35]

If quantity offsets inequality, there is the question of how much it takes. Consider the epistemic damage done by a given departure from equality. Now, holding that level of inequality constant, how much must the quantity be raised to undo the epistemic damage? More precisely, what must the initial sum be multiplied by to epistemically offset for the inequality? Call this the problem of the *epistemic compensation factor*. If the marginal epistemic value of input were constant rather than diminishing, or at least if we had good reason for fixing on some particular rate of diminution (rather than merely on a family of rates),[36] this would still be a daunting question. Under the circumstances, we cannot hope to arrive at anything like a strong reason for any very precise answer, and I will therefore proceed without one.

Even without knowing how much quantity is required to epistemically offset a level of inequality, we can at least make one assumption that grants more epistemic value to equality for the sake of argument. When inequality is increased by some people gaining input, let us assume that the epistemic damage of the inequality outweighs the epistemic enhancement from the added quantity whenever the increases of those who gain are not shared with all who have less. (There is no reason to suppose that those [if any] with more than the gainers must also gain, since with respect to them alone inequality has been reduced rather than increased. There is no epistemic threat in that segment of the distribution.) Thus, we will assume that:

Gains Must Be Shared Downward: Any less equal distribution is epistemically inferior unless gains are shared downward. (In that case it still depends on whether the inequality is too great.)

Inequality can be produced or increased either by some getting disproportionately more than before, or by some getting disproportionately less, or both. When some get disproportionately more, we have just said that this is epistemically inferior unless the gains are shared downward. If inequality is produced or increased solely by some getting disproportionately less than before, then this both increases inequality and reduces the quantity, so this is always epistemically inferior. Suppose some get less and some get more, with the total quantity and inequality increasing. Here the gains are not shared downward, and therefore the result is epistemically inferior.

These considerations lead to the following notable principle:

Epistemic Difference Principle: No deviation from strict equality is epistemically superior unless everyone gains input.

We can see this as follows: First, no distribution can epistemically top equality unless it is a higher quantity (Epistemic Value of Equality). But from strict equality, any increase in the quantity in which increases are shared downward (as required by the principle that Gains Must Be Shared Downward) must increase the input for all, which gives us the Epistemic Difference Principle.

Since I am criticizing political egalitarianism, it makes sense to let any errors work to the advantage of equality. Again, the Epistemic Difference Principle (and the assumptions from which it follows) may give too much epistemic weight to equality, but this will not harm my eventual conclusion that inequality of input will still often be justified.[37]

Clearly, a defense of inequality on epistemic grounds will rest on the possibility of (strongly) politically Pareto-superior cases, where equality would reduce everyone's absolute level of input. Keep in mind that strongly Pareto-superior options will not be sufficient for epistemic gain, since this depends on the degree of inequality involved and the unknown epistemic compensation factor.

Is more better?

Even theorists who acknowledge the epistemic value of political deliberation often argue that, above a certain quantity of input, there is little or no epistemic value in having more. Ronald Dworkin argues that current levels of political campaign advertising in the U.S. could easily be cut (by stronger contribution or spending limits) in the interest of fairness, without damaging the epistemic quality of the process, since current advertising is often repetitive and negative. "Such limits [would not] seriously risk keeping from the public any argument or information it would otherwise have."[38] Obviously the same could not be said if existing levels of spending were already very low, and thus Dworkin implicitly grants that, up to a point, more campaign speech tends to be epistemically better.

I am granting for the sake of argument that any increase in equality that does not lower everyone's level of input is an epistemic gain (from the

Epistemic Difference Principle), but this is a way of assuming an epistemic value of equality strong enough to offset the epistemic damage of the lost speech. Dworkin's argument is different. He doubts that, at current levels, speech that would be lost by limiting spending has any epistemic value in the first place, and so there is little or no loss to offset. If correct, his arguments would call into question my assumption of the Epistemic Value of Quantity: that at a given level of inequality, more input is epistemically better. The arguments, though, are not persuasive.

First, the repetitive and negative nature of campaign discourse (assuming it to be so) by itself hardly damns it as epistemically worthless. The educative power of current campaign advertising is an empirical matter, with a number of studies suggesting that Dworkin's speculation is mistaken and that such advertising adds to the information and understanding of the electorate.[39] Common sense also suggests that repetition of facts, ideas, and reasons can be an important component of learning of all kinds, and that "negative" claims about opponents can be valuable and informative even if some different mix of negative and positive claims would be even better. Simply eliminating some mostly negative ads might very well be an epistemic loss.[40]

Second, even if some portion of current speech by big-spending campaigns were epistemically worthless, Dworkin seems to conclude that trimming the big campaigns back to the level of approximate parity with the smallest campaigns would still not entail great epistemic losses. This is certainly less likely to be true, and depends a great deal on how much cutting would be required. Bill Clinton and Bob Dole might produce little epistemic bang for the marginal buck at their high levels of spending; but we cannot conclude, and it seems clearly false, that little would be lost if they were only allowed to spend roughly as much as was available to, say, Ralph Nader. The epistemic cost of equalizing expenditures downward cannot be easily dismissed, though of course this leaves open the possibility that the epistemic value of the increased equality of input might offset the epistemic cost of the lost quantity. Indeed, the Epistemic Difference Principle could probably not condone the present vastly unequal distributions of input that Dworkin is criticizing; but he is too dismissive of the epistemic costs of *equalizing*, and is led to an implausibly strong political egalitarianism.[41]

Finally, it must be acknowledged, if only speculatively, that there are a number of ways that higher levels of input might damage the epistemic value of discussion. Perhaps at high levels of input, campaigning gets negative. Perhaps it gets increasingly repetitive. Perhaps these or other features of discussion at high levels of input drive away voters. Perhaps the more people hear, the more confused they get. Perhaps the more people argue, the more intransigent they get. Even if some of these are true, though, the main conclusions of this essay would continue to apply at quantities of input below these turning points. And even if these effects were known to be genuine in principle, it would often be very difficult to know whether any actual level of input approached the turning point in question. But I must leave the matter here.

In general, the sorry state of present campaign discourse does not support in any simple way the proposition that the quantity could be reduced by imposing spending limits without doing damage to the epistemic value of the process. It may well be that at high levels of spending the epistemic value of the marginal campaign dollar is too low to be epistemically worth the inequality it causes, but that is not our question. The goal at this point is only a defense of the Epistemic Value of Quantity: the claim that at a fixed level of inequality of input, more input is epistemically better. For reasons like Dworkin's, some may doubt that this is true for the combination of high levels of spending and high levels of inequality. But the doubts are not well founded.

If equality and quantity serve quality in something like the way I have assumed, then some inequality could be justified as a part of an arrangement that promotes quantity and thereby promotes the expected quality of decisions. I turn now, in the next two sections, to whether circumstances favoring inequality on these grounds could actually occur.

IV. An Incentive Argument for Political Inequality

Consider a case where inequality has been introduced but the quantity of input has been increased enough to epistemically offset the inequality. Why distribute the extra quantity unequally? The Epistemic Value of Equality tells us that distributing that same new quantity of input equally would be epistemically even better, so why not do that? If you do not distribute input unequally, you will not need to epistemically compensate for it with quantity, says an important objection.

Under some circumstances, though, a higher quantity is impossible without diverging from equality. Suppose, for example, that input is currently equal, but that no more resources are forthcoming so long as the distribution remains equal. Some citizens are willing to produce more input (say, through money contributions) but only if they get more of this input than others and it is not simply redistributed equally. Thus, the quantity can be increased, but only at the cost of introducing inequality. The higher quantity would indeed produce even more epistemic value if it were distributed equally rather than unequally, but unless it is distributed unequally in a certain way it will not be produced in the first place. One natural explanation would be that those who could produce more input will not do it without special incentives. Let us call this the *incentive argument for unequal input*.

The parallel with disputes about the application of Rawls's difference principle is striking, but limited. Rawls holds that (roughly)[42] economic inequality is not justified unless it benefits the least well-off, and calls this the difference principle. He considers the possibility that certain schemes of inequality might be required to provide incentives for talented people to be more socially productive. If so, and if this extra productivity redounds to the benefit of the least well-off, then the inequality would be justified. Many believe that this is indeed the case and that it justifies wide economic inequalities, though Rawls is noncommittal on this empirical question. This *incentive argument for inequality* and the incentive argument for unequal input are similar.

There are differences, however. In Rawls's theory, equality and efficiency compete as moral values of a basic social structure. It is not that inequality causally limits productivity; rather, equality (in the form of the difference principle) is a moral constraint on productivity. In our case, the overriding value is the epistemic value of the procedure (in terms that are beyond reasonable objection). Equality of political input is not placed as a moral constraint on maximizing epistemic value or increasing the quantity of input. Inequality itself (so we are assuming) damages epistemic value. Epistemic value is what establishes the tension between quantity and inequality, and not any independent moral value of an equal distribution.[43]

What is the highest equal level?

The incentive argument shows how it may not be possible to take the gains from a political Pareto-improvement, and have them distributed so as to preserve equality of influence. The gains may not be produced but for the incentives provided by the unequal distribution. For example, some people might contribute a great deal to the political process only if the money buys them a certain amount of input that cannot be supplied to everyone. The highest possible equal level of input might be lower than the levels that can be provided to all under certain unequal schemes of distribution. Before illustrating this with an imaginary voucher scheme, notice that the idea of the highest possible equal level could mean several different things. It is important to be clear which one is in question when I claim that there can be political Pareto-improvements over the highest equal level.

One thing the highest possible equal level might mean is the *de facto* highest possible level: the highest equal level that is possible given the attitudes and motives that people actually have, justifiably or not. This concept will not suit our purposes, since it may only be due to some people's injustice that some higher equal level cannot be achieved. In that case, the inequality that is needed in order to surpass that *de facto* highest equal level is not entirely just, but represents a capitulation to some unreasonable citizens in order to do the best that can be done under unjust circumstances.

A more appropriate idea of the maximum equal level of input is the highest equal level of input that could be achieved while neither capitulating to any citizen's unjust motives, nor demanding more of citizens than is required by the idea of a fully just society. We might call this the *de jure* equal maximum, but for brevity I will simply call this, the pertinent concept of the equal maximum, *E-max*.

Whatever the epistemic value of E-max, we know that there are logically possible unequal distributions that would be epistemically superior. This is because any given level of inequality, while doing some epistemic damage, can occur at a high enough level of input to have compensating epistemic advantages (see the Epistemic Value of Quantity assumption in Section III). We ought to ask, then, is there a causally possible distribution of input that is unequal but epistemically superior to E-max? If so, we might provisionally suppose that this inequality of input will be at least permitted and perhaps required, keeping in mind that formal political equality is guaranteed.

Next, we will consider a scenario for such epistemic improvements over E-max using an application of the incentive argument for unequal input.

V. How Could Unequal Political Influence Increase Input for All?

Having granted considerable epistemic weight to more equal distributions of input, the fact remains that inequality may yet be called for on epistemic grounds, so long as it is politically Pareto-superior and not too unequal. In this section I argue that this is more than a mere logical possibility.

Suppose a society is supporting elections at the level of E-max[44] – equal available input at the highest level compatible with equality, given citizens' permissible (e.g., not unjust) motives. We know that there are logically possible unequal distributions of input that are epistemically superior to

E-max. Some of these may not even require political Pareto-improvements; but to give lots of weight to the epistemic value of equality, for the sake of argument we are assuming that no departure from equal input is epistemically superior unless it is politically Pareto-superior – that is, unless it gives everyone more input. (See the Epistemic Difference Principle discussed above.)

I want to sketch a simple voucher scheme that represents one way such improvements may actually be induced. My goal here is not to solve the many logistical problems involved in implementing such a scheme but to present a basic causal mechanism that appears to have this potential. It is important to keep in mind that the inequalities introduced may be so great as to cancel the epistemic advantage of the increased quantity. However, we can see that the inequalities might sometimes be very modest, and that this general strategy admits of many variations, some of which might be able to do even better than my examples.

Progressive Vouchers

Assume that a society supports elections at the level of E-max. Now allow additional expenditures through and only through government-supplied vouchers. These have a cash value when contributed to certain political endeavors such as election campaigns, and no value otherwise. Each next or marginal voucher a person buys costs more than the previous, but has only the same value as the last. The cash value of the voucher is then paid, by the administering agency, to the campaign that receives the voucher from a citizen. But the purchase price was more than this, and the extra amount retained by the agency goes into a fund that is used to subsidize the price of vouchers, making them more affordable. This subsidy can be structured in countless ways, and I will sketch only one, which I will call the Singular Voucher version of Progressive Vouchers:[45] suppose the money in the fund is distributed among all those who are happy to receive only their one government-supplied voucher (call this the Singular Voucher). These Singular Vouchers are available for free, or if it seems wise to charge some fee, to avoid frivolous uses, then they are cheap. Their value is determined by the size of the fund and the number of people who want the Singular Voucher. Anyone who wants to contribute more than the Singular Voucher will have to purchase Progressive Vouchers and may not receive a Singular Voucher. This will become clearer with the examples provided below. But first some general points.

If we assume that some citizens would pay more than the cash value for Progressive Vouchers if this were the only way to have additional political input, then this will raise money to pay for Singular Vouchers that are free or very cheap for anyone who wants one. The result would be a politically Pareto-superior distribution of political input. In presenting examples, I will simplify in several ways: (1) I will assume that it is known (say, by experience) how many vouchers will be purchased by how many people. This avoids temporal and strategic complications about setting prices and values of the vouchers. (2) I will consider possible purchase patterns in a pretty arbitrary and speculative way without any argumentative support. My purpose is illustrative, and therefore I only need the examples to be plausible enough to warrant further study and refinement by economists, political scientists, and others. (3) I ignore any administrative or transaction costs. (4) I assume that all available input is actually employed.[46]

Consider a community of 200,000 voters, the size of a small city such as Providence, Rhode Island. Suppose that the maximum equal level of contribution would be $5 per voter per election cycle, yielding a total expenditure of $1,000,000. Now suppose we allow vouchers in addition. Let each Progressive Voucher have a value (redeemable by campaigns) of $50, but remember that each one (beyond the first) will cost more than this. To buy one costs $50; to buy a second costs $87.50; a third, $153.13; a fourth, $267.97; and the fifth and final permissible voucher costs $468.95. (The marginal rate of increase is 75 percent, but this can easily be varied for other scenarios.) Alternatively, suppose citizens may buy more vouchers at correspondingly higher prices, but no one does. (This difference matters for First Amendment purposes discussed below.) Each voucher is still worth only $50, but people who can afford it and want to have more political input may well pay more than the cash value; indeed, the cash value has nothing to do with what a voucher will be worth to a citizen. Nevertheless, I will assume in this example that not many citizens will buy many of these increasingly expensive vouchers.[47] Suppose that only 5 percent of voters buy any progressive vouchers: 1 percent buy one; 1 percent buy two; 1 percent buy three; 1 percent buy four; and 1 percent buy all five. Buying all five costs $1,027.55, but a person's input is only $50 times the number of Progressive Vouchers she buys and uses, in this case $250, plus the amount that was already being spent under E-max, or $5. The total input for the maximum spender under these assumptions is $255. Rounded to the nearest dollar, these purchases build up a fund of $2,628,560. Dividing this into a free or cheap Singular Voucher for every voter who chose not to purchase Progressive Vouchers (95 percent of all voters) yields a Singular Voucher worth about $14. I assume for simplicity that all remaining voters receive and use a Singular Voucher (though if not, these vouchers can be worth more).[48] What is the result of this arrangement?

First, there is a Pareto-superior distribution of political input. Whereas before no voter contributed more than $5 to political campaigns, now no one contributes less than $19 since no one is without the $14 voucher. Second, we have introduced inequality of input. The vast majority are contributing at a value of $19, and a few at a value of $255, and some in between. The input of the highest contributors is about thirteen times that of the lowest; on the other hand, a campaign can get as much by winning over a small coffee meeting of thirteen of the poorest voters as it can by wooing any single fat cat. Third, since the distribution is Pareto-superior, the total contribution is also greater. It has gone from $1,000,000 to $5,128,560 – more than quintupled.[49] This greater quantity, we are assuming, has positive consequences for the epistemic value of the process, at least under favorable conditions, and so long as it is not too unequally distributed among participants.

The degree of inequality is certainly minuscule by the standard of actually existing politics in the U.S.,[50] and the increase in the total (with political Pareto-superiority) is enormous by any standard. We have no basis for saying that there is, or is not, a net epistemic gain, but this should be enough to suggest that the general strategy of Progressive Vouchers may offer a way of combining the epistemic values of the quantity of input and of equal distribution in a way that political egalitarianism cannot. Political egalitarianism would have mandated the E-max level of $5 per person for a total of $1,000,000 of input, forgoing the additional $4.1 million of input that could be induced if a certain (modest?) amount of inequality (with no invidious comparisons) were acceptable.[51]

Patriot versus Progressive Vouchers

Bruce Ackerman has proposed a different kind of voucher plan to reform campaign financing.[52] Under the Patriot plan each eligible voter would be given a voucher worth, say, $10 which could be spent only on political campaigns, while contributions of regular money would be prohibited. In one stroke this would equalize the availability of a major means of political input. Ackerman, like few others, takes the overall quantity of political speech very seriously. He recognizes that if equality comes at the cost of quantity, it is not an easy choice. However, his proposal fails to face that difficult trade-off. At the $10 level, Ackerman argues that (assuming most or all of the vouchers are spent – a simplification I join him in) aggregate political spending would go up compared to current levels. The more difficult question comes when it is recognized that there must be a maximum level to this equal voucher: maybe it is $5; maybe it is $20.

Whatever the equal maximum, or E-max as I have called it, we must ask whether it is worth insisting on equality even if modest inequality could increase aggregate spending dramatically. This is a question Ackerman asks ("Do we really want equality at the cost of shutting down debate?")[53] but does not answer, since he fails to recognize the potential for aggregate increases over the levels provided by his equalized Patriot vouchers.

Ackerman's proposal is apparently to be funded by taxes. We might think about where the highest level of Patriot funding (E-max) lies by considering the following question: Assuming citizens were properly just and public-spirited, how high a tax should they institute in order to pay for Patriot vouchers? (I leave aside the real political challenges under less ideal circumstances.) There is, I assume, no limit to the epistemic value of bigger vouchers (from the principle of Epistemic Value of Quantity), but there must be a limit on how much should be raised for this purpose through taxes. For example, suppose, in a crude model, that there is a limit to how much a citizen should be required to pay in taxes (assume a "progressive" structure of higher rates for wealthier citizens).[54] Add to this all the other important uses for tax money, and Patriot vouchers find themselves with a limited piece of a limited pie, even where the limits are not due to anyone's unjust stinginess or distorted priorities. Ackerman may be right that this would still support aggregate spending that is greater than current levels, though he does not give any argument for that conclusion. In any case, my main point does not depend on challenging that claim. For even if it is correct, there is the question of the potential further aggregate increases that would be allowed by a properly structured incentive scheme such as Progressive Vouchers. If more debate is as important as Ackerman says, then it may be worth accepting some inequality in order to promote it. My aim is to explore under what conditions this might be so.

Free speech implications

This is not the place to fully consider the constitutional questions raised by a scheme like Progressive Vouchers. In the United States, campaign finance reform has recently faced First Amendment obstacles stemming from the important role that campaign contributions and expenditures have in citizens' expression of political views. There remains a wide range of informed opinion about what regulations would be constitutionally permissible. Progressive Vouchers have some advantages in this connection, and I limit myself to briefly laying them out. Comparison with Ackerman's Patriot plan will help illustrate the main points.

The decision in *Buckley v. Valeo* asserted that "the concept that government may restrict the speech of some elements of our society in order to enhance the relative voice of others is wholly foreign to the First Amendment."[55] The Court showed no reservations about public subsidies or "floors." Given the Court's formulation, it is unclear whether its objection was to (a) reduction in the *quantity* of speech, (b) *prohibition* of speech above a certain financial level, (c) a *leveling* motive behind the regulation, or some mix of these. Consider the Progressive Voucher idea in light of these three possible concerns.

First, the Progressive Voucher idea is designed to increase the aggregate quantity of political spending over E-max; thus, if the egalitarian Patriot plan raises the quantity (as compared to current real-world spending), then so do Progressive Vouchers. On this assumption, there is no loss of quantity in either plan. Second, the method of regulation employed by Progressive Vouchers need not be a prohibition of any input at any level of expenditure. Rather, input is made progressively more expensive at higher quantities for a given contributor, but is permissible if paid for. The number of vouchers was limited to five in the earlier example for simplicity. It could equally well be unlimited. Third, it must be confessed that the argument is partly a leveling one, but not entirely. A separate motive is subsidy of political input. This is a motive that is above constitutional reproach (according to the *Buckley* Court), though that does not mean that it can be pursued in just any manner. The motive is to increase the quantity without too much inequality, and this is achieved without prohibiting speech at any level. If the *Buckley* decision precludes any regulation that has limiting inequality of influence as part of its aim, then Progressive Vouchers would be unconstitutional. But the *Buckley* opinion contains no language that requires that reading. The famous sentence rejecting "restrict[ing] the speech of some elements of our society in order to enhance the relative voice of others" might be meant only to apply to *restricting* speech, which may not include attaching certain taxes or surcharges to it on a viewpoint-neutral basis and without any aim of preventing any particular speech, or any effect of reducing the quantity of speech.

Ackerman's Patriot proposal shares with Progressive Vouchers a leveling motive, but a much more ambitious leveling is involved. In addition, the Patriot plan involves ceilings, outright restrictions prohibiting spending beyond the level of the fixed voucher everyone receives. The Patriot plan may not involve reductions in spending compared with current levels (this depends on what level would or should be supported by taxpayers), but it does forgo the additional quantity of spending that Progressive Vouchers could induce. Ackerman may be right that the Patriot plan is not constitutionally doomed, but from *Buckley*'s point of view Progressive Vouchers have important advantages over the political egalitarian scheme embodied in the Patriot plan. Progressive Vouchers have a stronger claim to promoting quantity of input; they involve no outright restrictions on spending; and their leveling ambition is far more modest and less central to their purpose. Progressive Vouchers are more likely than the Patriot plan to be compatible with the *Buckley* decision.

VI. Final Objections Considered

Why formal equality is preserved

The epistemic argument against political egalitarianism may seem difficult to contain. It is natural to suspect that an argument that places great importance on the epistemic value of the political process is bound, in the end, to recommend what we might call epistocracy: rule by the wise. But this is prevented by the liberal criterion of legitimacy; since the supposedly superior wisdom of any proposed epistocrat will be open to reasonable disagreement, no invidious comparison of that kind is available in a valid political justification. The argument against political egalitarianism permits an epistemic justification for inequality of political influence that does not make any such invidious comparisons.

But if inequality of political influence can be given a noninvidious justification, what is to stop similar arguments from condoning even formal, legal political inequality? In particular, mightn't there be ways of tinkering with the equal political liberties so as to improve the epistemic value of political procedures? If so, the epistemic argument would be led, embarrassingly, to recommend even unequal political rights and liberties under the law.

One way the embarrassment is avoided is by noticing how many possible violations of equal formal political liberties rely on invidious comparisons that are precluded by the liberal principle of legitimacy. Mill suggested that college graduates and certain others be given extra votes;[56] others might propose that Christians, or parents, or pet-owners are specially qualified to have extra influence as a matter of law. But none of these proposals is countenanced by an epistemic approach constrained by the liberal principle of legitimacy.

On the other hand, there are formal political inequalities that make no invidious comparison but, arguably, promote the epistemic value of the political process; but it is no embarrassment to endorse them. For example, members of the U.S. Senate and House of Representatives have more political power, as a matter of formal legal status, than other citizens. They are permitted to vote on momentous matters that you and I are not. One possible justification for the formal inequality involved in representative democracy is epistemic: having a small group of decision makers who can train and accumulate experience, and devote their full time to politics, serves the quality of the outcomes under the right conditions. If so, this is a good epistemic reason for formal political inequality of the most obvious kind, but one that makes no invidious comparison among groups of citizens.[57] No one is given extra political power on the basis of any supposedly greater wisdom or worth. People gain the extra political power of being a representative as a result of election, and the reasons for having a system of elected representatives to serve as legislators nowhere rely on invidious comparisons among citizens.[58]

Thus, the epistemic argument against political egalitarianism can be suitably contained. It is not led to endorse any erosion of formal political equality as it is normally understood.

VII. Conclusion

Insistence on equality of political input would preclude even modest inequalities that increase input for everyone. Under favorable conditions, a greater quantity of input improves the expected quality of political decisions; thus, we need a good reason if we are to stand in its way. It would be perfectly proper to object to inequality of influence if it were based on invidious comparisons among citizens. It may even be illegitimate to base such inequality on putative rights to liberty or property, though I have not considered that question here. But modest inequalities that significantly increase input for all without any implication of disrespect or controversial pre-political rights may be capable of improving the tendency of political decisions to be substantively just and proper in a way that it would be unreasonable to deny. If so, incentive structures such as Progressive Vouchers may be practical devices for pursuing this liberal epistemic conception of political equality.

Notes

I am grateful for useful discussions of this material with Reed Caster, Joshua Cohen, Norman Daniels, Gary Gates, Andy Hoffman, Andy Levine, Erin Kelly, the depart-

ment of Political Science at the University of Chicago, and the other contributors
[to this volume *of Social Philosophy and Policy*].

1   Some political egalitarians would not limit the view's scope in this way, but it
    simplifies matters to consider this narrower view. If it is not correct, then the
    broader version couldn't be either.
2   I describe an epistemic approach to democratic legitimacy called *epistemic pro-
    ceduralism* in my essay "Beyond Fairness and Deliberation: The Epistemic
    Dimension of Democratic Authority," in *Deliberative Democracy: Essays in
    Reason and Politics*, ed. James Bohman and William Rehg (Cambridge: MIT
    Press, 1997). I explain the pertinent idea of an independent standard there, and
    at greater length in "Making Truth Safe for Democracy," in *The Idea of Democ-
    racy*, ed. David Copp, Jean Hampton, and John Roemer (Cambridge: Cam-
    bridge University Press, 1993), 71–100.
3   My criticism of fair proceduralism in "Beyond Fairness and Deliberation"
    leaves the question of political egalitarianism open. Here I take it up directly.
4   On the distinction between justice and legitimacy in a liberal theory, see my
    essay "The Survival of Egalitarian Justice in John Rawls's *Political Liberalism*,"
    Journal of Political Philosophy 4, no. 1 (1996): 68–78.
5   Robert Dahl endorses political egalitarianism in *Democracy and Its Critics* (New
    Haven: Yale University Press, 1989), 109, 114–15. Joshua Cohen, in "Deliber-
    ation and Democratic Legitimacy," reprinted in Bohman and Rehg, eds., *Delib-
    erative Democracy*, sketches an "ideal deliberative procedure" which "is meant to
    provide a model for institutions to mirror" (73). One feature is that "the
    participants are substantively equal in that the existing distribution of power
    and resources does not shape their chances to contribute to deliberation..."
    (74). Cass Sunstein, in "Political Equality and Unintended Consequences,"
    Columbia Law Review 94 (1994): 1394, says: "Disparities in wealth ought not
    lead to disparities in power over government." Thomas Christiano writes:
    "Justice requires that individuals have political equality, that is, equal resources
    to influence decisions regarding the collective properties of society" (Christiano,
    The Rule of the Many [Boulder, CO: Westview Press, 1996], 87). Harry Brig-
    house advocates "equal availability of political influence," which "requires the
    insulation of the political process from [income and wealth] inequalities" (Brig-
    house, "Egalitarianism and Equal Availability of Political Influence," *Journal of
    Political Philosophy* 4, no. 2 [1996]: 120). Jack Knight and James Johnson
    ("What Sort of Political Equality Does Deliberative Democracy Require?" in
    Bohman and Rehg, eds., *Deliberative Democracy*) advocate "equal opportunity of
    access to political influence" (280), including "equality in the resources that any
    participant be allowed to employ in the deliberative process" (293). In addition,
    Rawls and Dworkin may be committed to versions of it; see notes 10 and 41,
    respectively. In criticizing political egalitarianism I do not expect to have fully
    refuted any of these authors, whose views differ in interesting ways from each
    other and from the simplified version of political egalitarianism that I discuss.

6   For quotations of several epistemic arguments used to disenfranchise the propertyless, blacks, and women, see Daniel Ortiz, "The Democratic Paradox of Campaign Finance Reform," *Stanford Law Review* 50 (February 1998): 906–9.

7   This label is meant only to name a view of political equality. I leave aside the question of the relation between this view and a more general libertarianism.

8   The difference principle states that inequalities can be justified if they benefit even the least well-off. See John Rawls, *A Theory of Justice* (Cambridge, MA: Harvard University Press, 1971), 302; and Rawls, *Political Liberalism* (New York: Columbia University Press, 1993), 56.

9   I will assume that where there is formal equality there is also full compliance.

10   Rawls stops short of insisting on perfect equality, but mentions approximately equal value of political liberties (*Political Liberalism*, 358). His name for this is "fair," not "equal," value, and this may reflect the view that equality is not the point. The challenge, then, as I see it, is to find a salient standard between merely formal equality and strictly equal substantive influence. It is not clear whether Rawls would include the fair value requirement of the first principle among the requirement of legitimacy, which is generally a lower standard than justice in Rawls's theory. (I discuss this in "The Survival of Egalitarian Justice in John Rawls's *Political Liberalism*.")

11   I am not making any assumptions about the particular nature of the discussion, or its civility, etc. Some of the literature on deliberative democracy revolves around implausible standards of politeness and reciprocity that I do not want to commit to here. Moreover, the term "discussion" is not meant to exclude nondiscursive contributions to public debate, such as protests or political art. There are important nondiscursive components of any discussion, including public political discussion.

12   See, e.g., Bruce Ackerman, "Crediting the Voters," *The American Prospect* 13 (Spring 1993): 71–80. I discuss Ackerman's view in more detail in Section V.

13   Rawls, *A Theory of Justice*, 78.

14   See Harry Brighouse, "Political Equality in Justice as Fairness," *Philosophical Studies* 86 (1997): 166–7.

15   By Pareto-superiority (political or not), I have in mind improvement in all positions in the distribution rather than effects on actual individuals. If two people switched places, so that one was worse off and the other better off, this would not yet count as a change at all from the perspective I want to consider. One distribution is Pareto-superior to the other if their graph lines flowing from lowest holdings to highest never cross, though they may touch (except in the case of strong Pareto-superiority).

16   One well-known competitive good structure is the "zero-sum game." But that is a special case. Competitive goods need not have a "zero" or fixed sum.

17   I address this simplification below, in a subsection titled "Input as money."

18   See the discussion below in Section V.

19 Of course, it would be unfair to formally give the two sides different time limits. But suppose both were allowed sixty minutes, but one side lacked leisure or strength enough to go beyond fifty minutes.

20 For some purposes, it is useful to distinguish between this general instrumental value, and a specifically epistemic route to it, e.g., via reasoning, knowledge, understanding, etc. This distinction is not important here.

21 Rawls, *Political Liberalism*, 137.

22 See my "Making Truth Safe." As William Galston and Steven Wall pointed out to me, citizens who reject the public conception of justice that I hold proper voting to address are very unlikely to promote it through their votes (whatever the value of their political speech), and this could be agreed upon by all reasonable citizens. This is because reasonable citizens all accept the conception. Thus, there is some uncomfortable pressure on my theory to disenfranchise those who reject the conception, or to weight their votes more lightly for legitimate epistemic reasons. There are several lines of reply worth considering, but here I will mention only that if, as I believe, the public conception of justice will consist in rather abstract principles that do not have straightforward practical consequences without interpretation, there may be no method that is beyond reasonable objection for identifying those who reject the conception.

23 There are complications. Certainly some bureaucratic or representative positions, e.g., entail greater power. The rule against invidious comparisons does not preclude hiring or electing the best-qualified applicants for such positions. But this would not be *basic* inequality so long as the position and its power and the hiring criteria are authorized, at least indirectly, by a legitimate democratic process that relies on no invidious comparisons.

24 Rawls holds that the fair value of the political liberties "is essential in order to establish just legislation" (*Political Liberalism*, 330).

25 Brighouse, "Egalitarianism," 123; Thomas Christiano, "The Significance of Public Deliberation," in *Deliberative Democracy*, ed. Bohman and Rehg, 256.

26 Christiano, "The Significance of Public Deliberation," 341.

27 Estlund, "Beyond Fairness and Deliberation."

28 We might distinguish between fairness to participants and fairness to candidates or potential beneficiaries. I am discussing fairness to participants.

29 Rawls, *A Theory of Justice*; Thomas Scanlon, "Contractualism and Utilitarianism," in *Utilitarianism and Beyond*, ed. Amartya Sen and Bernard Williams (Cambridge: Cambridge University Press, 1982); Charles Beitz, *Political Equality* (Princeton: Princeton University Press, 1989), esp. ch. 5.

30 Sidney Verba, Kay Lehman Schlozman, and Henry E. Brady, *Voice and Equality* (Cambridge, MA: Harvard University Press, 1995).

31 Christiano (in "The Significance of Public Deliberation") explores the epistemic basis of political egalitarianism in addition to fair proceduralism. "[E]quality in the process of democratic discussion . . . improves the quality of the outcomes of democratic decision making" (256). Since Christiano

advocates equal *access* rather than equal actual input (253), it is not entirely clear how his approach would have epistemic advantages.

32   By a more equal distribution, I shall mean as measured by the so-called Gini coefficient (a measure of inequality sometimes used by economists). There are various alternative measures, some more appropriate than others for different purposes, but the Gini measure is simple and has no significant disadvantages that I know of for our purposes. The choice between various measures will not matter for my main points, and readers can safely proceed with only an intuitive idea of greater or lesser distributed equality. See Larry S. Temkin, *Inequality* (Oxford: Oxford University Press, 1993), ch. 5, for a critical discussion of several alternative measures of inequality; see esp. p. 129f. for a discussion of the Gini coefficient.

33   See the discussion below in the subsection entitled "Is more better?"

34   Increased quantity at a constant level of Gini inequality (see note 32 above) may seem to guarantee political Pareto-improvement, but it does not. Here is one category of counterexample: Consider a distribution, call it *Distribution 1* among ten people. Suppose the bottom person has 0 units of input and the top person has 1,000, and each of the middle eight people has 50. Gini inequality rounds to .58, and the total is 1,400. Now the level of inequality can be maintained even through a Pareto loss, as follows: reduce the middle eight to 48 each (the Pareto loss), but raise the bottom person to 40.8 and the top person to 1,200. This is *Distribution 2*. This also rounds to Gini = .58 (and the remaining difference can be completely expunged by precisely tinkering with the numbers, but I am keeping it simple here). But the total has gone up to 1,424.8. Distribution 2 has a Gini-constant increased quantity, but is not Pareto-superior to Distribution 1.

35   One very simple way to model the decreasing epistemic value of input is to suppose that, so long as the level of inequality is kept constant, a given extra unit of input produces an epistemic increase that is some constant fraction of the gap between the *ex ante* epistemic value and infallibility. So, for example, each extra unit of input (suppose this is some amount of money spent) might get you 10 percent of the remaining way toward infallibility. The next unit gets you 10 percent of the remaining way, which is less progress than the first unit. Any value for the marginal unit (e.g., \$1, \$1,000), and any constant setting of this fraction of the gap (1 percent, 20 percent), will allow increasing quantities to converge on infallibility. I will proceed on the assumption that the marginal epistemic value of input at a given level of inequality has this structure. This says nothing about how fast an extra unit of input increases epistemic value, since this can be set very low or very high consistent with my assumption.

> *Decreasing Marginal Epistemic Value of Input*: Assuming inequality stays the same, then for any quantity, and any epistemic value, there is some constant fraction F, such that a unit of extra input moves the epistemic value of the scheme forward by removing that fraction F of the gap to infallibility.

This assumption is one way of representing the intuitive thought that quantity improves epistemic value, other things being equal. I offer no argument for placing no limit on this improvement short of infallibility, though this seems the simpler position in the absence of any reason to believe there are more severe limits. A weaker claim, placing such limits, would probably be sufficient for practical purposes, but it is difficult to know *which* weaker claim. With this in place, we are entitled to our assumption that quantity compensates inequality.

One odd feature of this model is that it is oblivious to the *ex ante* level of input, but notices only the *ex ante* epistemic value. In one scenario, then, the total input might be $1 million with an epistemic value of .5. Another scenario might find total input at $100 and an epistemic value of .5. If $1,000 moves a distribution 10 percent of the way toward infallibility, it would do this in both cases. This might seem to ignore the apparently greater epistemic value of each unit of input in the latter scenario, which has the same epistemic value as the former but with less input. I leave these complexities aside, but perhaps a more refined model should take account of them.

36 See note 35.

37 If the left-out group is very small, we could increase inequality only a little, increase quantity a lot, and still fail to share downward. Is it plausible to say this does more harm than good? What if only one person out of a million is left out of the increase? Here we should allow that the quantity probably outweighs the inequality. We can avoid this problem if we limit our purview to changes that affect groups that make up a substantial fraction of the whole. Then leaving one group out of an inequality-increasing input increase will raise inequality significantly so long as the quantity is increased significantly. Let us also assume that we mean no more here by social groups than groupings according to amount of political input. So the membership of, for example, the lowest group can change. If two sets of people were to end up with completely exchanged levels of input (set A now has as much input as set B had, and vice versa), the distribution of input would not have changed for present purposes.

38 Ronald Dworkin, "The Curse of American Politics," *New York Review of Books*, October 17, 1996, 21.

39 See, for example, Stephen Ansolabehere and Shanto Iyengar, *Going Negative* (New York: Free Press, 1997): "As we have shown in several chapters of this book, television actually fosters the democratic ideals of an informed and reasoning electorate" (145). Their worries about political advertising lie elsewhere.

40 Ansolabehere and Iyengar also argue (in *Going Negative*) that negative campaigning drives voters away from the polls. This might itself have epistemic disvalue to be weighed against the value of the information provided. But this is not a point specially about high levels of campaign spending, unless for some reason high levels of spending increase negativity. And even then, in order to

suppose that limits could be imposed without epistemic loss, it would need to be shown that the bad epistemic effects of the marginal speech outweigh the good.

41   Dworkin is not explicit about how much equality of influence should be sought through campaign finance regulations or other means. But he does say: "Each citizen must have a fair and reasonably equal opportunity... to command attention for his own views" (Dworkin, "The Curse of American Politics," 23).

42   I say "roughly" because he concentrates on primary goods, which are not limited to what is usually understood as economic matters.

43   The similarities between these two incentive arguments for inequality are sufficient, however, to force us to answer an important objection advanced by G. A. Cohen. Cohen argues that it is not clear that a proper citizen in a fully just society could have the motives that the incentive argument assumes. He wonders what would justify a citizen's holding out for more pay than others when he or she is capable of doing the work without it. Cohen has developed this criticism in a series of essays, including "Incentives, Inequality, and Community," in *The Tanner Lectures on Human Values*, vol. 13, ed. G. Peterson (Salt Lake City: University of Utah Press, 1992), 263–329; "The Pareto Argument for Inequality," in *Contemporary Political and Social Philosophy*, ed. Ellen Frankel Paul, Fred D. Miller, Jr., and Jeffrey Paul (Cambridge: Cambridge University Press, 1995), 160–85; and "Where the Action Is: On the Site of Distributive Justice," *Philosophy and Public Affairs* 26, no. 1 (Winter 1997): 3–30. I have defended Rawlsian inequality against Cohen's arguments in "Liberalism, Equality, and Fraternity in Cohen's Critique of Rawls," *Journal of Political Philosophy* 6, no. 1 (March 1998): 99–112, and those arguments apply fairly directly here as well.

44   For example, suppose Ackerman's Patriot plan (discussed below, in Section V) is already in effect at the maximum equal level.

45   The name "Progressive Vouchers" might connote three relevant things: that the voucher plan promotes quantity of input in a politically Pareto-superior way; that it promotes quality of decisions by independent standards of, e.g., justice; and that it involves progressive rates for marginal vouchers.

46   The Progressive Voucher plan suggests that it is possible to epistemically improve upon an equal distribution of actual input. However, political egalitarianism, the egalitarian alternative we are considering, advocates an equal distribution of availability of, or opportunity for, input, not an equal distribution of actual input. Even if Progressive Vouchers can epistemically beat E-max, which involves equal input, can it beat the pattern of actual input that would emerge under equal availability of input?

The epistemic value of democracy under political egalitarianism depends upon the level and distribution of actual input, even though what it seeks to equalize is availability of input. Since Progressive Vouchers can beat the epistemic value of E-max, the highest level of equal actual input, then it would suffice to show that E-max epistemically beats actual patterns of input under political egalitarianism. This is easily shown, and derives from the fact that a scheme of equally available input has no tendency to allow a greater quantity of input than would be present under E-max. In that case, since the distribution of this lower or equal quantity will be a less equal distribution than E-max, which is exactly equal, then by the principle of Epistemic Value of Equality, the epistemic value under political egalitarianism will be less than that under E-max. Therefore, if, as I claim, a Progressive Voucher program can epistemically beat E-max, it can also beat political egalitarianism.

47 This grants something congenial to opponents of my thesis. If more bought vouchers, it would simply mean that my conclusion would follow more easily.

48 As Ackerman points out, vouchers can be spent with no opportunity cost, unlike ordinary contributions of money. This fact should vastly increase participation. Still, full spending of the vouchers is an unrealistic assumption made to simplify the model.

49 This $5,128,560 figure is arrived at by adding to the original $1 million (from E-max) the proceeds from the sale of vouchers. Two thousand voters pay at each of the following five levels: $50 for one voucher, $137.50 ($50 plus $87.50) for two vouchers, $290.63 for three vouchers, $558.60 for four vouchers, and $1,027.55 for five vouchers. Rounding to the nearest dollar, this yields $4,128,560, which, added to the $1 million from E-max, gives us a total of $5,128,560.

50 Only about 8 percent of eligible voters contribute any money to political campaigns. See Warren E. Miller, and the National Election Studies, *American National Election Studies Cumulative Data File, 1952–1992* (computer file), 6th release (Ann Arbor, MI: University of Michigan, Center for Political Studies [producer], 1994; Ann Arbor, MI: Inter-University Consortium for Political and Social Research [distributor], 1991).

51 It might seem useful to know the Gini index for any such set of data. But no single Gini level can be assumed to be epistemically too much or too little. It follows from the Compensation of Quantity for Inequality assumption that higher levels of Gini inequality are epistemically acceptable at sufficiently higher quantities.

52 Ackerman, "Crediting the Voters."

53 Ibid., 72.

54 Note the political problem of the wealthier being required by law to transfer resources to the less wealthy in order to subsidize political activity that may well be antithetical to their interests. But this may be just, and thus so I will not harp on the fact that my Progressive Voucher plan would avoid this political problem.

55 *Buckley v. Valeo*, 424 U.S. 1, 48–9 (1976).

56 John Stuart Mill, *Representative Government* (New York: E. P. Dutton and Co., 1950), ch. 8.

57 Political egalitarianism apparently cannot account for this kind of inequality.

58   For a more difficult case, suppose it could be established beyond reasonable dispute that the quality of political decisions would be enhanced by selecting a small number of voters from the millions who register, and depriving all others of voting privileges. I do not think this has much plausibility, but suppose it were true. Giving only a few adult citizens the right to vote must be reckoned a version of formal political inequality. Now if the voting citizens were selected according to whether they were college-educated, or Christians, or pet-owners, and if this were done on the hypothesis that members of these groups were likely to make better decisions, or more fully deserved the power to vote than others, then the scheme would be utterly illegitimate. But if instead they were chosen randomly, and this still were reliably shown to have advantages for the quality of political decisions, it is no longer clear that the formal political inequality is objectionable. In truth, such a scheme would probably do more epistemic harm than good; but if it had overriding epistemic advantages, implementing it would not express disrespect for anyone.

8

Difference as a Resource for Democratic Communication

Iris Young

Recently, certain liberal and New Left writers have charged the politics of difference with bringing democracy to a new crisis. By a "politics of difference" I mean social movements that make a political claim that groups suffer oppression or disadvantage on account of cultural or structural social positions with which they are associated. To combat dominant stereotypes that construct members of such groups as despised and devalued Others, these movements have expressed uniquely situated understandings of members of society as arising from their group position. The perspectives of privileged and powerful groups tend to dominate public discourse and policy, these movements have asserted, and continue to exclude and marginalize others even when law and public rhetoric state a commitment to equality. The only remedies for these disadvantages and exclusions, according to these movements, require attending to the specific situations of differentiated social groups in politics and policy.

According to the critics, such assertion of group specificity has issued in nothing but confrontation and separation, resulting in the evacuation of the public space of coalition and cooperation. In the words of Todd Gitlin, the politics of difference is "a very bad turn, a detour into quicksand,"[1] and we had better pull ourselves out and get back on the main road of general citizenship and the common good.

Critics such as Gitlin and Jean Elshtain interpret the politics of difference as identity politics. According to these critics, the politics of difference encourages people to give primary loyalty to identity groups rigidly opposed to one another, instead of committing themselves to a common polity that transcends the groups. People claim a victim status for these identities, and thus claim special rights for themselves without accepting any parallel responsibilities. The politics of difference produces a backlash, when those who previously thought of themselves as just "people" go looking for their group identities and then claim their own special rights. A cacophony of particular claims for recognition and redress soon fills the public sphere, and in disgust people turn away from public exchange and discussion as a means for solving problems cooperatively. So says Jean Elshtain:

> To the extent that citizens begin to retribalize into ethnic or other "fixed identity" groups, democracy falters. Any possibility for human dialogue, for democratic communication and commonality, vanishes as so much froth on the polluted sea of phony equality. Difference becomes more and more exclusivist. If you are black and I am white, by definition I do not and cannot in principle "get it." There is no way that we can negotiate the space between our given differences. We are just stuck with them in what political theorists used to call "ascriptive characteristics" – things we cannot change about ourselves. Mired in the cement of our own identities, we need never deal with one another. Not really. One of us will win and one of us will lose the cultural war or the political struggle. That's what it's all about: power in the most reductive, impositional sort.[2]

Thus these critics also reduce the politics of difference to the most crass form of interest-group politics in which people simply compete to get the most for themselves. This interest-group politics precludes discussion and exchange where people revise their claims in response to criticism and aim to reach a solution acceptable to all. For the critics, the politics of difference understood as identity politics removes both the motivation and the capacity for citizens to talk to one another and solve problems together.

Doubtless feminists, multiculturalists, and activists for gay liberation, indigenous peoples, people of color, migrants, and people with disabilities have sometimes been overly separatist, essentialist, and inward looking in their promotion of group specificity and its political claims. Attributing such excesses to the movements as a whole or to the very logic of their existence, however, and laying in their lap responsibility for an alleged crisis of democracy, in my view, greatly misrepresents their meaning. Regression and repression are the likely outcomes of a political position that dismisses these movements as a gross error, and seeks a renewed commitment to a mythic neutral state, national unity, and the proposition that we are all just human, simply individuals, and that social, cultural and economic differences among us should be ignored in politics.

In this essay I argue against the identification of a politics of difference with a politics of identity. Group differentiation is best understood as a function of structural relations rather than constituted from some common attributes or dispositions of group members. A relational interpretation of difference conceives groups less rigidly and exclusively, as more open and fluid. Individuals are not positioned as social group members because they have common identities or interests, I argue, that distinguish them entirely from others. Instead the social positioning of group differentiation gives to individuals some shared *perspectives* on social life.

The idea that social perspective arises from group differentiation, I argue, contrary to the critics, helps us think of difference as a necessary resource for a discussion-based politics in which participants aim to cooperate, reach understanding, and do justice. Aiming to do justice through democratic public processes, I suggest, entails at least two things. First, democratic discussion and decision making must include all social perspectives. Second, participants in the discussion must develop a more comprehensive and objective account of the social relations, consequences of action, and relative advantage and disadvantage, than each begins with from their partial social perspective. Neither of these conditions can occur without communication across group-differentiated perspectives. Properly understood, then, and under conditions of mutual commitment to public discussion that aims to solve collective problems, expression of and attention to social group differentiation is an important resource for democratic communication.

I. Dilemmas of Difference

Some critics of group differentiated politics write as though racial, ethnic, class, or gender conflict would not exist if it were not for the corresponding movements. Such attitudes reverse the causal story. These movements have arisen in response to experiences of oppression and disadvantage that are attached to group designation. Racist and xenophobic language positions people in groups and subjects them to invidious stereotypes. Racist and xenophobic behavior discriminates against them, treats them with disdain, avoids them, and excludes them from benefits. Culturally imperialist policies or attitudes devalue or refuse to recognize the particular practices of some people, or subject them to unfair social disadvantages because of their particular practices. Sexist assumptions about male proprietary rights over women make us vulnerable to physical, sexual, and psychological abuse and often enough to unwanted pregnancy. So it goes with many other groups of people – poor people, who are treated as lazy and stupid, people with disabilities, whose needs are often ignored and lives stereotypically misrepresented.

People speak and act as though social groups are real; they treat others and themselves as though social group affinity is meaningful. Social group designation and experience is meaningful for the expectations we have of one another, the assumptions we make about one another, and the status we assign to ourselves and others. These social group designations have serious consequences for people's relative privilege or disadvantage. The politics of difference arose from a frustration with exhortations that everyone should just be thought of as a unique individual person, that group ascriptions are arbitrary and accidental, that liberal politics should transcend such petty affiliations and create a public world of equal citizenship where no particularist differences matter to the allocation of benefits and opportunities. Oppressed groups found that this humanist ideology resulted in ignoring rather than transcending the real material consequences of social group difference, often forcing some people to devalue their own particular cultural styles and forms of life because they did not fit the allegedly neutral mainstream. Thus movements affirming group difference called for attending to rather than ignoring the consequences of such difference for issues of freedom and equality. For many, such affirmation also entailed asserting group solidarity and a positive group identity to subvert demeaning stereotypes.

We did not need to wait for recent critics of a politics of difference for its aporiae and dilemmas to surface.[3] Much of the academic and political writing of these movements of the last ten years has explored problems with a politics of difference as the positive assertion of group identity, and has often itself argued against a politics of identity. While most people would agree that categorizations such as *women, Quebecois, African-Americans, old people*, or *Muslims* are meaningful, they founder as soon as they try to define any one of these groups. Most reject an essentialism which would define a group by a particular set of attributes or dispositions that all members share and that constitutes their identity in some respect. The objections to such essentialism are fatal indeed.

Attempts to define the essential attributes of persons belonging to social groups, whether imposed by outsiders or constructed by insiders to the group, fall prey to the problem that there always seem to be persons without the required attributes but whom experience tends to include in the group. The essentialist approach to defining social groups freezes the experienced fluidity of social relations by setting up rigid inside–outside distinctions among groups. If a politics of difference entails such internal unity coupled with external borders to the concept of social group, then its critics are right to claim that such politics divides and fragments people, encouraging conflict and parochialism.

A politics that seeks to form oppositional groups on the basis of a group identity all members share, moreover, must confront the fact that many people deny that group positioning is significant for their identity. Many women, for example, deny reflective awareness of womanly identity as constitutive of their identity, and they deny any particular identification with other women. Many French people deny the existence of a French identity and will claim that being French is nothing particularly important to their personal identities; indeed, many of these would be likely to say that the search for French identity that constitutes the personal identities of individual French men and women is a dangerous form of nationalism. Even when people affirm group affinity as important to their identities, they often chafe at the tendency to enforce norms of behavior or identity that essentialist definitions of the groups entail.

Thirdly, the tendency to conceive group difference as the basis of a common identity, which can assert itself in politics, would seem to imply that group members all have the same interests and agree on the values, strategies and policies that will promote those interests. In fact, however, there is usually wide disagreement among people in a given social group on political ideology. Though members of a group oppressed by gender or racial stereotypes may share interests in the elimination of discrimination and dehumanizing imagery, such a concern is too abstract to constitute a strategic goal. At a more concrete level members of such groups usually express divergent and even contradictory interests.[4]

The most important criticism of the idea of an essential group identity that members share, however, concerns its apparent denial of differentiation within and across groups. Everyone relates to a plurality of social groups; every social group has other social groups cutting across it. The group "men" is differentiated by class, race, religion, age, and so on; the group "Muslim" differentiated by gender, nationality, and so on. If group identity constitutes individual identity, and if individuals can identify with one another by means of group identity, then how do we deal theoretically and practically with the fact of multiple group positioning? Is my individual identity somehow an aggregate of my gender identity, race identity, class identity, like a string of beads, to use Elizabeth Spelman's image?[5] Such an additive image does not match my intuition that my life is of a piece. Spelman, Lugones and others also argue that the attempt to define a common group identity tends to normalize the experience and perspective of some of the group members while marginalizing or silencing that of others.[6]

Many conclude from these arguments and uncomfortable feelings that a discourse of group difference is incoherent and politically dangerous. Groups do not exist; there are only arbitrary categories and strategic performances, fluid and pastiche identities. Or there are only interest groups that form associations to promote certain ends, whether the legalization of same sex marriage, a raise in the minimum wage, or the right to wear a hijab to school. We are just only individuals, after all. This move, however, finds no way of accounting for or perhaps even noticing continuing patterns of privilege, disadvantage and exclusion that structure opportunity and capacity in modern societies. Group difference is a political issue because inequalities that are structured along lines of class, race, gender, physical ability, ethnicity, and relationships can usually be traced between that group specific situation of culture or division of labor and the advantages or disadvantages one has.

This, then, is one form of the dilemma of difference.[7] On the one hand, any attempt to describe just what differentiates a social group from others and to define a common identity of its members tends to normalize some life experiences and sets up group borders that wrongly exclude. On the other hand, to deny a reality to social groupings both devalues processes of cultural and social affinities and makes political actors unable to analyze patterns of oppression, inequality, and exclusion that are nevertheless sources of conflict and claims for redress. In the next section I will argue that the way out of this dilemma is to disengage the social logic of difference from the logic of identity.

II. Disengaging Difference from Identity

Critics are right to argue against defining groups in terms of essential attributes that all members share. They are wrong, however, to reject conceptualization of group differentiation altogether. Groups should be understood in relational terms rather than as self-identical substantial entities with essential attributes.[8] A social group is a collective of persons differentiated from others by cultural forms, practices, special needs or capacities, structures of power or prestige. Social grouping emerges from the way people encounter one another as different in form of life or association, even if they also regard each other as belonging to the same society. A group will not regard itself as having a distinct language, for example, unless its members encounter another group whose speech they cannot understand. In a relational conceptualization, what constitutes a social group is not internal to the attributes and self-understanding of its members. Rather, what makes the group a group is the relation in which it stands to others.

For political theory the relations that most matter are structural relations of hierarchy and inequality. Social structures are the relatively permanent constraints and enablements that condition people's actions and possibilities in relation to others and in relation to the natural and built environment. Hierarchical social structures denote differential relations of power, resource allocation, and normative hegemony. Class, gender, and race are some of the most far-reaching and enduring structural relations of hierarchy and inequality in modern societies. Differentiations of class or racism often rely on cultural group differentiation as a mechanism for structuring inequalities of resource allocation, power, or normative hegemony, but such structures cannot be reduced to culture or ethnicity. In some societies, age, caste, or religion also serve as the differentiating factors for structuring social relations of hierarchy and unequal access to resources, power, or prestige. Insofar as structures enable some people to have significant control over the conditions of their lives and those of others, or to develop and exercise their capacities while the same structures inhibit others, leave them less free, or deprive them of what they need, the structures are unjust. Thus groups defined by structural relations of privilege are most important for political theory because they often generate political conflicts and struggles.

So far I have aimed to disengage group difference from identity by suggesting that social groups do not themselves have substantive, unified identities, but rather are constituted through differentiated relations. The other task of this disengagement concerns the relation of individuals to groups. Some critics rightly resist a politics of identity that suggests that personal identity is determined in specific ways by group membership. This interpretation of a politics of identity suggests that members of the "same" group have a common set of group-based dispositions or attributes that constitutes them as individuals. Such a notion of personal identity as constituted by group identity fails both to give sufficient force to individual freedom and to account for the multiplicity of group affiliations that intersect with people's lives. From these failings it does not follow, however, that groups are fictions, or have no significant relation to individual possibilities.

It has been important for oppositional movements of subordinate social groups to reclaim and revalue the activities, cultural styles, and modes of affiliation associated with their social-group positions in order to subvert devaluation and negative stereotyping in dominant culture. This subversion has often encouraged cultivation of group solidarity by asserting a group identity. When the assertion of group identity is a self-conscious project of cultural creation and resistance, it can be positive and empowering, even though it corresponds to no pre-established group essence and inevitably involves only some of those associated with the group more than others. Too often, however, this political use of group identity does indeed speak as though it represents a given group identity that all associated with the group do or ought to share. The relation of individual identities to social groups, however, is more indirect than this conceptualization allows. Social groups do indeed position individuals, but a person's identity is her own, formed in active relation to that social positioning, among other things, rather than constituted by it. Individual subjects make their own identities, but not under conditions they choose.

Pierre Bourdieu theorizes the social world as a set of fields each of which is constituted by structural relations of power, resource allocation, or prestige.[9] Particular social agents can be understood in terms of their relative positions in these fields. While no individual is in exactly the same position as any other, agents are "closer" or "farther" from one another in their location with respect to the structural relations that define the field. Agents who are similarly positioned experience similar constraints or enablements as produced by the structural organization of power, resource allocation, or normative hegemony. On this view, social groups are collections of persons similarly situated in social fields structured by power and resources, but this says nothing about their particular identity as persons.

The idea that language and social processes position individual subjects in structured social fields makes this positioning process prior to individual subjectivity, both ontologically and historically.[10] Persons are thrown into a world with a given history of sedimented meanings and material landscape, and interaction with others in the social field locates us in terms of the given meanings, expected activities, and rules.[11] We find ourselves positioned, thrown, into the structured field of class, gender, race, nationality, religion, and so on, and in our daily lives we have no choice but to deal with this situation.

In an earlier essay I suggested that Sartre's concept of "seriality" can be useful for theorizing this structural positioning that conditions the possibility of social agents without constituting their identities. In Sartre's theory, to be working class (or capitalist class) is to be part of a series that is passively constituted by the material organization of labor ownership, and the power of capital in relation to labor. In the earlier essay I suggest that being a woman does not itself imply sharing social attributes and identity with all those others called "women." Instead, "women" is the name of a series in which some individuals find themselves by virtue of norms of enforced heterosexuality and the sexual division of labor.[12]

Social processes and interactions position individual subjects in prior structures, and this positioning conditions who one is. But positioning neither determines nor defines individual identity. Individuals are agents:

we constitute our own identities, and each person's identity is unique. We do not choose the conditions under which we form our identities, and we have no choice but to become ourselves under the conditions that position us in determinate relation to others. We act in situation, in relation to the structural conditions and their interaction into which we are thrown. Individuals can and do respond to and take up their positioning in many possible ways, however, and these actions-in-situation constitute individual identity.[13] Gloria Anzaldua expresses this active appropriation of one's own multiple group positionalities as a process of "making faces."[14] We are unique individuals, with our own identities created from the way we have taken up the histories, cultural constructs, language, and social relations of hierarchy and subordination, that condition our lives.

The gendered position of women, for example, continues to put greater obstacles in the way of girls achieving recognition for technical intelligence than boys experience. One girl may react to these obstacles by internalizing a sense of incapacity, while another may take them as a challenge to overcome, and each of these reactions will differently contribute to a girl's identity. Different people may experience and act in relation to similar positional intersections in different ways.

Complex societies position individuals in multiple ways, insofar as there exist multiple structures of privilege and subordination in respect to power, resource allocation, and normative hegemony. Which structures and positions intersect in an individual's life, and how they do so, conditions her particular situation. Kimberle Crenshaw theorizes this concept of the "intersectionality" of positioning for Black women. Being located in a position where racist and sexist structures meet, she suggests, sometimes produces constraints, dilemmas, tensions, and indeed possibilities that are specific to that intersecting position, and cannot be understood simply as summing up the experiences of being female and white and being black and male.[15] Other intersectionalities – say, of being upper class, female, and old – produce other specific conditions of structural reinforcement or weakening of privilege. This concept of intersectionality retains a generality to each social-group position without requiring a merely additive approach to the fact that individuals are multiply positioned. Each person's identity is a product of how he or she deals with his or her intersecting social positions.

Disengaging group difference from identity thus addresses many of the problems of more essentialist understandings of social group I discussed above. For many, certain social group positionings are important to their identities, and they find strong affinity with others on the basis of these relationally constituted groups. Doing so, however, is an active project of the person and does not arise from essential group attributes. The disengagement of difference from identity also addresses the "pop-bead" problem. Since groups do not themselves constitute individual identities there is no problem of how to conceive of myself as a combination of several group identities. I have only my own identity, fashioned in relation to my multiple group positionings.

III. Social Perspective

Because they assume that giving importance to social group differentiation entails that fixed group identities make the groups entirely separate and opposed, critics claim that a politics of difference produces only division. I have argued, however, that group differentiation should be understood with a more relational logic that does not entail substantive and mutually exclusive group identities. The primary resource that structural positioning offers to democratic communication, I shall now argue, is not a self-regarding identity or interest, but rather a perspective on the structures, relations, and events of the society.

The idea of social perspective presumes that differentiated groups dwell together within social processes with history, present arrangement, and future trajectories larger than all of them, which are constituted by their interactions. Each differentiated group position has a particular experience of a point of view on those social processes precisely because each is a part of and has helped produce the patterned processes. Especially insofar as people are situated on different sides of relations of structural inequality, they have differing understandings of those relations and their consequences.

Following the logic of the metaphor of group differentiation as arising from differing positions in social fields, the idea of social perspective suggests that agents who are "close" in the social field have a similar point of view on the field and the occurrences within it, while those who are socially distant see things differently. Though different, these social perspectives may not be incompatible. Each social perspective is particular and partial with respect to the whole social field, and from each perspective some aspects of the reality of social processes are more visible than others.

Each social group perspective offers what Donna Haraway calls a "situated knowledge." Individuals in each social location experience one another, their group relations and events, and the institutions in which they move in particular ways; their cultural and material resources afford them differing assumptions from which to process their experiences or different terms in which to articulate them. Among the sorts of situated knowledge people in each social location have are: (i) an understanding of their position, and how it stands in relation to other positions; (ii) a social map of other salient positions, how they are defined, and the relation in which they stand to their position; (iii) a point of view on the history of the society; (iv) an interpretation of how the relations and processes of the whole society operate, especially as they impact on their own position; and (v) a position-specific experience and point of view on the natural and physical environment. A social perspective is a certain way of being sensitive to particular aspects of social life, meanings, and interactions, and perhaps less sensitive to others. It is a form of attentiveness that brings some things into view while possibly obscuring others. The insights each perspective carries are partial with respect to the whole society.

Thus a social perspective does not contain a determinate, specific content. In this respect perspective is different from interest or opinion. Social perspective consists in a set of questions, kinds of experiences, and assumptions with which reasoning begins, rather than the conclusions drawn. Critiques of essentialism rightly show that those said to belong to the same social group often have different and even conflicting interests and opinions. People who have a similar perspective on social processes and issues – on the norms of heterosexual interaction, for example – nevertheless often have different interests or opinions, because they reason differently from what they experience or have different goals and projects. When Senator Robert Packwood was accused of sexual harassment, for example, nearly all the women in the U.S. Congress stood together to say that this was a serious issue while many men were inclined to remain silent or even joke. The women legislators did not agree on political values or even on what course should be pursued in the Packwood case, but they nevertheless expressed a similar perspective on the meaning and gravity of the accusations.

Perspective is a way of looking at social processes without determining what one sees. Thus two people may share a social perspective and still experience their positionality differently because they are attending to different elements of the society. As sharing a perspective, however, each is likely to have an affinity with the other's way of describing what he experiences, an affinity that those differently situated do not experience. This lesser affinity does not imply that those differently positioned cannot understand the description of an element of social reality from another social perspective, only that it takes more work to understand the expression of different social perspectives than those they share.[16]

Social perspective as the point of view group members have on certain aspects of social processes because of their position in them may be more or less self-conscious, both between different individuals associated within a group and between groups. The cultural expressions of ethnic, national, or religious groups, as well as groups responding to a history of grievance or structural oppression, often offer refined interpretations of the group's situation and its relations to others. Perspective may appear in story and song, humor and word play, as well as in more assertive and analytical forms of expression.

As Linda Alcoff suggests, Paul Gilroy offers an extended example of group differentiation as providing social perspective in his book *The Black Atlantic*.[17] Gilroy accepts anti-essentialist critiques and thus denies that blacks of the diaspora are a homogeneous group. He also confronts tendencies to treat social groups as unified ethnic or national groups. But he strongly rejects the suggestion that social groups are fictions. Instead, he aims to conceptualize the black experience as a particular structural location within modern history, a location initially constituted by the enslavement of Africans and their transportation across and around the Atlantic. The facts of slavery and exile produce specific experiences whose traces remain in cultural and political expression even into the present, according to Gilroy. They give black Europeans, Americans, and many Africans a distinct perspective on the events and ideas of modernity: "The distinctive historical experiences of this diaspora's populations have created a unique body of reflections on modernity and its discontents which is an enduring presence in the cultural and political struggles of their descendants today." (p. 45)

Gilroy argues that black experience and social location produce a black perspective on modernity. As with the concept of perspective I have developed here, this does not mean a fixed and self-identical set of beliefs shared by group members, but rather an orientation on the ideas and events of modern Western history.

> Blacks in the west eavesdropped on and then took over a fundamental question from the intellectual obsessions of their enlightened rulers. Their progress from the status of slaves to the status of citizens led them to enquire into what the best possible forms of social and political existence might be. The memory of slavery, actively preserved as a living intellectual resource in their expressive political culture, helped them to generate a new set of answers to this inquiry. They had to fight – often through their spirituality – to hold on to the unity of ethics and politics sundered from each other by modernity's insistence that the true, the good, and the beautiful had distinct origins and belong to different domains of knowledge. . . . Their subculture often appears to be the intuitive expression of some racial essence but is in fact an elementary historical acquisition produced from the viscera of an alternative body of

cultural and political expression that considers the world critically from the point of view of its emancipatory transformation. (p. 39)

Far from thinking of this black Atlantic perspective as homogeneous, self-identical and self-enclosed, Gilroy specifically articulates it as hybrid, in the sense that it consists of multiple political and cultural expressions both differentiated from and influencing one another, and influenced by their internal relation to and differentiation from white bourgeois, democratic, and imperialist culture and politics. Black intellectuals are a product of Enlightenment ideas, but they query them in specific ways. Black social movement activists are cultural hybrids of African cultural experience and the experience of racial subordination with European dominated culture and institutions which also form their experience and identities. Black diasporatic music, literature, and political rhetoric have traveled back and forth and up and down the Atlantic since the eighteenth century, proliferating hybrid differentiations. One of the purposes for theorizing a black Atlantic perspective, however, is to increase understanding of modern Western history generally, and not simply of the experience of the black diaspora.

Suppose we accept this claim that individuals positioned in similar ways in the social field have a similar group perspective on that society. What does this imply for individuals who are positioned in terms of many group-differentiated relations? Since individuals are multiply positioned in complexly structured societies, they interpret the society from a multiplicity of social group perspectives. Some of these may intersect to constitute a distinctive hybrid perspective, a black woman's perspective, perhaps, or a working class youth perspective. But individuals may also move around the social perspectives available to them depending on the people with whom they interact or the aspect of social reality to which they attend. The multiple perspectives from which persons may see society given their social-group positioning may reinforce and enhance one another, or it may be impossible to take one without obscuring another, as in a duck-rabbit figure. The perspectives available to a person may be incommensurable, producing ambiguity or confusion in the person's experience and understanding of social life; or their multiplicity may help the person form a composite picture of social processes. However experienced, the availability of multiple perspectives provides everyone with the resources to take a distance on any one of them, and to communicate in one way with people with whom one does not share perspectives. Thus understanding what is shared by members of a social group as perspective rather than identity diffuses a tendency to interpret groups as fixed, closed, and bounded.

V. Group Difference as a Deliberative Resource

Critics of the politics of difference assume that the expression of group specificity in public life is necessarily and only the expression of a narrow and rigidly defined group interest, set against the interests of other groups in a win-lose relation. This inward-looking pressing of interests, according to them, is precisely why the politics of difference makes democracy or coalition unworkable. In contrast to this image of politics as war by other means, critics wish to promote a neo-republican image of politics as civic deliberation, oriented toward a common good in which participants transcend their particularist interests and commitments.

Thus Jean Elshtain conceptualizes genuine democratic process as one in which participants assume a public mantle of citizenship, which cloaks the private and partial concerns of local culture and familiar interaction. She is not alone among democratic theorists in setting up an opposition between the partial and differentiated, on the one hand, and the impartial and unitary, on the other. Either politics is nothing but competition among private interests, in which case there is no public spirit; or politics is a commitment to equal respect for other citizens in a civil public discussion that puts aside private affiliation and interest to seek the common good.

When confronted so starkly with an opposition between difference and civility, most must opt for civility. But a conception of deliberative politics that insists that equal respect in public discussion requires putting aside or transcending partial and particularist differences forgets or denies the lesson that the politics of difference claims to teach. Where there are real group-based positional differences that give to some people greater power, material and cultural resources, and authoritative voice, social norms that appear impartial are often biased. Under circumstances of social and economic inequality among groups, the definition of the common good often devalues or excludes some of the legitimate frameworks of thinking, interests, and priorities in the polity. A common consequence of social privilege is the ability of a group to convert its perspective on some issues into authoritative knowledge without being challenged by those who have reason to see things differently. As long as such unequal circumstances persist, a politics that aims to do justice through public discussion and decision making must theorize and aim to practice a third alternative to both a private interest competition and one that denies the reality of difference in public discussions of the common good. This third way consists in a process of public discussion and decision making that includes and affirms all particular social group perspectives in the society and draws on their situated knowledge as a resource for enlarging the understanding of everyone and moving them beyond their own parochial interests.[18] In this section I articulate this alternative meaning of politics as public discussion and decision making and argue that the particular social perspectives groups bring to the public are a necessary resource for making the wisest and most just decisions.

Gitlin mocks the perspectivism he sees to be typical of postmodernism. He interprets an account of social difference as positionality with perspective as a form of crass relativism and subjectivism:

> How you see is a function of who you are – that is, where you stand or, in clunkier language, your "subject position," the two nouns constituting an unacknowledged gesture toward an objective grid that prescribes where you stand whether or not you know it. (p. 201)

> Perspective may lead to falsity or to truth, may be conducive to some truths and not to others. Perspective may be conducive to accurate observations or distorted inferences, may lead to promising notions or idiotic ideas – but to elevate the observations, inferences, or ideas, we need to do more than inquire into their origins.... To know whether the science is good or bad requires a perspective different from all other perspectives: a commitment to truth-seeking above all else. (p. 205)

This interpretation of a theory of social perspective as relativist begs the question. For just what is truth in social knowledge, what is the truth about social justice, and how do we achieve them? Gitlin correctly suggests that perspectives can only be starting points and not conclusions, and that by itself no perspective is "objective." Political discussion and debate can sort out the more from the less true, the better from the worse political judgments, however, only by encouraging the expression of all the particular social groups perspectives relevant and salient to an issue. This is the argument I shall now make.

With the neo-republican position, I assume that the democratic process ought not properly to be an adversarial process of competition among self-regarding interests, in which each seeks only to get the most for himself, whatever the costs to others. Instead, democracy should be conceived and as far as possible institutionalized as a process of discussion, debate, and criticism that aims to solve collective problems. Political actors should promote their own interests in such a process, but must also be answerable to others to justify their proposals. This means that actors must be prepared to take the interests of others into account. With theorists of deliberative democracy, I define the democratic process as a form of practical reason for conflict resolution and collective problem solving. So defined, democratic process entails that participants have a commitment to cooperation and to looking for the most just solution. These conditions of openness are much weaker, I believe, than what many thinkers mean by seeking a common good or a common interest.

If we understand democracy as a process of practical reason, then democracy has an epistemic as well as a normative meaning. Democracy is not only a process where citizens aim to promote their interests knowing that others are doing the same, though it is that. It is also a method for determining the best and most just solution to conflicts and other collective problems. Though there is not necessarily only one right answer to political problems, some proposals and policies are more just and wise than others, and the democratic task is to identify and implement the best solutions. Ideally, this epistemic function of democracy requires a political equality that includes the expression of all perspectives equally and neutralizes the ability of powerful interests to distort discussion with threats or coercion.[19] Especially in the absence of such ideal conditions, acquiring the social knowledge needed to formulate the best solutions to conflict and collective problems requires learning from the social perspectives of people positioned differently in structures of power, resource allocation, or normative hegemony.

Elshtain correctly evokes a special status for democratic publicity. She rightly claims that workable democratic politics entails that people look beyond their own parochial and private concerns. She is wrong, however, to suggest that adopting a public-spirited stance entails leaving particular group interests and perspectives behind. On the contrary, decision making takes place under conditions of publicity only if it explicitly includes critical dialogue among the plurality of socially differentiated perspectives present in the social field. For this understanding of publicity as entailing group-differentiated social perspective I rely on recent interpretations of Hannah Arendt's idea of the public.

For Arendt, the defining characteristic of a public is plurality. The public consists of multiple histories and perspectives relatively unfamiliar to one another, distant yet connected and irreducible to one another. A conception of publicity that requires its members to put aside their differences in order to uncover their common good destroys the very meaning of publicity because it aims to turn the many into one. In the words of commentator Lisa Disch,

> The definitive quality of the public space is particularity: that the plurality of perspectives that constitute it is irreducible to a single common denominator.

A claim to decisive authority reduces those perspectives to a single one, effectively discrediting the claims of other political actors and closing off public discussion. Meaning is not inherent in an action, but public, which is to say, constituted by the interpretive context among the plurality of perspectives in the public realm that confer plurality on action and thereby make it real.[20]

The public is not a comfortable place of conversation among those who share language, assumptions, and ways of looking at issues. Arendt conceives the public as a place of *appearance* where actors stand before others and are subject to mutual scrutiny and judgment from a plurality of perspectives. The public is open in the sense of being both exposed and inclusive; a genuinely public discussion is in principle open to anyone.

If differently positioned citizens engage in public discussion with the aim of solving problems with a spirit of openness and mutual accountability, then these conditions are sufficient for transformative deliberation. They need not be committed to a common interest or a common good; indeed, their stance of openness and mutual accountability requires them to attend to their particular differences in order to understand the situation and perspective of others. They share problems to be solved, to be sure; otherwise they would have no need for discussion. It does not follow, however, that they share a good or an interest beyond that.

Public critical discussion that includes the expression of and exchange between all relevant differentiated social perspectives transforms the partial and parochial interests and ideas of each into more reflective and objective judgment. By "objective" I do not mean a neutral point of view outside of and transcending those particular social perspectives. I mean only the contrary of subjective, that is, a reflective stance and substantive understanding that is not merely self-regarding. Judgment is objective in this sense when it situates one's own particular perspectives in a wider context that takes other perspectives into account as well. Objectivity in this sense means only that judgment has taken account of the experience, knowledge, and interests of others. Such objectivity is possible only if those particular perspectives are expressed publicly to everyone.[21]

If citizens participate in public discussion that includes all social perspectives in their partiality and gives them a hearing, they are most likely to arrive at just and wise solutions to their shared problems. Group difference is a necessary resource for making more just and wise decisions by means of democratic discussion due to at least three functions dialogue across such difference serves.

1 Plurality of perspectives motivates claimants to express their proposals as appeals to justice rather than expressions of mere self-interest or preference. Proposals for collective policies need not be expressed in terms of common interest, an interest all can share. Especially where there are structural injustices – and these are everywhere today – at least some claims that correctly appeal to justice are likely not to express a common interest. Even without rectifying injustices, just solutions to many political problems can entail obligations on the part of the public to recognize and provide for some unique needs of uniquely situated persons. The presence of a plurality of social perspectives in public discussion helps frame the discourse in terms of legitimate claims of justice. Because others are not likely to accept "I want this" or "this policy is in my interest" as good reasons for them to accept a proposal, the need to be accountable to others with different perspectives on collective problems motivates participants in a discussion to frame their proposals in terms of justice.

2 Confrontation with different perspectives, interests, and cultural meanings teaches individuals the partiality of their own, and reveals to them their own experience as perspectival. Listening to those differently situated than myself and my close associates teaches me how my situation looks to them, what relation they think I stand to them. Such a contextualizing of perspective is especially important for groups that have power, authority, or privilege. Too often those in structurally superior positions take their experience, preferences, and opinions to be general, uncontroversial, ordinary and even an expression of suffering or disadvantage. Having to answer to others who speak from a different, less privileged perspective on their social relations exposes their partiality and relative blindness. Where such exposure does not lead them to shut down dialogue and attempt to force their preferences on policy, it can lead to a better understanding of the requirements of justice. Nor does the perspective of those less socially privileged carry unquestionable "epistemic privilege." They also may need the perspectives of others to understand the social causes of their disadvantage or to realize that they lay blame in the wrong place.

3 Expressing, questioning, and challenging differently situated knowledge adds to social knowledge. While not abandoning their own perspectives, people who listen across differences come to understand something about the ways that proposals and policies affect others differently situated. They gain knowledge of what is going on in different social locations and how social processes appear to connect and conflict from different points of view. By internalizing such a mediated understanding, participants in democratic discussion and decision making gain a wider picture of the

social processes in which their own partial experience is embedded. Such a more comprehensive social knowledge better enables them to arrive at wise solutions to collective problems to the extent that they are committed to doing so.

This account of democratic communication, which uses the differences in group perspectives as a resource for enlarging the understanding of everyone to take account of the perspectives of others, is of course an ideal. This ideal extrapolates from real elements and tendencies in public communication across differences present within the unjust and power-oriented politics we usually experience. This ideal can serve at least three functions: to justify a principle of the inclusion of specific group perspectives in discussion; to serve as a standard against which the inclusiveness of actual public communication can be measured; and to motivate action to bring real politics more into line with the ideal.

Notes

I am grateful to Linda Alcoff, David Alexander, Bill Rehg, and Steve Seidman for comments on earlier versions of this paper.

1   Todd Gitlin, *Twilight of Common Dreams* (New York: Henry Holt, 1995), p. 36.
2   Jean Elshtain, *Democracy on Trial* (New York: Basic Books, 1995), p. 74.
3   For some examples of critiques of essentialism and a politics of identity from within theories and movements that support a politics of difference, see Elizabeth V. Spelman, *Inessential Woman* (Boston: Beacon Press, 1988); Anna Yeatman, "Minorities and the Politics of Difference," in *Postmodern Revisionings of the Political* (New York: Routledge, 1994); Michael Dyson, "Essentialism and the Complexities of Racial Identity," in David Theo Goldberg, ed., *Multiculturalism* (Cambridge: Blackwell, 1994), pp. 218–29.
4   Compare Anne Phillips, *The Politics of Presence* (Oxford: Oxford University Press, 1995).
5   Spelman, *Inessential Woman*, pp. 15; 136.
6   Ibid.; Maria Lugones, "Parity, Imparity, and Separation: Forum," *Signs* (14), 458–77.
7   See Martha Minow, *Making All the Difference* (Ithaca: Cornell University Press, 1990), chapter 1, for the phrase "dilemma of difference," and for some formulations of the dilemma.
8   Martha Minow proposes a relational understanding of group difference in *Making All the Difference*, especially in part II; I have introduced a relational analysis of group difference in *Justice and the Politics of Difference* (Princeton:

Princeton University Press, 1990), chapter 2; in the earlier formulation, however, I do not distinguish group affiliation from personal identity as strongly as I do in this essay.

9   Pierre Bourdieu, "Social Space and the Genesis of Groups," *Theory and Society*, 14 (1985), 723–44.

10 See Rosalind Coward and John Ellis, *Language and Materialism* (London: Routledge and Kegan Paul, 1977), pp. 49–60. See also Diana Fuss, *Essentially Speaking: Feminism, Nature and Difference* (New York: Routledge, 1989); Bill Martin, *Matrix and Line* (Albany: SUNY Press, 1993).

11 I refer here to Heidegger's concept of "thrownness," as the existential condition of not being one's own origin, of the facticity of history. See *Being and Time* (New York: Harper & Row, 1965), division one, chapter V. I have developed a more extended discussion of being "thrown" into group membership in *Justice and the Politics of Difference*, p. 46.

12 Young, "Gender as Seriality: Thinking about Women as a Social Collective," *Signs: Journal of Women in Culture and Society*, vol. 19, no. 3, 1994, pp. 713–38.

13 I mean here to evoke Sartre's concepts of facticity and situation. In Sartre's early existentialism, agents are always free insofar as they choose to make of themselves what they are, but they always must do so within an unchosen historical and social situation.

14 Gloria Anzaldua, "Haciendo Caras, una entrada/an Introduction," in *Making Face, Making South/Haciendo Caras*, ed., Gloria Anzaldua (San Francisco: Aunt Lute Foundation, 1990).

15 Kimberle Crenshaw, "Mapping the Margins: Intersectionality, Identity Politics, and Violence Against Women of Color," *Stanford Law Review*, vol. 43 (July 1991), pp. 1241–99.

16 I develop this point more in my essay, "Asymmetrical Reciprocity: On Moral Respect, Wonder, and Enlarged Thought," *Constellations*, 3 (1997), 340–63.

17 See Linda Alcoff, "Philosophy and Racial Identity," *Radical Philosophy*, 75 (January–February 1996), pp. 5–14; Paul Gilroy, *The Black Atlantic* (Cambridge: Harvard University Press, 1993).

18 James Bohman develops a version of this third alternative between the parochial and the unitary in *Public Deliberation: Pluralism, Complexity, and Democracy* (Cambridge, MA: MIT Press, 1996), especially in chapters 2 and 3.

19 For statements of this epistemic function of democracy, see Hilary Putnam, "A Reconsideration of Deweyan Democracy," *Southern California Law Review*, vol. 63, no. 6, Sept. 1990, pp. 1671–97; Joshua Cohen, "An Epistemic Conception of Democracy," *Ethics*, 97 (October 1986), pp. 26–38; David Estlund, "Making Truth Safe for Democracy," in Copp, Hampton, Roemer, eds., *The Idea of Democracy* (Cambridge: Cambridge University Press, 1993); and Estlund, "Beyond Fairness and Deliberation: The Epistemic Dimension of Democratic Authority," in *Deliberative Democracy*, from which the present chapter in this volume is taken.

20   Lisa Disch, *Hannah Arendt and the Limits of Philosophy* (Ithaca: Cornell University Press, 1994), p. 80.

21   For such a meaning of objectivity I draw on feminist epistemologies. See, for example, Sandra Harding's notion of "strong objectivity," which relies on oppositional theories produced from the perspective of historically marginalized groups to produce objectivity in science, especially social science, in *Whose Science? Whose Knowledge? Thinking from Women's Lives* (Ithaca: Cornell University Press, 1991). See also Ismay Barwell, "Towards a Defence of Objectivity," in Kathleen Lennon and Margaret Whitford, eds., *Knowing the Difference: Feminist Perspectives in Epistemology* (London: Routledge, 1994), pp. 79–94.

Part V

Why Vote?

9

Toward a Democratic Morality

Geoffrey Brennan and Loren Lomasky

> A phenomenon noticeable throughout history regardless of place or period is the pursuit by governments of policies contrary to their own interests. Mankind, it seems, makes a poorer performance of government than of almost any other human activity. In this sphere, wisdom – which may be defined as the exercise of judgment acting on experience, common sense and available information – is less operative and more frustrated than it should be. Why do holders of high office so often act contrary to the way reason points and enlightened self-interest suggests? Why does intelligent mental process seem so often not to function?
>
> Barbara Tuchman, *The March of Folly*

By the People?

Democracy, so the popular maxim assures us, is government of the people, *by* the people, *for* the people – and it is unique among political regimes in being so. In this chapter we seek to interrogate that species of democratic piety. To be more precise, we shall question two-thirds of it. That democracy is government of the people is hardly to be denied. But this is not what makes democracy unique: All functioning political regimes govern "the people." It is rather democracy's status as rule *by* the people and *for* the people that is the distinctive core of the democrat's faith.

The two elements – the by-ness and for-ness – are not unrelated. Although government for the people by a beneficent elite is a conceptual possibility, it is a highly improbable one. Elites cannot be relied on to pursue individuals' interests with anything like the consistency or intensity that the individuals themselves regularly do: Benevolent despots are considerably more likely to remain despotic than benevolent. Moreover, effective benevolence requires that one determine what genuinely constitutes the interests of others, and such judgments are deeply problematic.[1] Even if the decision maker is sincerely motivated to pursue the good of others, identification of that good, almost inescapably, will be colored by his own views as to human flourishing. Accordingly, so the argument goes, government for the people enjoys some decent likelihood if government is by the people, and it is wildly unlikely otherwise.

The formulation of an appropriate morality of democracy begins, therefore, on the more or less straightforwardly consequentialist grounds that people tend to fare better in democratic regimes than they do under alternative political structures. The by-ness of democracy possesses instrumental value insofar as it promotes for-ness. If, as Tuchman argues, the history of political rule is a march of follies, then democracy is to be endorsed insofar as it breaks step. For two reasons, though, that is too slender a reed on which to construct a robust democratic faith. First, while democracies may slow down folly's march, sometimes they rush pell-mell along it. To wit, Tuchman's rendition of the American experience in Vietnam, public choice's lengthy catalog of the woes of collective decision making, and, indeed, the additions to that dispiriting catalog broached in the preceding chapters [of *Democracy and Decision*]. Democratic procedures neither reliably elicit citizens' preferences over outcomes nor rationally aggregate the results of balloting. That other regimes typically do even worse may be true, but that observation hardly fires the imagination.

That democracy does have a capacity to fire the imagination, that individuals have been observed willing to fight and die under its banner, suggests the second deficiency of a purely instrumental account. Governance by the people is valued not only because it conduces to social welfare, but also because it is an intrinsic good. It matters to a person not only how well things go, but also who it is that is making them go. One might, for example, be convinced that arranged marriages are likely to enjoy more long-term success than those contracted independently and yet prefer a system in which people choose their own mates. "It's *my* marriage" may not only be a report of who the wedded party is to be, but an insistence on an entitlement to tend to the arranging oneself. Similarly, a colonial people may wish to strike out for independence even if the rule of the imperial government has been more efficient and fair minded than the indigenous alternative promises to be. On both the personal and political level we value self-determination, and not simply because we are convinced that we shall choose better for ourselves than others will do on our behalf. The capacity to make one's own mistakes may be a valued component of autonomy irrespective of any judgment as to whether some other person or group will make decisions for one that are less "mistaken" than one's own. To be treated as a cloistered minor is demeaning to one who has morally come of age.

It is, therefore, a central element of the democratic brief that the people genuinely have the status of responsible political actors if and only if they are self-governing. Accordingly, should the coherence of government by the people be at risk, then the notion of political responsibility will have to be rethought, and with it much in the lexicon of democratic civic morality: How should I vote? Should I vote at all? Why? And so on. And, as we shall argue, if the construction of a democratic civic morality is problematic, so is much that passes for justification of democratic institutions.

It is helpful to a normative analysis of the practice of democracy to distinguish between democratic "macroethics" and democratic "micro-ethics." The former embraces questions of global institutional design: Are decisions of such and such kind to be made collectively or through decen-tralized individual choice? If collectively, are determinations to be made democratically or via some other procedure? If democratically, what should the voting rules be, and should they be constrained or unconstrained (e.g., by judicial review)? Who will be permitted/required to participate in elec-tions? And so on. Microethical questions concern the performances of individual voters: Should I vote? If I do vote, how should I determine the direction of my ballot? How much investment should I make in securing political information? And so on.

In this chapter, we want to refocus the argument [of the foregoing chapters] on microethical issues specifically. The linchpin of the analysis is the concept of political responsibility, the alleged by-ness of democratic procedures. We shall argue in the upcoming section that that concept, as normally construed, is highly dubious. We thereafter ask whether the idea of democracy being for the people might nevertheless be rescued to some extent, and what would be required to make any such rescue operation successful. The following section constitutes the bulk of this chapter and is where we consider whether and how one might construct a civic morality that coherently engages individuals on the level of their particular voting performances. We argue that an expressively based understanding of voting not only does service as a positive theory of electoral phenomena, but also affords the most plausible grounding of democratic microethics that can be constructed. The final section builds on these results to show how one can effect a transition from judgments of individual voter responsibility to the global macroethical concern that democratic govern-ance be reliably for the people. [That, in turn, prepares the way for the book's final chapter in which we turn to macroethical democratic policy making.]

The Dubious Status of "Collective Self-Determination"

The proposition that democracy is government by the people and thus for the people depends, in its naive version, on a picture of democratic action as individual choice writ large. The intuition is that just as an individual chooses among options to produce intended results in the private arena, so all individuals, acting in concert, choose among social outcomes via explicit collective decision-making processes. When an individual chooses the maximally preferred set of achievable outcomes from among the alternatives open to her, she thereby acts rationally. Similarly, collective choice is rational insofar as "society" has evaluated alternatives and chooses from them those deemed best. This organic conception of society currently enjoys much less currency than it once did – an eclipse we applaud. Within the rational actor tradition with which we associate our own work, the organicist view embodies a gross conceptual confusion. As countless examples of the prisoners' dilemma attest, the processes through which individual actions are translated into social outcomes are complex and sometimes perverse. Any theory that treats social aggregates as choosing entities, much like individuals, sweeps away many of the most interesting intellectual questions in social analysis and many of the most pressing practical problems in social policy design.

Consider the simple analogy of the littered beach. The litter arises as a result of human action – we can plausibly say that the beach is littered *by* the people. But there can be no suggestion that the litter arises as a result of users' careful computations of alternative states of the beach and that the litter is there because the people prefer it. While there may be a natural presumption that a choice made by an individual is for that individual, no such presumption applies in the collective case. Even if there is an intelligible sense in which beach litter is by the people, that sense does not legitimate the inference that a littered beach is their preferred outcome, that it is expressive of their will – that the outcome brought about by the people is, therefore, *for* the people. Because the littered beach is not in any meaningful sense collectively *chosen* (or, for that matter, chosen by any one of the individual litterers), the sense in which the litter is by the people must be quite different from that involved in the individual case. Individual and collective choice are sharply disanalogous in this respect.

The robustness or lack of same of such analogies would matter little in practice if we could be sure that democratic procedures ruled out prisoners' dilemma problems. But this is what needs to be proved. And, of course, both public choice orthodoxy and the alternative theory [developed in the preceding chapters] emphasize the relevance of prisoners' dilemma problems to majoritarian decision-making procedures. Public choice orthodoxy focuses on the problems of revolving coalitions and political instability; our alternative emphasizes the disproportionate influence of expressive considerations at the ballot box. In the development of our central propositions [in Chapter 2], we took particular care to stress the underlying prisoners' dilemma potential of the collective decision-making problem. Because of that potential, the fact that government is by the people does not necessarily mean that it is for the people – and we would expect that in a significant number of cases it will not be. The alleged connection between by-ness and for-ness, the fulcrum of the democratic faith, is severed.

A yet deeper question needs to be broached. Is there any significant sense in which democracy constitutes government by the people? It may seem that this must be so. In a democracy political outcomes do not merely *happen* but rather are the product – even if not a collectively chosen product – of the various voting acts of the citizenry. It is through their agency, and not some other thing, that outcomes are determined, and since they are, taken together, "the people," democratic governance – whatever its deviations from a hypothesized social welfare optimum – is government by them.

The conclusion is too quick, at least if there is to remain any link whatsoever between government by the people and citizens' political responsibility. To see that that is so, consider the following "electoral" setting. As with our elections, every two or four or some other number of years voters march to the polls and select levers to pull. As with our elections, the quantity of pulls determines the success of one of the standing candidates/policies/parties. Unlike the running of our elections, however, these levers are unmarked. No voter knows which lever-pulling action supports which candidate. Nonetheless, levers get pulled, totals cumulated, winners determined, and policies enacted. Do we have here an instance of government by the people?

Well, one could choose to *call* it such. But this is very cheap talk indeed. Clearly it is talk too impoverished to support any imputation of moral responsibility for what has been brought about "by" the voters. Government by unmarked levers is government by lottery. As with other (fair) lottery forms, it induces no attempt on the part of candidates to secure support. And voters will have no reason to pull one lever rather than another – or at least no reason connected with an intention to secure a particular political outcome. The role of levers is purely causal. But by-ness in this attenuated sense is palpably insufficient to sustain an argument that governance in a democracy is something that the people do, that it is something for which they bear moral responsibility (and not just causal responsibility in the way a lightning strike is causally responsible for the felling of the tree). If democratic governance is to be an activity of the people, we need not merely causation but also, at a minimum, *intent*. There lies the democrat's problem. In elections where the numbers are even modestly large, the political outcome is, for each and every voter, essentially incidental to his action – and that is so whether or not the levers are identified. That is, what presents itself for the voter's choice is not the political outcome, and any voter who believes otherwise must be deluded. One who intends through his vote to bring about the election of candidate X is on all fours with someone who steps on a crack with the intention thereby of breaking his grandmother's back. Irrespective of what they may believe they are doing, they are in fact not acting intentionally to secure favored outcomes. Each is in need of a patient course of instruction in the workings of the causal order. Conversely, undeluded *X*-voters are doing something other than intentionally choosing political outcomes. And when a large number of persons all engaged in doing something *else* produce as an incidental byproduct of their action a particular state of affairs, then the insinuation that this state of affairs is, in some meaningful sense, expressive of their *will* must be regarded as highly suspect.

We do not mean by this observation to imply that any state of affairs so generated will necessarily be the worse for being undesigned. It has been a familiar theme in political economy since Mandeville and Smith that benign outcomes may be produced by invisible hand mechanisms rather than via deliberate construction. Whether a possible invisible hand lurks nearby in this case is, however, a quite complex matter – as far as we know unargued in the literature on democracy, or at least unargued in any explicit way. Some such argument would, however, seem to be crucial to any reasoned defense of democracy, and so it is to that argument we now turn.

Quasi-Invisible Hands and Public-Interested Voting

The most familiar picture of the operation of invisible hand institutions is that offered by Smith in his description of well-ordered markets, nowadays thoroughly absorbed (with some modification) into mainstream welfare economics. In this context, agents who are predominantly egoistic promote through their actions the interest of others. Competitive markets locate each actor in a network of what may be conceived as bribes – less pejoratively, prices – paid to the actor to modify her conduct in the interest of others.

The institutional structure is crucial here. In the absence of well-defined property rights and appropriate arrangements to enforce them, and without the possibility of enforceable contracts between agents, the alchemy of the idealized market cannot work. And it is worth emphasizing that this institutional structure is supported by a range of benign prisoners' dilemma interactions. It will often be in the interest of a subset of the community to coordinate behavior at the expense of nonmembers of that subset: This is precisely what happens when sellers of a commodity form a monopolistic cartel. However, any member of such a cartel can typically steal a personal advantage by free-riding on other members; and it is this free-riding behavior that inhibits the emergence of cartels, undermines those that do materialize, allows the freely competitive market to flourish, and empowers the invisible hand to shower its blessings on the multitude. The implication of the Smithian analysis is that there is no warrant for the assumption that prisoners' dilemma interactions are necessarily welfare diminishing for all affected parties. We must examine and assess the outcomes of such interactions as best we can on a case-by-case basis.

Does the democratic political process with electoral competition under majority rule constitute an incentive structure that induces political agents (specifically, political decision makers, whether politicians or bureaucrats) to act in the interests of citizens? Is politics like the market in this sense? The answer generally offered by public choice scholarship is no! Majority rule does not aggregate preferences in a determinate way, and in the absence of further restriction there is no bound on the political outcomes to which majority rule can give rise. To that difficulty, we insist, must be added another – namely, that the *inputs* to the majoritarian aggregation process are not of the right kind: They are not reflections of voter preferences over political outcomes.

Perhaps, though, the second difficulty *mitigates* rather than exacerbates the first. It will do so if voter inconsequentiality itself ("as if by an invisible hand") induces persons to forgo in some measure the political predation they would undertake were they to enjoy the capacity to act decisively. The suggestion carries credibility because inconsequentiality radically lowers the costs of indulging one's benign sentiments toward others. The preference aggregation that external institutional procedures are unable to effect may, then, occur internally in the minds of appropriately motivated individuals. Suppose specifically that citizen-voters are impelled not by self-interest but by a desire to express the public interest as they perceive it. If their perceptions are not too divergent, it seems plausible that the kinds of instability emphasized in public choice orthodoxy might be significantly moderated if not totally solved.[2] To majority rule would be left the modest role of sorting out minor differences in voter judgments of the public interest, rather than settling irreconcilable conflicts over whose particular interests are to be served.[3] This scenario may strike the economist (and political skeptics, cynics, and other low forms of life) as hopelessly quixotic. Nonetheless, other political theorists, notably those who situate themselves in the republican tradition,[4] do seriously entertain the likelihood of a vigorously public-spirited citizenry, and the expressive theory of electoral preference may buttress their hope that the propensities of democratic governance are fundamentally benign. That hypothesis now merits further attention.

The clear message of the redistribution example [discussed at length in Chapter 3] is that the collective nature of voting does indeed lower the cost of "voting morally." Individuals who believe in the abstract that poverty ought to be relieved, that they have a strict duty to aid the poor, may in the arena of private action be observed to relinquish a very small percentage of their assets toward redistributive ends. This is hardly puzzling. Although aiding the poor is judged to be the morally right thing to do and therefore assigned a positive valuation in utility functions, a yet higher valuation is assigned to personal consumption. A dollar given away to the poor is a dollar's consumption forgone, and so the poor will fare quite badly. If, though, the cost of a dollar's worth of poverty alleviation dropped to a dime, to a fraction of a penny, then the poor might make out much better.

Because voting does lower the cost of acting on one's perceived moral duties, individuals will find it less onerous to vote morally than they would if they stood to bear the full costs of their actions. Self-interest, we might say, no longer blinds them from seeing where their moral duty lies, and weakness of will does not hobble them from carrying it out. The voter's dilemma [of Table 3.1; not included here] is, from this perspective, altogether auspicious rather than symptomatic of some deep-seated pathology of democratic procedures. True, each voter gets the outcome he desires less, but it is nonetheless the outcome that he acknowledges to be the morally better one.[5] It can hardly be a damning indictment of democracy that voting substantially mutes the voracious acquisitive appetite that dominates market behavior and thereby amplifies the too often inaudible voice of conscience. In this vein, J. S. Mill says of the individual who participates in public functions:

> He is called upon, while so engaged, to weigh interests not his own: to be guided, in case of conflicting claims, by another rule than his private partialities; to apply at every turn, principles and maxims which have for their reason

of existence the common good. He is made to feel himself one of the public, and whatever is for their benefit to be for his benefit. (1958, p. 54)

By way of contrast, where citizens are generally excluded from political activity, Mill states:

Scarcely any sense is entertained that private persons, in no eminent social situation, owe any duties to society, except to obey the laws and submit to the government. There is no unselfish sentiment of identification with the public. Every thought or feeling, either of interest or of duty, is absorbed in the individual and in the family. The man never thinks of any collective interest, of any objects to be pursued jointly with others, but only in competition with them, and in some measure at their expense. Thus even private morality suffers, while public is actually extinct. (pp. 54–5)

Mill is, of course, speaking of public participation extending beyond the mere exercise of the franchise, but his reasoning nicely fits the narrower case of voting. Society, he believes, is the recipient of substantial benefits when citizens actively involve themselves in the conduct of public business. Individuals have not only one persona but at least two: the practical but unlovely visage of homo economicus and a public-spirited self of greater comeliness but lamentable shyness. Mill, and exponents of democracy more generally, can present the following syllogism: Institutional structures that encourage a shift in concern away from the acquisitive, reflexively absorbed self toward the greater community merit support. Democratic institutions do encourage this shift. Therefore democratic institutions ought to be supported.

But we must be careful, not least because it would be so reassuring to be persuaded by the argument. Such reassurance, it seems to us, is precarious for at least three reasons. First, although voter inconsequentiality lowers the cost of voting one's moral principles, it also lowers the cost of voting on the basis of whim, fancy, or prejudice. That is, although public-interest considerations are among those that may drive individuals' expressive activities, expressive preferences can, as a pure matter of logic, take any content whatever. It is a pious hope to imagine otherwise. Expressions of malice and/or envy no less than expressions of altruism are cheaper in the voting booth than in the market. A German voter who in 1933 cast a ballot for Hitler was able to indulge his antisemitic sentiments at much less cost than he would have borne by organizing a pogrom.

Second, there are grounds for fearing that voting, particularly voting under conditions of secrecy, favors more than does market activity the "darker side of the force." Because votes are anonymous, recipients of altruistic concern expressed through the voting act will be unable to identify and express gratitude toward their benefactors. If someone places value not only on *helping* other persons, but also on *being seen by them to have helped*, he will receive a greater return from a dollar of direct giving than from incurring an equal expense through his vote. Although voting remains a relative bargain for one prone to economize on the expression of altruism, there is at least some countervailing tendency for persons to channel their altruistic impulses into private giving rather than philanthropic ballots. The reverse is true with respect to malice. Here, anonymity stands to be a benefit rather than a cost because it insulates one from the reproach and reciprocation of one's victim. Admittedly, the sadistic and vengeful may not only desire to harm someone but also desire that their target know whence his harm comes. But this is surely the exception; more people will vote for capital punishment than will volunteer for duty in the firing squad, and many Germans noted with equanimity the disappearance of the Jewish population from their communities without desiring to become more deeply involved in the machinations of the Third Reich. Between altruism and malice, there is some grounds for anxiety that democratic procedures tend to favor the latter.[6] Consequently, an apology for democracy on the grounds that it encourages greater public-interestedness than would be observed in private transactions is in some jeopardy – at least under conditions of secret voting. Whether unveiling the vote might encourage increased "civic virtue" is a matter we take up in Chapter 11 [of *Democracy and Decision*]. The point to be made here is that because voting is virtually cost free, it is likely to prove conducive to extremes of expression, both altruistic and malicious and that at least under prevailing conditions of secrecy, the malicious extreme might be differentially encouraged.

Third, even if voting does engage the moral impulses of the citizenry, there can be no guarantee that these moral impulses will in fact generate social goods. We have already referred to the difficulty that some commentators, and most notably Hayek, have identified as attaching to judgments of others' interests. On this argument, even if voters were to *aim* at some internal analogue of the aggregation process that serves public interest in the market case, their success could not be assumed. Moreover, voters are far more likely to fasten onto emotionally vivid features of candidates and policy proposals as a vehicle for the identification and expression of their moral principles than onto broader and more subtle components of the public interest. Where the candidates stand on, say, abortion or South Africa may influence votes even though the office in question has virtually nothing to do with the formulation of policy in those areas. Political folklore informs us that kissing babies garners votes – and that kissing episodes that reach the front pages of the lurid tabloids sold in supermarkets do rather the opposite. Are moral impulses at work in these cases? No doubt. Do they reliably advance a public interest? That is considerably more dubious.

Responsibility and Voter Morality

If public-interest voting, or morally defensible voting more generally, is to predominate in large-scale settings, electoral conduct will have to be the subject of a prevailing civic morality, one that gives a satisfactory account of why individuals should exercise the franchise and why they should do so in a publicly interested way. As noted earlier, the inconsequentiality of individual votes seems to provide fertile soil in which such a civic morality might take root, since moral injunctions do not have to overcome the clamorous urgings of self-interest. And certainly there is no shortage of moral charges to the effect that, as citizens, we ought to vote, that we ought to do so in an informed and responsible manner, that one who takes the performance of voting lightly is derelict in civic duty, and so on. The question is, How can such injunctions be grounded? The very inconsequentiality of the individual vote – that which suggests the possible potency of electoral morality – also seems to undermine the most natural route toward justification; for how can it be the case that a citizen can properly be blamed or praised for an action the performance or nonperformance of which almost certainly makes no difference? And for an action, moreover, that she *knows* will almost certainly make no difference? Unless some plausible account can be given, democratic macroethics will entirely lack an adequate microethical foundation.

To the question Why vote? there are broadly three kinds of answers. The first focuses on the *probability of being decisive*. It claims that it is wrong to suggest that a vote will "almost certainly" make no difference – that, in fact, there is a reasonable chance of exercising some effect. The second fastens instead on the *magnitude of the moral stakes* involved. It accepts that the chances of actually deciding the electoral outcome are extremely remote but argues that the consequences of generating the wrong electoral outcome are sufficiently grave most of the time to justify voting, and voting in the right way. The third focuses directly on the *content of expressive preferences*. It maintains that one is morally obligated to express one's views on significant political issues whether or not one is likely to have an impact on electoral outcomes, and that one is morally answerable for one's views as such (or for failing to have any) and for giving them expression in appropriate forums, as well as for the political (or other) outcomes that may result from such expression.

In what follows, we shall explore these three possibilities. And we explore them in relation to the two questions that we see as central in any democratic civic morality: Why should I vote, and how should I vote? The latter is ultimately the more salient because participation in elections would have no moral point but for the fact that voters' decisions about the direction in which to cast their ballots determines the quality of political outcomes. (Recall the example of the unmarked levers. Under such conditions could any sense be given to the proposition that to vote is better than to refrain from voting?) The interest in democratic microethics is, whatever its further ramifications, directed by a quest for a civic morality consistent with eliciting satisfactory electoral outcomes from democratic processes. That interest is more than theoretical because the preceding chapters' [of *Democracy and Decision*] analysis of rational voter behavior indicates that large-scale elections have a propensity to produce political outcomes that the voters themselves do not want.

The exploration of issues in democratic microethics is, then, framed by macroethical concerns: Ultimately we are going to want to evaluate the particular performances of individual citizen-voters within a context of democratic institutions in which their actions give rise to outcomes that significantly affect their weal and woe. This is not, however, to presuppose that an adequate civic morality must be consequentialistic. For at least three reasons, no such implication follows. First, direct concern for consequences could be self-defeating. It may be that prevalence of an option-oriented or expressive civic morality makes democracy "work better" than would be the case if people were motivated exclusively by consequentialist considerations. Second, although democratic institutions would not exist if people did not care about their outcomes, to proceed forthwith to a consequentialist rendering of civic morality begs all the crucial questions in the debate between teleology and deontology in ethics. Consider the following analogy: There would be no practice of promise making if people had no concern for whether that which is promised will be forthcoming, and moral principles that adequately regulate the making and keeping of promises are predicated on that concern. It does not follow that one is morally obligated to keep (or make) some promise if and only if doing so yields the greatest utilitarian sum. Third, and this we will argue at length, ordinary consequentialism is unable to provide any cogent reasons why it is generally morally better to vote than not to vote, why individuals should invest time and resources in investigating the issues, or even why one who does vote is morally obligated to vote for the candidate whose victory would most advance overall well-being. These are central tenets of the democratic faith, yet a straightforward consequentialism leaves them embarrassingly vulnerable. The failure of consequentialism to ground a civic morality does not, however, entail the demise of democratic microethics. Although we stop short of categorically maintaining that individuals do have a duty to vote, do have a duty to investigate the issues, and do have a duty to cast ballots for the candidate/policy deemed best for the polity, we argue that these injunctions derive at least some prima facie support from an expressive ethics. To put it another way, if there does exist a well-grounded democratic microethics, its contours are expressive rather than directly consequentialist.

Why should I vote?

We take it as given that voting is costly, in both the objective and the opportunity cost sense. The fact that not all citizens vote (even in places like Australia where voting is nominally compulsory) and that *many* do not vote on some occasions in other places, indicates that citizens place positive value on alternative uses of their time and energy. Even if turnouts were total, the time and energy used up in voting would have alternative uses that may be deemed to be of higher value. Those California voters, for example, who voted in the Reagan and Bush elections when the outcomes were already known, could arguably have devoted their energies to more personally or socially productive activities than voting. To the extent that they voted out of civic duty, for example, an act utilitarian could argue that they behaved on the basis of a mistaken morality and that a correct utilitarian calculus would have indicated some other activity as more desirable.[7] If the satisfaction they derived from the act of voting was sufficiently great, then these "irrelevant" Californian voters do right to vote, but there is no basis for encouraging other citizens to follow their example. In any event, we take it to be nonaxiomatic that everyone ought to vote, that the optimal turnout is the entire set of enfranchised persons. Whether one ought to vote, whether one's responsibility to vote is a matter simply of getting the optimal turnout, and, if so, what that optimal turnout is are all matters to be determined.

We also take it to be nonaxiomatic that actual turnouts are necessarily suboptimal. One might argue that, although optimal turnouts may be less than 100%, the importance of a vibrant civic morality constitutes strong presumptive reason for believing that turnouts in which a significant slice of the eligible citizenry fails to vote are suboptimal. However, once it is accepted that citizens may have reasons to go to the polls that are independent of moral duty, or that civic morality can be potent (and potentially excessively so) in promoting electoral activity, the possibility that turnouts may be too large cannot be ruled out: A less rather than more vigorous civic morality may be preferable. Interestingly, this possibility is virtually never mentioned in discussions of the subject. It is simply taken for granted that larger turnout is better than smaller, and that the aim of moral admonition is to increase political participation. We find this literature unpersuasive. Turnout can in principle – and in fact – be too large as well as too small. Restricting ourselves for the moment to purely consequential consider- ations, the rule for optimal turnout is that the expected value from an additional vote (in whatever terms that value is specified) should be equal to the cost of that vote. Accordingly, at optimal turnout we should be effectively morally indifferent as to whether one additional person votes or not. What that optimal turnout will be in any particular case is, of course, a function of the circumstances – how much is at stake in the election, how many others are voting, how those other voters are likely to vote, and so on – as well as any good consequences that derive from participation per se.

One possible source of the common intuition that more turnout is better than less lies in the prospect that there are good consequences deriving from participation over and above any influence on electoral outcomes. It can be argued, for example, that participation *legitimizes* the electoral outcome to participants, and that increased legitimation promotes wider voluntary compliance with public decrees and, more generally, enhanced political stability. Or one might join Mill in maintaining that voting incorp- orates a contemplation of the public interest, the effects of which spill over into other arenas of conduct that are consequential (e.g., private provision of public goods). Such arguments provide presumptive reason for prefer- ring larger turnouts to smaller. Or, they do at least in those cases where the electoral outcomes are appropriately satisfactory: One might doubt whether it is a desirable thing to have citizens regard as legitimate outcomes that are truly disastrous (such as undertaking horrendously destructive wars; see Tuchman, 1984, for further details). And, returning to the central question of this chapter, one might doubt whether legitimacy does properly attach to outcomes that are not truly chosen by the people in the relevant sense. In other words, the alleged benefits of increased participation are dependent on how people vote and whether the resultant outcomes correspond toler- ably well to citizen preferences over them. And even supposing that, other things (and specifically the quality of collective decisions) being equal, benefits from increased turnout tend to be positive, the magnitude of these positive externalities may well in any large-scale election be dwarfed by the costs to a reluctant voter of an unwanted trip to the polls. If these factors support a consequentialist case for increased political participation, they do so only at the periphery. Accordingly, we turn to the central microethical justificatory routes.

The influence factor. Consider the three alternative foci for morally based admonitions to vote: the probability of influence, the magnitude of the stakes, and the moral content of expressive preferences as such. As a representative example of the first genre, we offer the following editorial comment, fortuitously encountered by one of us (invisible hand?), while trying to break the boredom of travel, in the October 1982 issue of United Airlines' in-flight magazine and penned by its CEO at the time, Richard J. Ferris:

> Why do so many Americans take for granted the right to vote? Perhaps it's because they are politically apathetic, distrustful of the system, unwilling to take the time, unbending in their belief that their vote can't possibly have an impact on the outcome of an election. How wrong and how wasteful. By voting, *a person chooses leaders, endows them with power, and holds them accountable.* (Emphasis added)

Heartening though it is to find among our great corporate executives such abiding respect for the political potency of the average (non)voter, the central empirical claims here are just plain wrong. A person does not, in fact, choose leaders; his influence on their power is asymptotically negligible; and since he cannot unilaterally bundle them out, it is hard to see how *he* can hold them accountable. *Pace* Mr. Ferris, the belief that a single voter is extremely unlikely to have an impact on the outcome of an election is true. Perhaps to assert otherwise is a noble lie, but it is a lie just the same.

But is it even noble? Suppose that the Ferris strategy worked, that voters came to believe that the probability of being decisive was considerable. Then individuals would presumably be encouraged to vote as they act in other arenas where they are decisive – that is, according to private outcome-oriented interest. Such private interest would, incidentally, be unlikely to be congruent with United's or Mr. Ferris's interests, which supports the suspicion that Ferris himself does not actually believe the propositions he is urging. More to the point for our purposes, all the traditional anxieties troubling an interest-based voting system, familiar from orthodox public choice, would reemerge. Suppose next, for the sake of argument, that Ferris is right, that one who does not vote would have a significant chance of affecting electoral outcomes if she did vote. Then it follows that democracy as it actually works, and in particular with the levels of turnout that actually prevail, generates electoral outcomes that we would expect to be very different if turnouts were larger. What authority then do the actual outcomes have? What confidence can we have that emergent outcomes reflect any reliable measure of the public interest? Surely the Ferris depiction is an *indictment* of American democracy as a process of collective decision making! To be sure, nondemocratic processes may be yet worse; but it must be sobering news for the democraphile that electoral outcomes are so arbitrary.

Our own view, as we said, is that Ferris is wrong on this matter. We may have grounds for anxiety about democratic outcomes, but sensitivity to small changes in voter turnout is not among them. There is, though, one qualification to be entered. Individuals may en masse refrain from voting as a means of expressing lack of support for the current incarnation of a traditionally favored party. A seasoned Democrat who finds it impossible to vote for the Republican candidate however much she detests her own party's candidate may simply stay away from the polls. If she is one among many such, the electoral outcome will respond – but the response is not arbitrary, and one presumably would not want to insist that such a non-voter should vote. Nonvoting is precisely the means whereby her preference is given effect.

The stakes. The second route to civic morality is to accept that each voter has a minute probability of being decisive, but to emphasize the magnitude of the stakes involved. Brian Barry (1978) pursues this consequentialist line in the voting context specifically:

> If an act-utilitarian really gives full weight to the consequences for *everyone* that he expects will be affected, this will normally provide an adequate reason for voting. If I think that one party will increase the GNP by 1/4 per cent over five years more than the other party, that for a utilitarian is a big aggregate difference. Are there *really* so many more beneficial things one could do with fifteen minutes! (p. 39)

On the more general issue of the moral grounds for taking account of small chances, Derek Parfit (1984) has this to say:

> It may be objected that it is *irrational* to consider very tiny chances. When our acts cannot affect more than a few people, this may be so. But this is because the stakes are here comparatively low. Consider the risks of causing accidental death. It may be irrational to give any thought to a one-in-a-million chance of killing one person. But if I was a nuclear engineer, would I be irrational to give any thought to the same chance of killing a million people? This is what most of us believe.... When the stakes are very high, no chance, however small, should be ignored. (pp. 74–5)

Barry and Parfit concede, in effect, that from a perspective of self-interested prudence, investment in a trip to the polls is irrational. The individual does not stand to gain enough *for himself*. However, when the relevant stake is the sum of benefits to the citizenry at large, calculations are radically transformed. And it is, of course, the overall social good on which the utilitarian fastens. So far so good. Those who maintain on consequentialist grounds that there is a moral duty to vote surely do not mean to say that the balance of advantage accrues exclusively or primarily to the individual voter. Such self-derived benefits are incidental. Their claim is that voting is a public good, and that an adequate civic morality bids us each to supply that good to our fellows.

Is the utilitarian ideal, then, a citizenry in which all participate at the polls? That question cannot be answered as it stands; for here, as elsewhere, what it is that I should do to produce the best overall consequences crucially depends on what *others* will do. Barry and Parfit fail to address the various possibilities; we now do so by exploring variants of the voter's dilemma [introduced in Chapter 3].

The standard "egoistic" version is depicted in table 9.1. Recalling that each voter's valuations are taken to be identical, the *total* cost of outcome A is not a benefit of 100 forgone but a benefit of 100 to each citizen-voter – that is, a total benefit of $100n$ (where n is the number of citizen-voters). Thus the matrix relevant to a utilitarian is the one depicted in table 9.2. An expected payoff calculation will require the agent to weigh the benefit (7) of voting for A against the benefit ($100n$) of voting for B. All that seems required to induce the agent to vote is a probability of being decisive larger

Table 9.1 The egoistic calculus

Each	All others		
	Majority for A	Majority for B	Tie
Votes for A	7	107	7
Votes for B	0	100	100

Table 9.2 The utilitarian calculus

Each	Majority for A	Majority for B	Tie
Votes for A	7	$100n + 7(S + 1)$	$7 + 7n/2$
Votes for B	$7m$	$100n + 7S$	$100n + 7n/2$

Note: m is the number of (other) voters for A when A wins, S is the number of (other) voters for A when B wins, and n is total citizen population (all of whom are assumed to vote).

than $7/100n$. With citizens numbering in the millions, this requirement seems a weak one.[8] So, one might conclude, each person should vote, and each should vote for B over A.

But this is too quick. One may not ignore what others are doing. So let us begin by universalizing table 9.2. Suppose that the utilitarian argument is a compelling one, and all voters can be relied on to vote for B over A. Then we should need only *one* voter to secure the preferred electoral outcome. To have n votes for B is to have $(n-1)$ too many. Resources are being squandered that could be employed elsewhere to generate utility.

Less restrictively, we can allow for mistakes in pulling levers and errors of judgment, but unless the probability of a representative individual supplying the correct vote is very close to one-half,[9] the proportion of the electorate required to vote in order to ensure that the right outcome emerges is very small. For example, the probability of my being decisive if 100 other voters vote for B with a probability of .9 is (using Equation (4.6)) 3.6×10^{-24}. If there are 100 million citizens (or otherwise affected parties), then the payoff *to each* would have to be of the order of 10 thousand trillion (10^{12}) dollars in order for it to be worth a forgone \$3.60 for the 101st person to vote. In other words, in a community composed entirely of individuals who are motivated by concern for the general weal and whose judgment of where the weal lies is fairly reliable, the turnout required to generate the correct outcome is quite small – only a tiny fraction of the enfranchised group. Of course, as we noted above, one would have to allow here for any benefits of increased legitimacy or compliance (whether soundly grounded or not) that flowed from electoral participation; if such benefits exceed the cost of voting for some or all voters, then turnout should be larger on that account. But such considerations do not seem to be connected to the stakes at issue in any election and are certainly not what Parfit and Barry have in mind, so we shall set them aside. There is, however, a further complication that is relevant to the utilitarian calculus. Note that there is an expressive return to the individual from going to the polls and *voting for A*. Since the probability for the 100th voter of doing any harm by voting for A when the other 99 all vote for B with probability .9 is truly negligible, it increases overall preference satisfaction for that voter to go to the polls and cast a ballot *against* the utilitarian-preferred candidate. Suppose we set aside the problem of mistakes. Then the true utilitarian ideal will not necessarily be where one person votes for B and no one else votes, but may instead be where everyone votes, with a simple majority of exactly one voter for B. This will be so if the expressive benefit from voting for A is at least *twice* the cost of voting, because for each additional A-voter we allow we must admit an additional B-voter to ensure that the correct outcome is assured. Of course, no such outcome is really feasible unless there is an appropriate coordination mechanism in place. If each must vote for A or B probabilistically, because she does not know deterministically how others will vote, then the ideal stochastic outcome will be one in which B defeats A (on average) but in which each votes for A with sufficient probability that the expected expressive benefit from voting exceeds the cost.

If we drop the assumption of identical voters, we can suppose that some will derive smaller expressive benefits from voting for A than will others. It is the former group that should vote for B, if indeed they should vote at all. And among the latter group, it may well be that some of them should not vote, even though it is individually rational for them to do so, because their voting in the "wrong way" requires that someone else may have to vote in the "right way" to ensure that getting the desired outcome is appropriately likely. Actual turnout could indeed be too large.

All this may seem like an excessively elaborate way of making the following simple point: Once expressive considerations are allowed for, what each ought to do depends critically on what all others do, even if the merits of the competing electoral contenders are unambiguous and even if all citizens are moved by concern for the public interest. That is, it may be best for me to vote for A, to vote for B, or not to vote at all, depending on what I think others are going to do. And this is so even if the stakes involved in the electoral success of B over A are quite large.

But how plausible is it to suppose, given assumptions of general public-spiritedness and reliable judgment, that the stakes are substantial? In that envisioned world, any forces of electoral competition that are operative will force parties to adopt policy platforms that are perceived by voters to aim at the overall social good. Thus, if the appeal to the public interest is compelling and parties respond to electoral demands, they will converge on roughly the same point in electoral space.[10] The electoral landscape simply will not exhibit contests such as those in table 9.2 in which there is a clear and significant consequentialist demarcation between the contending parties. Differences will be almost entirely matters of "style," alternate paths to the political summum bonum, rather than differences of substance. Insofar as individuals accrue greater or lesser or negligible expressive returns from one of these paths, they will rationally vote for A, vote for B, or not vote at all. But the claim that each is morally obligated to vote in virtue of the gravity of the stakes evaporates.

Barry and Parfit could protest that the preceding analysis is beside the point. We do not, alas, live in a world in which each intends the public interest. If we did live in such a world, all the prisoners' dilemma problems on which so much of welfare economics and political philosophy hang would be solved. Provision of public goods would no longer be a problem that required for its solution large-scale collective action. To be sure, coordination problems of various kinds might still arise, and so anarchy would not necessarily provide the optimal level of spending on public goods, but the standard cases of internal and external defense provision, littered beaches, excessive greenhouse-gas emissions, and so on would be removed. But this is a pipe dream. The average level of benevolence we in fact experience is distinctly subutopian, and there is considerable variance around that mean. We do better, therefore, to take Barry and Parfit to be prescribing for the actual world and its near neighbors rather than an envisioned utilitarian paradise. Specifically, we can take them to be assuming that many individuals will not vote even if there would be a nonnegligible public benefit to their exercise of the franchise, and that many of those who do bestir themselves to vote will be moved by a private interest that diverges from the public interest. Moreover, the argument will not be directed toward the moral saints, of whom there are too few within electoral precincts to have any discernible impact, but rather toward men and women who can be induced to do the moral thing if the costs are not too great and if they perceive that benefits to the general public are substantial. This revised scenario is analytically messy. Eschewing as it does any neatly simplifying hypothesis about what "all others" will do, it is indeterminate. Still, we can say something about it – and we had better if we hope to assess the consequentialist argument as it applies to the actual world.

The question then becomes: In a world where special interest as well as whim, malice, and ideology are dominant electoral forces, should I vote? And if I do vote, should I cast my ballot for the candidate whose election I judge would maximize the utilitarian sum? We take Barry and Parfit to be answering in the affirmative to them both, explicitly concerning the former and implicitly with regard to the latter. Both answers, we contend, are undersupported by consequentialist considerations.

Consider first the claim that voting is morally preferable to not voting (or, yet stronger, that voting is a moral duty). There are at least four points to be noted against this version of the utilitarian argument. First, as noted previously, the argument rests on the assumption that it is not generally compelling. If it were a compelling argument, then the "moral equilibrium" would be one in which we should be morally indifferent as to whether turnout was marginally larger or not, and the political equilibrium would be one in which differences in policy platforms would be small in utilitarian terms. The more the argument persuades, the less inherently persuasive it becomes.

Second, since we are being called on to assume that we are located a long way from any such moral equilibrium, it follows that collective decision making produced under real-world democratic situations is likely to be extremely inadequate. If the stakes are sufficiently high that individuals are morally obligated to vote even though the probability of being decisive is very low, then the expected cost of getting the "wrong outcome" must also be high enough to cause alarm. In other words, there are echoes here of the implication of Ferris's argument on turnout: If it is so manifestly clear that one ought to vote in the kinds of electoral situations that actually prevail (whether because one is likely to be decisive or because the stakes are so high), prevailing electoral situations must be held to be highly defective. The democrat's faith has, then, a distinctly otherworldly tenor.

Third, the Barry–Parfit "real-world" consequentialist analysis is itself infected by a disabling unrealism. Barry stylizes the electoral choice as one for or against higher GNP; Parfit analogizes it to a nuclear accident in which one million perish. Can one imagine any actual electoral contests being waged under such banners? Party platforms do not declare, "We promise exactly what our opponents do – except that we will give you less economic growth or nuclear safety." (The electoral prospects of any such platform would merit derision rather than disquiet.) A realistic construal of political competition in democracies will instead recognize that all credible candidates insist that it is through enactment of *their* platforms that the public interest will be best served, that they endeavor through their public actions to render this claim persuasive to a skeptical electorate, that they adopt policies that can never be known with anything approaching certainty to be efficacious in achieving their declared ends, and that they must necessarily endorse trading off more of one good for less of another, the net balancing of which is excruciatingly difficult. So instead of a transparently facile choice between more or less GNP, more or less nuclear safety, an electorate will instead confront the alternative of slightly more economic growth versus slightly lower inflation, increased safety but higher energy costs. How clear is it in these cases where the utility balance lies?

Let us then reformulate Barry's calculus. Suppose one judges that the victory of party B will result in a 0.25% increase in GNP compared with what would result from the victory of A. Performing the straightforward utilitarian calculation of multiplying the probability that one's vote will be decisive times the utility of such an increase in GNP will be justified only if one *knows* with a certainty approaching 1.0 that those consequences have been estimated correctly. But political life simply does not admit of such certainty. So one must bring into one's accounting a whole host of additional considerations: the likelihood that party B will indeed, should it gain power, pursue the policy that it says it will; the likelihood that one's theory about the determinants of GNP is correct; the likelihood that party A would, if elected, pursue a less optimific policy; the adequacy of one's judgment that a heightened GNP will produce more aggregate well-being than the alternative under which, perhaps, the inflation rate would be a percentage point lower; and a host of ceteris paribus conditions.

Voters are prone to claim great prodigies of knowledge and insight for themselves, and many will contend that they do indeed know such relevant facts.[11] We confess ourselves guilty of such hubris from time to time. A more accurate epistemic test, then, might be to ask what degree of confidence one has that one's neighbor (political affiliation unknown) has the degree of knowledge and moral motivation required for the expected payoff to his vote to be strongly positive. We believe it is not implausible to maintain that if political prejudices are recognized for what they are and appropriately discounted, it will generally be the case that the likelihood that any given voter will hit on the utility-enhancing line is not appreciably greater than the chance that he will select the one that is utility diminishing. It is the difference between these two possibilities that gives the net expected payoff to a vote. When that sharply reduced sum is multiplied by the probability of being decisive, the utilitarian rationale for a vote becomes exceedingly problematic.

Fourth, individuals are not homogeneous with regard to their ability to assess accurately the effects of political policies. Some are more easily gulled by sharp-talking political operatives; some have a greater understanding of what genuinely comprises the public interest. It follows that a blanket consequentialist endorsement of voting is unjustifiable. If electoral participation is a serious business, then it ought to be consigned to those with the expertise to conduct it most responsibly. A consequentialist argument that properly attends to voter heterogeneity, therefore, does not extend to the general electorate; it is, rather, addressed to the Wise and the Good. Persons who lack a full quota of wisdom and moral motivation do better not to vote at all. Their ballots add "noise" (that is at best random) to the total electoral outpouring, thus making it more likely that those best equipped to ascertain the common good will find themselves among the overall minority. Rather than an argument for democracy, the argument becomes a curiously backhanded brief for a reign of philosopher-kings.

The upshot is, then, that we can find no good utilitarian case for increased turnout as such. Expressive returns to the individual voter aside, it is very likely that one could do better for overall utility by doing something else. A perhaps surprising corollary of this result is that there is no good utilitarian reason why one who does vote should cast a ballot for the candidate whose election it is judged would be most conducive to the greatest good of the greatest number. Given the minute chance of being decisive and the imponderables surrounding political prognostication, little stands to be gained through so directing a ballot. If, however, the individual can accrue significant expressive returns through a vote for some one of the (nonutilitarian preferred) candidates, then a concern for consequences dictates that she snatch the bird in the hand rather than stalk utility in a bush that is almost certainly unreachable and that may not even exist. Ordinary standard consequentialism, we therefore conclude, cannot sustain a robust democratic faith.

The expressive domain. To this point the quest for for an adequate democratic microethics has been unavailing. This suggests that it may be a mistake to construe the moral significance of voting as a matter of achieving "optimal turnout" and wrong to think of voters as bearing responsibility for their electoral behavior only insofar as it affects, or seems likely to affect, electoral outcomes. Suppose that in an election involving two outcomes A and B, it is a foregone conclusion that A will win. Clearly, a vote for either option will not alter the probabilities in any non-negligible way. Nonetheless, we might want to say that the A-voters bear responsibility for their candidate's victory, and that they bear it no less fully when the preelection polls indicate a 70–30% margin for A than they would if the polls had indicated the election too close to call. To approach the point from a slightly different direction, it seems intuitively acceptable to hold up to reproach someone who voted for the Ku Klux Klan party candidate for president even though the Klandidate was not listed on the ballots of enough states to comprise a majority of the Electoral College, and hence could never win. One who registers himself as supporting the thoroughly unsavory is culpable irrespective of the tendency that such expression has to generate the repugnant state of affairs. Why that should be so deserves a closer look.

To cast a Klan ballot is to *identify oneself* in a morally significant way with the racist policies that the organization espouses. One thereby lays oneself open to associated moral liability whether that candidate has a small, large, or zero probability of gaining victory, and whether or not one's own vote has an appreciable likelihood of affecting the election result. Even stronger, to express such support in a forum in which no outcomes will be decided, such as in casual conversation or in response to a survey, is also odious. That is not, of course, to deny that any influence on electoral outcomes is morally relevant: To express support for A and to bring about the victory of

A is worse than merely to express support for A. The point is not that effects on political outcomes do not matter, but they are not all that matters.

It may be that outcome considerations enter not so much into the choice of action as in assessing the significance of the context within which the expression of one's views takes place. If one cheers as the lion devours a Christian, the act is laden with more significance than is cheering at a football game in which the Lions are devouring the Bears; the moral stakes are higher. Nothing in this necessarily commits one to a view of cheering as a means to bring about a preferred result. Neither, importantly, does it entail an outcome-oriented account of why cheering one way or another merits commendation.

One who writes a letter to a newspaper in which it is contended that Hitler's assumption of the chancellorship was a good thing, as were the events that followed therefrom, throws oneself open to rebuke. The grounds for criticism are not simply that one has made an intellectual error – for which correction and not castigation would be the appropriate response – nor any alleged tendency of one's public expression to influence others to build a Fourth Reich that resembles the Third. Even assuming that such manifestos have any discernible public impact at all, they cannot be assumed more likely to generate increased bigotry than to renew vigilance against bigotry. But we need not indulge in such far-fetched causal speculations to identify sufficient grounds for moral disapproval. Persons are morally responsible not only for what they *bring about*, what they *intend* to bring about, and what they help to bring about; they are also responsible for what they *endorse* and for that with which they choose to *identify themselves*.

One might indeed go further and maintain that persons bear responsibility for their characters and attitudes whether or not they choose to give them expression. An antisemite who never expresses her loathing for the Jews may still be accounted morally defective, and this whether she refrains from public expression because she judges it to be imprudent or because she herself recognizes and loathes the bigotry to which she finds herself chained. If that is correct, then persons are responsible not only for that which they voluntarily perform, but for that which, quite nonvoluntarily, they are.[12] This reflection matches common intuitions and would, we believe, be seen more widely as plausible were it not for the continuing grip of philosophical theories insisting that the connection between willing and responsibility must be universal. There is nothing unusual or paradoxical about esteeming someone who is unreflectively and instinctively kind and compassionate toward others despite querulous Kantian suggestions that benevolent states resulting from natural inclination merit no moral credit. It would be extravagant to push this line of argument further. Whether or not individuals bear responsibility for their characters and attitudes, all we need to maintain for present purposes is that they are accountable for that which they choose to express.

There is, then, a logic of moral discourse appropriate to expressive activity. It is impossible here to do more than to begin to sketch its contours, but no involved exercise in cartography is needed to render its likeness familiar; our ordinary activity richly exemplifies the play of normative considerations underlying expressive acts. When we sympathize with a sick friend (or are left cold by someone "too busy" to do so), mourn the irretrievably lost, and bristle at injustice, our activity is laden with moral significance. These entirely familiar performances are, in the first instance, expressive. They may be indirectly consequential for good or ill, but that is not their point. Similarly explicable as expressively based are versions of the frequently voiced claim that citizens in a democracy have a *duty* to vote. Such appeals reach a crescendo in the flurry of media pronouncements preceding national elections. One who turns on a television set will be regaled with emotive messages about patriots who have done their part by defending the nation at the cost of their lives. One is solemnly informed that the least an ordinary citizen can do to fulfill his end of the social compact is to exercise the franchise. In Australia this sentiment is given legal force via a requirement backed up by fines that all adult citizens able to vote do so. And many of those who do not recognize the existence of a strict duty to vote will nonetheless concede that it is a good thing that citizens vote, that voting is an act to the individual's moral credit.

As we have noted, these pronouncements are often buttressed with strained claims about the chances of being decisive or the magnitude of the stakes involved. No such claims, even where plausible, seem to be required. What is wrong with abstention does not need to be tied to any effect on outcomes: The wrong inheres in the apathy thereby displayed.[13] In great national elections or referenda, principles of undeniable moral salience are at stake. Political parties prepare lengthy platforms stating their positions on the major issues of the day, and candidates contend with each other concerning the ends to which the nation ought to devote itself and the appropriateness of rival means to those ends. What is done and how burdens and benefits come to be assigned will depend on who gets in and who is tossed out. This is the stuff of which serious commitment is made. By the stand one takes, one displays to oneself and to others what sort of person one is.

Or rather, one who takes some stand or other does so. But the individual who declines to get involved, who is so unmoved by the debate before her that she will not give up a few minutes of her time to register her views in the electoral precincts provided for that purpose can present the appearance of a political neuter. She is too diffident or too detached from events of great moment to bestir herself. In showing herself unmoved by that to which her fellow citizens assign considerable weight, she displays an insensitivity for which they can reasonably take her to task.

We believe that this is, in embryo, the strongest argument that can be made for the claim that individuals do wrong by not voting. Is it compelling? To adjudicate that point we would have to develop a full-fledged normative theory of expression and that is beyond our current aspirations. What we claim here for the expressive argument is not conclusiveness but intrinsic cogency. It is a *contender* as an account of why citizens ought to vote, while consequentialist arguments that one should vote because the chance of being decisive is substantial or because the magnitude of the stakes mandates a trip to the polls are summarily dismissible.

How ought I vote?

The question of which considerations should weigh in deciding how to vote is, in our view, a more significant one than persuading persons to go to the polls, at least in Western democracies as they actually function. Whether because they are impelled by a civic morality of electoral participation or for other reasons, voters turn out for significant elections in sufficient numbers to make the possibility of excessive influence by any one voter suitably remote and to confer on electoral verdicts whatever legitimacy may be forthcoming from the vox populi. The important macroethical consideration is to secure tolerable outcomes, not merely to get more voters to the polls. And in that process, the critical thing is to induce voters to vote in an appropriate way.

As we have emphasized, the question of *how* I should vote is closely connected with the question of *whether* I should vote, and much of the foregoing discussion is obviously germane. We can therefore be brief in discussing this second question.

Directly consequentialist considerations are, except in the most exceptional circumstances, mute. Virtually nothing (in the relevant expected sense) pertaining to political outcomes hinges on how the individual chooses to direct his ballot. So he might as well – indeed, he *must* if he is to give due weight to his own utility – vote as he prefers. Whether these preferences are egoistic or other-directed, well considered or whimsical, is immaterial. For a consistent consequentialism, voting behavior is the procurement of consumer goods from which externalities are almost entirely absent. *De gustibus non est disputandum.*

An expressively grounded theory of democratic microethics will have rather more to say. If the quality of expressive acts matters, it is not enough merely to go to the polls and vote any old how. Unless the act of voting is performed with the requisite preparation and attentiveness, it will not satisfy canons of good citizenship. Certainly this view accords with the message of common morality. Merely to vote, we are told, is insufficient; one who goes to the polls only vaguely aware of who the candidates are and what they stand for, and who pulls the lever closest to his hand so that he can be done with the business and return to his couch and television, stands hardly, if at all, higher than one who never left the couch. That is in part because one who votes in so desultory and absent-minded a fashion is not to be credited with taking a stand on anything. One may also fault the voter who knows well enough what he favors but does not have any good reason for favoring it. He has voted the straight Republican ticket in every election since he came of age, and his mother and father did so before him; therefore, he will vote the Republican ticket again in this election. The phenomenon may be common, but nonetheless can be judged an inadequate performance. One who votes should know the issues, scrutinize candidates' statements, and make up one's mind after weighing all the facts: This is how the voter's duty is often expressed.

It is often observed that the return to voters' expenditures of time and resources in the pursuit of political information is minuscule. When the probability of the direction of one's vote being improved by more information is multiplied by the probability that one's vote will be decisive, an investment in political information seems to be one of the lowest return ventures one might undertake. In the light of such demonstrations of the irrationality of the exercise, it might seem utterly incongruous that "knowing the issues" is so widely endorsed by common democratic morality. However, that incongruity dissolves once we drop the assumptions that voting behavior is to be justified on the basis of effects on outcomes and that the basis for evaluating the pursuit of political information is derived from such effects. The proposition that individuals ought to take a principled stand on issues of great moment includes the notion that they ought to do so *intelligently*. If expressive activity matters in its own right, then high-quality expression is valuable irrespective of its causal product. A utilitarian calculus exhibits little difference with respect to overall optimization between an ignorant voter and one who is well informed (and none at all should they happen to support the same candidates), but a normative theory of expressive discourse can present such voters as sharply separated.

Again, what we claim for that theory is considerable congruence with the dictates of common morality. That is not to insist on its truth. But it is to locate the position within the wider framework common morality affords. One who comes down on the "right side" of an issue but does so for largely irrelevant and ill-informed reasons can be held up to criticism. This is so with respect to voting decisions but also holds, and for essentially the same reasons, for other expressive acts. An ignorant and poorly reasoned letter to the editor is disreputable for much the same reasons as is an ignorant ballot. To express disdain for the Nazis because they swaggered a lot, made interminable speeches, and wore those horridly unstylish brown shirts is simply to get the grounds for disapproval wrong. Both inside and outside voting booths, it matters what one stands for and why one stands for it.

The upshot of these considerations is this: Sense can be made of the assertion that individuals in a democracy are responsible for how and whether they vote. Even though an individual ballot is causally inefficacious, people are nonetheless morally answerable for their electoral conduct. To be sure, consequences up the moral ante. Moral deeds do speak louder than mere words. And in contexts where an agent acts to bring about a particular outcome, its characteristics will be a central part of any moral appraisal. So one can understand the temptation to construe civic morality as outcome oriented. But the standard arguments advanced in this connection are, upon analysis, found to be unpersuasive.

A more promising line focuses on the expressive dimension of voting. The object of an expressive civic morality is to inculcate an ethic of well-informed, responsible political participation more or less for its own sake. It directs attention to the character of the citizen rather than to the alternative electoral outcomes that the citizen might leave in her wake. Whether such an ethic can ultimately be vindicated and, if it can, whether it will be supportive of a satisfactory democratic macroethics must be left here as somewhat open questions. We can, though, offer a conditional judgment: If the democratic faith in government by a politically responsible people is sustainable, that faith will hinge on the potency of a largely expressive ethic of political conduct among citizen-voters.

Notes

1   The difficulty of such judgments has been an important theme in the Austrian discussion of the feasibility of "socialist calculation." For a recent relevant statement, see Hayek (1988).

2   Although the respective contexts differ markedly, this proposed solution to the problem of distilling a public interest from the interplay of private interests is interestingly reminiscent of Rousseau's project of extracting from citizens' particular judgments political outcomes that are authentically indicative of general will.

3   See Chapter 5 of *Democracy and Decision,* from which the present chapter in this volume is taken, for a more detailed discussion of the implications of expressive voting for public choice orthodoxy.

4   See, e.g., Pettit (1989) and Braithwaite and Pettit (1990).

5   This argument receives more extended treatment in Chapter 8 of *Democracy and Decision.*

6   This argument was initially suggested to us by a reading of the account of sympathy in Adam Smith's *The Theory of Moral Sentiments* (1982), especially pp. 113–34. It is buttressed by Smith's reflections in *The Wealth of Nations* concerning the "man of low condition": "While he remains in a country village, his conduct may be attended to, and he may be obliged to attend to it himself. In this situation, and in this situation only, he may have what is called a character to lose. But as soon as he comes into a great city, he is sunk in obscurity and darkness. His conduct is observed and attended to by nobody, and he is therefore very likely to neglect it himself, and to abandon himself to every sort of low profligacy and vice" (1930, Bk. V p. 705). The parallel between the anonymity of urban existence and that of the voting booth is suggestive. A Smithian moral psychology is extremely congenial to our argument though not strictly presupposed by it. See Brennan and Lomasky (1985) for a fuller discussion.

7   To avoid complexities not directly relevant to the issue under consideration, we note but do not further discuss the fact that those California ballots also contained local races and referenda. If, for one already at the polls, a further lever pull comes at virtually zero utility cost, then a presidential vote does not display a calculative error. Neither, though, is it, from a utilitarian perspective, morally preferable to abstention.

8   It is weaker still if, as will often be the case, benefits extend to individuals beyond the polity's boundaries. Recurring to Barry's example, if America's GNP increases by 0.25%, the consequences for those who trade with Americans will also be positive. Should it be an issue of war or peace on which the election turns, such external effects will be yet more pronounced.

9   If that probability is less than .5, then the *smaller* the turnout, the greater the likelihood of the correct outcome. If that probability is more than slightly greater than .5, larger turnouts are wasteful of resources.

10 Note that this analysis, unlike those assuming predominantly egoistic voters, is not sensitive to the number of contending parties.

11 Why, in the face of a multitude of factors that should incline one toward caution, do individuals tend to be so obdurately convinced of the soundness of their political judgments? Although we disclaim expertise in political

psychology, two explanations suggest themselves. First, it is the business of political parties and candidates to sell unquestioning conviction. True believers vote more reliably than do those who profess Socratic ignorance, and so it is to the creation of true belief and the destruction of doubts that political actors bend their efforts. Political evangelism is, in this regard, very much akin to religious evangelism. Second, expressive returns will usually be an increasing function of strength of conviction. We can presume that the fans who cheer most vociferously and unyieldingly are the ones who most enjoy themselves. To delight in following the shifting fortunes of the Yankees is incompatible with persistently questioning whether they deserve one's support. For the political analogue, substitute, for Yankees, Republicans or Democrats.

12   Some will object that a person can be morally accountable for her attitudes and character only to the extent that she acted to *produce* them in herself or to the extent that it is now up to her whether to *change* them. The contention is that individuals are responsible only so far as their voluntary agency extends. We do not find it obvious that that is so. Indeed, the claim is especially questionable in the first-person case. To recognize in oneself a vice, and to recognize it *as a vice* is, we think, incompatible with taking the trait to be a matter of utter moral indifference. What of third-person ascriptions? Again, we find it implausible that the nonvoluntary is necessarily immune from moral categorization. There may be no point to *blaming* or *punishing* someone for that which is not within her voluntary control, but other moral stances (e.g., scorn, contempt) may nonetheless be appropriate.

13   Conscientious abstention is, on this reading, to be accounted very differently, though the effect, if any, on electoral outcomes is the same. Indeed, this observation exposes one strength of the expressive account – that it not only provides a case for why individuals typically ought to vote but also enables one to draw moral distinctions between different reasons for nonvoting. Consider someone who declines to vote not out of apathy or inertia but as a principled protest against the grounds on which the election is fought or because he believes the political process of which it is a part to be corrupt. We might disagree with the substantive position taken by this person, but we could hardly contend that his abstention on grounds of principle is dereliction of an obligation to take a stand on momentous issues. On strictly outcome-related grounds, however, the efficacy of a lazy abstention and a principled one are exactly the same.

10

A Causal Responsibility Approach to Voting

Alvin Goldman

I. Some Rationales for Voting

Why should a citizen vote? There are two ways to interpret this question: in a *prudential* sense, and in a *moral* (or *quasi-moral*) sense. Under the first interpretation, the question asks why – or under what circumstances – it is in a citizen's self-interest to vote. Under the second interpretation, it asks what moral (or quasi-moral) reasons citizens have for voting. I shall mainly try to answer the moral version of the question, but my answer may also, in some circumstances, bear on the prudential question. Before proceeding to my own approach, let me briefly survey alternatives in the field.

Many theorists approach the issue from an *economic* or *rational-choice* perspective, and they usually have in mind the prudential question. On a standard version of this approach, it is considered rational for a citizen to vote if and only if the expected personal benefit of voting exceeds the expected cost. Confronted with a choice between two candidates, C and C', a prospective voter should ask how much he values getting his more preferred candidate as compared with his less preferred one. This differ-ence in value should be multiplied by the probability that his ballot, if cast, would change what would otherwise happen. The resulting expected value should then be compared with the expected cost of voting, which might include the time lost from work, and the inconvenience of traveling to the polling site, standing in line, and so forth. Voting is prudentially rational if and only if the expected benefit exceeds the expected cost. Most theorists who analyze the subject from this angle conclude that it is rarely rational for a citizen to vote, especially in large elections. The expected benefit from voting is usually quite small because the probability of casting the deciding ballot in large elections is tiny. The expected cost of casting a vote, on the other hand, is not insignificant.[1]

A different version of the expected-value approach incorporates the benefits that would accrue to the entire electorate, not merely to the voter himself. Derek Parfit argues that the benefits to the entire populace of electing the superior candidate must be taken into account, and the magnitude of these collective benefits, even when multiplied by the voter's tiny probability of being decisive, might make the expected benefits substantial.[2] Parfit's analysis is presumably addressed to the second interpretation – the moral or quasi-moral interpretation – of the "Why vote?" question.

A second possible moral rationale for voting is the *Kantian* approach. According to Kant's categorical imperative, one must not act according to a principle (maxim) which cannot be willed to become a universal law.[3] Thus, the Kantian approach would lead us to ask whether one can will it to become a universal law that everybody abstains from voting when it does not suit his or her personal economic calculus. Since the upshot would obviously be unacceptable for political democracy, the Kantian approach would not allow citizens to abstain on grounds of personal inconvenience. Presumably, according to Kantianism, only the general practice of voting can be universalized, and that is why one should vote. It is difficult to find full-fledged endorsements of the Kantian theme in the recent literature, but Paul Meehl comes close.[4] He says that you cannot get people to go "rationally" to the polls unless you introduce some sort of quasi-Kantian principle with a distinctly ethical content.[5]

A third rationale for voting is the *expressivist* rationale. Geoffrey Brennan and Loren Lomasky give the following motivating examples.[6] When you send a get-well card to a hospitalized friend, you do not expect the card to effect a therapeutic outcome. When a sports fan goes to the stadium to cheer for his team, he does not expect his scream from the bleachers to enhance the probability of his team's winning. These are "expressive" acts; they express certain desires or preferences of the actor, without any accompanying assumption that they will *cause* the desired outcome. Similarly, Brennan and Lomasky suggest, voting for candidate A can be a bona fide and appropriate expression of support even when one knows that the effect on the outcome is minuscule. Stanley Benn endorses the expressivist approach in the following passage: "I am suggesting, in short, that political activity may be a form of moral self-expression, necessary ... because one could not seriously claim, even to oneself, to be on [the side of the right] without expressing the attitude by the action most appropriate to it in the paradigm situation."[7]

I shall not try to assess the merits of these approaches in any detail. I shall not pick a quarrel, for example, with the economic analysis of whether and when it is prudent to vote. However, voting might be morally commendable even if it is not prudent. Nor shall I spend time evaluating the three foregoing approaches to the morality of voting. Although each has its difficulties, I believe, it is not essential for me to prove them wrong. This is because the approach I favor is not necessarily a rival to these other approaches; in principle, they could all be legitimate rationales for voting.

The approach I favor – a novel approach, as far as I know – may be called the *causal responsibility* approach. The first claim of the causal responsibility approach is that a voter can make a partial causal contribution toward the election of a given candidate even if he is not a swing or decisive voter. Even a non-swing voter can *help* elect a winner. Second, voting in favor of the actual winner counts as a greater causal contribution to her election than merely abstaining. Thus, if the election of a given candidate would be a (socially) *good* outcome, a person can earn more "credit" by helping to produce that outcome than by sitting on the sidelines. Conversely, if an election might result in a *bad* candidate being chosen, potential voters who sit on the sidelines may not escape partial blame for that possible outcome, should it occur. They could contribute (more) toward the defeat of that candidate by voting for a rival; and their failure to do so may carry with it some culpability or blameworthiness. They do not avert such blameworthiness or culpability simply because their vote would not have been a decisive, or swing, vote. So potential voters should vote either to help produce a good outcome or to avoid a bad one.

Exactly what kind of credit or blame is in question here? Is it *moral* credit and blame, or some other kind? This is an issue I shall not try to settle fully. Certainly in some cases moral credit or blame may be apt. In legislative voting and popular referenda, there may be votes on policies that are morally desirable or objectionable; failure to help enact or defeat such policies would be morally culpable. Similarly, in some elections one candidate may be morally inferior to a rival. A voter's failure to contribute as much as possible to the election of the morally preferable candidate may be a moral blemish. More commonly, credit or blame might be in order that is less clearly of a moral stripe. Consider the election of a chair for a social club or professional organization in which neither candidate is morally superior to the other but one is vastly more competent than her rival. She would advance the collective interests of the social entity much more than the rival. If a potential voter, knowing who would be the better officer, nonetheless declines to vote, this might be regarded as a socially irresponsible or socially culpable omission. Is it a *morally* culpable omission? I doubt it; but it does seem to be culpable in a *quasi-moral* sense. In either case, the voter's culpability seems to arise in part from the fact that his action causally influences the outcome. The first step that needs to be taken, then, is to establish that voting or abstaining, even when one is not a prospective swing voter, can nonetheless involve causal responsibility for the outcome. This problem will occupy me for a large chunk of the essay.

II. Overdetermination and Causal Responsibility

According to one view of causation, a particular vote causes a particular electoral outcome only if a different outcome would have eventuated if that vote had not occurred. This is a *simple counterfactual* analysis of event causation. More generally, the theory says that event c causes event e just in case c and e actually occur but if c had not occurred e would not have occurred. A theory very close to this is advocated by David Lewis.[8] Lewis does not require precisely this counterfactual, because he says there might be a causal chain from c to d to e such that d would not have occurred without c, and e would not have occurred without d, yet e might have occurred via a different causal route than through c. These types of cases, however, do not matter for the analysis of voting. So I shall write as if Lewis's account were equivalent to the simple counterfactual analysis. This analysis deals fairly adequately with acts of voting which are decisive. If the citizen had not voted as he did, the outcome would have been different (a tie, at any rate, if not a victory for a different candidate).[9] Such a case will qualify as a cause of the actual electoral outcome under the simple counter-factual analysis. But wherever a citizen's alternative action would not be enough to single-handedly cancel the outcome, his vote will not qualify as a cause of the outcome.

So much the worse, I say, for the simple counterfactual analysis. It is a defect of this account that it restricts causation to these cases. All but a few large elections are decided by a margin of more than one vote. In all of these cases, the simple counterfactual account implies that *no* voter's action is a cause of the outcome. But surely some of the votes – at least those cast for the actual winner – exercised *some* causal influence toward the outcome. Compare this situation with two others. Consider a firing squad with ten members who all fire simultaneously at a victim and all hit their mark. Is it not bizarre to declare that none of their individual actions has any causal influence on the outcome? Moral responsibility for the death is presumably contingent on playing at least some causal role in the death, so if we declare each shooter causally irrelevant to the death, we commit ourselves to absolving each shooter from any moral responsibility. That seems misguided. Any prospective murderer could then protect himself against culpability by recruiting an accomplice to commit the crime simultaneously.

Analogously, suppose that ten friends are recruited to push a car out of a snow bank, when three would suffice for the job. If all ten push simultaneously, the car's being freed does not depend counterfactually on the pushing of any one. But surely this is a case in which each exerts *some* causal influence, and each deserves some degree of credit and thanks, which are presumably predicated on his partial causal responsibility.[10]

Both civil and criminal law support the view that in these types of (concurrent) overdetermination cases, each separate set of sufficient conditions qualifies as a cause.[11] Where two defendants ride their motorcycles past the victim's horse, which is startled and injures the victim, each defendant causes the injury, despite the sufficiency of the noise from each motorcycle to have done the job. Where two defendants independently stab or shoot the victim, who dies of loss of blood, each is liable for the victim's death.

Lewis groups these types of cases under a category he labels "symmetric overdetermination."[12] He says that these are cases in which common sense does not deliver a clear answer as to whether the individual act causes the outcome, so theory can safely say what it likes.[13] This strikes me as wrong, or at least inadequate. Although it may not be clear that these are cases of "full" causation, they are at least instances of a weak species of causation, call it *partial* causation, or *contributory* causation, or causal *influence*.[14] Lewis points out that in cases of symmetric overdetermination we can always find a larger event that qualifies as a cause, an event that consists in the "sum" of the various causes.[15] Returning to our earlier examples, the sum of the ten shootings or the ten pushings will satisfy the counterfactual analysis, even if the individual shootings or pushings do not, because the death would not have occurred without the ten shootings, and the freeing of the car would not have occurred without the ten pushings. This *may* be right, but it does not go far enough.[16] A satisfactory theory must also assign some causal influence to the individual shootings and pushings; and a satisfactory theory must assign causal influence to individual acts of voting even in wide-margin elections where no single vote is decisive.

Another approach to the theory of causation, which seems more promising for our purposes than the simple counterfactual approach, is presented by J. L. Mackie.[17] Mackie considers the example of a fire started by a short-circuit. The short-circuit combines with other conditions, such as the presence of flammable material, the absence of a suitably placed sprinkler, and so on, to constitute a complex condition that is sufficient for the fire. Also, the short-circuit is an indispensable part of this complex condition; the other parts of this condition, in the absence of the short-circuit, would not have produced the fire.[18] Mackie calls this an INUS condition: an *insufficient* but *necessary* part of a condition which is itself *unnecessary* but *sufficient* for the result. Thus, in typical cases, a cause is an indispensable part of a sufficient condition.

This formulation would nicely handle standard election cases in which the margin of victory is more than one. Consider an electorate of 100 persons, all of whom vote in a given election in which Jones defeats Smith by a 60-to-40 margin. Let citizen Z be one of those who votes for Jones. Is Z's ballot a (partial) cause of Jones's victory? If we focus on all 60 votes for Jones, which is a condition sufficient for Jones's victory, Z's vote does not meet the INUS requirement. Although Z's vote is part of that 60-vote condition, his vote is not a *necessary* or *indispensable* part of that sufficient condition. The other 59 votes for Jones still suffice for Jones's victory, even if we subtract Z's vote. Let us instead consider any set of 51 actual votes for Jones, including Z's vote. Such a set of 51 votes is also sufficient for Jones's victory, and Z's vote is a necessary or indispensable part of that sufficient condition (given the 100-member electorate). Z's vote is indispensable because if his vote is subtracted from the 51 – that is, if it is left open what Z will do – a Jones victory is not guaranteed. So Z's vote does satisfy the INUS condition.

It is true, of course, that any other set of 51 Jones votes, not including Z's vote, is also sufficient for Jones's victory. Z's vote is not an indispensable part of *those* sufficient conditions. But if the INUS approach is going to authorize overdetermining causes to qualify as causes, this should not matter. It should be enough that a given event is an indispensable member of *some* sufficient condition for the effect. It is not clear that Mackie himself means to allow this. In the fire example, he adds the requirement that "no other sufficient condition of the house's catching fire was present on this occasion."[19] This seems intended to exclude overdeterminers as causes, and would thereby exclude wide-margin electoral results from having any causes. This follows, at any rate, if "another sufficient condition" means any sufficient condition not identical with, but possibly overlapping, a selected one. For reasons already adduced, however, this addendum is unfortunate, precisely because it would exclude overdeterminers from qualifying as causes. This is especially unfortunate relative to our project of analyzing the concept of *partial* or *contributory* cause (as opposed to the concept of "*the* cause," for example). We do better to work with the initial formulation I took from Mackie, not the final formulation he provides.

To clarify how the INUS analysis works, let us ask whether someone's vote for Jones could ever serve as a partial cause of an opponent's victory. Setting aside "indirect" effects – for example, one's own vote influencing the votes of others – the answer is no. If Z votes for Jones but Smith wins by a 60-to-40 margin, there is no (actually present) condition sufficient for Smith's victory of which Z's vote is an indispensable part. To be sure, there is the set of votes consisting of 51 votes for Smith plus Z's vote for Jones. That set is sufficient for Smith's victory. But even if we subtract Z's vote for Jones, the remaining votes are still sufficient for Smith's victory.

What about abstentions? Can they qualify as partial causes under the INUS approach? Yes. But it depends on whether the number of potential voters is even or odd. If the number is even, an abstention can satisfy the INUS condition; if the number is odd, it cannot. To illustrate, consider first a 100-person electorate. Suppose Z abstains and Jones wins by a 59-to-40 margin. Consider the set of decisions consisting of 50 votes for Jones plus Z's abstention. This set of decisions suffices for Jones's victory, because only 49 potential voters remain and they cannot prevent Jones's victory. If we subtract Z's abstention, however, there is no longer a guarantee of Jones's victory. Because 50 voting decisions are still open, there could be a tie. So Z's abstention is an indispensable part of the originally designated set of conditions for Jones's victory. In the case of an odd-numbered electorate, however, this scenario cannot happen. To illustrate, consider a 101-person electorate. Where Jones wins with a minimum of 51 votes, we can consider a set consisting of 51 Jones votes plus Z's abstention. This suffices for Jones's victory; but subtracting Z's abstention, there is still enough to guarantee Jones's victory. So Z's abstention is not an indispensable member of such a set.[20]

Proceeding from this analysis, let us ask what can be said to citizen Z who is deciding whether to vote in a forthcoming election. Suppose he knows *how* he will vote if he votes at all but has not yet decided *whether* to vote. Assume that candidate Brown, for whom Z would vote, is indeed the best candidate in the race.[21] Here is what we can say to citizen Z, to justify his voting: "If you vote for Brown and Brown wins, you will deserve partial causal credit for her victory. If you vote for Brown but her (inferior) opponent Johnson wins, you will be absolved from any causal responsibility for Johnson's victory. A tie is possible but so improbable that it can be ignored. Thus, if you vote, you are guaranteed either partial causal credit for a good outcome or no causal discredit for a bad outcome. On the other hand, if you abstain from voting, there is no guarantee that either of these scenarios will transpire. If there is an even-numbered electorate, you will earn partial causal credit by abstention in case Brown wins, but you will also earn partial causal discredit if Brown loses. If there is an odd-numbered electorate, you will earn neither causal credit nor causal discredit. So in terms of causal credit or discredit, you are better off voting than abstaining."

If we adopt the INUS approach to causation, then, we have a rationale for voting in terms of causal responsibility. It is not as smooth and intuitive as one might like; and therefore in the next section, I shall propose an alternative approach. We see, however, how at least one familiar approach to causation provides a basis for rationalizing voting in terms of causal responsibility.

I should emphasize that this type of rationale requires certain explanations, qualifications, and/or provisos. Let me introduce these qualifications by reversing the earlier assumption that the candidate for whom citizen Z plans to vote is the superior candidate. Suppose instead that Z's preferred candidate Brown is the inferior candidate. Does Z still have good reasons to vote? In other words, should a citizen vote whether or not his preferred candidate is the objectively best choice? Or should he vote only when the preferred candidate is objectively best?

First let us ask what might be meant by the phrase "objectively best candidate." Elsewhere[22] I have suggested that if candidate A would produce a set of outcomes higher on the preference-ordering of a majority of citizens than the set of outcomes candidate B would produce, then A is a democratically better candidate than B. This is one possible way to give content to the phrase "objectively best candidate," though others, of course, might be proposed. Now a voter might be said to have *objectively good reasons* to vote for a certain candidate if that candidate is objectively best. But what if a citizen does not know, and indeed has no idea, which candidate is objectively best? Should such a citizen still be encouraged to vote rather than abstain?

On the approach I favor, citizens should not be encouraged to vote, *full stop*. Instead they should be encouraged first to gather enough information and then to vote. The point of becoming informed, of course, is to increase the probability of making a good choice, that is, of choosing the objectively best candidate.[23] The upshot is that voting is not necessarily and without qualification a desirable or dutiful act. Consider an uninformed citizen, late on election day, who has no time to become informed before the polls close, but wonders whether he should vote. The present approach would not justify his voting. In this respect, the present rationale differs from both the Kantian and expressivist approaches, which presumably urge people to vote under all circumstances. I do not regard it as a defect of the current rationale that it has this qualified aspect. I am unconvinced that a person ought to vote, or has a duty to vote, even when he is both uninformed and no longer has time to become informed.[24]

Even if a voter collects substantial information about the candidates, he might still be wrong about which would be the best one to elect. Can he still have good reasons to vote under this scenario? Here I introduce the notion of *subjectively* good reasons to vote, which I define in terms of what a voter is *justified* in believing about the candidates, rather than what is *true* of them. Citizen Z's information might *justify* him in believing that Brown is the best candidate in the race, even if she is not. Z would then be justified in believing that by voting for Brown he would either achieve partial causal responsibility for the election of the best candidate or at least avoid all causal responsibility for the best candidate's defeat. His being justified in believing this gives him subjectively good reasons to vote for Brown.

Which class of reasons is more important, one might ask, objective reasons or subjective reasons? Which class of reasons is crucial in determining whether a citizen really should vote? These questions have no answers, I submit. The question of whether a person should vote is simply ambiguous as between an objective sense of "should" and a subjective sense of "should." There are simply two distinct questions here, and there is no reason to expect one of them to take precedence over the other. The important thing, for present purposes, is that in *each* sense of "should" our account shows why citizens will often be in a situation in which it is true that they should vote.

III. Vectorial and Conventional Causal Systems

Although the INUS analysis of causation provides one basis for justifying a decision to vote, that analysis does not adequately capture the intuitive difference in causal role between voting and abstaining. I shall try to do a better job of capturing that difference by introducing another model of causation: the *vectorial* model. This is not intended to be a general analysis of causation, for it applies only to a restricted subset of causal relationships, which I shall call *vectorial causal systems*. Electoral systems are prime examples of such systems.

A vectorial causal system is a system in which states and state-changes result from the interplay among forces that can be represented as vectors. A simple illustration of a natural vectorial system is a tug-of-war. Forces are exerted on a rope in opposite directions, and movements of the rope – and of participants clinging to the rope – are the results of the sum of the vectorial forces. When an element in a vectorial causal system moves in a given direction, this is because the sum of the forces on that element are positive in that direction. This sum is computed from three kinds of forces: (1) forces that are positive in the direction of movement, (2) forces that are negative in the direction of movement, and (3) forces that are zero in the direction of movement.[25] Finally, when thinking about the causation of a given movement, we think of each positive force as a *contributing factor* in the production of the movement, each negative force as a *counteracting*, or *resisting*, factor in the production of the movement, and each zero force as a *neutral factor* vis-à-vis the production of the movement.

Elections are what we may call *conventional* vectorial causal systems. Given the conventions of vote counting, a vote for candidate C is a positive vector vis-à-vis C's possible election. A vote for a rival candidate is a negative vector vis-à-vis C's possible election. And an abstention from voting is a zero vector vis-à-vis C's (and anybody else's) possible election. Now how should we link vector forces with event causation in electoral contexts? The following seems plausible. If the target candidate actually wins, each vote for her is a partial cause of her victory; but neither votes against her nor abstentions from voting are partial causes of her victory.

When we turn to an *agent's* causal responsibility, however, things are a little different. When we address the responsibility of an agent, we take into account all of the options available to him. We consider not only the options he chooses but those he could have chosen instead. If an available option is not chosen, but would have exerted a causal influence had it been chosen, this is certainly germane in assessing the agent's responsibility. Suppose citizen Z votes for candidate C, but C loses nonetheless. Is Z in any way responsible for C's defeat? No. Z did everything in his electoral power to elect C, so he cannot be held responsible.[26] Now suppose that Z abstains and C loses. Here Z can certainly be held partly responsible for C's loss, because an option available to Z – namely, voting for C – would have been a counteracting causal factor vis-à-vis C's loss. Thus, an abstention certainly opens an agent to charges of causal responsibility, despite the fact that the agent's act of abstention does not qualify as an event-cause of the outcome (under the vectorial model of causation). Of course, this analysis can be flipped on the other side. If an agent can be held partly responsible for a candidate's defeat by virtue of his abstention, shouldn't he equally be held partly responsible for a candidate's victory if he abstains? After all, he *could* have voted for a rival candidate but did not. This seems to me plausible, as long as we insist that an abstainer bears *less* responsibility for C's victory than someone who actually voted for C. That seems a clear implication of the vectorial model of causation. Obviously, a positive vote exerts greater causal influence toward a victory than an abstention, and that should weigh heavily in assigning responsibility.

Let us now link this responsibility-based approach to the rationale for voting that can be offered to citizens. The story is similar to the one presented at the end of Section II, but without the complications encountered there (e.g., those relating to odd- or even-numbered electorates). If Brown is the superior candidate, then Z's voting for her rather than abstaining places him in the following position. If Brown wins, Z will have had greater responsibility than an abstainer for the election of the better candidate; if she loses, Z will have had no responsibility for her loss. Furthermore, if Z is justified in believing that Brown is the better candidate, then he is justified in believing that he will have some measure of responsibility for the victory (or no responsibility for the loss) of the better candidate if he votes for Brown. Thus, Z has either objectively good reasons to vote for Brown, or subjectively good reasons, or both.

At this point an important objection must be confronted. The cases I have discussed of overdetermining causes are instances of what Lewis calls "symmetric" overdetermination, where all the redundant causes occur simultaneously. In the case of voting, though, many of the votes occur in sequence. Moreover, by the time many voters cast their ballots, the outcome has already been decided. This is particularly striking in the case of presidential elections in the United States, where several time zones are involved. By the time voters in California or Hawaii go to the polls, the earlier-voting states may already have determined the victor. How can voters in these later-voting districts rationalize their voting? Do their votes really qualify as partial causes of the outcome (even if they vote for the winner)?[27] Are they really responsible for the outcome?

These voting cases, the objection continues, are instances of what is commonly called causal *preemption*. In preemption, an event c_1 occurs and actually causes e, but another event, c_2, also occurs and would have caused e if it were not preempted by c_1. As Lewis puts it: "There is the beginning of a causal process running from the preempted alternative to the effect. But this process does not go to completion."[28] An example would be a case in which a would-be assassin sets a timer to fire a gun at an intended victim at the stroke of midnight. A moment before midnight, another assassin shoots and kills the victim. Here intuition dictates that the preempted alternative is not a cause at all of the victim's death. Nor is the agent who sets the timer responsible for the death. Doesn't this equally apply to voters who cast their ballots for Brown but who get preempted by earlier votes for Brown, which suffice for her election?

To deal with this objection, we need to make greater use of the notion of a conventional causal system, introduced earlier in this section. A conventional causal system is one in which causal upshots are defined or stipulated by social conventions. For example, property ownership is conventionally conferred and changed as a function of various symbolic acts. When two people make certain verbal utterances and money is exchanged, this conventionally causes the transfer of ownership of some item of property from one individual to the other. Elections are another prime example of a conventional causal system, in which certain types of outcomes are conventionally stipulated to result from assorted collections of voting acts.

An important feature of conventional causal systems is that the time of an outcome is one of the conventionally determined elements. Certain types of sales, for example, do not go into effect until a certain time period has elapsed after the main transactions, to allow a party (especially a buyer) to reconsider. Similarly, I contend, elections standardly feature a certain conventional element with respect to time. Even if voters cast their ballots at different times on election day (or through earlier absentee ballots), the system conventionally abstracts from this actual or "natural" order and considers all the votes on an equal basis. This is reflected in the fact that the votes are not *counted*, and have no conventional causal upshot, until all votes in a given electoral district are cast, that is, until the polls close. Nor does the order of counting make any official difference. For these reasons, the temporal asymmetry among different votes is officially voided or obliterated by the conventions of the electoral process. In the United States House or Senate, for example, a roll-call vote is completed even if the outcome is clear long before the last vote has been voiced. This is because, officially, votes are not counted or "registered" until all have been voiced. Because of this conventional feature, the causal impact of a late vote is not really preempted by a collection of early votes. From the official, conventional perspective, they are all simultaneous; hence, their causal statuses are perfectly symmetric.[29]

Admittedly, this conventional perspective is obscured by national elections featuring different time zones, or by different poll-closing times among districts within the same time zone. All such cases, I would say, are flawed executions of the traditional conceptualization of elections. The idea behind a democratic election is that all votes should have equal weight, and that idea is, to some degree, undercut by counting some people's ballots before other citizens have had an opportunity to vote.[30]

IV. Objections and Replies

The heart of my (quasi-) moral rationale for voting is that one stands to earn more "credit" for helping to elect the best candidate or stands to avoid "discredit" for letting the best candidate lose. But, it may be asked, who is handing out this credit?[31] Other citizens? God? What I mean to say, in saying that a voter "earns credit" for voting, is that the voter attains a certain (quasi-) moral status, whether or not anybody else knows about this status or does anything about it. Analogously, if someone (appropriately) fulfills a promise to a deceased friend or relative, he thereby attains a certain moral status, whether or not anybody else knows of his promise-keeping or compliments him for it. People of certain persuasions may doubt that the prospect of attaining a certain moral status would be very *motivating* for prospective voters. I am inclined to disagree with these doubts; but, in any case, I have not yet claimed that the rationale proffered here will necessarily succeed in motivating citizens. Insofar as I am interested in providing a (quasi-) moral rationale for voting, I merely wish to offer normatively sound reasons for voting, however successful or unsuccessful these reasons might be in motivational terms.

It is but a small step, however, from this normative rationale to scenarios that provide voting incentives. Citizens often disclose their voting actions or inactions to their friends and associates. A voter who informs his chums that he voted for their mutually approved candidate may be greeted with verbal approval (credit), whereas an acknowledgment that he did not manage to vote may be greeted with disapproval (discredit). These responses may arise precisely because friends and associates recognize the respective causal effects of voting and abstaining. If a citizen *expects* approval for voting and disapproval for abstaining, such an expectation creates an incentive in favor of voting.[32] Thus, insofar as my (quasi-) moral rationale underpins peer approval and disapproval, it can also indirectly affect a citizen's *prudential* rationale for voting. But I do not wish to make much of this.[33]

Let me return, then, to the moral rationale. Readers who are persuaded that causal responsibility gives a citizen a moral reason to vote might still want to know more about this reason; in particular, they might want to know how *weighty* it is. After all, voting is still somewhat costly, and it would be good to know how to weigh the moral value of helping elect a good candidate – especially when one's help is not essential – against the personal cost of voting. More generally, how is moral credit to be divided when there are more than enough contributors to a socially valuable outcome?[34] It would indeed be nice to have answers to these further questions, but I do not have them. This in no way suggests, however, that my type of voting rationale is on the wrong track; it merely suggests (unsurprisingly) that more work is left to be done.

Personal cost, moreover, is not the only reason to abstain from casting a vote. At least two other considerations of an entirely different nature can also militate against voting. First, if both candidates in a given race are terrible, a citizen might wish to avoid complicity in electing even the lesser of the two evils.[35] Second, one might sometimes wish to abstain in order to "send a message" of some sort. For example, if a citizen objects to the placement of a questionable referendum on the ballot, he might express his opposition by means of abstention.[36] Once again, however, the fact that there are sometimes these kinds of reasons to abstain does not cut against the proposal that causal responsibility creates a positive reason to vote. Nor does it undercut the possibility that *normally*, if citizens become sufficiently informed, their on-balance reasons will favor voting.

The final objection I wish to consider concerns the epistemic conditions of citizens in the contemporary age of scientific polling and rapid communication. Given pollsters' predictions prior to election day, or the reports of exit polls on election day itself, a prospective voter may either know or be highly justified in believing that one of the candidates is a shoo-in and that his own vote will make no difference to the outcome. In the face of such knowledge or justified belief, how can the responsibility rationale properly move him? How can he incur moral or quasi-moral culpability by not voting?[37]

This line of argument restates the rational-choice perspective on the voting problem. No doubt it has intuitive appeal, but I do not think it deserves to be either the sole or the dominant perspective on the problem. According to the argument I have offered, when a prospective voter knows or justifiably believes that candidate X will win with or without his vote, this does not cancel his partial responsibility for the electoral outcome. If partial responsibility for the outcome gives him a reason to vote, as I have argued it does, the prospective voter's epistemic condition does not undercut this reason.

To appreciate the force of my reply, return to the firing-squad example. Suppose a member of a firing-squad offers himself the following argument: "People have counseled me not to shoot because then I won't incur any moral responsibility for the victim's death. But I won't incur any responsibility even if I do shoot. After all, I *know* that my comrades are all going to shoot, so the outcome will be the same whether I shoot or not. I cannot single-handedly change the outcome, so I won't be responsible. Therefore, I might as well shoot and not get in trouble with my superiors for abstaining." This argument is unconvincing, because our criterion of moral responsibility is not tied to the make-a-difference, or decisiveness, criterion. Nor does knowledge that one will not make a difference to the outcome entail absence of moral responsibility. Our criterion of moral responsibility is tied to being a *contributing* (though possibly redundant) cause, not to being a *decisive* cause. A member of a firing squad who shoots (accurately) *is* a contributing cause of the victim's death. If he shoots, he does bear partial responsibility, although he could not have reversed the outcome by abstaining. *Mutatis mutandis*, the same applies to a voter. He can earn (more) moral credit by voting for the good candidate even if his vote is not decisive for victory; and he can incur moral culpability by abstaining even if his abstention is not decisive for the candidate's loss.[38]

Another possible objection by appeal to epistemic conditions might run as follows: "Even if you (Goldman) are right in claiming that partial causation rather than decisiveness is the crucial de facto ingredient in culpability, there is still a further, epistemic ingredient. To be culpable for an act or omission the agent must know, or be justified in believing, that this act or omission would instantiate that de facto ingredient. Do citizens satisfy this epistemic constraint?"

The answer to this is easy. Since citizens understand the conventional causal system that comprises the electoral process, it is pretty trivial for them to appreciate (at least at a tacit level) the causal role that their voting or abstaining will play in a given election. So the indicated epistemic condition, I suspect, is regularly met. Indeed, I am tempted to speculate that the reason so many people *do* vote, as a matter of fact, is precisely because of their grasp of the rationale offered here, including their grasp of the "contributing cause" role that their voting occupies within the system. As we saw earlier, if voting is approached from the standard economic or rational-choice perspective (which incorporates the decisiveness test), it seems irrational for most people to vote. From this perspective, it is perplexing why so many people do vote. The current approach offers a possible explanation of this phenomenon. Conceivably, then, the account presented here fulfills the dual function of both *normative* and *explanatory* theory. It can explain why people *should* vote (after obtaining sufficient information), and it can explain why people *do* vote (in fairly substantial numbers).

V. Conclusion

Political theorists have been hard put to explain why citizens should vote – or why they *do* vote – because the theorists have largely focused on the expected consequences of an individual's voting versus not voting. This essay proposes a different approach to the problem.[39] It argues that citizens often have good reasons to vote because they bear partial responsibility for the electoral outcome. Even if an individual's vote is not decisive for a given candidate's victory, such a vote can still qualify as a partial cause of that victory. So a voter can earn moral or quasi-moral credit for an electoral outcome even if he is not a swing voter. Thus, the proper treatment of partial causation and causal responsibility provides the underpinning of a good rationale for voting. If citizens intuitively grasp this rationale – and it is not implausible that they do – it may also explain why they actually vote (a fair amount of the time).

Notes

I am indebted to Tom Christiano, Holly Smith, and Ellen Frankel Paul, for valuable discussion and suggestions. Christiano's pointers to relevant literature on voting rationales were especially helpful.

1   William Riker and Peter Ordeshook have estimated the probability of an individual voter being decisive to the outcome of a U.S. presidential election as p $= 10^{-8}$ – that is, a 1 in 100,000,000 chance. See Riker and Ordeshook, "A Theory of the Calculus of Voting," *American Political Science Review* 62 (March 1968): 25. Perhaps the earliest formulation of the economic approach is due to Anthony Downs, *An Economic Theory of Democracy* (New York: Harper and Row, 1957), ch. 14. Downs formulates matters in terms of the "party differential" rather than the differential between the two individual candidates, but this difference is incidental.

2   Derek Parfit, *Reasons and Persons* (Oxford: Clarendon Press, 1984), 73–5.

3   Immanuel Kant, *Foundations of the Metaphysics of Morals*, trans. L. W. Beck (Indianapolis: Bobbs-Merrill, 1959), 39.

4   Paul Meehl, "The Selfish Voter Paradox and the Thrown-Away Vote Argument," *American Political Science Review* 71 (March 1977): 11–30.

5   Ibid., 13. Later, Meehl sketches his favored rationale as follows: "I would say that some sort of prima facie obligation or obligation vector exists for me as a voter to participate in the electoral process, relying on the general principle that unless people do, the system won't work..." (ibid., 21).

6   Geoffrey Brennan and Loren Lomasky, "Large Numbers, Small Costs: The Uneasy Foundation of Democratic Rule," in *Politics and Process: New Essays in Democratic Thought*, ed. Geoffrey Brennan and Loren Lomasky (Cambridge: Cambridge University Press, 1989), 49–50.

7   Stanley Benn, "The Problematic Rationality of Political Participation," in *Philosophy, Politics, and Society, Fifth Series*, ed. Peter Laslett and James Fishkin (New Haven: Yale University Press, 1979), 310.

8   David Lewis, "Causation," in Lewis, *Philosophical Papers*, vol. 2 (New York: Oxford University Press, 1986).

9   The term "swing vote" perhaps suggests a vote that tilts the outcome either toward one candidate or toward the other; it does not suggest a tie as a possible outcome. In the present context, however, we want to consider possible abstentions as well as votes for different candidates. And a decision to abstain rather

than vote could change the outcome from a victory for one candidate to a tie – perhaps requiring a run-off election. (For that matter, even switching a vote from one candidate to another can result in a tie, when the number of votes is even.) The counterfactual analysis also invites consideration of abstentions. If a citizen votes for candidate X and we ask, "What would have happened if the citizen had not cast this vote?," one possible scenario is that the citizen abstains rather than votes for an opposing candidate.

10 In other cases, of course, credit or thanks might be given for mere *effort*, even if it makes no causal contribution. In this case, however, the effort plays a causal role; it is not merely fruitless effort.

11 I draw the examples that follow from Michael S. Moore, "Causation and Responsibility," *Social Philosophy And Policy* 16 (1999). Moore, in turn, cites Richard Wright, "Causation in Tort Law," *California Law Review* 73 (1985): 1775–98, as an excellent discussion of such cases.

12 See David Lewis, "Postscripts to 'Causation'," in Lewis, *Philosophical Papers*, 2:193–212.

13 Ibid., 194, 212.

14 In a similar spirit, Louis Loeb offers an account of causation that includes overdetermining causes. See his "Causal Theories and Causal Overdetermination," *Journal of Philosophy* 71, no. 15 (1974): 525–44.

15 Lewis, "Postscripts," 212.

16 I say it "may" be right because it is not entirely clear. If the ten pushings had not occurred, would *no* pushings have occurred? Not obviously. Perhaps five pushings would still have occurred, which would have been sufficient to free the car.

17 J. L. Mackie, "Causes and Conditions," *American Philosophical Quarterly* 2, no. 4 (October 1965): 245–64.

18 Ibid., 245.

19 Ibid.

20 There are a number of objections to Mackie's INUS account. One of them is that it requires causation to feature sufficient conditions, and this ostensibly implies that there is no causation without determinism. This is too restrictive, as many writers point out. Causation can take place even in chancy situations, where merely probabilistic laws hold sway. See Patrick Suppes, *A Probabilistic Theory of Causality* (Amsterdam: North-Holland, 1970); Nancy Cartwright, "Causal Laws and Effective Strategies," *Nôus* 13 (1979): 419–37; Wesley Salmon, *Scientific Explanation and the Causal Structure of the World* (Princeton, NJ: Princeton University Press, 1984); and Lewis, "Postscripts," 175–84. I concede this point, and therefore grant that the INUS account is not fully comprehensive. In the context of voting, however, we do not need to worry about probabilistic causation. Wherever an electoral outcome occurs, some set of votes is sufficient for the outcome. So the analysis sketched above is adequate for present purposes.

21 For simplicity, I assume an election with a single race.

22 Alvin I. Goldman, *Knowledge in a Social World* (Oxford: Oxford University Press, 1999), ch. 10.
23 The types of relevant information to gather would not be exhausted, of course, by campaign promises and accusations against one's opponent. Other relevant types of information would include each candidate's past experience and track record, her party affiliation and supporters, and so forth.
24 The critical role of political information in producing good outcomes is elaborated in my *Knowledge in a Social World,* ch. 10.
25 John Staddon points out that these forces can be treated as *scalars* rather than *vectors,* because there is just one dimension of movement, and forces can be treated as either positive or negative along this dimension. In election cases, however, at least in races where there are more than two candidates, the scalar approach will not work. In any case, the term "vector" is here used loosely to depict an interplay of conflicting forces.
26 There may be ways to influence the outcome above and beyond one's personal vote, for example, by persuading other voters. But this goes beyond the present subject.
27 Thanks to Tom Christiano for calling my attention to this problem and for highlighting its importance.
28 Lewis, "Postscripts," 199.
29 There are, to be sure, all sorts of deals made by members of Congress that depend upon voting order. This is not the occasion to enter into a close analysis of what such deals imply or presuppose.
30 It might be objected that not all votes do have equal weights under all systems. For example, under the American system of electing presidents, the electoral college, not all citizens' votes count equally. However, this is not a clear instance of unequal weights. The electoral college involves a two-step system, in which citizens first choose electors who then choose a president. In the race for any given elector, all votes count equally; and in the race for president, all electors' ballots count equally.
31 Thanks to Ellen Frankel Paul for highlighting this issue.
32 In principle, of course, someone who votes for Brown might incur the wrath of those who oppose Brown's election. But a voter for Brown will probably have fewer associations with people who oppose Brown's election, and is less likely to inform them of his vote.
33 Feeling as if one is part of a team that is working toward victory is undoubtedly a major factor in the psychology of political participation. But the integrity of team spirit derives from the fact that team members can all make causal contributions toward mutually sought outcomes.
34 This question was properly urged on me by David Sobel.
35 This consideration was suggested by Roderick Long and Susan Sauvé Meyer.
36 David Schmidtz suggested this consideration.
37 Thanks to Tom Christiano for pressing this problem on me.

38 Similarly, many commentators on the Holocaust morally censure people – especially people in official capacities – who failed to speak out against it at the time, even if such speech would not have single-handedly changed the outcome.

39 Strictly, the causal responsibility approach I propose could be subsumed under the expected-consequences, or rational-choice, perspective. Suppose we view the state of being a partial cause of a good electoral result, or the state of deserving moral credit (or discredit), as themselves possible *outcomes* or *consequences* of voting or not voting. Then the approach I favor may just be a special case of the rational-choice framework. The choice matrix now confronting the voter will differ from the matrix that would exist under the standard analysis. In addition to the outcomes being different, the probability of getting a more preferred outcome from voting than from abstaining is no longer linked to the probability of being a swing voter. Even if one is not a swing voter, one's act of voting can raise the probability of one's earning more causal credit for a superior candidate's victory and of avoiding causal discredit for such a candidate's loss. If citizens value some of these kinds of outcomes over others to a sufficient degree, the new choice matrix might make it "rational" for them to vote on numerous occasions. Since the outcomes have a moral nature, however, it may be controversial whether the choices should be considered a matter of "prudence" or "self-interest." I do not try to address this issue here.

Part VI

Formal Models and Normative Theory

11

Deliberative Democracy and Social Choice

David Miller

The paper contrasts the liberal conception of democracy as the aggregation of individual preferences with the deliberative conception of democracy as a process of open discussion leading to an agreed judgement on policy. Social choice theory has identified problems – the arbitrariness of decision rules, vulnerability to strategic voting – which are often held to undermine democratic ideals. Contrary to common opinion, I argue that deliberative democracy is less vulnerable to these difficulties than liberal democracy. The process of discussion tends to produce sets of policy preferences that are 'single peaked'; and within a deliberative setting it may be possible to vary the decision rule according to the nature of the issue to be decided.

If we are in the business of thinking about liberal democracy and possible alternatives to it, we must begin by drawing a distinction between institutions and their regulative ideals. Liberal democracy may be taken to refer to the set of institutions – free elections, competing parties, freedom of speech – that make up the political system with which we are familiar in the west; or it may refer to the conception of democracy that underlies and justifies that system. The relationship between institutions and regulative ideals is not necessarily simple or one-to-one. The same institution may be justified from different points of view, although characteristically those who favour contrasting regulative ideals will aim to shape the institution in different ways. Thus, to take a familiar case, the practice of electing representatives to a legislative assembly may be seen as a way of subjecting legislators to popular control; alternatively, it may be seen simply as a means of removing visibly corrupt legislators from office. Which of these views you take will affect your preferences as to the form of the practice. (How frequent should elections be? Should the voting system be first-past-the-post or something else? And so forth.)

The argument that follows has mainly to do with competing regulative ideals of democracy. In comparing liberal democracy with what I shall call deliberative democracy, my aim is to contrast two basic ways of understanding the democratic process. In favouring deliberative democracy, therefore, I am not recommending wholesale abolition of the present institutions of liberal democracy but rather a reshaping of those institutions in the light of a different regulative ideal from that which I take to be prevalent now. I shall only address the institutional questions briefly. My main aim is to bring out what is at stake between liberal and deliberative democracy, particularly in the light of social choice theory, which appears to challenge the cogency of anything beyond the most minimal of democratic ideals.

Let me now sketch the contrast between liberal and deliberative democracy as regulative ideals. In the liberal view, the aim of democracy is to aggregate individual preferences into a collective choice in as fair and efficient a way as possible.[1] In a democracy there will be many different views as to what should be done politically, reflecting the many different interests and beliefs present in society. Each person's preferences should be accorded equal weight. Moreover, preferences are sacrosanct because they reflect the individuality of each member of the political community (an exception to this arises only in the case of preferences that violate the canons of liberal democracy itself, such as racist beliefs that deny the equal rights of all citizens). The problem then is to find the institutional structure that best meets the requirements of equality and efficiency. Thus liberal democrats may divide on the question of whether majoritarian decision-making is to be preferred, or whether the ideal is a pluralist system which gives various groups in society different amounts of influence over decisions in proportion to their interest in those decisions. This, however, is a family quarrel in which both sides are guided by the same underlying ideal, namely how to reach a fair and efficient compromise given the many conflicting preferences expressed in the political community.

The deliberative ideal also starts from the premise that political preferences will conflict and that the purpose of democratic institutions must be to resolve this conflict. But it envisages this occurring through an open and uncoerced discussion of the issue at stake with the aim of arriving at an agreed judgement.[2] The process of reaching a decision will also be a process whereby initial preferences are transformed to take account of the views of others. That is, the need to reach an agreement forces each participant to put forward proposals under the rubric of general principles or policy considerations that others could accept. Thus even if initially my aim is to support the claims of a particular group to which I belong or which I represent, I cannot in a general discussion simply say 'I claim that group *A*

– farmers, say, or policemen – should get more money'. I have to give reasons for the claim. These might be that the group in question has special needs, or that it is in the common interest to improve the living standards of the group. By giving these reasons, however, I am committing myself to a general principle, which by implication applies to any other similarly placed group. Thus I am forced to take a wider view, and either defend the claim I am making when applied not only to my group but to groups B, C and D, which are like A in the relevant respects, or else to back down and moderate the claim to something I am prepared to accept in these other cases too. Although finally when a decision has to be reached there may still need to be a vote taken between two or more options, what participants are doing at that point is something like rendering a judgement or a verdict on the basis of what they have heard. They are expressing an opinion about which policy best meets the various claims that have been advanced, or represents the fairest compromise between the competing points of view that have been expressed.

The deliberative view clearly rests on a different conception of 'human nature in politics' from the liberal view. Whereas the latter stresses the importance of giving due weight to each individual's distinct preferences, the former relies upon a person's capacity to be swayed by rational arguments and to lay aside particular interests and opinions in deference to overall fairness and the common interest of the collectivity. It supposes people to be to some degree communally orientated in their outlook. It also seems to be more vulnerable to exploitation, in the sense that the practice of deliberative democracy can be abused by people who pay lip-service to the ideal of open discussion but actually attempt to manipulate their colleagues to reach decisions that serve private interests.[3] We shall shortly see, however, that liberal democratic procedures are themselves vulnerable to political manipulation. At this stage, therefore, we must take it as an open question which of the two democratic ideals is more likely to be subverted by manipulative individuals or groups.

In presenting my account of deliberative democracy, I mean to distinguish it not only from liberal democracy but from what has been called 'epistemic' democracy.[4] The epistemic conception of democracy sees the aim of democratic procedures as being to arrive at a correct answer to some question facing the political community. It is assumed here, in other words, that there is some objectively right or valid answer to the question that has been posed, but because there is uncertainty as to what the answer is, a decision-procedure is needed, and democracy, in the form of majority voting, is the procedure most likely to produce the right answer. This was, for instance, the view of Condorcet[5] and it has also been attributed to Rousseau,[6] although my own belief is that Rousseau's view is ambiguous as between deliberative and epistemic conceptions of democracy.[7]

I believe the epistemic conception sets an unrealistically high standard for political decision-making. Although occasionally a political community may have to decide on some question to which it is plausible to suppose a correct answer exists (say some scientific question in circumstances where there is complete consensus on the ends which the decision should serve), it is much more likely that the issue will concern competing claims which cannot all be met simultaneously in circumstances where no resolution of the competition can be deemed objectively right. In the deliberative conception, the aim is to reach agreement, which might be achieved in different ways. One way is for the participants to agree on a substantive norm, which all concur in thinking is the appropriate norm for the case in hand. Another way is to agree on a procedure, which abstracts from the merits of the arguments advanced by particular claimants. (Thus suppose the question is how an available resource such as a tract of land should be allocated as between several groups that lay claim with it. One possibility would be to agree on a principle such as that the resource should go to the group which needs it most or which could use it most productively, and then on the basis of the arguments advanced decide which group that was. Alternatively the deliberating body might feel that it was not competent to make such a judgement, and opt instead for a procedural solution, such as sharing the resource out equally between the groups, rotating it between them, or deciding by lot.) In either case, the outcome is a decision which all the parties involved may feel to be reasonable, but this does not entail that it reflects any transcendent standard of justice or rightness. The emphasis in the deliberative conception is on the way in which a process of open discussion in which all points of view can be heard may legitimate the outcome when this is seen to reflect the discussion that has preceded it, not on deliberation as a discovery procedure in search of a correct answer.[8]

My aim in this paper is to see whether deliberative democracy may be less vulnerable than liberal democracy to the problems posed by social choice theory for democracy in general. In arguing in this way, I am apparently reversing a common opinion which is that social choice obliges us to abandon 'populist' models of democracy in which democratic decisions are represented as expressions of 'the people's choice' or the 'popular will' in favour of 'liberal' models in which democratic elections are construed merely as a safeguard against the emergence of tyrannical rulers. Democracy on this view is a matter of the voters having the right, at periodic intervals, to remove from office governments which they have come to dislike. Any notion that the voters should in some more positive way determine public policy is misguided. This argument plays some role in the classic defences of liberal democracy by Schumpeter and Dahl[9] and has recently been developed at length and with great intellectual force by William Riker.[10]

From my perspective, however, both liberalism and populism as understood by Riker count as variants on the liberal ideal of democracy. For populism is the view that individuals' preferences should be amalgamated, by voting, to yield a general will which then guides policy. Liberalism in Riker's sense is less ambitious in that it sees the purpose of elections in negative terms as involving the removal of unpopular leaders. Both views see democracy as a matter of aggregating voters' preferences: they differ over the question of whether policy can be chosen in this way, or only the personnel of government. The idea that democratic decisions are not a matter of aggregating preferences at all but of reaching agreed judgements is foreign to both.

Let me now remind readers of the challenge which social choice theory poses for these liberal views of democracy. Suppose a voting public has to decide between a number of policy options – suppose, to take a concrete case, that the issue is how Britain should generate its electricity, and the public has to choose between coal-fired, oil-fired, gas-fired and nuclear power stations. The message of social choice theory, and in particular its most celebrated constituent, Arrow's general possibility theorem,[11] is that one cannot devise a mechanism for making such decisions which simultaneously meets a number of quite weak and reasonable-sounding conditions that we might want to impose, such as monotonicity or the requirement that if a voter raises the position of one option in his own personal ranking, this cannot have the effect of lowering it in the social ranking.

This, one might say, is *the* problem posed by social choice for democracy – that is, in general there is no fair and rational way of amalgamating voters' preferences to reach a social decision – but it entails two more specific problems. The first is the arbitrariness of decision rules and the second is the near-unavoidability of strategic voting, or more strictly of opportunities for strategic voting. Decision rules fall broadly speaking into two classes, which following Riker we may call majoritarian and positional methods of selecting a preferred outcome. Majoritarian rules proceed by offering voters a series of binary choices and, depending on which option wins which encounters, identify an overall winner. So, in our example, voters would be asked to choose between coal and oil for generating electricity, between coal and gas, and so forth. There would be a series of majorities on the questions asked, and then some rule for discovering the overall choice. Positional rules ask voters to rank the available options and then compute a winner using all or part of this fuller information. Thus voters might be asked to rank the energy options from 1 to 4 on their ballot papers and then a winner found by some rule such as giving an option two points each time it is someone's first choice and one point each time it comes second.

The problem of arbitrariness arises because it is not clear which of the many possible rules best matches our intuitive sense of 'finding the option which the voters most prefer', or to put the point another way, for any given rule it is possible to give examples where using that rule produces an outcome that seems repugnant to our sense of what a democratic decision should be. Among majoritarian rules, a strong contender is the Condorcet rule that any option which beats all the others in a series of binary choices should be the social choice. But there is no guarantee in any particular case that such a Condorcet winner can be found, so the rule is incomplete. Thus gas might beat coal and oil but lose to nuclear power, which in turn was beaten by one of the other options. If the rule is to be complete it has then to be extended to cope with this possibility, but there is no extension that is obviously the right one.[12] Among positional rules, the one most often favoured is the Borda count, which scores each option according to the place it holds in each voter's ranking, so that my top option gets n points, my second option $n - 1$ points and so on right the way down. One problem with this is that it may make the decision among quite popular options depend upon the way some voters rank way-out or eccentric options if these are on the ballot paper. Finally, it is an embarrassment that the Condorcet and Borda rules do not necessarily converge; that is, a Condorcet winner may exist, but a different option may be selected by use of the Borda count. This might occur where the Condorcet winner – nuclear power, let's say – was the first choice of a fair number of people but tended to be ranked very low by those who were against it, whereas another option – gas, let's say – was the first preference of just a few, but ranked second by quite a lot. Here it is not at all clear which way we should jump. There is a case for the option with most first preferences, and a case for the compromise proposal which comes reasonably high in most people's rankings.

The second problem is strategic voting, which means misrepresenting your true preferences when you vote with the aim of increasing the chances of your favoured option. Obviously the success of this depends on your having some knowledge of the preferences of other voters. It can be shown that there is virtually no decision rule that is not vulnerable to strategic manipulation if some voters choose to act in this way.[13] Again a couple of examples may help to bring this out. Suppose we are using a majoritarian decision rule. It is possible by strategic voting to block the emergence of a Condorcet winner. Thus suppose in our example nuclear power is the

Condorcet winner if everyone votes sincerely. I am not particularly averse to nuclear power, but I am very strongly committed to coal-fired stations. I cannot prevent nuclear power defeating coal in a run-off between these options, but if others think like me we can stop the nuclear power bandwagon by voting insincerely for gas when the choice between gas and nuclear power is posed, thus preventing the emergence of nuclear power as a Condorcet winner and triggering whatever subsidiary rule is being employed in the hope that coal will win. Equally, if a Borda count is being used and I know that gas, say, is the likely winner, then I can boost the chances of coal by insincerely pushing gas down into fourth place. There is of course no guarantee that my strategy will work, since my opponents may behave strategically too. But this only serves to underline the arbitrariness of the eventual decision which in these circumstances would have very little claim to be called anything like a popular will.

So the challenge posed by social choice to democratic theory can be reduced to two basic claims: that there is no rule for aggregating individual preferences that is obviously fair and rational and thus superior to other possible rules; and that virtually every rule is subject to strategic manipulation, so that even if it would produce a plausible outcome for a given set of preferences if everyone voted sincerely, the actual outcome is liable to be distorted by strategic voting.

Working from within the liberal view of democracy, pessimists such as Riker respond to this challenge by reducing the significance of the electoral process to that of providing a safeguard against what Riker calls 'tyranny'. But even this safeguard is quite weak, since if the outcome of elections is to some degree arbitrary (as the social choice analysis shows), it is not apparent why they should pick out for removal unpopular or 'tyrannical' leaders. Coleman and Ferejohn put this point well:

> Nonreasoned removal from office is precisely what follows if Riker is correct in interpreting the instability results of social choice theory as demonstrating the meaninglessness of voting. If outcomes are arbitrarily connected to the preferences of the electorate, we cannot infer from his removal from office that an officeholder's conduct was in fact disapproved of by the voters. This is hardly the ideal of officeholders being put at risk by elections that we associate with liberalism.[14]

Social choice theory seems to undermine the liberal view of democracy in a systematic way, regardless of the precise function that is assigned to the act of voting in elections.

Can the problems of social choice be avoided altogether by switching to the deliberative ideal of democracy? Social choice theory postulates voters with given preferences over outcomes, and it is sometimes suggested that, once we allow that voters' preferences may alter in the course of decision-making, its results no longer apply.[15] But this response is too simple-minded. So long as there is a problem of amalgamating the voters' wishes at the point of decision – so long, to be more precise, as three or more policy outcomes are still in play and there is no unanimous preference for one of these outcomes – the social choice results apply. A decision rule must be found and this is potentially vulnerable to the problems of arbitrariness and strategic manipulation. In my account of deliberative democracy I indicated that, although full consensus was the ideal guiding discussion, it would be quite unrealistic to suppose that every instance of deliberation would culminate in unanimous agreement. Votes will still have to be taken, and where voting occurs so, potentially, will social choice problems.

Rather than sweeping away social choice theory at a stroke, my aim is the more limited one of showing that deliberative democracy has the resources to attenuate the social choice problems faced by the political community. The case I shall make has two main aspects. The first concerns the way in which deliberation may limit the range of preferences that have to be amalgamated in the final judgement. The second concerns the way in which knowledge of the structure of opinion in the deliberating body may influence the choice of decision rule.

The first part of the argument addresses one of the axioms of Arrow's original theorem, namely the requirement that the social choice procedure should be able to accommodate any possible set of individual rank orderings of outcomes. This axiom may indeed seem self-evident; it appears to pick up the liberal idea that each person is entitled to express whatever preferences he chooses, so that any limits on individual rank orderings would be discriminatory [as Riker puts the point, 'any rule or command that prohibits a person from choosing some preference order is morally unacceptable (or at least unfair) from the point of view of democracy'[16]]. But rather than some external prohibition of possible ways of ranking alternatives, the possibility I wish to contemplate is that some initial sets of preferences might spontaneously be transformed through the process of deliberation, so that the final set of rankings from which a decision had to be reached was much smaller than the original set. If this were so, we could drop Arrow's unrestricted condition in favour of the weaker requirement that the social decision procedure should be able to cope with all possible sets of *post-deliberation* rankings.

I shall shortly suggest how this might help to resolve the social choice problems we have identified. But first we need to consider why some initial preferences might be eliminated in this way. The most straightforward case is that of preference orders that are irrational because they are based on false empirical beliefs. To use the energy policy example, someone might judge energy sources entirely on the basis of environmental soundness and begin with the rank order coal, gas, oil, nuclear power. However, in the course of debate strong evidence is produced about the atmospheric effects of coal-burning power stations which decisively pushes coal below gas and oil from an environmental point of view. This is not to say that the original rank order is completely untenable because there may be other value stances from which it remains appropriate. But then again it may be that no one or virtually no one holds these value stances, so the effect of debate is to crystallize the rank orderings into a smaller number of coherent patterns.

A second case is that of preferences that are so repugnant to the moral beliefs of the society within which the decisions are being made that no one is willing to advance them in a public context. This seems to be roughly the position with racist beliefs in contemporary Britain: a number of people hold them privately, but it is generally recognized that they cannot be articulated in political forums like Parliament. And this does constrain the set of policies that can be supported. You may favour immigration restrictions for racist reasons, but the fact that you cannot present these reasons publicly means that the policies you advocate have to be general in form; that is, they cannot explicitly discriminate between black and white immigrants.

The most important way in which deliberation may alter initial preferences, however, is that outlined in my original description of the deliberative ideal. Preferences that are not so much immoral as narrowly self-regarding will tend to be eliminated by the process of public debate. To be seen to be engaged in political debate we must argue in terms that any other participant would potentially accept, and 'It's good for me' is not such an argument. Or as Bob Goodin has put the point, when we adopt a public role, we must launder our preferences so that only public-orientated ones are expressed.[17] I discount here the possibility of people expressing one set of preferences in debate and voting according to another set at decision time. If voting is public, this could only occur at the cost of immediate loss of future credibility, and this may be a good reason for having an open voting system under conditions that approximate to deliberative democracy, as Brennan and Pettit have recently argued.[18] However, even under a secret ballot, it seems to me quite unlikely that we would witness widespread hypocrisy such as is involved in arguing for one position and then voting for another. This is a claim about human psychology: it says that if you have committed yourself to one position publicly you would find it demeaning to retreat to a more selfish posture at the point of material decision.[19] I do not say this is universally true, but I think it is widely true.

Since this claim about the moralizing effect of public discussion is crucial to my argument about deliberative democracy, I would like at this point to illustrate it with some empirical evidence, although not alas drawn directly from the field of politics. The first piece of evidence comes from psychological experiments which try to simulate the behaviour of juries.[20] In these experiments, a number of subjects are shown a video recording of a trial in which the evidence for and against the accused is fairly evenly balanced. They are then asked to give their private guilty/not-guilty verdict and on the basis of this formed into a number of mock juries divided evenly between the two views. The question is: which verdict will the jury eventually reach? *A priori* one would predict some hung juries, and then equal proportions of guilty and not-guilty verdicts. In fact, however, there is a marked tilt towards the not-guilty side, which the researchers attribute to the presence of a 'leniency norm'. That is, where the presence of conflicting opinions suggests that there is real doubt as to the guilt or innocence of the accused, you should give the accused the benefit of that doubt by returning a not-guilty verdict. Now the leniency norm is always present to some degree, but the point to which I want to draw attention is that allowing the 'jurors' a period of discussion before asking them to give their collective verdict shifted the outcome noticeably in the not-guilty direction. The best explanation seems to be that the effect of discussion was to activate the norm so that some participants who went in thinking 'Yes, he did it' ended up thinking 'We can't agree on this, so I'd better give him the benefit of the doubt'. In other words, the effect of discussion was to shift at least some people from a particular judgement to a general norm which people in liberal societies tend to apply to cases of this sort.

I want, however, to claim not only that discussion can activate norms but also that it can create norms by inducing participants to think of themselves as forming a certain kind of group. Broadly speaking, discussion has the effect of turning a collection of separate individuals into a group who see one another as cooperators. Perhaps I can again illustrate this with some experimental evidence, this time involving groups confronting a classic Prisoner's Dilemma. Each member is given a small sum of money and told that he can either keep it himself, or donate it to a common pool whereupon it will be doubled in value and shared equally among all members of the group. Obviously if everyone donates, everyone doubles their income, but the individually rational thing to do is to hold back the money. In the experiment I am describing, a ten-minute period of discussion more than doubled the rate of cooperation, from 37.5 per cent to 78.6 per cent.[21] Exactly what the normative mechanism at work here is may be open to question, but plainly the effect of debate was to generate a norm of cooperation within the group strong enough in the great majority of cases to override individual self-interest. A group of friends would have no difficulty extricating themselves from a Prisoner's Dilemma – they would trust one another already. Talking to one another appears to be a fairly effective way of simulating friendship in this case.

The upshot of this argument is that we have good reason to expect the deliberative process to transform initial policy preferences (which may be based on private interest, sectional interest, prejudice and so on) into ethical judgements on the matter in hand; and this will sharply curtail the set of rankings of policy outcomes with which the final decision procedure has to deal. How does this help to eliminate the social choice problems we identified earlier? Take first the indeterminacy problem, and our observation that the Condorcet rule may be defeated by the existence of voting cycles (where, say, majorities favour gas over coal, coal over nuclear power, and nuclear power over gas in two-way comparisons). Here I wish to appeal to the well-known finding that cycles of this kind (and the Arrow problem more generally) can be avoided on condition that voters' rank orderings are 'single peaked'.[22] That is to say, the alternatives can be arrayed on a continuum such that if, say, a voter ranks the alternative on the left the highest, he does not rank the alternative on the right above that in the centre.[23] Where preferences are single peaked in this sense, one option must be the Condorcet winner and it would be possible to find this by repeated binary votes.

What does single-peakedness reveal about voters' preferences? It shows that they understand the choice before them in the same way, even though they adopt different positions on the spectrum. Thus suppose in the example we are using that coal is the cheapest of the three fuels but environmentally the most harmful; that oil is the most expensive but environmentally the best; and that gas stands between coal and oil in both respects. Then we might see the choice facing the voters as essentially that between economic cost and environmental soundness, and they would naturally divide into economizers (who put coal first but prefer gas to oil), greens (who put oil first but prefer gas to coal) and moderates, who favour gas as the best trade-off between the two values. A single dimension of choice underlies the various positions, and this is sufficient to guarantee that the rank orderings will be single peaked.

In many cases we may expect ethically informed judgements to display this property: the policy options represent a choice between two values, and different groups of voters weight these values differently.[24] However, it is still possible for single-peakedness to fail even where ethical judgements are involved. For an example of this consider the following. Suppose nuclear power replaces oil as the third possible source of energy, and the facts about it are these: it is moderately cheap, it is environmentally sound in general, but it carries with it the risk of a major accident. We might then have three groups of voters: economizers, whose ranking is (1) coal, (2) nuclear power and (3) gas; pessimistic greens, whose ranking is (1) gas, (2) coal and (3) nuclear power; and a more optimistic group of greenish voters who believe that the risk of a nuclear accident can be borne in the light of the all-round benefits of nuclear power, and whose ranking is therefore (1) nuclear power, (2) gas and (3) coal. As a moment's inspection shows, if no group of voters forms a majority we have a voting cycle in which each energy option can defeat one of the others.

How has this come about? There are two dimensions of disagreement underlying the decision in this case. One is the balance to be struck between cost and environmental safety; the other is the relative weighting to be given to predictable pollution as against the risk of a nuclear accident *within* the fold of environmental concern. The economizers think the issue is only about costs; the out-and-out greens think it is only about environmental safety; the third group think it is about both, but they also disagree with the greens about what environmental safety consists in. It is this condition of cross-cutting disagreement that produces rank orders that are not single peaked and threatens to produce a voting cycle.

Now consider how such a choice might be handled within the context of deliberative democracy. Participants in the debate, aiming to convince others to support the alternative that they favour, must inevitably give grounds for their preference. As the various views are articulated, one thing that will be revealed is whether there is just a single dimension of disagreement underlying the original set of alternatives, or more than one dimension. If there is more than one dimension, then it may be possible to split the original decision into components. I say 'may be' here because it is of course possible that the original alternatives were discrete and irreducible. Consider again the choice between types of power station. It looks as though this might be a case where the alternatives are discrete (a station must *either* be coal or gas fired and so on), whereas many possible dimensions of disagreement underlie the choice: relative costs, levels of employment, issues of environmental safety and so on. However, I do not think that the choice is really so discrete. For instance, coal-fired stations might in general be favoured on cost grounds, but there could be a separate issue as to whether they should be fitted with filters to reduce emissions of sulphur or carbon dioxide at the cost of some loss of output. If it became clear in the course of debate that the major reason why some speakers were opposing coal-fired stations was their polluting emissions, then the obvious solution would be to have two votes, or series of votes, one concerning the basic technology, another concerning the environment/efficiency trade-off given that technology.

Such a solution is obvious in the sense that it enables a final outcome to emerge that can reasonably be regarded as the majority's choice, even in cases where it is not a Condorcet winner.[25] Here one is taking an Olympian perspective and saying what ought to happen. From the point of view of the participants, some may have an incentive to prevent the issues being disaggregated because they envisage that the alternative they favour will lose when this is done.[26] Indeed they may have an incentive artificially to yoke issues together – I am not a student of Labour Party politics, but I suppose this is the art of compositing as practised at party conferences; that is, running together motions to create artificial majorities encompassing the particular position you are interested in. However, the conditions for this technique to work appear to be that there is a group of people who are in a privileged position to manipulate the agenda in the sense of deciding which decisions will be taken separately and which together; and that this group also has a better sense of the pattern of preferences among ordinary participants than those participants do themselves. In a deliberative democracy the pattern of opinion – the extent to which opinions on one issue correlate or fail to correlate with opinions on others – should become public knowledge as different speakers argue for and against the various composite proposals on the table. It would then be difficult to make a public argument against the disaggregation of decisions where it was clear that the original choice was multidimensional. In cases where it was not so clear, speakers might of course try to bamboozle their fellows into choosing simply between composite proposals in the hope that their favoured composite might win.

Let me try to summarize the point I have just made. I have suggested that the major reason apart from empirical error why preference orders are likely not to be single peaked is that the issue under discussion amalgamates separate dimensions of choice to which different voters attach different weights. I am claiming that it is a virtue of deliberative democracy (unlike, say, simple opinion-polling) that it will reveal this to be the case. Unless a lot of people are prepared to behave strategically, there should be a general willingness to break the decision down along its several dimensions, on each of which we should expect to find a winning position. Putting the bits together again, we would have an overall result which can fairly be said to represent the will of the majority, since it follows the majority's judgement on each dimension of policy choice.

In the foregoing discussion the Condorcet criterion has been used as the test of a democratic choice. Starting with preference orders that produce cycles, we have looked at ways in which the process of discussion might be expected to change either the preference orders or the decision agenda so that non-cyclical majorities emerge. However, earlier in the paper I observed that majoritarian methods of decision-making competed with positional methods as represented, for example, by the Borda count, and this particular dilemma has still to be addressed.

The Condorcet criterion invites us to look for the policy option that can win a majority vote against any other, if one can be found. The Borda count invites us to look at voters' complete rank orderings and to choose the alternative with the highest overall score. What is at stake in the choice between these potentially conflicting decision rules? I think the question can best be brought into focus by citing Michael Dummett's case for preferring the Borda count to majoritarian methods of decision-making:

> The question turns on whether it be thought more important to please as many people as possible or to please everyone collectively as much as possible. The latter is surely more reasonable. The rule to do as the majority wishes does not appear to have any better justification than as a rough-and-ready test for what will secure the maximum total satisfaction: to accord it greater importance is to fall victim to the mystique of the majority.[27]

What is noticeable about this is that it treats political decisions as delivering variable amounts of satisfaction to those who vote for them. Now some decisions approximate to this stereotype. If, say, we have to take a vote on what dish is to be served at the annual College feast, then Dummett's argument that it matters much more that overall satisfaction is maximized than that a majority's will prevails seems a good one, and it would be perfectly sensible to use a Borda count to decide this matter. Equally, though, many other decisions are better represented as judgements about what is the right thing to do – say a decision about whether to impose the death penalty for a particular crime – and here it would be very odd to defend the Borda count in the way that Dummett does. Indeed it seems here that the natural procedure would be to use one of the majoritarian methods, since what seems important is that whatever is done is done by the will of the majority – if possible what the majority wills in preference to all other options.[28]

If that intuition is right, then the best and fairest decision procedure to use will depend on the issue at hand. Now one virtue of deliberative democracy here is that the process of deliberation will reveal what sort of issue is at stake if indeed that is not obvious from the outset. In my presentation of the deliberative model, I focused on its most distinctive aspect, namely the process whereby individual preferences are transformed into ethically based judgements about matters of common concern. However, in any real democracy there are going to be other issues that come closer to the College feast stereotype in the sense that personal preferences should reasonably play a large role in deciding them. This will be true of many ordinary public goods, for instance. If we have to make a budget allocation as between football pitches and the swimming pool in the local park, the main consideration is likely to be the general direction and strength of preference between these options. So here once the alternatives are identified, it would be sensible to use a Borda count to find the most satisfactory way of allocating funds, and if no other considerations intervene, the final decision would simply amount to ratifying that result. This is a case where the role of deliberation is to identify a procedure for making a decision rather than to arrive at a substantive agreed judgement.

What we have seen here is that standard social choice theory invites us to pick a mechanism for aggregating preferences regardless of the content of those preferences; whereas deliberative democracy, precisely because the content of people's preferences emerges in the course of deliberation, can in theory select the decision procedure most appropriate to the case in hand. Now clearly once we allow that the decision procedure might be flexible in this way, we open the door to manipulation by those who opt for a procedure not on grounds of its appropriateness to the issue but because they believe it enhances the chances of their preferred policy being adopted. This highlights the point that, for deliberative democracy to work well, people must exercise what we might call democratic self-restraint: they must think it more important that the decision reached should be a genuinely democratic one than that it is the decision that they themselves favour. This depends in turn on the level of trust that exists in the deliberating body: people will tend to behave in a democratic spirit to the extent that they believe that others can be trusted to behave likewise. Here the evidence cited earlier, showing that discussion itself is a good way of building up trust among the participants, is relevant. But this evidence, obtained from research in small group contexts, does also raise the question of the scale on which deliberative democracy can be expected to operate.

It is a mistake to think that the deliberative ideal requires us to treat the citizens of a modern nation-state as a single deliberating body. Although it is a requirement of democracy that every citizen should have the opportunity to participate in collective decision-making in some way, this requirement can be met in a system embodying a high degree of pluralism. Pluralism may work in either or both of two ways: decisions may be parcelled out to the sub-constituencies that are best placed to make them, or most affected by the outcome; or else lower-level deliberating bodies may act as feeders for higher-level ones, with arguments and verdicts being transmitted from one to the other by representatives. Thus one might, for instance, envisage primary assemblies at town or city level making decisions on local matters, and at the same time debating issues of national concern in the presence of their parliamentary representatives: the latter would not be bound by the outcome, since they would themselves be involved in a deliberative process in which new arguments might be presented, but part of their job would be to convey the sense of the local meeting to the national body.[29]

For citizens to be directly involved in deliberation even at local level poses major problems of organization, although recent technological developments can help us see how relatively large bodies of people might be brought together to engage in something we would recognize as common debate.[30] Nor do I want to consider the question whether citizens will be sufficiently motivated to take part in debating assemblies if these are brought into existence. Clearly these are key issues when considering the extent to which the deliberative ideal can be realized in a large society. My focus here has been on what I take to be a key weakness in the liberal conception of democracy – the vulnerability of preference-aggregating procedures to problems of social choice – and the way in which deliberative democracy can overcome that weakness. If we take social choice seriously, as I do, then rather than retreating to a minimal form of liberalism, we can seek to shift democratic practice towards the deliberative ideal, encouraging people not merely to *express* their political opinions (through opinion polls, referendums and the like), but to *form* those opinions through debate in public settings.

Notes

I should like to thank Joshua Cohen, David Held, Iain McLean, William Riker and Albert Weale, as well as the participants in the *Political Studies* conference on Alternatives to Liberal Democracy, for their very helpful comments on earlier versions of this paper.

1   This is how liberal democracy, *qua* regulative ideal, will be understood for the purposes of the paper. Some liberals may protest at this appropriation of the

term. However, although my interpretation only fastens upon one strand of liberalism – the importance it attaches to individual preferences and their expression – I take it to be an important stand. It is also the strand that prevails in contemporary liberal societies, where democracy is predominantly understood as involving the aggregation of independently formed preferences.

2 The ideal of deliberative democracy has recently been advocated and discussed by a number of political theorists. The most incisive presentation is probably J. Cohen, 'Deliberation and democratic legitimacy', in A. Hamlin and P. Pettit (eds), *The Good Polity* (Oxford, Basil Blackwell, 1989). See also B. Manin, 'On legitimacy and political deliberation', *Political Theory*, 15 (1987), 338–68; J. Dryzek, *Discursive Democracy* (Cambridge, Cambridge University Press, 1990); and my own earlier discussion in D. Miller, *Market, State and Community* (Oxford, Clarendon Press, 1989), Ch. 10.

3 This point is well made in J. Elster, *Sour Grapes* (Cambridge, Cambridge University Press, 1983), Ch. I. 5.

4 See J. Coleman and J. Ferejohn, 'Democracy and social choice', *Ethics*, 97 (1986–7), 6–25 for this view.

5 See H. P. Young, 'Condorcet's theory of voting', *American Political Science Review*, 82 (1988), 1231–44.

6 See B. Barry, 'The public interest', in A. Quinton (ed.), *Political Philosophy* (London, Oxford University Press, 1967); B. Grofman and S. L. Feld, 'Rousseau's General Will: a Condorcetian perspective', *American Political Science Review*, 82 (1988), 567–76.

7 Some of the ambiguities are brought out in the exchange between D. Estlund, J. Waldron, B. Grofman and S. L. Feld, 'Democratic theory and the public interest: Condorcet and Rousseau revisited', *American Political Science Review*, 83 (1989), 1317–40.

8 This is not to deny that deliberation tends to improve the quality of decisions. It may indeed be part of the process of reaching a decision that alternatives which initially find favour with some people are eliminated because these preferences rest on empirical misapprehensions which discussion exposes (I give an example of this later on). But it is wrong to suppose that this is the only or in many cases the main purpose of deliberation.

9 J. A. Schumpeter, *Capitalism, Socialism and Democracy* (London, Allen and Unwin, 5th edn, 1976); R. A. Dahl, *A Preface to Democratic Theory* (Chicago, University of Chicago Press, 1956). Schumpeter wrote before Arrow had stated his theorem, but I believe it is informally anticipated in some of Schumpeter's remarks. Dahl refers explicitly to Arrow.

10 W. H. Riker, *Liberalism Against Populism* (San Francisco, W. H. Freeman, 1982).

11 K. J. Arrow, *Social Choice and Individual Values* (New York, Wiley, 2nd edn, 1963).

12 See Riker, *Liberalism Against Populism*, Ch. 4.

13 This is the so-called Gibbard-Satterthwaite theorem after A. Gibbard, 'Manipulation of voting schemes: a general result', *Econometrica*, 41 (1973), 587–601 and M. Satterthwaite, 'Strategy-proofness and Arrow's conditions', *Journal of Economic Theory*, 10 (1975), 187–217.

14 Coleman and Ferejohn, 'Democracy and social choice', p. 22. See also the discussion in J. Cohen, 'An epistemic conception of democracy', *Ethics*, 97 (1986–7), 26–38, especially pp. 29–31.

15 The literature of social choice theory may give the impression that voters' preferences are taken as immutable, with apparent changes being explained in terms of changes in the choice set. But in fact a social choice theorist can quite readily concede that preferences vary, are subject to social influences and so forth, so long as for any particular decision or set of decisions they are taken as fixed and identifiable. The shift of approach occurs when we see preferences as altering within the process of decision-making itself, so that individuals end up making judgements which do not necessarily correspond to their initial preferences.

16 Riker, *Liberalism Against Populism* p. 117. Arrow himself, however, concedes that the condition may be too strong, and indeed in his original proof of the Possibility Theorem used a somewhat weaker version; see *Social Choice and Individual Values*, pp. 24–5 and 96–7.

17 R. Goodin, 'Laundering preferences', in J. Elster and A. Hylland (eds), *Foundations of Social Choice Theory* (Cambridge, Cambridge University Press, 1986).

18 G. Brennan and P. Pettit, 'Unveiling the vote', *British Journal of Political Science*, 20 (1990), 311–33.

19 Jon Elster argues along similar lines in *Sour Grapes*, p. 36.

20 See J. Davis, M. Stasson, K. Ono and S. Zimmerman, 'Effects of straw polls on group decision-making: sequential voting pattern, timing and local majorities', *Journal of Personality and Social Psychology*, 55 (1988), 918–26.

21 J. M. Orbell, A. van der Kragt and R. Dawes, 'Explaining discussion-induced co-operation', *Journal of Personality and Social Psychology*, 54 (1988), 811–19.

22 This idea was first introduced and explored in D. Black, *The Theory of Committees and Elections* (Cambridge, Cambridge University Press, 1958).

23 Suppose the alternatives are coal, gas and oil and they are arranged from left to right in that order. For single-peakedness to obtain, each voter must rank them in one of the four following ways: (1) coal, (2) gas, (3) oil; (1) gas, (2) coal, (3) oil; (1) gas, (2) oil, (3) coal; or (1) oil, (2) gas, and (3) coal. Conversely, no voter may have (1) coal, (2) oil, (3) gas or (1) oil, (2) coal, (3) gas. The requirement is not that voters should agree, but that there should be a certain logic to their disagreement.

24 Arrow himself accepts that if decisions are made on impartial, rather than self-interested grounds, voting cycles are less likely to occur. 'If voters acted like Kantian judges, they might still differ, but the chances of coming to an agreement by majority decision would be much greater than if voters consulted

egoistic values only.' See K. J. Arrow, 'Tullock and an existence theorem', in *Collected Papers of Kenneth J. Arrow. Vol. I* (Oxford, Blackwell, 1984), p. 87.

25 The majority position on the two dimensions may still be defeated when run against the minority position on both. Thus suppose the first issue is whether to have coal- or oil-fired stations and the second is whether to fit pollution filters or not. Majorities may judge that coal is preferable to oil and that filters are desirable; yet if we were to take a vote between coal-with-filters and oil-with-no-filters, the latter might still win by attracting the support of enough people strongly committed to oil together with people strongly opposed to filters. In my view we should still regard coal-with-filters as the majority choice in these circumstances.

26 This is so even where their support for that alternative is based on ethical beliefs: convictions as well as interests may give people a motive to manipulate democratic procedures.

27 M. Dummett, *Voting Procedures* (Oxford, Clarendon Press, 1984), p. 142.

28 The assumption here is that we have an issue about which reasonable people may disagree, but on which some collective decision is needed: in such a case the decision with the greatest democratic legitimacy will be that which follows the will of the majority, which points us towards the Condorcet criterion. If, however, we took the epistemic view – that is, we thought that there was indeed a right answer to the question being posed, and justified democratic decision-making as the most likely means of finding it – then with more than two options on the table the best method will probably be to take a Borda count. See Young, 'Condorcet's theory of voting' for this result.

29 This is not the only way in which deliberative institutions might be created, and advocates of deliberative democracy disagree to some extent about the best institutional setting for their ideal. Tocqueville, one of the founders of this tradition, pointed to voluntary associations as well as to town meetings as sites of public debate. Others have emphasized the role of political parties as institutions within which policies are put together in coherent packages, enabling ordinary voters to arrive at more rational decisions. See Manin, 'On legitimacy and political deliberation' and J. Cohen and J. Rogers, *On Democracy* (New York, Penguin, 1983), Ch. 6 for the latter view.

30 For a good discussion, see I. McLean, *Democracy and New Technology* (Cambridge, Polity Press, 1989).

12

Rousseau's General Will: A Condorcetian Perspective

Bernard Grofman and Scott Feld

We identify three basic elements of Rousseau's theory of the general will: (1) there is a common good; (2) citizens are not always accurate in their judgments about what is in the common good; and (3) when citizens strive to identify the common good and vote in accordance with their perceptions of it, the vote of the Assembly of the People can be taken to be the most reliable means for ascertaining the common good. We then show that Condorcet's (1785) model of collective judgment shares these assumptions with Rousseau and that understanding the implications of Condorcet's (1785) "jury theorem" enables us to clarify many of the most obscure aspects of Rousseau's treatment of the general will, including his discussion of the debilitating effects of factions and his confidence in the ability of the Assembly of the People to discern the general will by means of voting.

Rousseau's seminal contributions to democratic theory are his views on the development of the social contract and his notion of the "general will." Although the "general will" has been given various interpretations, there has been little understanding of how, in practice, political institutions might ascertain the general will for the purpose of effectuating public policy.

We illuminate the logic underlying Rousseau's notion of the general will by making use of long-neglected ideas of Rousseau's contemporary, Condorcet, especially those about the judgmental competence of individuals and groups. We also present some new results about the linkages between (individual and collective) preferences and (individual and collective) judgments about the nature of the public good. In the process, we show how some of the most obscure passages in Rousseau can be clarified by referring to results about features of majority rule first demonstrated by Condorcet some decades after *Of the Social Contract* was published. In particular, we examine the relationship between the general will and the will of all, the likelihood that the general will will err, and the subordination of individual opinions to the collective judgment. Our aim is to understand how collective decision-making processes may be appropriately used to ascertain the general will.

Almost no scholars dealing with Rousseau mention Condorcet (for important exceptions see Barry 1964, 1965, and Baker 1980), and even those who mention him customarily cite not his 1785 essay on voting but other works dealing with quite different topics (see, e.g., Ellenburg 1976, 46, 84, 85). A leading interpretation of Rousseau's general will, made famous by Runciman and Sen (1965), interprets it in the context of a prisoner's dilemma game, and treats it as a problem of reconciling conflicting individual preferences rather than as a problem of developing a reliable judgment of what is in the collective interest. We view our approach, with its focus on social judgments, as complementary to that of Runciman and Sen, and providing a needed corrective to a current focus, in social choice theory, on treating all value questions in democratic theory as if they could be reduced to some aspect of the problem of aggregation of preferences.

Rousseau's General Will

> The general will can only direct the forces of the State in keeping with the end for which it was instituted, which is the common good; for if the opposition of private interests has made the establishment of societies necessary, the harmony of these same interests has made it possible. That which is common to these different interests forms the social bond; and if there were not some point in which all interests agree, no society could exist. Now it is only on this common interest that the society should be governed. (Rousseau 1984, 66 [3.1])

In this quote from Book 3 of *Of the Social Contract*, Rousseau recognizes that people differ in their interests but asserts that there is a common (or public) interest on which all humankind can agree in principle – even though not all would wish to pursue it: "Indeed, each individual may, as a man, have a particular will contrary to, or divergent from, the general will which he has as a citizen. His private interest may speak to him quite differently from the common interest; his absolute and naturally independent existence may make him regard what he owes to the common cause as a gratuitous contribution, the loss of which will be less harmful to others than will the payment of it be onerous to him" (p. 53 [1.7]).

How is the general will to be ascertained? Rousseau's answer is, by voting: "The voice of the greater number always obliges all the others"

(p. 328 [4.2]). However, the vote is not to be an aggregation of self-interested preferences. Rather, "when a law is proposed in the Assembly of the People, what is asked of them is not precisely whether they approve the proposition or reject it; but whether or not it conforms to the general will which is their own: each in giving his vote states his opinion on that question, and from the counting of the voting is taken the declaration of the general will" (p. 329 [4.2]).

This passage in Rousseau is often misunderstood. It represents an understanding of the process of voting not as a means of combining divergent interests but rather as a process that searches for "truth." Somewhere in the course of the development of capitalism, what we may think of as an essentially religious idea of voting – a search for God's mandate as revealed through man's finite cognitions (still present in some contemporary religious groups, e.g., the Bruderhof Commune [Zablocki 1971]) was replaced with a much more individual interest-based notion (Riley 1986).[1] Contemporary social welfare economics, beginning with Arrow's work (1963), has focused entirely on voting as a means of preference aggregation. The notion of voting as a process that can be thought of as a direct search for the common good – indeed, the very notion that there can be a common good that is something other than some form of summation or reconciliation of the *preferences* of individuals – has been lost.

There is another important implication of this quote about the nature of voting in the Assembly of the People, namely, that even those individuals whose vote is based on their perception of the common good may err in that perception:[2] "When the opinion contrary to mine prevails, that only proves that I was mistaken, and that what I had considered to be the general will was not" (Rousseau 1984, 329 [4.2]).

Because the voters who seek the general will are fallible in their judgments, the collective judgment can also sometimes be wrong: "The general will is always upright and always tends toward the public utility, but it does not follow that the deliberations of the people always have the same rectitude. One wishes always his own good but does not always discern it. The people is never corrupted, though often deceived, and then only does it seem to will that which is bad" (p. 75 [2.3]).[2]

Nonetheless, Rousseau expects the vote of the popular assembly (i.e., its "declaration of the general will") to coincide with the general will under reasonable conditions: "If, when an adequately informed people deliberate, the citizens having no communication among themselves, ... the general will would always result" (p. 75 [2.3]).

We should also note that Rousseau, in the passage quoted directly above, sees the "deliberative process" as one taking place within individuals rather than in terms of a process of group debate. Thus, each voter is seen as seeking to reach an individual and independent judgment about alternatives.

There are three elements of Rousseau's theory of the general will that we wish to single out:

1 There is a common good.[4]
2 Citizens are not always accurate in their judgments about what is in the common good.[5]
3 When citizens strive to identify this common good and vote in accordance with their perceptions of it, the vote of the Assembly of the People can be taken to be the most reliable means for ascertaining the common good.[6]

Condorcet's Jury Theorem as a Formalization of Rousseau's General Will

Rousseau has long been acknowledged as one of the great political philosophers. In contrast, Rousseau's contemporary, Condorcet, languished long in obscurity until his idea of the "paradox of cyclical majorities" was rediscovered by Black (1950, 1958) and helped lay the foundation for modern social choice theory (see, e.g., Arrow 1963; Farquharson 1969; Plott 1976; Riker 1964; Sen 1966; and a host of others). However, the idea for which Condorcet is now most famous, the paradox of cyclical majorities, was actually only an incidental by-product of the problem on which he was working, which was the problem of ascertaining how groups could best make choices that were collectively optimal (Black 1958; Grofman, Owen, and Feld 1983; Pinkham and Urken 1982; Young 1986).

Two hundred years ago Condorcet (1785) recognized that majorities of individuals are likely to be more often correct than individuals. Whether understood by the participants or not, this is one fact that makes democracy "work." Condorcet's result, however, was lost for most of the next two hundred years (Black 1958) and even today is nowhere near as well known as it deserves to be (Barry 1965; Grofman 1975; Grofman and Owen 1986a, 1986b; Miller 1986). The Condorcet jury theorem (Black 1958; Condorcet 1785; Grofman 1975) says that if each individual is somewhat more likely than not to make the "better" choice between some pair of alternatives (along some specified evaluative dimension) and each individual has the same probability of being correct in this choice, then (with each voter voting independently) the probability of the group majority being correct increases as the number of individuals increases, towards a limiting value of 1. Moreover, even if individuals have varying competence – where by *competence* we mean the individual probabilities of making the "correct" (dichotomous) choice (i.e., the choice that has the higher value along the specified evaluative dimension) – then so long as the *average* competence is greater than .5, the probability of the group majority being correct still increases to 1 as the group gets large (see Grofman, Owen, and Feld 1983).[7]

We can provide a statement of Condorcet's jury theorem in a form in which its resemblance to Rousseau's theory of the "general will" will be readily apparent. We assume that

1 There is a common good and a set of alternatives that more or less share in its virtues. Thus, alternatives can in principle be evaluated with respect to the underlying normative dimension of consonance with the public interest (general will), and this evaluative dimension permits us, in principle, to rank-order alternatives.
2 With respect to choice between any pair of alternatives, each citizen i has a probability $p_i(0 \leq p_i \leq 1)$ of choosing that alternative which is more in the public interest (closer to the general will).
3 A group of size N chooses between any two alternatives by means of a majority vote in which each voter is polled about his or her independently reached choice, without any group deliberation.

Though Rousseau was not at all a formal mathematical thinker, and despite the fact that some of the basic probabilistic ideas needed to make sense of the Condorcet jury theorem were still in a very preliminary stage of development in the 1750s, we believe that the Condorcet jury theorem accurately captures the basic ideas underlying Rousseau's notion of the general will. It seems virtually certain that ideas similar to those later to be formally developed by Condorcet were "in the wind," and influenced both Rousseau and, later, Condorcet; and there certainly were various social and intellectual linkages between Rousseau and Condorcet. One connection is via the *Encyclopédie* project, in which Diderot and D'Alembert were involved. Condorcet became a close friend of the mathematician and philosopher D'Alembert, whose notion of the pursuit of the common good anticipated that of Condorcet; Rousseau, as a close friend of Diderot, may have learned of these ideas.[8]

There are five key points in understanding the relationship between the ideas of Rousseau and those of Condorcet: *First*, the Condorcet jury theorem is based on a notion of common judgment, not separate individual preferences. It thus permits us to understand better how Rousseau's distinction between the general will and the "will of all" can be implemented in a voting assembly. In Rousseau's own language, "There is often a great difference between the will of all and the general will. The latter regards only the common interest; the other regards private interests and is only the sum of particular wills."

Second, the Condorcet jury theorem permits us to understand how the majority can be a representation of the general will (when its members act in judgment of the common good and not in terms of their particularized self-interests) without the majority will being *identical to* the general will. The Condorcet jury theorem states the "limit result" that as the group size grows large, if the average citizen is more likely than not to judge correctly which of any pair of alternatives is more nearly in the public interest, the majority vote of the group will be *almost certain to be correct* in its judgment *of the public interest.*[9]

Nonetheless, the general will may err, or – in Rousseau's terminology – "the characteristics" of the general will "may not reside in the majority" (1984, 102 [4.3]). However, even for average group competence $\bar{p}$ near .5, the expected judgmental accuracy of large assemblies is considerable.[10] For example, even if $\bar{p}$ is only .51, a 399-member assembly has a competence of .66, while if $\bar{p} = .55$, a 399-member assembly has a competence of .98. For a reasonable level of $\bar{p}$ (e.g., $\bar{p} = .6$), even relatively small assemblies (of size greater than 41) have a group competence level P_N above .9 (see Grofman 1975; Miller 1986). For $p = .7$, an assembly of only size 11 will have a group competence level of above .9.

Third, knowledge of the Condorcet jury theorem (and recent extensions, e.g., Miller 1986; Owen 1986) helps us better understand the logic undergirding another somewhat puzzling passage in Rousseau:

> But when factions are formed, partial associations at the expense of the whole, the will of each of these associations becomes general with regard to its members and particular with regard to the state: one is then able to say that there are no longer as many voters as there are men, but only as many as there are associations... and [this] yield[s] *a less general result*. Finally, when one of these associations is so large that it overcomes the rest,... then there no longer is a general will, and the opinion which dominates is only a private opinion. (1984, 27 [2.3], emphasis ours)

We translate this remark of Rousseau in Condorcetian terms as an observation about factions reducing the *effective* size of the assembly. As the *effective* size of the assembly is reduced – because people vote as a herd (part of a faction) not as separately thinking and independently acting individuals – the Condorcet jury theorem tells us, group accuracy will be reduced. Indeed, at the extreme, if there is a majority faction, this faction is equivalent to a single voice deciding things; thus the benefits of large numbers are lost completely.[11] More generally, if individual choices are positively correlated with one another beyond the correlation to be expected from similarities in competence alone, group accuracy will be reduced (Owen 1986; Shapley and Grofman 1984).

Fourth, a focus on the judgmental basis of voting allows us to provide a mathematical foundation for Rousseau's observation that "the closer opinions approach unanimity, the more dominant is the general will" (1984, 322 [4.2]).

Using the Condorcetian probability framework, it can be shown that the more votes there are on the majority side, the more likely is the group majority to be correct.[12]

Fifth, a probabilistic approach to group judgment allows us better to understand Rousseau's views as to when supermajoritarian decision rules are called for: "The more important and serious the deliberations, the closer the prevailing opinion should approach unanimity; [on the other hand,] in decisions that must be resolved immediately, a majority of one vote should suffice" (p. 103 [4.2]).

If certain kinds of decisions are more subject to error than others (or are simply more important than others so that we wish to have a higher level of confidence that the group vote is an accurate expression of the general will), we might wish to require more than a bare majority vote, since this will reduce the error level since it can be shown that the more votes there are in favor, the more likely is the group judgment to be correct (Grofman 1978; Nitzan and Paroush 1985; cf. Buchanan and Tullock 1962; Rae 1969).[13]

Our emphasis has been on how individual judgments about what is in the public interest aggregate to indicate the general will. We believe that this approach captures the central notion of Rousseau's concept of the general will. However, Rousseau recognized that individuals were not always so nobly motivated and that they sometimes expressed their personal preferences, rather than seeking the general will (see n. 5). He also noted that the general will could sometimes emerge as the residue from the canceling out of individual self-interest in the process of aggregation: "The [general will] looks only to the common interest. The [will of all] looks only to private interest and is only the sum of particular wills: but take away from these same wills the pluses and minuses which cancel each other out and the general will remains as the sum of the differences" (1984, 76 [2.3]).

While this language has proved incomprehensible or nonsensical to some (e.g., Plamenatz quoted in Gildin 1983, p. 55), Gildin (1983, 55–7) provides a simple illustration of what Rousseau almost certainly meant. In Gildin's illustration of a Common's Dilemma, each fisherman would like to fish above the limit set by long-run social advantage, since, ceteris paribus, the few fish netted will not be sufficient to drive the fish population to extinction; yet if each fisherman "cheats," all will suffer (cf. Goodin 1982). Clearly, each fisherman wishes the rule to be one where *all other* fishermen must obey the limit. If we subtract out these egocentric peculiarities, the "common" preference is for a ban on fishing above the socially optimal limit for *all* fishermen (see Gildin 1983; cf. Runciman and Sen 1965).

However, as is clear from many passages from him, Rousseau believed that the most certain route to finding the general will was one in which individuals were primarily oriented toward the general will rather than to their own narrow self-interest.

Conclusions

We hope that our reconstruction of Rousseau's theory can lead to a broader understanding of democracy as a means to collective ends, rather than as just as a means for aggregating narrow interests residing in, and confined to, individuals. While it is often assumed that democracy should be based upon individuals following their own self-interests, Rousseau's and Condorcet's contributions suggest that democracy "works" better when individuals try to see beyond their narrow self-interests to the collective good. Democracy may require a certain amount of shared collective consciousness to achieve competent collective judgments; consequently, polities that lack such consciousness may not function well as democracies.[14]

Even while many politicians and researchers recognize that voters often vote to further the collective rather than their individual interests, other researchers and theorists (especially those working in a social choice framework) tend to overlook the importance of these collective orientations. Politicians obviously recognize that appeals to "right," "good," and "fair" policies have some political appeal. Similarly, empirical research consistently shows that norms of citizen duty are one of the main determinants of whether citizens vote at all. However, theorists of democracy may fail to recognize that even relatively small amounts of collective orientation (i.e., only slightly more than none), especially in the context of negatively correlated individual interests, can aggregate to collective decisions with a high probability of serving the public good. That small differences in each individual's amount of collective orientation can make large differences in the likely ability of the electorate as a whole to make collectively beneficial judgments is one of the clear implications of the Condorcet jury theorem. Thus, it may not matter that individuals are not very "sociotropic" in their voting, as long as there are *some* elements of sociotropic voting present in a significant number of voters (cf. Miller 1986).[15]

We see Rousseau as a propounder of enlightened democracy, not dehumanized collectivism.[16] For Rousseau, as for Condorcet, the process of voting is a means whereby the common good can be identified and implemented, albeit imperfectly.[17] In voting, however, social judgments, not individual preferences, are to be the basis of voter choice.[18] Democracy as a process for making good decisions based upon the aggregation of individual judgments has only recently begun to receive the attention that it deserves (Grofman and Owen 1986a, 1986b; Miller 1986; Nitzan and Paroush 1985; Pinkham and Urken 1982; Young 1986).[19] We hope our reinterpretation of Rousseau's views may encourage others to pursue the topic of collective judgments in terms of both descriptive and normative theory of democratic behavior.[20]

Notes

This research was begun while Grofman was a fellow at the Center for Advanced Study in the Behavioral Sciences, Stanford. We are indebted to the staff of the Word Processing Center, School of Social Sciences, UCI for typing and table preparation and to Dorothy Gormick for bibliographic assistance.

1   Riley (1986, ix) characterizes his book as "a study of the transformation of a theological idea, the general will of God to save all men, into a political one, the general will of the citizen to place common good of the city above his particular will as a private self, and thereby to 'save the polity.'"

2   Compare this idea with that of the "impartial spectator" that, according to Adam Smith in his *Theory of Moral Sentiments* (1971, 171) is contained within each of us and would be "forced" to agree on what is right. Such intuitionist notions of moral judgment are common in the seventeenth and eighteenth centuries.

3   We have omitted the continuation of this quote, which indicates what happens when the assembly is divided into factions. We will return to this problem later.

4   "If there were not some point in which all interests agree, no society could exist" (Rousseau 1984, 66 [2.1]).

5   Moreover, individuals may falter in their allegiance to the common good over self-interest: "If it is not impossible that a private will will agree at some point

with the general, it is at least impossible that this agreement should be lasting and constant; for the private will naturally tends to preferences, and the general will to equality" (Rousseau 1984, 68 [2.1]).

6   Thus, from the vote of the Assembly "is taken the declaration of the general will" (Rousseau 1984, 329 [4.2]).

7   Let P_N be the majority judgmental accuracy of a group of size $N(m = (N + 1)/2$, if we assume, for convenience, N odd), i.e., let P_N be the probability that the group majority will, in a pairwise comparison, pick the alternative that is better with respect to the common interest. Let $\bar{p}$ be the average accuracy level of voters. Then, if voter choices are mutually independent,

$$P_N \approx \sum_{h=m}^{N} \binom{N}{h}(\bar{p})^h(1 - \bar{p})^{N-h}$$

and if $\bar{p} > .5$,

$$\lim_{N \to \infty} P_N \to 1.$$

If $\bar{p} < .5$,

$$\lim_{N \to \infty} P_N \to 0,$$

while if $\bar{p} = .5$, then, not so intuitively,

$$1 - e^{1/2} < \lim_{N \to \infty} P_N < e^{-1/2}$$

(Grofman, Owen, and Feld 1983).

8   In his *Encyclopédie* essays on natural rights and on the ancient Greeks, Diderot himself deals with the conflict between individual wills and the general will (see Riley 1986, 203–5). We are not, however, aware of any mention of Rousseau by Condorcet in his 1785 essay.

9   Grofman (1975) characterizes this aspect of the Condorcet jury theorem as "vox populi, vox dei," i.e., the voice of the people approaches infallibility.

10 The calculations below are based on a normal approximation to the situation in which all group members have identical accuracy levels. However, for $m > 10$ or so, distributional effects of competence are minimal, and the results given above may be used even for extreme cases (e.g., ones where some members of the group have $p_i = 0$ or 1). Grofman, Owen, and Feld (1983) and Grofman, Feld, and Owen (1982) give precise bounds.

11 See n. 10.

12 To look at the differing competences of group judgments with differing margins of votes, we make use of the formula for the ratio of the probability of the correct choice by a group majority of size $m + k$ to the probability of an incorrect choice by a group majority of that same size, where m is a

simple majority ($= (N + 1)/2$ if N odd), and $\bar{p}$ is mean group competence. We have

$$\frac{(\bar{p})^{m+k}(1 - \bar{p})^{N-m-k}}{(\bar{p})^{N-m-k}(1 - \bar{p})^{m+k}} = \frac{\bar{p}^{(2m+2k-N)}}{(1 - \bar{p})^{N-2m-2k}}.$$

It is apparent that the above expression increases with k.

It should be clear that no single will can ever be expected to divine the general will reliably (i.e., more formally, we would not expect any p_i to equal 1). Furthermore it is likely that any long-lasting faction, even if a majority, will turn away from a search for the common good to a concern for the private good of its own members (see n. 5; cf. *Federalist Papers*, no. 10).

13 If we insist on a supermajority, of course, then we must risk deadlock; e.g., if juries require unanimity, this opens the possibility of hung juries (see Grofman 1979, 1981; cf. Buchanan and Tullock 1962).

14 Thomas Schwartz (personal communication, March 1985) has proposed that "Rousseau and other radical democrats want to have a society without politics." In one sense, this is correct; but we prefer to stress the way in which, for Rousseau, politics in effect becomes redefined as the search for the general will.

15 Compare the view of Tocqueville: "Not only is common opinion the only guide which private judgment retains among a democratic people, but amongst such a people it possesses a power infinitely beyond what it has elsewhere. At periods of equality men have no faith in one another, by reason of their common resemblance; but this very resemblance gives them almost unbounded confidence in the judgment of the public; for it would not seem probable, as they are all endowed with equal means of judging, but that the greater truth should go with the greater number" (1945, 2:11).

16 Some of the same language we have cited to show how the majority will can become the general will if citizens strive to identify the common good and vote in accordance with their perceptions of it, other authors interpret to mean that Rousseau takes the position that individuals do not count, only society matters. For example, Peter Drucker contends that Rousseau believes that

> whatever human existence there is; whatever freedom, rights and duties the individual has; whatever meaning there is in individual life – all is determined by society according to society's objective need of survival. The individual, in other words, is not autonomous. He is determined by society. He is free only in matters that do not matter. He has rights only because society concedes them. He has a will only if he wills what society needs. His life has meaning only insofar as it relates to the social meaning and as it fulfills itself in fulfilling the objective goal of society. There is, in short, no human existence, there is only social existence. There is no individual, there is only the citizen. (1971, 51)

This seems far too extreme a reading of Rousseau. Certainly, the language in Rousseau about the "general will" is susceptible to a much more straightforward interpretation. Rousseau merely sees a public interest that is the proper concern of citizens acting in the legislative arena but does not make the extravagant claim that the legislative arena is the sole, or even the superordinate, arena (see Riley 1986, 248–50; cf. Cobban 1964).

17 The clause "albeit imperfectly" is a critical one. It is sometimes claimed that Arrow's theorem demonstrates the inherent impossibility of there being such a thing as a general will: "The theorem provides an unambiguous answer to the question 'Is there a foolproof way to derive complete and transitive social preference relations?' The answer is no. This clearly negative result casts doubts on all assertions that there is a 'general will,' a 'social contract,' a 'social good,' a 'will of the people,' a 'people's government,' a 'people's voice,' a 'social benefit,' and so forth" (Feldman 1980, 191). We believe this (common) view of what Arrow's theorem allegedly demonstrates about democratic theory is simply wrong. Our position, like Rousseau's, is that the general will may exist but that the outcome of any voting process is but an imperfect reflection of it.

18 As previously noted, we believe that the Condorcetian perspective on social judgments provides a useful corrective to the standard emphasis of economists on social welfare as the aggregation of *individual preferences* (cf. Dummett 1984, 170; Grofman, Owen, and Feld 1983; Lehrer and Wagner 1981; Margolis 1982, 66–9; Nurmi 1984). We also believe that the educative role of politicians in the political process must also be acknowledged (cf. Kelly 1987; Shklar 1969, 186–7). Similarly, accounts of political actors as vote maximizers neglect the role of politicians as innovators of organizational solutions to common problems (Glazer and McMillan 1987).

19 As we have seen, Condorcet, who was concerned with the search for the public good, is remembered only for his analysis of the effects of combining individual *preferences* in such a fashion as to give rise to intransitivities (the paradox of cyclical majorities).

20 One such application might be the analysis of judicial decision making. Clearly, Supreme Court justices are not supposed to be reconciling competing personal preferences for policy when they vote; rather they are seeking to arrive at a judgment of what the Constitution – or some statute – means (in the given context). Thus, to use terminology from early U.S. (and Continental) political thought, Supreme Court justices are to exercise "judgment," not "will" (Chamberlin n.d.). Whether such distinction is meaningful and, even if meaningful, whether human beings can be expected to restrain their will and exercise only their judgment are questions relevant to the present debate over the proper role of evaluation of judicial philosophies as a factor in shaping Senate nonconfirmation of U.S. Supreme Court justices such as Robert Bork.

Bibliography

Ackerman, B. "The Storrs Lectures: Discovering the Constitution." *Yale Law Journal* 93 (1984): 1013–72.

——. "Discovering the Constitution." Unpublished manuscript, 1986.

——. "Crediting the Voters," *The American Prospect* 13 (1993): 71–80.

Alcoff, L. "Philosophy and Racial Identity," *Radical Philosophy* 75 (1996): 5–14.

Ansolabehere, S. and S. Iyengar. *Going Negative*. New York: Free Press, 1997.

Anzaldua, G. "Haciendo Caras, una entrada/ an Introduction." In *Making Face, Making Soul/ Haciendo Caras*, edited by G. Anzaldua, xv–xxviii. San Francisco: Aunt Lute Foundation, 1990.

——, ed. *Making Face, Making Soul/ Haciendo Caras*. San Francisco: Aunt Lute Foundation, 1990.

Aristotle. *Politics*, translated by Benjamin Jowett, in *The Basic Works of Aristotle*, edited by Richard McKeon. New York: Random House, 1941.

Arrow, K. "A Difficulty in Social Welfare," *Journal of Poltical Economy* 68 (1950): 328–46.

Arrow, K. *Social Choice and Individual Values*. 2nd edn. New York: Wiley, 1963.

——. *Collected Papers of Kenneth J. Arrow*, vol. 1. Oxford: Blackwell, 1984.

Baker, K. *Condorcet*. Chicago: Chicago University Press, 1980.

Barry, B. "The Public Interest," *Proceedings of the Aristotelian Society* 38 (1964): 9–14.

——. *Political Argument*. London: Routledge and Kegan Paul, 1965.

——and R. Hardin, eds. *Rational Man and Irrational Society?* Beverly Hills, CA: Sage Publications, 1982.

Barwell, I. "Towards a Defence of Objectivity." In *Knowing the Difference: Feminist Perspectives in Epistemology*, edited by K. Lennon and M. Whitford, 79–94. London: Routledge, 1994.

Becker, W. *Die Freiheit, die wir meinen: Entscheidung für die liberale Demokratie*. Munich: Piper, 1982.

Beitz, C. *Political Equality*. Princeton, NJ: Princeton University Press, 1989.

Benhabib, S., ed. *Democracy and Difference: Contesting the Boundaries of the Political*. Princeton, NJ: Princeton University Press, 1996.

Benn, S. I. and R. S. Peters. *The Principles of Political Thought*. New York: Free Press, 1965.

——. "The Problematic Rationality of Political Participation." In *Philosophy, Politics, and Society*. 5th Series, edited by P. Laslett and J. Fishkin, 291–312. New Haven, CN: Yale University Press, 1979.

Black, Charles L. *A New Birth of Freedom*. New York: Grosset/Putnam, 1997.

Black, D. "The Unity of Political and Economic Science," *Economic Journal* 60 (1950): 506–14.

——. *The Theory of Committees and Elections*. Cambridge: Cambridge University Press, 1958.

Bobbio, Norberto. *The Future of Democracy*, translated by Roger Griffin, edited by Richard Bellamy. Cambridge: Polity Press, 1987.

Bohman, J. *Public Deliberation: Pluralism, Complexity, and Democracy*. Cambridge, MA: MIT Press, 1996.

—— and W. Rehg, eds. *Deliberative Democracy: Essays on Reason and Politics*. Cambridge, MA: MIT Press, 1997.

Bourdieu, P. "Social Space and the Genesis of Groups," *Theory and Society* 14 (1985): 723–44.

Braithwaite, J. and P. Pettit. *Not Just Deserts: A Republican Theory of Criminal Justice*. Oxford: Oxford University Press, 1990.

Brennan, G. and L. Lomasky. "The Impartial Spectator Goes to Washington: Towards a Smithian Model of Electoral Politics," *Economics and Philosophy* 1 (1985): 189–212.

——. "Large Numbers, Small Costs: The Uneasy Foundation of Democratic Rule." In *Politics and Process: New Essays in Democratic Thought*, edited by G. Brennan and L. Lomasky, 42–59. Cambridge: Cambridge University Press, 1989.

——. *Democracy and Decision*. Cambridge: Cambridge University Press, 1993.

Brennan, G. and L. Lomasky, eds. *Politics and Process: New Essays in Democratic Thought*. Cambridge: Cambridge University Press, 1989.

Brennan, G. and P. Pettit. "Unveiling the Vote," *British Journal of Political Science* 20 (1990): 311–33.

Brighouse, H. "Egalitarianism and Equal Availability of Political Influence," *Journal of Political Philosophy* 4 (1996): 118–41.

——. "Political Equality in Justice as Fairness," *Philosophical Studies* 86 (1997): 155–84.

Buchanan, J. and G. Tullock. *The Calculus of Consent*. Ann Arbor, MI: University of Michigan Press, 1962.

Buckley v. Valeo, 424 U. S. 1 (1976).

Burnham, W. D. *The Current Crisis in American Politics*. Oxford: Oxford University Press, 1982.

Cartwright, N. "Causal Laws and Effective Strategies," *Noûs* 13 (1979): 419–37.

Chamberlin, J. "Assessing the Power of the Supreme Court." In *The "Federalist Papers" and the New Institutionalism*, edited by B. Grofman and D. Wittman, 142–9. New York: Agathon, 1989.

Chambers, S. *Reasonable Democracy: Jürgen Habermas and the Politics of Discourse.* Ithaca, NY: Cornell University Press, 1996.

Christiano, T. *The Rule of the Many.* Boulder, CO: Westview Press, 1996.

——. "The Significance of Public Deliberation." In *Deliberative Democracy: Essays on Reason and Politics,* edited by J. Bohman and W. Rehg, 243–77. Cambridge, MA: MIT Press, 1997.

Cobban, A. *Rousseau and the Modern State.* 2nd edn. London: Allen and Unwin, 1964.

Cohen, C. *Democracy.* Athens: University of Georgia Press, 1971.

Cohen, G. A. "On the Currency of Egalitarian Justice." *Ethics* 99 (1989), 906–44.

——. "Incentives, Inequality, and Community." In *The Tanner Lectures on Human Values,* vol. 13, edited by G. Peterson, 263–9. Salt Lake City, UT: University of Utah Press, 1992.

——. "The Pareto Argument for Inequality." In *Contemporary Political and Social Philosophy,* edited by E. F. Paul, F. D. Miller and J. Paul, 160–85. Cambridge: Cambridge University Press, 1995.

——. "Where the Action Is: On the Site of Distributive Justice," *Philosophy and Public Affairs* 26 (1997): 3–30.

Cohen, J. "An Epistemic Conception of Democracy," *Ethics* 97 (1986): 26–38.

——. "Autonomy and Democracy: Reflections on Rousseau." *Philosophy and Public Affairs* 15 (1986): 275–97.

——. "Deliberation and Democratic Legitimacy." In *The Good Polity,* edited by A. Hamlin and P. Pettit, 17–34. Oxford: Blackwell, 1989.

——. "The Economic Basis of Deliberative Democracy." *Social Philosophy and Policy* 6 (1989): 25–50.

Cohen, J. and J. Rogers. *On Democracy.* New York: Penguin, 1983.

Coleman, J. and J. Ferejohn. "Democracy and Social Choice," *Ethics* 97 (1986–7): 6–25.

Condorcet, M. *Essai sur l'application de l'analyse à la probabilité des decisions rendues à la pluralité des voix.* Paris 1785.

Connolly, W. *The Terms of Political Discourse.* Lexington: Heath, 1974.

Copp, D., J. Hampton and J. Roemer, eds. *The Idea of Democracy.* Cambridge: Cambridge University Press, 1993.

Coward, R. and J. Ellis. *Language and Materialism.* London: Routledge and Kegan Paul, 1977.

Crenshaw, K. "Mapping the Margins: Intersectionality, Identity Politics, and Violence Against Women of Color," *Stanford Law Review* 43 (1991): 1241–99.

Dahl, R. A. *A Preface to Democratic Theory.* Chicago: Chicago University Press, 1956.

——. *Pluralist Democracy in the United States.* Chicago: Rand McNally, 1967.

——. *After the Revolution.* New Haven: Yale University Press, 1970.

——. "Democracy and the Chinese Boxes" in *Frontiers of Democratic Theory* edited by H. Kariel, 370–94. New York: Random House, 1970.

——. "Procedural Democracy," in *Philosophy, Politics and Society,* edited by James Fishkin and Peter Laslett. New Haven: Yale University Press, 1979.

——. *Democracy and Its Critics*. New Haven: Yale University Press, 1989.

Davis, J. C. "The Levellers and Democracy." *Past and Present* 40 (1968): 174–80.

Davis, J., M. Strasson, K. Ono, and S. Zimmerman. "Effects of Straw Polls on Group Decision-making: Sequential Voting Pattern, Timing and Local Majorities," *Journal of Personality and Social Psychology* 55 (1988): 918–26.

Devlin, P. *The Enforcement of Morals*. Oxford: Oxford University Press, 1965.

Dewey, J. *The Public and Its Problems*. Chicago: Swallow Press, 1954.

Disch, L. *Hannah Arendt and the Limits of Philosophy*. Ithaca, NY: Cornell University Press, 1994.

Downs, A. *An Economic Theory of Democracy*. New York: Harper & Row, 1957.

Drucker, P. *Men, Ideas, and Politics*. New York: Harper and Row, 1971.

Dryzek, J. *Discursive Democracy: Politics, Policy, and Political Science*. Cambridge: Cambridge University Press, 1990.

Dummett, M. *Voting Procedures*. Oxford: Clarendon Press, 1984.

Dworkin, R. "What is Equality? Part I: Equality of Welfare." *Philosophy and Public Affairs* 10 (1981): 185–246.

——. *A Matter of Principle*. Cambridge MA: Harvard University Press, 1985.

——. *Law's Empire*. Cambridge, MA: Harvard University Press, 1986.

——. *A Bill of Rights for Britain*. London: Chatto and Windus, 1990.

——. *Freedom's Law: The Moral Reading of the American Constitution*. Cambridge: Harvard University Press, 1996.

——. "The Curse of American Politics," *New York Review of Books*, October 17, 1996, p. 21.

Dyson, M. "Essentialism and the Complexities of Racial Identity." In *Multiculturalism*, edited by D. Goldberg, 218–29. Cambridge: Blackwell, 1994.

Ellenburg, S. *Rousseau's Political Philosophy*. Ithaca, NY: Cornell University Press, 1976.

Elshtain, J. *Democracy on Trial*. New York: Basic Books, 1995.

Elster, J. "Sour Grapes," in *Utilitarianism and Beyond*, edited by A. Sen and B. Williams, 219–38. Cambridge: Cambridge University Press, 1982.

——. *Sour Grapes*. Cambridge: Cambridge University Press, 1983.

——. "The Market and the Forum: Three Varieties of Political Theory," in *The Foundations of Social Choice Theory*, edited by J. Elster and A. Hylland, 103–32. Cambridge: Cambridge University Press, 1986.

Elster, J. ed. *Deliberative Democracy*. Cambridge: Cambridge University Press, 1998.

Elster, J. and A. Hylland, eds. *Foundations of Social Choice Theory*. Cambridge: Cambridge University Press, 1986.

Ely, John Hart. *Democracy and Distrust: A Theory of Judicial Review*. Cambridge, MA: Harvard University Press, 1980.

Estlund, D. "Making Truth Safe for Democracy." In *The Idea of Democracy*, edited by D. Copp, J. Hampton, and J. Roemer, 71–100. Cambridge: Cambridge University Press, 1993.

——. "Opinion Leaders, Independence, and Condorcet's Jury Theorem," *Theory and Decision* 36 (1994): 131–62.

——. "The Survival of Egalitarian Justice in John Rawls's *Political Liberalism*," *The Journal of Political Philosophy* 4 (1996): 68–78.

——. "Beyond Fairness and Deliberation: The Epistemic Dimension of Democratic Authority." In *Deliberative Democracy: Essays in Reason and Politics*, edited by J. Bohman and W. Rehg, 173–204. Cambridge, MA: MIT Press, 1997.

——. "Liberalism, Equality, and Fraternity in Cohen's Critique of Rawls," *Journal of Political Philosophy* 6 (1998): 99–112.

——. "Political Quality," *Social Philosophy and Policy* 17 (2000): 127–60.

——. "Waldron on *Law and Disagreement*," *Philosophical Studies* 99 (2000): 111–28.

——. "Deliberation Down and Dirty: Must Political Expression Be Civil?" In *The Boundaries of Freedom of Expression and Order in American Democracy*, edited by T. Hensley, 49–67. Kent, Ohio: Kent State University Press, 2001.

Estlund, D., J. Waldron, B. Grofman, and S. Feld. "Democratic Theory and the Public Interest: Condorcet and Rousseau Revisited," *American Political Science Review* 83 (1989): 1317–40.

Farquharson, R. *Theory of Voting*. New Haven, CT: Yale University Press, 1969.

Feldman, A. *Welfare Economics and Social Choice Theory*. Boston: Martinus Nijhoff, 1980.

Fishkin, J. *Deliberative Democracy*. New Haven, CT: Yale University Press, 1991.

Foot, P. "Moral Beliefs." *Proceedings of the Aristotelian Society* 58 (1958–9).

——. "Morality as a System of Hypothetical Imperatives." *Philosophical Review* 81 (1972), 305–16.

Forbath, W. E. *Law and the Shaping of the American Labor Movement*. Cambridge MA: Harvard University Press, 1991.

Fraser, N. "Rethinking the Public Sphere: A Contribution to the Critique of Actually Existing Democracy," in *Habermas and the Public Sphere*, edited by Craig Calhoun, 109–42. Cambridge MA: MIT Press, 1992.

Fuss, D. *Essentially Speaking: Feminism, Nature and Difference*. New York: Routledge, 1989.

Gauthier, D. "Morality and Advantage." *Philosophical Review* 76 (1967): 460–75.

——. "David Hume, Contractarian." *Philosophical Review* 88 (1979): 3–38.

——. *Morals by Agreement*. Oxford: Clarendon Press, 1986.

Geyer, F. and H. van der Zouwen, eds. *Dependence and Inequality*. New York: Pergamon, 1982.

Gibbard, A. "Manipulation of Voting Schemes: A General Result," *Econometrica* 41 (1973): 587–601.

Gildin, H. *Rousseau's Social Contract: The Design of the Argument*. Chicago: University of Chicago Press, 1983.

Gilroy, P. *The Black Atlantic*. Cambridge, MA: Harvard University Press, 1993.

Gitlin, T. *Twilight of Common Dreams*. New York: Henry Holt, 1995.

Glazer, A. and H. McMillan. "Legislation and the Cost of Making Proposals." Irvine, CA: University of California, Irvine. Photo-offset, 1987.

Glendon, M. *Rights Talk: The Impoverishment of Political Discourse*. New York: Free Press, 1991.

Goldberg, D., ed. *Multiculturalism*. Cambridge: Blackwell, 1994.

Goldman, A. "A Causal Responsibility Approach to Voting," *Social Philosophy and Policy* 16 (1999): 201–17.

———. *Knowledge in a Social World*. Oxford: Oxford University Press, 1999.

Goodin, R. *Political Theory and Public Policy*. Chicago: University of Chicago Press, 1982.

———. "Laundering Preferences." In *Foundations of Social Choice Theory*, edited by J. Elster and A. Hylland, 75–101. Cambridge: Cambridge University Press, 1986.

Grofman, B. "A Comment on Democratic Theory: A Preliminary Mathematical Model," *Public Choice* 21 (1975): 99–104.

———. "Judgmental Competence of Individuals and Groups in a Dichotomous Choice Situation: Is a Majority of Heads Better than One?," *Journal of Mathematical Sociology* 6 (1978): 47–60.

———. "A Preliminary Model of Jury Decision Making as a Function of Jury Size, Effective Jury Decision Rule, and Mean Juror Judgmental Competence." In *Frontiers of Economics*, vol. 3, edited by G. Tullock, 98–110. Blacksburg, VA: Center for Study of Public Choice, 1979.

———. "Mathematical Models of Juror and Jury Decision Making: The State of the Art." In *Perspectives in Law and Psychology*, vol. 2, *The Trial Processes*, edited by B. Sales, 305–51. New York: Plenum, 1981.

Grofman, B. and S. Feld. "Rousseau's General Will: A Condorcetian Perspective," *American Political Science Review* 82 (1988): 567–76.

Grofman, B., S. Feld, and G. Owen. "Evaluating the Competence of Experts, Pooling Individual Judgments into a Collective Choice, and Delegating Decision Responsibility to Subgroups." In *Dependence and Inequality*, edited by F. Geyer and H. van der Zouwen, 221–38. New York: Pergamon, 1982.

Grofman, B. and G. Owen, eds. *Information Pooling and Group Decision Making*. Greenwich, CT: JAI, 1986.

Grofman, B. and G. Owen. "Condorcet Models: Avenues for Future Research." In *Information Pooling and Group Decision Making*, edited by B. Grofman and G. Owen, 93–102. Greenwich, CT: JAI, 1986.

Grofman, B., G. Owen, and S. Feld. "Thirteen Theorems in Search of the Truth," *Theory and Decision* 15 (1983): 261–78.

Grofman, B. and D. Wittman, eds. *The "Federalist Papers" and the New Institutionalism*. New York: Agathon, 1989.

Gutmann, A. and D. Thompson. *Democracy and Disagreement*. Cambridge, MA: Harvard University Press, 1998.

Habermas, J. *The Legitimation Crisis of Late Capitalism*, translated by T. McCarthy. Boston: Beacon Press, 1975.

———. *Communication and the Evolution of Society*, translated by T. McCarthy. Boston: Beacon Press, 1979.

———. *The Theory of Communicative Action*, translated by T. McCarthy. Boston: Beacon Press, 1984.

——. *Between Facts and Norms: Contributions to a Discourse Theory of Law and Democracy*, translated by W. Rehg. Cambridge, MA: MIT Press, 1996.

Hamlin, A. and P. Pettit, eds. *The Good Polity*. Oxford: Blackwell, 1989.

Hampton, J. *Hobbes and the Social Contract Tradition*. Cambridge: Cambridge University Press, 1986.

Harding, S. *Whose Science? Whose Knowledge? Thinking from Women's Lives*. Ithaca, NY: Cornell University Press, 1991.

Harman, G. "Moral Relativism Defended." *Philosophical Review* 84 (1975): 3–22.

——. *The Nature of Morality*. New York: Oxford University Press, 1977.

——. "Relativistic Ethics: Morality as Politics." *Midwest Studies in Philosophy*, 3 (1978).

Hart, H. L. A. *Law, Liberty and Morality*. Oxford: Oxford University Press, 1963.

Hayek, F. *New Studies in Philosophy, Politics, Economics and the History of Ideas*. London: Routledge and Kegan Paul, 1978.

——. *The Fatal Conceit: The Errors of Socialism*. London: Routledge & Kegan Paul, 1988.

Heidegger, M. *Being and Time*, translated by J. Macquarrie and E. Robinson. New York: Harper & Row, 1965.

Held, D. *Models of Democracy*. Stanford: Stanford University Press, 1987.

Hempel, C. "Empiricist Criteria of Cognitive Significance: Problems and Changes," in *Aspects of Scientific Explanation*. Chicago: Free Press, 1956.

Hirshman, A. *Exit, Voice, and Loyalty*. Cambridge, MA: Harvard University Press, 1970.

Hobbes, T. *Leviathan*. New York: Collier Books, 1962.

——. *De Cive: The English Version*, edited by Howard Warrender. Oxford: Clarendon Press, 1983.

Hohfeld, Wesley N. *Fundamental Legal Conceptions*. New Haven: Yale University Press, 1923.

Jones, Peter. "Political Equality and Majority Rule," in *The Nature of Political Theory*, edited by David Miller and Larry Seidentop, 155–82. Oxford: Oxford University Press, 1983.

Kant, I. *Foundations of the Metaphysics of Morals*, translated by L. W. Beck. Indianapolis, IN: Bobbs-Merrill, 1959.

——. "On the Common Saying: 'This May be True in Theory, but it does not Apply in Practice'," in *Kant's Political Writings*, edited by Hans Reiss and translated by H. B. Nisbet, 61–92. Cambridge: Cambridge University Press, 1970.

——. "To Perpetual Peace: A Philosophical Sketch," in *Perpetual Peace and Other Essays*, translated by T. Humphrey, 107–43. Indianapolis: Hackett, 1983.

Kelly, C. "To Persuade without Convincing: The Language of Rousseau's Legislator," *American Journal of Political Science* 31 (1987): 321–35.

Kelly, E. "Habermas on Moral Justification," *Social Theory and Practice* 26 (2000): 223–49.

Knight, J. and J. Johnson. "What Sort of Political Equality Does Deliberative Democracy Require?" In *Deliberative Democracy: Essays on Reason and Politics*, edited by J. Bohman and W. Rehg, 279–319. Cambridge, MA: MIT Press, 1997.

Laslett, P. and J. Fishkin, eds. *Philosophy, Politics, and Society*, 5th Series. New Haven, CT: Yale University Press, 1979.

Lehrer, K. and C. Wagner. *Rational Consensus in Science and Society*. Dordrecht: D. Reidel, 1981.

Lennon, K. and M. Whitford, eds. *Knowing the Difference: Feminist Perspectives in Epistemology*. London: Routledge, 1994.

Lewis, D. *Convention: A Philosophical Study*. Harvard University Press, 1969.

——. "Languages, Language, and Grammar," in *On Noam Chomsky: Critical Essays*, edited by Gilbert Harman, 253–67. Garden City, New York: Doubleday: 1974.

——. *Philosophical Papers*, vol. 2. New York: Oxford University Press, 1986.

Lindsay, A. D. *The Essentials of Democracy*. Philadelphia: University of Pennsylvania Press, 1929.

Lipset, S. M. *Political Man*. New York: Doubleday, 1960.

——. "The Paradox of American Politics." *The Public Interest* 41 (1975).

List, C. and R. Goodin. "Epistemic Democracy: Generalizing the Condorcet Jury Theorem," *The Journal of Political Philosophy* 9 (2001).

Lively, Jack. *Democracy*. Oxford: Basil Blackwell, 1975.

Locke, J. *An Essay Concerning Human Understanding*, edited by P. Nidditch. Oxford: Clarendon Press, 1975.

——. *Two Treatises of Government*, edited by Peter Laslett. Cambridge: Cambridge University Press, 1988.

Loeb, L. "Causal Theories and Causal Overdetermination," *Journal of Philosophy* 71 (1974): 525–44.

Luce, R. Duncan and Howard Raiffa. *Games and Decisions*. New York: Wiley, 1957.

Lugones, M. "Parity, Imparity, and Separation: Forum," *Signs: Journal of Women in Culture and Society* 14 (1994): 458–77.

MacIntyre, A. *After Virtue*. Notre Dame: University of Notre Dame Press, 1981.

Mackie, J. L. "Causes and Conditions," *American Philosophical Quarterly* 2 (1965): 245–64.

Manin, B. "On Legitimacy and Political Deliberation." *Political Theory* 15 (1987) 338–68.

Manning, B. *The English People and the English Revolution*. London: Heinemann, 1975.

Mansbridge, J. *Beyond Adversary Democracy*. Chicago: University of Chicago Press, 1983.

Margolis, H. *Selfishness, Altruism, and Rationality: A Theory of Social Choice*. Chicago: University of Chicago Press, 1982.

Marshall, T. H. "Citizenship and Social Class," in *Class, Citizenship, and Social Development*. Garden City: Doubleday, 1964.

Martin, B. *Matrix and Line*. Albany, NY: SUNY Press, 1993.

Maus, I. *Zur Aufklärung der Demokratietheorie*. Frankfurt am Main: Suhrkamp, 1992.

McCarthy, T. *The Critical Theory of Jürgen Habermas*. Cambridge, MA: MIT Press, 1982.

McLean, I. *Democracy and New Technology*. Cambridge: Polity Press, 1989.

Meehl, P. "The Selfish Voter Paradox and the Thrown-Away Vote Argument," *American Political Science Review* 71 (1977): 11–30.

Meiklejohn, A. *Free Speech and its Relation to Self-Government*. New York: Harper and Row, 1948.

Michelman, F. I. "The Supreme Court, 1985 Term – Foreword: Traces of Self-Government." *Harvard Law Review* 100 (1986): 4–77.

Mill, J. S. *Considerations on Representative Government*, 2nd edn. London: Parker, Son and Bourn, 1861.

——. *Representative Government*. New York: E. P. Dutton and Co., 1950.

——. *On Liberty*. Indianapolis: Bobbs-Merill, 1955.

——. *Considerations on Representative Government*. New York: Bobbs-Merill, 1958.

——. *Considerations on Representative Government*. Buffalo: Prometheus Books, 1991.

Miller, D. *Market, State and Community*. Oxford: Clarendon Press, 1989. "Deliberative Democracy and Social Choice," *Political Studies* 40 (1992): 54–67.

Miller, N. "Information, Electorates, and Democracy: Some Extensions and Interpretations of the Condorcet Jury Theorem." In *Information Pooling and Group Decision Making*, edited by B. Grofman and G. Owen, 173–92. Greenwich, CT: JAI, 1986.

Miller, W. and the National Election Studies. *American National Election Studies Cumulative Data File, 1952–1992* (computer file), 6th release. Ann Arbor, MI: University of Michigan Center for Political Studies [producer], 1994; Ann Arbor, MI: Inter-University Consortium for Political and Social Research [distributor], 1991.

Minow, M. *Making All the Difference*. Ithaca, NY: Cornell University Press, 1990.

Moore, M. "Causation and Responsibility," *Social Philosophy and Policy* 16 (1999): 1–51.

Nagel, T. "Rawls on Justice." *Philosophical Review*, 82 (1973), 220–34.

——. "Equality." In *Mortal Questions*. Cambridge: Cambridge University Press, 1979.

——. *The View From Nowhere*. New York: Oxford University Press, 1986.

Nelson, W. *On Justifying Democracy*. London: Routledge & Kegan Paul, 1980.

Nino, C. S. *The Constitution of Deliberative Democracy*. New Haven, CT: Yale University Press, 1996.

Nitzan, S. and J. Paroush. *Collective Decision Making: An Economic Approach*. New York: Cambridge University Press, 1985.

Nurmi, H. "Social Choice Theory and Democracy: A Comparison of Two Recent Views," *European Journal of Political Research* 12 (1984): 325–33.

Okin, S. M. *Justice, Gender and the Family*. New York: Basic Books, 1989.

Orbell, J. M., A. van der Kragt, and R. Dawes. "Explaining Discussion-induced Co-operation," *Journal of Personality and Social Psychology* 54 (1988): 811–19.

Ortiz, D. "The Democratic Paradox of Campaign Finance Reform," *Stanford Law Review* 50 (1998): 893–914.

Owen, G. " 'Fair' Indirect Majority Rules." In *Information Pooling and Group Decision Making*, edited by B. Grofman and G. Owen, 223–30. Greenwich, CT: JAI, 1986.

Pangle, T. *The Spirit of Modern Republicanism*. Chicago: University of Chicago Press, 1988.

Parfit, D. *Reasons and Persons*. Oxford: Clarendon Press, 1984.

Pateman, C. *Participation and Democratic Theory*. Cambridge: Cambridge University Press, 1970.

Patterson, O. *Slavery and Social Death*. Cambridge, MA: Harvard University Press, 1982.

Paul, E. F., F. D. Miller, and J. Paul, eds. *Contemporary Political and Social Philosophy*. Cambridge: Cambridge University Press, 1995.

Perlman, L. "Parties, Democracy and Consent." Unpublished manuscript, 1987.

Pettit, P. "The Freedom of the City: A Republican Ideal." In *The Good Polity*, edited by A. Hamlin and P. Pettit, 141–68. Oxford: Blackwell Publishers, 1989.

Phillips, A. *Democracy and Difference*. University Park, PA: University of Pennsylvania Press, 1993.

——. *The Politics of Presence*. Oxford: Oxford University Press, 1995.

Pinkham, R. and A. Urken. "Competence and the Choice of a Voting System." (Typescript) Stevens Institute of Technology, 1982.

Plott, C. "Axiomatic Social Choice Theory: An Overview and Interpretation," *American Journal of Political Science* 20 (1976): 511–96.

Putnam, H. "A Reconsideration of Deweyan Democracy," *Southern California Law Review* 63 (1990): 1671–97.

Rae, D. "Decision Rules and Individual Values in Constitutional Choice," *American Political Science Review* 63 (1969): 40–56.

Rainsborough, Thomas. "The Putney Debates: The Debate on the Franchise (1647)," in *Divine Right and Democracy*, edited by David Wootton, 283–317. Harmondsworth: Penguin Books, 1986.

Rawls, J. *A Theory of Justice*. Cambridge, MA: Harvard University Press, 1971.

——. "Fairness to Goodness." *Philosophical Review*, 84 (1975), 536–54.

——. "Kantian Constructivism in Moral Theory." *Journal of Philosophy* 77 (1980): 515–72.

——. "The Basic Liberties and Their Priority." In *The Tanner Lectures on Human Values, III (1982)*, edited by S. McMurrin, 1–87. Salt Lake City: University of Utah Press; Cambridge: Cambridge University Press, 1982.

——. "Justice as Fairness: Political not Metaphysical." *Philosophy and Public Affairs* 14 (1985): 243.

——. "The Idea of an Overlapping Consensus." *Oxford Journal of Legal Studies* 7 (1987): 1–25.

——. *Political Liberalism*. New York: Columbia University Press, 1993.

Rehg, W. *Insight And Solidarity: The Discourse Ethics of Jürgen Habermas*. Berkeley: University of California Press, 1997.

Riker, W. "Voting and the Summation of Preferences," *American Political Science Review* 58 (1964): 341–9.

——. *Liberalism Against Populism*. San Francisco: W. H. Freeman, 1982.

Riker, W. and P. Ordeshook. "A Theory of the Calculus of Voting," *American Political Science Review* 62 (1968): 25–42.

Riley, P. *The General Will Before Rousseau*. Princeton, NJ: Princeton University Press, 1986.

Rosenberg, G. N. *The Hollow Hope: Can Courts Bring About Social Change?* Chicago: University of Chicago Press, 1991.

Rousseau, J. J. *The Social Contract*, in *The Social Contract and Discourses*, translated by G. D. H. Cole. London: J. M. Dent, 1973.

——. *Of The Social Contract*, translated by C. Sherover. New York: Harper and Row, 1984.

Runciman, W. and A. Sen. "Games, Justice and the General Will," *Mind* 74 (1965): 554–62.

Sales, B, ed. *Perspectives in Law and Psychology*: vol. 2, *The Jury, Judicial, and Trial Processes*. New York: Plenum, 1981.

Salmon, W. *Scientific Explanation and the Causal Structure of the World*. Princeton, NJ: Princeton University Press, 1984.

Sandel, M. *Liberalism and the Limits of Justice*. Cambridge: Cambridge University Press, 1982.

Sartori, G. *The Theory of Democracy Revisited*. Chatham: Chatham House, 1987.

Satterthwaite, M. "Strategy-proofness and Arrow's Conditions," *Journal of Economic Theory* 10 (1975): 187–217.

Scanlon, T. M. "Preference and Urgency." *Journal of Philosophy* 72 (1975): 655–69.

——. "Liberty, Contract, and Contribution," in *Morals and Markets*, edited by Gerald Dworkin, Gordon Bermant, and Peter G. Brown, 43–67. Washington, D.C.: Hemisphere, 1977.

——. "Contractualism and Utilitarianism." In *Utilitarianism and Beyond*, edited by Amartya Sen and Bernard Williams, 103–28. Cambridge: Cambridge University Press, 1982.

Schmitt, C. *The Crisis of Parliamentary Democracy*, translated by E. Kennedy. Cambridge, MA: MIT Press, 1985.

Schumpeter, J. A. *Capitalism, Socialism and Democracy*. 5th edn. London: Allen and Unwin, 1976.

Sen, A. "A Possibility Theorem on Majority Decisions," *Econometrica* 34 (1966): 491–9.

——. *Collective Choice and Social Welfare*. San Francisco: Holden-Day, 1970.

——. "Rational Fools," *Philosophy and Public Affairs* 6 (1977): 317–44.

——. "Well-being, Agency and Freedom: The Dewey Lectures," *Journal of Philosophy* 82 (1984): 169–203.

Sen, A. and B. Williams. *Utilitarianism and Beyond*. Cambridge: Cambridge University Press, 1982.

Shapley, L. and B. Grofman. "Optimizing Group Judgmental Accuracy in the Presence of Interdependencies," *Public Choice* 43 (1984): 329–43.

Shklar, J. *Men and Citizens: A Study of Rousseau's Social Theory.* London: Cambridge University Press, 1969.

Shue, H. *Basic Rights: Subsistence, Affluence and U. S. Foreign Policy.* Princeton: Princeton University Press, 1980.

Simon, H. *Reason in Human Affairs.* Stanford: Stanford University Press, 1983.

Smith, A. *An Inquiry into the Nature and Causes of the Wealth of Nations.* 5th edn. London: Methuen and Co., 1930.

——. *The Theory of Moral Sentiments*, edited by D. Raphael and A. MacFields. Oxford: Oxford University Press, 1982.

Spelman, E. *Inessential Woman.* Boston: Beacon Press, 1988.

Stone, G. "Content-Neutral Restrictions." *University of Chicago Law Review* 54 (1987): 46–118.

Sunstein, C. "Naked Preferences and the Constitution." *Columbia Law Review* 84 (1984): 1689–732.

——. "Interest Groups in American Public Law." *Stanford Law Review* 38 (1985): 29–87.

——. "Legal Interference with Private Preferences." *University of Chicago Law Review* 53 (1986): 1129–84.

——. "Political Equality and Unintended Consequence," *Columbia Law Review* 94 (1994): 1390–414.

Suppes, P. *A Probabilistic Theory of Causality.* Amsterdam: North-Holland, 1970.

Temkin, L. S. *Inequality.* Oxford: Oxford University Press, 1993.

Thomas, K. "The Levellers and the Franchise." In *The Interregnum: The Quest for Settlement 1646–1660*, edited by G. E. Aylmer, 57–78. London: Archon, 1972.

Thucydides. *The Peloponnesian War*, translated by John H. Finley, Jr. New York: Modern Library, 1951.

Tocqueville, A. *Democracy in America.* New York: Random House Vintage, 1945.

Tribe, L. *American Constitutional Law.* Mineola: Foundation Press, 1978.

——. *Constitutional Choices.* Cambridge: Harvard University Press, 1985.

Tuchman, B. *The March of Folly: From Troy to Vietnam.* Worcester, MA: Billing, 1984.

Tullock, G., ed. *Frontiers of Economics*, vol. 3. Blacksburg, VA: Center for Study of Public Choice, 1979.

Unger, R. *False Necessity.* Cambridge: Cambridge University Press, 1987.

Verba, S., K. L. Schlozman, and H. Brady. *Voice and Equality.* Cambridge, MA: Harvard University Press, 1995.

Waldron, J. "Theoretical Foundations of Liberalism." *Philosophical Quarterly* 37 (1987): 135–40.

——. "A Right-Based Critique of Constitutional Rights." *Oxford Journal of Legal Studies* 13 (1993).

——. "The Wisdom of the Multitude: Some Reflections on Book 3, Chapter 11 of Aristotle's Politics," *Political Theory* 23 (1995): 563–84.

———. "What Plato Would Allow," in *Nomos XXXVII: Theory and Practice*, edited by Ian Shapiro and Judith Decew. New York: New York University Press, 1995.

———. *Law and Disagreement*. Oxford: Clarendon Press, 1999.

———. *The Dignity of Legislation*. Cambridge: Cambridge University Press, 1999.

Walker, J. "Normative Consequences of 'Democratic' Theory" in *Frontiers of Democratic Theory* edited by H. Kariel, 227–47. New York: Random House, 1970.

Walzer, M. "The Communitarian Critique of Liberalism." *Political Theory* 18 (1990), 6–23.

Weber, M. *Economy and Society*, edited by G. Roth and C. Wittich. Berkeley: University of California Press, 1968.

Wertheimer, R. *The Significance of Sense*. Ithaca: Cornell University Press, 1972.

Williams, B. *Ethics and the Limits of Philosophy*. London: Fontana, 1985.

Woolrych, A. *Soldiers and Statesmen: The General Council of the Army and Its Debates, 1647–1648*. Oxford: Clarendon Press, 1987.

Wright, R. "Causation in Tort Law," *California Law Review* 73 (1985): 1775–98.

Yeatman, A. *Postmodern Revisionings of the Political*. New York: Routledge, 1994.

Young, H. P. "Optimal Ranking and Choice from Pairwise Comparisons." In *Information Pooling and Group Decision Making*, edited by B. Grofman and G. Owen, 113–22. Greenwich, CT: JAI, 1986.

———. "Condorcet's Theory of Voting," *American Political Science Review* 82 (1988): 1231–44.

Young, I. *Justice and the Politics of Difference*. Princeton, NJ: Princeton University Press, 1990.

———. "Gender as Seriality: Thinking about Women as a Social Collective," *Signs: Journal of Women in Culture and Society* 19 (1994): 713–38.

———. "Asymmetrical Reciprocity: On Moral Respect, Wonder, and Enlarged Thought," *Constellations* 3 (1997): 340–63.

———. "Difference as a Resource for Democratic Communication." In *Deliberative Democracy: Essays on Reason and Politics*, edited by J. Bohman and W. Rehg, 383–406. Cambridge, MA: MIT Press, 1997.

———. *Inclusion and Democracy*. Oxford: Oxford University Press, 2000.

Zablocki, B. *The Joyful Community*. New York: Pelican, 1971.

Index

As democracy and its subdivisions form the subject matter of this book, no attempt has been made to index these topics exhaustively. Passing and casual references to any topic have been ignored. Page numbers in bold type indicate a main or detailed reference. Where endnotes do not contain direct information, or an author or topic is not identified by name in the text, the relevant page in the text is given in brackets after the note reference.

abortion, 58, 59
abstaining, 252, 266 n.13, 273, 276, 279–80, 282–3 n.9
accommodationist preferences, 96
Ackerman, Bruce, 104 n.2 (88), 200–1, 202, 206 n.12 (179), 211 n.48, nn.52–3
adaptive preferences, 95–6
advertising, political, 193–5
administrative power, 107
agency contracts, 169–70 n.2
agency, 4, 220, 276
aggregation of preferences,
    Arrow's impossibility theorem, 3, 4, 22–3
    general will and, 310, 314–15
    liberalism and, 289, 290, 293
    populism and, 293
    social choice theory and, 295, 303, 309
Alcoff, Linda, 224, 232 n.17
d'Alembert, Jean, 312
alienation, 37, 47, 48–9
alienation contracts, 169 n.2

alterability condition, 37
altruism, 246
America see United States
anonymity, 245–6
Ansolabehere, Stephen, 209–10 nn.39–40
Anzaldua, Gloria, 221, 232 n.14
arbitrariness of decision rules, 289, **293–4**
Arendt, Hannah, 114, 228
Aristotle, 16, 26 n.8, 49, 50 n.10, 98
Arrow, Kenneth, 2, 4, 169, 22–3, 45, 305 n.9, 310, 319 n.17
    Jury Theorem and, 27 n.14 (25), 299, 306–7 n.24, 311, 319 n.27
    Miller and, 4, 22–3, 293, 296, 299, 305 n.11
    Riker and, 3, 296, 306 n.16
Assembly of the People, 308, 310, 311
Australia, 249, 261
autonomy, 87, **95–6**

Baker, K., 309
balkanization, 16–17

Barry, Brian, 24, 252, 254, 256, 257, 305 n.6 (292), 309, 311
Barwell, Ismay, 233 n.21 (229)
Becker, Werner, **108–12**, 123–4 nn.2–9
Beitz, Charles, 6, 7, **13–15**, 22, 80 n.2 (52), 186, 207 n.29
benefits of voting, 267, 268
benevolence, 237–8, 256
Benhabib, Seyla, 2
Benn, Stanley, 150 n.13 (142), 151 n.16 (147), 268, 282 n.7
Black, Charles L., 81 n.10 (55)
Black, D., 24, 306 n.22 (299), 311
black Atlantic perspective, 224–5
Black women, 221
Bobbio, Norberto, 119, 124 nn.13–16
Bodin, Jean, 117
Bohman, James, 2, 232 n.18 (227)
Borda count, 294, 302, 303, 307 n.28
Bourdieu, Pierre, 220, 232 n.9
Bowers v. Hardwick, 59
Brady, Henry E., 189, 207 n.30
Braithwaite, J., 265 n.4 (244)
Brennan, Geoffrey, 19, 265 n.6 (246), 268, 282 n.6, 297, 306 n.18
Brighouse, Harry, 205 n.5, 206 n.14 (181), 207 n.25 (185)
Bruderhof Commune, 310
Buchanan, J., 130, 314, 318 n.13
Buckley v. Valeo, 202, 203
Burnham, Walter Dean, 106 n.29 (102)

campaign advertising, 193–5
Cartwright, Nancy, 283 n.20 (273)
caste societies, 135
causal influence, 20, **271**
causal preemption, 277
causal responsibility, **19–21, 269–70**, 285 n.39
  overdetermination and, 270–5
Chamberlin, J., 319 n.20
changeability of preferences, 41
Christiano, Thomas, 6–7, 8, 9, 14, 284 n.27 (277), n.37 (282)

on political equality, 7, 205 n.5, 207 nn.25–6 (185), 207–8 n.31
Cobban, A., 319 n.16 (316)
cognitive bias, 47
Cohen, Carl, 150 n.13 (142)
Cohen, G. A., 50 n.5 (39), 210 n.43
Cohen, Joshua, 6, 12, 22, 103, 104 n.3 (88), 232 n.19 (228), 306 n.14 (295), 307 n.29 (304)
  Habermas and, 5, 9, 10, 11, 26 n.2, 120–1
  on ideal deliberation, 105 n.21 (98), 106 n.29 (102), 124 nn.18–22, 205 n.5, 305 n.2 (290)
  on political equality, 50 n.8 (42), 97, 106 n.29 (102), 125 nn.23–4, 205 n.5
Coleman, J., 105 n.21 (98), 295, 305 n.4 (291), 306 n.14
collective properties of society, **35–8**, 44, 45, 50 n.3
common good, 6, 87, 88, 90, **94–5**, 100, 125 n.23, 308, 311, 312
Common's Dilemmas, 315
Compensation of Quantity for Inequality principle, 191, 211 n.51
competence, 308, 312, 313, 317–18 n.12
complex proceduralism, **153–5**, 167–9
  regulative interests, 154, **160–7**, 168
  social contract framework, 155, **157–60**
compositing of motions, 301
Condorcet, Marie Jean, 291, 294–5, 299, 301, 302, 319 n.19
  Jury Theorem, **24–6**, 307 n.28, 317 n.9
  Rousseau and, 308, 309, **311–15**, 316, 317 n.8
Connolly, W. E., 125 n.23 (121)
consequentialism, 2, 248–9, 262–3
constitutional democracy,
  disagreements and, 63–4
  judicial review and, 54–7, 60–3
  justice and, 56–7

legitimacy and, 66–70
public debate and, 58–60
rights and, 51–4
contestability of comparisons argument, 41
contractualism, 12, 13, 22
contributory causation, 20, **271**
conventional causal systems, 276, **277–8**
costs of voting, 249, 267
Coward, Rosalind, 232 n.10 (220)
Crenshaw, Kimberle, 221, 232 n.15
cyclical majorities, 311, 319 n.19

Dahl, Robert, 49 n.1 (32), 81 n.16 (57), 129, 151 n.15 (146), 205 n.5, 293
on Madison, 130, 148
Davis, J., 306 n.20 (298)
Davis, J. C., 170 n.10 (156)
Dawes, R., 306 n.21 (299)
decision-making, 31–2, 35, 38, 45, 46, 47, 48, 87
Jury Theorem, 311–15
Rousseau's view, 309–11
see also deliberative democracy; public debate
decision rules, 293–4
Decreasing Marginal Epistemic Value of Input, 208 n.35
deliberation *see* public debate
deliberative democracy, **2–6**, 87, **120–3**
autonomy and, 95–6
common good and, 94–5
formal conception of, **91–2**, 94
ideal deliberative procedure, 92–4
objections to, 98–103
Rawls's view, 88–91
as regulative ideal, 290–2
sectarianism objection, 98
social choice theory and, 292, **296–304**
deliberative responsibility interest, 154, **164–6**
democracy, 82 n.34, 118–20, 129–30, 228, **237–42**

Locke's view, 76–8
Mill's view, 139–45
see also constitutional democracy; deliberative democracy; direct democracy; epistemic democracy; liberalism
democratic institutions, 13–14, 43, 97, 245, 289
Descartes, René, 65
Devlin, Lord, 59, 81 n.24
Dewey, John, 120, 124 n.17
Diderot, Denis, 312, 317 n.8
difference principle, 88, 89, 104 n.7, 178, 180–1, 196, 206 n.8
direct democracy, 8, 101, 142–3
disagreement, **63–4**, 75–6, 79
Disch, Lisa, 228–9, 233 n.20
discourse theory, 115–16
distributive justice, 2
Downs, Anthony, 3, 282 n.1
Dryzek, J., 305 n.2 (290)
Drucker, Peter, 318 n.16
Dummett, Michael, 302, 307 n.27, 319 n.18 (316)
Dworkin, Ronald, 50 n.7 (41), 105 n.20 (98), n.23 (100), 124 n.10, 171 n.15 (160), 205 n.5
on campaign advertising, 193, 194, 209 n.38, 210 n.41
on community, 52–3
on constitutional design, **63**, 65, 81 n.28
on judicial review, 52, **54–6**, 57–8, 60–1, 62, 70–1, 81 n.9, nn.11–13, n.21
on public debate, **58**, 59, 60
on rights, 52, **54–6**, 63, 65, 67, 68, 71, 81 nn.8–9
Dyson, Michael, 231 n.3 (216)

economic theories, 2, 3, 16, 242
voting and, 267
egalitarianism 6, 14, 31–2
egoistic calculus, 253

elections, 241, 275, 276, 278 *see also* voting
elites, 237
Ellenburg, S., 309
Ellis, John, 232 n.10 (220)
Elshtain, Jean, 213, 214, 226, 228, 231 n.2
Elster, Jon, 2, 5, 27 n.14 (25), 104 n.12 (91), 105 n.17 (94), 305 n.3 (291), 306 n.19 (298)
  on preference formation, 4, 95
Ely, John Hart, 54, 64, 81 nn.6–7, n.29, 105 n.22
empiricism, 107, 108, 111, 112–13
environmental protection, 35, 36
epistemic compensation factor, 192
epistemic democracy, 7, 8, **175–9**, 291–2
  incentive argument, 195–8
  justice and, 175, **182–4**, 185
  Paretianism and, 179–89
  value of input, 189–95
  voucher systems, 198–203
Epistemic Difference Principle, 186, 193, 194
Epistemic Value of Equality, 190, 193, 195
Epistemic Value of Quantity, 190, 194, 195, 201
equality, 6, 39, 45, 93
  of interests, 7, **32–4**, 35, 39, 44, **46–8**
  of political influence, 175–9, 184–8
  of well-being, 34, **38–44**
  see also fairness; inequality; injustice; justice
equitable treatment interest, 154, **162–4**
Estlund, David, 6, 7, 25, 232 n.19 (228), 305 n.7 (292)
ethical subjectivism, 109–10
expected-value voting rationale, 267–8
expressivist voting rationale, 247–8, **259–62**, 268
external procedural fairness, 186–7

factions, 308, **313–14**
fair proceduralism, 185, 189
fair value of political liberties, 88, 89–90, 104 n.6, n.7, 206 n.10, 207 n.24
fairness, **88–91**, 150–1 n.14
  procedural, **6–9**, 13–15, 186–7
  see also equality; inequality; injustice; justice
Farquharson, R., 311
Feld, Scott, 24, 305 nn.6–7 (292), 311, 312, 317 n.7, n.10 (313), 319 n.18 (316)
Feldman, A., 319 n.17
Ferejohn, J., 105 n.21 (98), 295, 305 n.4 (291), 306 n.14
Ferris, Richard J., 251, 252, 257
First Amendment, US Constitution, 201–2
Foot, Philippa, 136, 150 n.10
Forbath, W. E., 81 nn.17–18 (57)
Fraser, N., 125 n.26
free speech, 52, **100–1**, 105 n.22
  voucher systems and, 201–3
freedom of association, 52
Fuss, Diana, 232 n.10 (220)

Gains Must Be Shared Downward principle, 192, 193
Galston, William, 207 n.22
Gauthier, David, 149 n.2 (131), 170 n.5 (156), n.7 (156)
general will, 265 n.2, 292, **308–11**, 316–17 nn.5–6, n.8, 318 n.14, n.16
  impossibility theorem and, 319 n.17
  Jury Theorem and, 311–15
Germany, 117
Gibbard, A., 306 n.13 (294)
Gibbard–Satterthwaite theorem, 306 n.13 (294)
Gildin, H., 315
Gilroy, Paul, 224–5, 232 n.17
Gini coefficient, 208 n.32, n.34, 211 n.51

Gitlin, Todd, 213, 227, 231 n.1
Glazer, A., 319 n.18 (316)
Glendon, Mary Ann, 59, 81 n.26
Goldman, Alvin, 19–21,
    284 n.22 (274)
Goodin, Bob, 26 n.13, 297, 306 n.17,
    315
government, **139–46**, 152
Grofman, Bernard, 24, 305 nn.6–7
    (292), 311, 312, 313, 314, 316,
    317 n.7, nn.9–10, 318 n.13,
    319 n.18
group competence levels, 313,
    317–18 n.12
group differentiation, 16–18,
    214–15
    attitudes to, 215–18
    deliberation and, 226–31
    identity and, 218–22
    social perspective and, 222–5

Habermas, Jürgen, 2, 6, 12, 22,
    26 nn.4–5, 104 n.12 (91), 105 n.17
    (94)
    Cohen and, 5, 9, 10, 11, 26 n.2,
        120–1
    ideal discourse, 4–5, **9–11**, 93
Hamilton, Alexander, 82 n.55
Haraway, Donna, 222
Harding, Sandra, 233 n.21 (229)
Harman, G., 149 n.5 (133)
Hart, H. L. A., 59, 81 n.24
Hayek, F., 246, 264 n.1 (238)
Heidegger, M., 232 n.11 (220)
Held, D., 124 n.10 (113)
Hirschman, Albert, 151 n.18 (148)
Hobbes, Thomas, 74, 82 n.34, n.40,
    156, 169–70 n.2 (152)
    Leviathan, 65, 77, 81 nn.32–3,
        82 n.48, 152, 169 n.1
Hohfeld, Wesley N., 81 n.5 (53)
homosexuality, 59
Hume, David, 170 n.7 (156)
Hylland, A., 2, 27 n.14 (25)

ideal deliberative procedure, 10–11, 87,
    92–4, 96, 97, 120, 121
ideal discourse, 4, 10, 11
ideal speech situation, 9
identity,
    difference and, 218–22
    social perspective and, 222–5
identity politics, 17–18, 213–14
impartial spectator view, 316 n.2
impossibility theorem, *see* Arrow,
    Keith
incoherence, 98–9
incompleteness of knowledge, 40–1
inequality, 16, **179–82**, 203–4
    incentive argument for, 195–7
    justice and, 182–4
    voucher schemes and, 197–203
    see also equality; fairness; injustice;
        justice
inevitability condition, 36–7
influence factor in voting, 247, **251–2**
injustice, 99–101 *see also* equality;
    fairness; inequality; justice
input, 188–9
    epistemic value of, 189–95
institutions *see* democratic institutions
interest-group politics, 214
interests,
    equal consideration of, 7, **32–4**, 35,
        39, 44, **45–9**
    interdependence of, 35, 37, 44–5
    regulative, of citizenship, 154,
        159–67, 168
    self-interest, 267, 314–15
internal procedural fairness, 186–7
intersectionality, 221
INUS conditions, **271–4**, 283 n.20
invisible hand mechanisms, 242–3
irrelevance, 101–3
Iyengar, Shanto, 209–10 n.39, 40

Jefferson, Thomas, 106 n.28
Johnson, James, 205 n.5
Jones, Peter, 49 n.1 (32)

judgment, 32, 46, 73, 82 n.38,
    319 n.20
judicial review, 8, 52, **54–6**, 71, 77,
    319 n.20
  justice and, 56–7
  public debate and, 58–60
juries, **298**, 318 n.13
Jury Theorem, **24–6**, 26–7 n.13
  general will and, 311–15
justice, 4, **6–9**, 33–4, 44, 89, 129,
    150–1 n.14, 207 n.22
  interests and, 7, **45–9**
  judicial review and, 56–7
  political inequality and, 182–4
  see also equality; fairness; inequality;
    injustice

Kant, Immanuel, 104 n.13 (92),
    171 n.12 (157), 268, 282 n.3
Kantian voting rationale, **268**, 274
Kelly, C., 319 n.18 (316)
Kelly, E., 26 n.5 (10)
Knight, Jack, 205 n.5

Labour Party, 301
language, 111, 125 n.25, 220
Laslett, Peter, 77, 82 n.46
Law of Large Numbers, 24
legitimacy, 63, 71, 91, 92, 108, 109,
    116, 250
  rights and, 53–4, **65–70**
  theories of, 177–9
Lehrer, K., 319 n.18 (316)
Levellers, 156, 170 n.11
Lewis, David, 149 n.2 (131), 150 n.11
    (139)
  on causation, 270, 271, 277, 282 n.8,
    283 nn.12–13, n.15, n.20 (273),
    284 n.28
liberalism, 2–3, 5–6, 113, 114, 117,
    178, 187, 304–5 n.1
  alternatives to, 289, 290, 291,
    292–5
liberty, 31, **78–80**

Lindsay, A. D., 156, 170 n.11
Lipset, S. M., 151 n.17 (147)
List, C., 26 n.13
Lively, Jack, 171 n.19 (162)
local-level deliberation, 304
Lochner era, 57
Locke, John, 65, **76–8**, 81 nn.31–2,
    82 nn.42–7, nn.49–51
Loeb, Louis, 283 n.14 (271)
Lomasky, Loren, 19, 265 n.6 (246),
    268, 282 n.6
Long, Roderick, 284 n.35 (280)
Luce, R. Duncan, 149 n.2 (131)
Lugones, Maria, 217, 231 n.6

MacIntyre, A., 105 n.20 (98)
Mackie, J. L., 271–2, 283 nn.17–20.
macroethics, 239
Madison, James, 105 n.23, 106 n.28,
    130, 148
majoritarian decision rules, 293, 294
majority rule, 33, **66–70**, 71, 93, 99,
    110, 147, 244
  Dewey on 120
  Jury Theorem, 311–15
Mandeville, Bernard, 242
Manin, B., 104 n.12 (91), 105 n.16
    (93), 305 n.2 (290),
    307 n.29 (304)
Manning, Brian, 170 n.10 (156)
Marcuse, Herbert, 10–11
Margolis, H., 319 n.18 (316)
markets, 242–3, 244
Marshall, T. H., 171 n.17 (161)
Martin, Bill, 232 n.10 (220)
Maus, I., 124 n.12 (117)
McCarthy, T., 26 n.4 (9)
McLean, I., 307 n.30 (304)
McMillan, H., 319 n.18 (316)
Meehl, Paul, 268, 282 nn.4–5
Meiklejohn, A., 105 n.22
Meyer, Susan Sauvé, 284 n.35 (280)
Michelman, F. I., 104 n.2 (88)
microethics, 239

Mill, John Stuart, 15, 50 n.9 (48), 203,
  211 n.56, 244–5
  on government, 13, **139–46**
  on liberty, **78–80**, 82 nn.53–4,
    83 nn.57–60
Miller, David, 3, 4, **22–3**
Miller, N., 311, 313, 316
Miller, Warren E., 211 n.50 (200)
minorities, 110–11
Minow, Martha, 231–2 nn.7–8 (218)
mobility, 125 n.25
moderate formalism, 178
money input, 188 *see also* voucher
  systems
Moore, Michael S., 283 n.11 (271)
moral voting rationales, 267, **268** *see also*
  causal responsibility
moral responsibility, 20, 260, 266 n.12,
  270
morality, 12, **129–39**, 150 n.6, n.11, 238
  voting and, 244–5

Nagel, Thomas, 149 n.6, 170 n.4 (156),
  171 n.16 (161)
nation-states, 114, 119, 303
negative campaigning, 194,
  209–10 n.40
Nelson, William, 6, 7, **12–13**, 14,
  171 n.21 (163)
nemo iudex in sua causa, **65–6**, 71
New Zealand, 59, 61
Nitzan, S., 314, 316
nonexclusivity condition, 36
normative theories of democracy, 2, 6,
  107–8, 113–14
  Becker, 108–12
  Habermas, 4–5, **9–11**
Nurmi, H., 319 n.18 (316)

objectivity, 274
Okin, S. M., 18
Ono, K., 306 n.20 (298)
open government, 12–13, **146–7**
Orbell, J. M., 306 n.21 (299)

Ordeshook, Peter, 282 n.1
Ortiz, Daniel, 206 n.6 (177)
'ought' judgments, 134
overdetermination, 20, **270–5**
Owen, G., 311, 312, 313, 314, 316,
  317 n.7, n.10, 319 n.18

Packwood, Robert, 223
Pangle, T., 82 n.52 (78)
Pareto improvements/superiority, 130,
  181, 182, 193, 196, 197, 198,
  206 n.15, 208 n.34
Parfit, Derek, 252, 254, 256, 257, 268,
  282 n.2
Parliament, 143–4
Paroush, J., 314, 316
partial causation, 20, **271**
participation, 244–5
participation principle, 104 n.9
participatory democracy, 2
Pateman, C., 2
Patriot Vouchers, **200–1**, 202–3
Patterson, Orlando, 171 n.18 (161)
Paul, Ellen Frankel, 284 n.31 (278)
Pericles, 171 n.25
Perlman, 106 n.29 (102)
Perry, Stephen, 81 n.27 (62)
Peters, R. S., 150 n.13 (142), 151 n.16
  (147)
Pettit, P., 265 n.4 (244), 297, 306 n.18
Phillips, Anne, 231 n.4 (217)
Philosopher's Index, 26 n.1
Pinkham, R., 311, 316
Plamenatz, John, 315
Plato, 16
Plott, C., 311
pluralism, 88, 90, 91, 104 n.5, 124 n.8,
  304
political egalitarianism, 175, 176–7,
  178, 179, 180, 187, 207–8 n.31
political input, 188–9
  equality of influence, 179–82
political parties, 102–3, 106 n.29
political power, 107, 108

politics of difference, **213–14**, 216
pollution control, 36
popular sovereignty, 116, **117–18**
populism, 292–3
positional decision rules, 293–4
preemption, 277
preference formation, 4–5, 32, 95
prisoners' dilemmas, 149 n.2, 240, 241,
    243, 298–9, 309
procedural fairness, **6–9**, 13–15, 186–7
Progressive Vouchers, 187, **198–200**,
    210–11 nn.45–6
  free speech and, 201–3
property, 6, 35–6, 44
prudential voting rationales, 267, 279
public choice, 2, 243–4
public debate,
  group difference and, 226–31
  quality of, **58–60**, 71
  see also decision-making
public opinion, 122–3
public space, 228–9
publicity condition, 36
Putnam, Hilary, 232 n.19 (228)

Rae, D., 314
racism, 17–18, 297
Raiffa, Howard, 149 n.2 (131)
Rainsborough, Thomas, 32, 49 n.2,
    156
rational-choice perspective, 267, 280,
    285 n.39
rationales for voting, 18–21, **267–9**
Rawls, John, 2, 10, 26 n.5, 80 n.1 (51),
    105 n.15 (92), n.20 (98), 124 n.10,
    161, 171 n.18, 186, 205 n.5,
    207 n.29
  burdens of judgment, 73, 82 n.38
  Cohen and, 5, 11
  on common good, 88, 89
  contractualism and, 22, 133, 149 n.5,
    157, 170 n.6 (156)
  difference principle, 88, 89, 104 n.7,
    178, 180–1, 196, 206 n.8, n. 13

on fair value, **88–90**, 104 nn.6–8,
    206 n.10, 207 n.24
on legitimacy, 104 n.13 (92),
    207 n.21 (184)
on morality, 149 n.3 (131), 150 n.9
    (135), n.10 (136), 196
original contractual position, 89,
    133–4, 149–50 n.6, 150–1 n.14
on participation, 89, 104 n.9
on primary goods, 180–1, 206 n.13,
    210 n.42 (196)
A Theory of Justice, 3–4, 63, 149 n.1
    (129), 150–1 n.14, 157
veil of ignorance, 3, 133, 171 n.14
    (158)
on well-ordered society, 132, 133,
    138, 145, 147, 149 n.4
recognition, interest in, 46–7, 154,
    161–2
regulative ideals, 289–90
  deliberative, 290–1
  epistemic, 291–2
  liberal, 289, 290, **292–5**, 304
regulative interests of citizenship, 154,
    159–67, 168
Rehg, William, 2, 26 n.5 (9)
religion, 310
representative democracy, 8, **139–42**,
    143, 145–6
republican view, 113, 114, 117, 244
resources, 39
responsibility,
  causal, 19–21, **269–75**
  moral, 20, 260, 266 n.12, 270
rhetoric, 111
rights, 2, 82 n.55
  democracy and, **51–4**, 64, 143, 148
  to equal influence, 184–8
  legitimacy and, 53–4, **65–70**
Riker, William, 3, 172 n.28 (169),
    282 n.1, 305 n.12 (294)
  on incoherence, 98–9, 105 n.21
  liberalism and, 293, 295, 296,
    305 n.10, 306 n.16

Riley, P., 310, 316 n.1, 317 n.8 (312),
    319 n.16 (316)
Roe v. Wade, 58
Rogers, Joel, 97, 103, 104 n.3 (88),
    106 n.29 (102), 125 n.23 (121),
    307 n.29 (304)
Rosenberg, G. N., 81 n.15 (57)
Rousseau, Jean-Jacques, 11, 82 n.36
    (65), 117, 171 n.19 (162)
  on common good, 23, 316 n.4 (311),
    316–17 nn.4–5
  on general will, 265 n.2, 292, **308–11**,
    316–17 nn.5–6, n.8, 318 n.14, n.16
  Jury Theorem and, 24, **312–15**
  on legitimacy, 21, 105–6 n.27
rules, moral, 131–2, 134, 150 n.11
Runciman, W., 309, 315

Salmon, Wesley, 283 n.20 (273)
Sandel, Michael, 50 n.4, 105 n.20 (98)
Sartori, Giovanni, 171 n.22 (163)
Sartre, Jean-Paul, 220, 232 n.13 (221)
Satterthwaite, M., 306 n.13 (294)
Scanlon, Thomas, 26 n.5, 171 n.16
    (161), 172 n.27 (168), 186,
    207 n.29
  contractualism and, 10, 12, 104 n.12
    (91), 155, 157, 170 n.3, n.9 (156),
    171 n.13
Schlozman, Kay Lehman, 188,
    207 n.30 (189)
Schmidtz, David, 284 n.36 (280)
Schmitt, C., 105 n.26 (101)
Schumpeter, J. A., 98, 293, 305 n.9
Schwartz, Thomas, 318 n.14
scientific value-neutrality, 2
secret ballots, 245–6, 297–8
sectarianism, 98
self-interest, 267, 314–15
Sen, Amartya, 2, 4, 309, 311, 315
seriality, 220
sexual harassment, 223
Shapley, L., 314
Shklar, J., 319 n.18 (316)

Shue, Henry, 53, 81 n.4
Simon, Herbert, 50 n.6 (40)
single-peakedness, 23, **299–300**
Singular Vouchers, 198–9
situated knowledge, 222–3
Smith, Adam, 242, 265 n.6, 316 n.2
Sobel, David, 284 n.34 (279)
social choice theory, 2, 3, 4, 21, 22–3,
    45, 289, 292, **295–7**
social contract tradition, 133, **155–7**,
    169–70 n.2, 308
  complex proceduralism and, 155,
    157–60
social groups, 215–18
social perspectives, 215, **222–5**, 227
social power, 107
sovereignty, popular, 116, **117–18**
Spelman, Elizabeth, 217, 231 n.3 (216),
    nn.5–6
Staddon, John, 284 n.25
stakes in voting, 247, **252–9**
Stasson, M., 306 n.20 (298)
Stone, G., 105 n.24 (101)
strategic voting, 289, **294–5**
strict formalism, 178
subjectivity, 275
sufficient conditions, 272
Sunstein, Cass, 104 n.1 (87), n.2 (88),
    n.5, 105 n.18 (95), 205 n.5
supermajorities, 314, 318 n.13
Suppes, Patrick, 283 n.20 (273)
symmetric overdetermination, 271,
    277

Taylor, Charles, 50 n.4
Temkin, Larry S., 208 n.32 (190)
Thomas, Keith, 170 n.10 (156)
Thucydides, 171–2 n.25 (164)
Tilden, Samuel J., 124 n.17 (120)
time input, 189
Tocqueville, Alexis de, 307 n.29,
    318 n.15
trade-offs problem, 31
Tribe, L., 105 n.22, n.24 (101)

Tuchman, Barbara, 237, 238, 250
Tullock, G., 130, 314, 318 n.13
turnouts, 249–50, 258
tyranny, 110, 295

Unger, R., 104 n.3 (88)
United Kingdom, 56, 59, 62
United States, 55, 56–7, 62, 71,
        104 n.5, 282 n.1
    First Amendment, 201–2
    Supreme Court, 59, 75–6, 319 n.20
Urken, A., 311, 316
utilitarian calculus, 253–4
utilitarianism, 2, 3, 4, 6, 155–6
    voting and, 249–59

van der Kragt, A., 306 n.21 (299)
vectorial causal systems, 275–6
veil of ignorance, 3, 133, 155, 158
Verba, Sidney, 188, 207 n.30 (189)
voting, **18–21**, 33, 38–9, 93, 315–16
    causal responsibility approach,
        19–21, **269–70**
    cycles, 306–7 n.24
    epistemic conditions, 280–1
    influence factor, 247, **251–2**
    INUS approach, **272–3**, 283 n.20
    Jury Theorem, 24–5, **311–15**
    morality and, 18–19, 244–5, **268–9**
    prudential rationales, 267
    Rousseau on, **309–11**, 316
    secret, 245–6, 297–8
    stakes involved, 247, **252–9**
    strategic, 289, **294–5**

see also elections
voucher systems, 198–203

Wagner, C., 319 n.18 (316)
Waldron, Jeremy, 6, 14, 26 n.8 (16),
        83 n.56 (79), 170 n.8 (156),
        305 n.7 (292)
    on judicial review, 5, 7
    on justice, **7–9**, 26 n.3
    on rights, 81 n.8 (54), n.30 (64)
Wall, Steven, 207 n.22
Walzer, Michael, 125 n.25, 169 n.1
        (152)
weak publics, 122–3, 125 n.26
Weber, M., 82 n.39 (74)
weighting of votes, 284 n.30
welfare economics, 3
well-ordered society, 132, 133, 137
Wertheimer, Roger, 134, 150 nn.7–8
Williams, B., 104 n.13 (92)
Wolfenden Report, 59
women, 221, 223
Woolrych, Austin, 170 nn.10–11 (156)
Wright, Richard, 283 n.11 (271)

Yeatman, Anna, 231 n.3 (216)
Young, H. P., 305 n.5 (291), 307 n.28
        (302)
Young, Iris, 6, 7, **16–18**, 232 n.12 (220),
        311, 316

Zablocki, B., 310
Zimmerman, S., 306 n.20 (298)
zoning laws, 35, 36